## Date Due

| MY 1 7 '56 | | | |
|---|---|---|---|
| | | | |
| | | | |
| | | | |
| | | | |
| | | | |
| | | | |
| | | | |
| | | | |
| | | | |
| | | | |
| | | | |
| | | | |
| | | | |
| | | | |
| | | | |
| | | | |
| | | | |

# AUDITING

# THEORY AND PROCEDURE

BY

## J. F. SHERWOOD

Certified Public Accountant and Auditor (Indiana)
Member Taxation and Legislative Committee, Cincinnati Chamber of Commerce
Instructor of Accounting, University of Cincinnati

AND

## ROY T. CULEY

Certified Public Accountant (California)
Instructor of Accounting, Los Angeles City College
Associate Member, American Institute of Accountants
Member, California State Society of Certified Public Accountants

PUBLISHED BY

## SOUTH-WESTERN PUBLISHING COMPANY

Cincinnati     Chicago     New York     San Francisco     Dallas

Copyright, 1939
SOUTH-WESTERN PUBLISHING CO.
Cincinnati, Ohio

Printed in the United States of America

# PREFACE

Professional or public accounting practice involves (a) system building or the designing of accounting systems, (b) bookkeeping or record keeping, and (c) the verification, analysis, and interpretation of the records. Auditing deals with the latter.

A thorough knowledge of the principles of accounting should be a prerequisite to the study of auditing. In this textbook the authors assume that the student has this background. This assumption makes it possible to offer an intensive presentation of auditing without an extensive discussion of accounting principles. This plan simplifies the presentation.

As the title indicates, the subject matter relates to both theory and procedure. Mere presentation of the theory of auditing is not sufficient. Too great emphasis on procedure without an adequate presentation of the theory would not constitute good pedagogy. The authors have, therefore, attempted to offer a well-balanced presentation of both theory and procedure. Following is a more specific statement of the method of presenting each topic as it is taken up:

(1) Each chapter is devoted to a particular topic or phase of auditing. The material in the chapter is arranged so that it may be subdivided into a number of assignments. Preceding the discussion in each chapter there is an outline which constitutes a preview of the discussion. Many instructors will find it helpful to use this outline as the basis for a preview of the subject when making study assignments.

(2) Presentation of the theory applicable to the topic discussed in each chapter consists of (a) discussion, (b) illustration, and (c) application. The discussion has been made as simple as possible, believing that this is in the interest of the pupil.

(3) Following the discussion in each chapter, beginning with Chapter Three through Chapter Fifteen, is an Application of Principles based on an illustrative audit of The Blank Manufacturing Company. The theory developed in each of these chapters is applied through the medium of this illustrative audit.

(4) Following the Application of Principles in each chapter is a brief summary of the most important principles developed in the chapter. It is anticipated that many students will use this summary as an aid in reviewing the chapter.

(5) Practice assignments are given at conclusion of each

5

chapter. These assignments provide three types of practice work as follows:

(a)  Questions relating to auditing theory

(b)  Practical auditing problems

(c)  An audit case.

(6) The theory questions are from three sources as follows:

(a)  Questions prepared by the authors relating to important points developed in the discussion of theory

(b)  Questions selected from the C. P. A. Examinations of different states

(c)  Questions selected from the examinations prepared by the American Institute of Accountants.

(7) The auditing problems were either compiled by the authors or selected from the C. P. A. and Institute Examinations. In solving these problems it is necessary for the student to apply his knowledge of the principles previously developed.

(8) Beginning with Chapter Three and ending with Chapter Fifteen there is an Audit Case which constitutes a continuous audit of the Beverly Supply Company. This audit is practically parallel to the audit of The Blank Manufacturing Company which constitutes an illustrative audit. In the audit of The Blank Manufacturing Company the student is shown how the principles may be applied, while in the audit of the Beverly Supply Company the student is required to demonstrate his ability to apply the knowledge gained from his study of auditing. These audits are based on actual experience and the work is identical with that required in that type of audit which public accountants are most frequently called upon to make.

Following Chapter Seventeen two audit projects are presented. In Project No. 1 a complete set of audit working papers is reproduced from which the student is required to prepare a certified audit report. In Project No. 2 the student is required to prepare the working papers from the data given and write an audit report for a lumber company. These projects provide auditing practice on as nearly a realistic basis as it is possible to provide in a textbook.

While there may not be any such thing as standard procedure in auditing, considerable progress has been made in recent years toward such a development. The interest and efforts of the American Institute of Accountants, the American Association of Certified Public Accountants, and other professional organizations of public accountants, the Federal Reserve Board, the Federal Trade Commission, the Securities and Exchange Commission, and other governmental agencies, the New York Stock

Exchange, and other similar exchanges, public accountants, bankers, and businessmen in general has had a marked influence on the development of uniform auditing procedure.

The authors desire to acknowledge their indebtedness to Mr. John L. Carey, Secretary of the American Institute of Accountants, for giving permission to quote from a bulletin entitled "Examination of Financial Statements by Independent Public Accountants" which was prepared and published by the Institute in January, 1936. Acknowledgment also is made of the assistance given by Mr. S. J. Broad, Chairman of the special committee named by the American Institute of Accountants to revise the Federal Reserve Bulletin which was originally published under the title of "Verification of Financial Statements". A number of instructors and accountants have also given valuable assistance in the preparation of this book for which the authors are exceedingly grateful. Suggestions from instructors who may use the book as a text will be welcome. Such suggestions may be of great help in the preparation of future editions.

J. F. SHERWOOD
ROY T. CULEY

# CONTENTS

9

# CONTENTS

# ILLUSTRATIONS

**Auditing
Theory and
Procedure**

# CHAPTER ONE

## INTRODUCTION TO AUDITING

## AUDITING

**Definition.** Auditing is the science of verifying the records and reports which reflect the financial condition and operating results of a business. It may comprehend a detailed verification of the recording of all of the operating transactions of a business for the purpose of confirmation of the results exhibited in the financial reports. On the other hand, it may comprehend merely a partial verification of the records or a testing of the accuracy of the information set forth in a balance sheet. The extent of an audit is determined by the condition of the records and the agreement existing between the auditor and his client.

**Purpose of Auditing.** The purpose of auditing is to promote accuracy in accounting. A periodic or continuous audit will have a tendency to prevent errors in the recording of transactions. Obviously bookkeepers who know that their work will be audited will use greater care in their work. An audit program will also have a tendency to prevent fraud or embezzlement. The prevention of either voluntary or involuntary mistakes whether they represent errors of omission or commission, is just as important as the detection of mistakes which have been made in the recording process.

The detection of fraud and the discovery of errors are not the only aims of an audit although in particular engagements either might be the primary aim. The development of the auditing profession and the character of the services rendered by professional auditors have relegated such considerations to positions of minor importance. The major purpose of auditing is to promote efficiency in accounting and to place before the management accurate information which may serve as an aid to the administration of the business.

## THE AUDITOR

**Qualifications.** The scope of the work of an auditor is such that certain definite qualifications are essential to success. While it is obviously difficult to state all of the desired qualifications the following may be considered essential:

(1) Honesty
(2) Analytical ability
(3) A thorough knowledge of the principles of accounting
(4) A broad business education
(5) A knowledge of business law
(6) Experience in accounting practice
(7) Familiarity with general office procedure
(8) A knowledge of mechanical accounting devices.

To be of the greatest value to a particular enterprise, an auditor should know not only the peculiar problems of the individual enterprise concerned and its financial and accounting methods and procedures, but he should have a wide knowledge of business practices of the industry and all allied industries which have similar problems to meet. The successful auditor must be aggressive and keep abreast of modern business methods. The extent of an auditor's knowledge and experience determines the value of the services he is prepared to render his clients.

**Duties of the Auditor.** The duties of an auditor depend upon a number of factors. An auditor may be an employee of a firm with specific duties assigned to him. Such an auditor is considered an internal auditor. Sometimes he is considered the head of the accounting department and is often looked upon as one of the principal officials of a company. In another case he may be merely an employee of the accounting department, being responsible to the chief accountant or some other official of the company.

The professional auditor is one who renders service for a fee. He may be engaged in business for himself or he may be in the employ of a firm of accountants. Professional accountants and auditors usually engage in business as individuals or partners and their employees usually are classified as junior and senior accountants. In large firms there may be several staffs located in different cities. Each staff may be under the supervision of a managing senior or partner of the firm. Juniors work under the supervision of seniors, and seniors usually work under the supervision of a manager or partner. Each class of employees is usually given specific duties to perform. Obviously these duties vary widely but there is sufficient uniformity of practice to give some idea of the distinction between the work of a junior and the work of a senior.

**The Duties of a Junior Accountant.** At first a junior accountant is usually assigned to work under the direct supervision of a senior accountant who is familiar with the different phases of the field work and he is instructed as to just what to do and how to go about it. In due time, however, he may be sent out only with general instructions from the senior, and he is expected to know how to proceed with the work.

Policies of the firm must be thoroughly understood. They may vary, but every firm has certain policies that it expects all employees to adhere to closely. Juniors, seniors, the managing senior, and even a partner are required by all firms to prepare and keep a set of working papers showing a complete record of work completed. The arrangement and scope of these working papers naturally vary. They are made up of schedules containing records and figures arranged in a systematic order so as to show conclusions; how the conclusions were arrived at; why, in some cases, the figures differ from the book figures; and to show items not appearing in the books of account at all.

The duties of the junior accountant may include the verification of bank and cash balances, checking footings, checking and testing postings, vouching entries, verifications of securities, taking trial balances, checking inventories, making schedules, etc.

**The Duties of a Senior Accountant.** Naturally the senior accountant has certain responsibilities that do not fall to the junior accountant. He may have one or several juniors under his supervision depending upon the nature and extent of each engagement. He is expected to plan and direct their work, decide difficult and complex questions arising from time to time, and make a complete report of each engagement completed, submitting all necessary working papers arranged to show in detail the work performed. As a rule, he is not expected to prepare final reports for the client, this being done in the office under the direction of a supervising senior or a partner of the firm. However, the senior who expects to become a manager or a partner of the firm should learn to prepare certificates and reports from a set of working papers.

**Responsibilities of the Auditor.** Anyone who holds himself out to be skillful in any trade or profession, and who is negligent in the performance of an undertaking and does not use the skill of an ordinarily skillful tradesman or professional man, becomes legally responsible and is subject to a suit and penalty for damages which may result from such negligence. This statement applies to an accountant or an auditor. His moral responsibility is, undoubtedly, higher than his legal responsibility. Legally, one is not required to measure up to the standard of the most skillful but only to the standard of an ordinarily skillful accountant and auditor. Morally, an auditor is responsible if he does not properly perform his duties in a manner which shall conform to the best practices of the profession.

**Rules of Professional Conduct.** As in every other profession, there are certain rules of professional conduct which are generally observed by reputable members of the accounting profession. Those accountants who are not members of any association may not be bound legally to observe the rules of professional conduct establised by the associations, but nevertheless any reputable accountant engaged in public practice will observe the ethics of the profession. The American Institute of Accountants has adopted the following rules of professional conduct:

"(1) A firm or partnership, all the individual members of which are members of the Institute (or in part members and in part associates, provided all the members of the firm are either members or associates), may describe itself as "Members of the American Institute of Accountants," but a firm or partnership, all the individual members of which are not members of the Institute (or in part members and in part associates), or an individual practicing under a style denoting a partnership when in fact there be no partner or partners or a corporation or an individual or individuals practicing under a style denoting a corporate organization shall not use the designation "Members (or Associates) of the American Institute of Accountants."

"(2) The preparation and certification of exhibits, statements, schedules or other forms of accountancy work, containing an essential misstatement of fact or omission therefrom of such a fact as would amount to an essential misstatement or a failure to put prospective investors on notice in respect of an essential or material fact not specifically shown in the balance sheet itself shall be, ipso facto, cause for expulsion or for such other discipline as the council may impose upon proper presentation of proof that such misstatement was either willful or the result of such gross negligence as to be inexcusable.

"(3) No member or associate shall allow any person to practice in his name as a public accountant who is not a member or an associate of the Institute or in partnership with him or in his employ on a salary.

"(4) No member or associate shall directly or indirectly allow or agree to allow a commission, brokerage or other participation by the laity in the fees or profits of his professional work; nor shall he accept directly or indirectly from the laity any commission, brokerage or other participation for professional or commercial business turned over to others as an incident of his services to clients.

"(5) No member or associate shall engage in any business or occupation conjointly with that of a public accountant, which in the opinion of the executive committee or of the council is incompatible or inconsistent therewith.

"(6) No member or associate shall certify to any accounts, exhibits, statements, schedules or other forms of accountancy work which have not been verified entirely under the supervision of himself, a member of his firm, one of his staff, a member or an associate of this Institute or a member of a similar association of good standing in a foreign country which has been approved by the council.

"(7) No member or associate shall take part in any effort to secure the enactment or amendment of any state or Federal law or of any regulation of any governmental or civic body, affecting the practice of the profession, without giving immediate notice thereof to the secretary of the Institute, who in turn shall at once advise the executive committee or the council.

"(8) No member or associate shall directly or indirectly solicit the clients or encroach upon the business of another member or associate, but it is the right of any member or associate to give proper service and advice to those asking such service or advice.

"(9) No member or associate shall directly or indirectly offer employment to an employee of a fellow member or associate without first informing said fellow member or associate of his intent. This rule shall not be construed so as to inhibit negotiations with any one who of his own initiative or in response to public advertisement shall apply to a member or an associate for employment.

"(10) No member or associate shall render or offer to render professional service, the fee for which shall be contingent upon his findings and the results thereof. This rule does not apply to cases such as those involving Federal, state, or other taxes in which the findings are those of the tax or other similar authorities and not those of the accountant.

"(11) No member or associate of the Institute shall advertise his or her professional attainments or service through the mails, in the public prints, by circular letters or by any other written word except that a member or an associate may cause to be published in the public prints what is technically known as a card. A card is hereby defined as an advertisement of the name title (member of American Institute of Accountants, C.P.A., or other professional affiliation or designation), class of service and address of the advertiser, without any further qualifying words or letters, or in the case of announcement of change of address or personnel of firm the plain statement of the fact for the publication of which the announcement purports to be made. Cards permitted by this rule when appearing in newspapers shall not exceed two columns in width and three inches in depth; when appearing in magazines, directories and similar publications, cards shall not exceed one-quarter page in size. This rule shall not be construed to inhibit the proper and professional dissemination of impersonal information among a member's own clients or personal associates or the properly restricted circulation of firm bulletins containing staff personnel and professional information.

"(12) No member or associate of the Institute shall be an officer, a director, stockholder, representative, an agent, a teacher or lecturer, nor participate in any other way in the activities or profits of any university, college or school which conducts its operations, solicits prospective students or advertises its courses by methods which in the opinion of the committee on professional ethics are discreditable to the profession."

## AUDITS

**Types of Audits.** The purpose for which an audit is to be made is an important factor in determining the extent of the audit. The condition of the records or the nature of the information may be such as to require detailed checking before reports may be certified. On the other hand, a partial or test audit may be sufficient to insure reasonable accuracy of the records. The auditor and his client should have a clear understanding of the purposes and scope of an audit. There should be a definite agreement covering these factors and also the terms of the audit. Naturally the cost of an audit will depend upon the amount of work involved, and the amount of work to be done will be controlled by the amount of checking required in ascertaining the information needed in certifying a report.

**Internal and External Audits.** Audits may be classified as internal and external audits. Many concerns have auditors within their organization whose duties consist of checking continuously the financial operations from day to day. It becomes the duty, for example, of the night auditor of a hotel to audit the records of the previous day's transactions. Such an auditor performs what is commonly known as an internal audit.

It is highly desirable that an internal audit be maintained where possible. It has a tendency to prevent carelessness and dishonesty on the part of the employees in the accounting department. It will not only prevent many errors but will permit the locating and correcting of errors currently. It is usually a comparatively simple matter to arrange the work in the accounting department, dividing it among the employees so as to provide for an internal check.

The typical internal audit is found in the large company with a large number of daily transactions, which are of sufficient importance to justify a daily check. Such conditions may be found in hotels in the larger cities, in most railroads, municipal, county and other political subdivisions, and in most large industrials. It is the purpose of the internal audit to see that proper accounting and operating methods are set up to care for the financial transactions as they occur; to see that these methods are followed; and that the records show the true financial conditions as they exist. The internal audit has the advantage that it is usually a daily verification of the financial operations of the business; it is a continuous check on the operations, while the periodic audit made by the public auditor is usually of necessity made some time after the transactions are consummated, and at times a little late to effect a satisfactory routine to adequately handle difficulties as they may arise.

Many companies in publishing their annual reports to their stockholders, rely on their internal audits and accounting methods for the accuracy of their statements, and publish them as correct over the signature of one or more of the officers of the corporation.

Financial statements, based upon internally audited reports due to policies and influences which may not be of the best, may not show true financial conditions. As a result there has steadily grown the demand for external, periodic audits made by public accountants, in addition to the regular internal audits made by the company employees. The advantages of such an external audit may be summarized as follows:

(1) It serves to assure the stockholders that the activities of the corporation are being properly accounted for.

(2) It serves as a periodic assurance to the responsible officials of their proper custodianship.

(3) It provides a periodic review of the methods and procedure of the office and accounting departments by an outside party whose knowledge should be much broader than that of the company's employees, hence providing a method of aiding the management to maintain up-to-date methods and policies.

(4) It provides a periodic analysis of operations by outside parties whose training and practice provide a broad background of experience usually not found among the employees of the company.

**Continuous and Periodic Audits.** A continuous audit, as the name implies, is carried on from day to day as the operations of an enterprise are taking place. A periodic audit, on the other hand, is one made quarterly, semi-annually, annually, or at some stated period. Continuous audits are usually made by internal auditors, though in some large corporations outside auditors continually maintain personnel within a company, thus eliminating the periodic rush to prepare certified statements at the end of a fiscal period. A proper continuous internal audit program greatly aids the external auditor in that much routine checking may be eliminated.

**Balance Sheet and Detailed Audits.** External audits are commonly classified as (a) Balance Sheet Audits, and (b) Detailed Audits. The balance sheet audit consists of a verification of the assets and equities of the enterprise as of a given time accompanied by a general check on the profit and loss accounts for a given period of operations. A balance sheet audit presupposes an adequate accounting system supported by a proper internal check within the organization. Where this condition exists, the auditor usually may proceed to verify the different property and equity values as shown by the records, test the operating accounts to satisfy himself that the accounts are being properly and adequately maintained, and check the routine methods existent to determine that the usual internal checks are properly functioning. Any possible contingencies are then investigated and finally the report may be drawn up and certified.

Corporations are more and more finding it advantageous to have a balance sheet audit prepared by external auditors. The independently certified statement carries much more weight in the minds of the readers, and has a tendency to create greater confidence in the management. It also acts as a check on the management, their measures and procedures, which periodically assures those responsible to the stockholders of a "bill of health" for the period concerned. The balance sheet audit accomplishes for the stockholders what the internal audit does for the management.

A proper routine internal check in a business satisfactorily assures the auditor that the transactions of a period are included in the proper records, and that the books will fairly reflect the true financial results of the business.

In many businesses adequate records are not kept and no internal check is provided. In such cases a balance sheet audit will hardly be satisfactory and a detailed audit may be highly advisable.

The detailed audit involves the checking of the transactions themselves from ledgers to journals, or vice versa, footing and checking for errors of omission and commission. This procedure does not necessarily involve the verification of every transaction of the period under audit, but does involve a check of a sufficient number of transactions to assure the auditor that the records as checked, adequately reflect true financial condition. The extent of the detailed audit will depend largely on the condition of the books, the underlying records, and the adequacy of both for the type and amount of business transacted. A detailed audit usually consists of essentially the same procedure as a balance sheet audit with additional detailed verification of the recorded transactions to insure proper reports.

The detailed audit is usually used for the same purposes as the balance sheet audit, the differences between the two being mostly the result of differing methods of verification due to variations in accounting procedure.

**Examination of Financial Statements.** The expression "examination of financial statements" may be used to describe a type of audit, commonly referred to as a balance sheet audit. The term is of comparatively recent origin. Its use probably originated with the bulletin, "Examination of Financial Statements", published by the American Institute of Accountants in January, 1936. The suggestions contained in this bulletin are intended to apply to examinations of financial statements by independent public accountants for credit purposes or for annual reports to stockholders.

Examination of financial statements expresses more clearly the nature of the audit than does the term balance sheet audit. Accounting authorities are not agreed as to exactly what is meant by a balance sheet audit. Some accountants state that the scope of a balance sheet audit is limited to verifying the balance sheet accounts, and that it includes a verification of the profit and loss accounts only in so far as it is necessary to verify certain of these accounts in connection with the verification of the asset or liability accounts to which they are related. Depreciation, bad debts, interest income, and interest expense are examples of profit and loss accounts that would be verified in connection with the examination of the related asset or liability accounts. Other accounting authorities maintain that a balance sheet audit should include in its scope the verification of both the balance sheet and the profit and loss accounts.

**Cash Audits.** A cash audit, as the name implies, consists of a detailed verification of the cash accounts and records. Prior to the development of modern organizations and the resultant accounting procedure, cash audits were a rather common occurrence. Today they are the exception rather than the rule. In cases of certain types of organizations, as fraternal organizations and some municipalities, cash records are still the principal records maintained. Here the cash audit is the only audit made. For other concerns, cash audits are usually made for the purposes of disclosing suspected irregularities and for the most part provide confidential information only. A cash audit is very similar as to procedure, to the detailed audit, though it concerns the cash records only.

**System Audits.** The purpose of a system audit is to obtain, through an investigation, the information needed in outlining improved accounting methods and in designing an appropriate system of accounts which will be suited to the needs of the company for which it is designed. Accounting systems frequently need to be revised in order that they may provide the information desired by the executives as an aid to management.

As industrial practices change, as new machines are invented for specific types of work and new methods are devised to properly record information, many companies find it profitable to employ auditors to analyze their accounting system and business methods to ascertain whether the practices are up-to-date and economical, and whether such records and practices may be changed so as to do the work better, quicker and at less cost under more modern conditions. As the new types of duplicate posting machines, analysis machines, receivable records, and other devices are developed, labor may usually be displaced or supplemented to advantage by machines, or a new device for recording, posting, and billing receivables, or some other type of transactions may often allow one operation in the place of several now performed to obtain the same record. The progressive executive is always on the alert for such improvements.

**Credit Investigations.** Another type of engagement which the auditor frequently encounters is that of making investigations for credit purposes. A corporation wishes to refinance and market a bond or stock issue. As a prerequisite to underwriting such an issue, investment bankers may request an audit of the corporation's books for several years, which will show the earnings available for interest on the bonds, or for dividends on the stock. Such an investigation requires careful analysis on the part of the auditor of the earnings statements and usually of the last balance sheet, as well as the proper segregation and elimination of non-recurring items, or the inclusion of expected additional charges.

**Special Investigations.** There are various other types of audits which are desired by clients for various reasons. The verification of the property or of any other accounts may be desired for some specific purpose. Such investigations are usually made at the request of the client for the purpose of ascertaining specific information which he may need. In such cases verification is made of only those items affected, and the audit is usually limited to a specific purpose and the accounts affecting that purpose.

**Advantages of Audits.** The advantages to be derived from a proper audit program are numerous. Business men have come to realize the value of having their records audited and their annual reports certified. Of course, not all business men have learned to know the importance and value of an audit. In fact, some business men look upon accounting as a necessary expense which should be kept to a minimum. Such men have not learned to use accounting information as an aid to management and as a means of control. The progressive executive realizes that he cannot efficiently operate a business without having the operations of the business properly accounted for and he knows that the professional accountant may render valuable service. He also realizes that certified statements are often desired by creditors, bankers and stockholders.

The work of an auditor is not limited to merely checking footings and posting. This phase of his work requires the least amount of ability and experience. It is the duty of an auditor to determine the accuracy of the figures stated on the books of account; to distinguish between capital and revenue expenditures; to determine the actual value of accounts with customers through a process of testing, or if necessary to correspond with each customer to secure a verification of the account; to determine a conservative and sound basis for estimating the depreciation of assets and to secure authority for making all necessary adjustments. He is not satisfied to submit statements of financial condition which are simply in accord with the books of account. He determines whether the assets are overvalued and whether all liabilities are correctly stated in the balance sheet.

The internal accountant may be influenced in his work by the wishes of the management but the professional accountant is morally and legally responsible for the reports which he certifies, and, therefore, he must of necessity prepare reports based upon facts, in which he must be impartial and unbiased in the application of his knowledge of accounting and auditing procedure. Following are a few of the outstanding advantages which can reasonably be expected from a proper audit program:

(1) The detection and prevention of errors
(2) The determination of the financial condition of a business
(3) The provision of information for credit purposes
(4) The provision of information to be used as the basis of a settlement between partners

(5) The provision of information to be used in adjusting a claim for fire loss

(6) The provision of information which will facilitate the sale of a business or securities

(7) The detection and prevention of fraud.

**Scope of Audits.** The scope of an audit varies widely. An internal audit, being a verification of transactions day by day, involves continuous checking to see that the records are being properly maintained, and that the actual transactions are properly recorded. An internal audit is of necessity a detailed job, and may be divided into different types of work with different auditors handling each type of transactions. The organization of the auditing department of a railroad well illustrates this tendency. One of the better known companies maintains an audit department in charge of a general auditor with assistants in charge of auditing disbursements, freight accounts, passenger accounts, freight overcharges, capital expenditures, coal and coke traffic, and miscellaneous accounts.

The scope of an external audit depends on the purpose of the audit, the type of auditing previously done by the client's force, and the condition of the books and records. In an audit for a company which maintains a well trained accounting and auditing force, records for which are kept in approved fashion, and which follows the established procedures and methods of good accounting and auditing practice, the auditor may simply verify the financial statements as prepared by the client's own force of employees. When he has satisfied himself that the routines and practices expected by such a system of accounts are being followed in order to adequately state the changes in condition, he may certify the statements. Such an audit will require comparatively little time and will involve a minimum of detail work. It will usually not disclose petty discrepancies in the accounts and possibly would fail to disclose misappropriations in that the tests and checks applied would not happen to catch a possible false entry, though the internal check if properly carried out usually has done this previously and the auditor may rely thereon.

In an audit of a small concern, where the bookkeeper is also cashier, auditor, and general office clerk, the work of the professional auditor may be of considerable length and detail, as the records are likely to be poorly maintained, with no satisfactory internal check. The auditor will be forced, due to the conditions existent, to provide through the various methods at his command detailed checks to satisfy himself that the records present the true financial condition, and that all transactions have been entered and accounted for.

As a result of these varying conditions, an auditing engagement for a comparatively large company may involve a small fee in comparison to that of a smaller company due to the fact that the internal checks and detailed auditing may be well handled in the former case and practically ignored in the latter. Where the auditor is forced to cover work which should and could be done by the client's staff, the resultant expense of an audit is bound to be increased. This accounts in large part for the differences in fees in different audits of the same nature as between different firms of comparatively the same size and type.

This matter of differing fees for an audit engagement is one which oftentimes causes considerable confusion to both corporation officials and directors. A corporation may have a cash audit made and inform the officials of another company that they have their books audited at a certain cost. Upon asking a firm of auditors to audit their books the latter officials find the cost two and three times that of the cost in the former case. They naturally cannot but wonder as to the reasons for the difference in audit fees. The main factors affecting the time required and the cost of making an audit are (1) the condition of the books and records, (2) the extent of the internal check provided through the ordinary routine of the organization, (3) the type of audit required, and (4) the length of time elapsing since previous audit. A detailed audit will usually be much more expensive than a balance sheet audit for the amount of detailed checking and verification will require a greater amount of time to be spent on the engagement than will be necessary in the latter case. Again, a firm of auditors may be engaged on an audit for the first time, and such an engagement will require verifying fixed asset valuations for some periods, or some other work may be needed which may require checking back in the records for several periods. On the other hand a second engagement in which the beginning balances of the period's operations

have already been verified by the firm, will require verification
from that point only, with a resultant saving in the auditor's
time.

**Limitations of Audits.** There are certain limitations connected with audits with which clients and readers of audited reports should be thoroughly acquainted. These limitations may be
roughly classified as those which are inherent in accounting as such,
and those resulting from the limitations on the auditor as such.

No financial statement, audited or otherwise, is capable of
expressing all the values accruing to a business enterprise, at
any one time. The best any auditor may do is to attempt to
present, within his best judgment, a financial statement presenting the results of financial transactions. There may be other
values accruing to the corporation not shown on the financial
statement. For example, a firm of accountants and auditors may
have a small amount of property shown on their financial statement; though the value of the business may be exceedingly large.
Their skill and reputation, two assets of exceedingly large value
to them, may not be stated on the financial statement as they
are not the result of financial transactions.

A financial statement is of value only in so far as the values
stated are reasonable, fair, and on an equitable basis. The
auditor is inclined to use historical cost as a basis of value. This
may or may not be fair under specific conditions. The value of a
certified statement, then, depends on the reasonableness, in the
light of practice, of the values shown, and the auditor is here
decidedly limited by practice, knowledge, and experience. The
best he may do is to use his better judgment in many cases in
collaboration with that of his client.

A balance sheet is a statement of financial condition as of a
given time. Values assigned to properties today may be largely
wiped out tomorrow by the result of factors which the auditor
or accountant cannot usually take into account when preparing
his statements and reports. Many factors might be named which
limit the value of the auditor's work. As these factors, however,
are relative, the value of the auditor's work lies in the degree
to which, recognizing the limitations under which he is working,
he is able to overcome the difficulties from a practical, workable
viewpoint.

Not only are there limitations as a result of the type of material and conditions with which the auditor must work, but there are also definite restrictions with which he must cope. Due to the limitations of time, expense, and the value to be received from his efforts, he is limited in his operations to obtaining, to the best of his ability, the information and records which are vital to his work. He must make tests, rather than detailed analyses, and from these tests he must approximate true conditions and state them to the best of his ability. He frequently enters an engagement several months, and at times years, after the transactions have been consummated. The records may be poor and he may be forced to use his best judgment on the basis of the facts and records as he finds them. In other words, one of the qualifications of the auditor must be good judgment, which should be coupled with training and practical experience in handling and interpreting relative, not absolute, facts and information.

The auditor is also limited by the terms of the engagement made with his client. Some engagements will require a general verification of the financial condition and changes in condition. Such an engagement may involve detailed checking, not only of the values shown on the financial statements, but of footings, postings, vouchers, and the system of recording. On the other hand, a cash audit may involve only a simple verification of the cash accounts involving a few hours' work, but providing no judgment or verification of the values accruing to the business, or any judgment as to the proper income for the period or periods under review. On the other hand, a credit investigation will usually involve a careful study of the income and expense figures for several years in the past with the purpose in view of determining what items included therein were recurring or non-recurring, and to determine whether expenses were properly stated so as to form a suitable basis to judge future earnings for some prospective security which may be issued.

**Classification of Accountancy Services.** There is no standard classification of accountancy services but considerable progress toward uniformity has been made as a result of the activity of the leading associations of accountants. The following classification was recommended by a committee appointed by the American Society of Certified Public Accountants:

### 1. Complete or Detailed Audits:

A complete or detailed audit contemplates verification of all assets, liabilities (actual and contingent), reserves, capital and surplus at a balance sheet date, together with the vouching of all transactions, the checking of all postings and footings, the checking of the classification of all entries, for a period ended on the balance sheet date.

The audit report may take the form of a balance sheet, and a statement of income and profit and loss, together with comments in which the certificate is incorporated, or, when no comments other than those which may be embodied in the certificate are necessary, the certificate may be appended to the financial statements.

### 2. General Audits:

A general audit contemplates verification of all assets, liabilities (actual and contingent), reserves, capital, and surplus at a balance sheet date, together with the verification, by means of tests (the character and extent of which are governed by the effectiveness of the system of internal control as determined by the accountant) of the transactions for a period ended on the balance sheet date.

The audit report may take the form of a balance sheet and a statement of income and profit and loss, together with comments in which the certificate is incorporated, or, when no comments other than those which may be embodied in the certificate are necessary, the certificate may be appended to the financial statements.

### 3. Miscellaneous Audits:

Miscellaneous audits comprehend the verification of a particular account or accounts, of which the following are examples:

(a) Cash

(b) Securities

(c) Pay roll

(d) Manufacturing cost

A cash audit contemplates the verification of all receipts and disbursements for which an accounting should have been made during a period, of the accuracy of the cash records, and of the balance at the beginning and end of the period.

An audit report on an account, or accounts, falling in the miscellaneous group, may take the form of a statement of the account or accounts verified, together with comments in which the certificate is incorporated, or the certificate may be appended to the statement.

### 4. General Examination:

A general examination contemplates verification of the stated assets, liabilities (actual and contingent), reserves, capital and surplus at a balance sheet date, together with analytical review, investigation, statistical and miscellaneous tests of the income, expense, profits and losses for a period ended on the balance sheet date.

The particular object of a general examination is to verify the representations made in respect to the party under examination and to determine that there is no overstatement of net assets or of net profits; that the net assets and net profits are as good at least as represented. It is not designed to detect lapses of fiduciary integrity.

A general examination is distinguished from a general audit by omission to audit the cash transactions, and by analytical study, investigation, statistical and miscellaneous tests of the income, expense, profits and losses rather than routine verification of transactions.

A general examination usually arises in connection with the proposed issuance of securities. In such cases the examination report containing, in addition to the balance sheet, statement of income and profit and loss, and certificate, statistical and other explanatory data which will be of assistance in interpreting the financial history and status of the company under review, is usually supplemented by a statement, or statements, duly certified, giving effect to financial transactions consummated, or to be consummated, subsequent to the date of the verified statements. Transactions to which effect is given in the supplementary statements should be fully verified.

### 5. Examinations of Financial Condition:

An examination of financial condition contemplates verification as of a given date of the stated assets, liabilities (actual and contingent), reserves, and capital, and an analysis of surplus, including as an incident to the verification, such examination of the complimentary accounts as may be necessary to give credence to the stated financial condition.

This type of service, while contemplating certain examination of the records with a view to substantiating the assets as represented and affording reasonable assurance that there are no liabilities (actual or contingent) other than those admitted, does not contemplate systematic verification of transactions, such as is required in a general audit, or review of the income, expense, profits and losses, as is required in a general examination, and may not be relied upon to disclose any understatement of assets which may have been concealed in the operating accounts.

A report on an examination of financial condition may contain properly a certified balance sheet, but if a statement of income and profit and loss is included in the report it should be qualified as having been prepared from the books without verification.

### 6. Investigations:

Investigations are examinations of one or more specific features of a business and are undertaken usually in connection with such matters as suspected fraud, disputes regarding payments of royalties, etc., reasons for increases or decreases of profits, financial policies, determination of civil liability, measurement of contract obligations, insolvency, bankruptcy, measurement of rate-making factors of utilities and carriers, and other financial or administrative matters.

In each case the accountant's instructions from his client should be specific as to the object of the investigation.

The scope of each investigation is determined by its objects and the extent to which the accountant considers it necessary to go in order to accomplish those objects.

The accountant's findings in an investigation usually are communicated to his client in the form of a detailed report. In such a report the general correctness of the conclusions is more important than meticulous accuracy of detail.

### 7. Preparation of Statements from Books or Records without Verification:

Statements prepared from the books or records without verification, should be made preferably on unwatermarked paper, bound (if at all) in a plain back, without any indication in the statements themselves or in anything attached to the statements that they were prepared by public accountants. If, on the other hand, watermarked or regular stationery is used, a footnote should be added to balance sheets or other statements showing that no verification has been made of them, but that they have been prepared from the books of account without verification.

In cases where it is necessary to include in a report any statements which have been prepared from the face of the books without verification, or with only partial verification, such statements should be marked under the descriptive heading and at the bottom, so as clearly to indicate that they were prepared from the books without verification or with only such verification as is indicated opposite the respective items, depending on the situation.

### 8. Tax Services:

Tax services may consist of:

Preparing or reviewing tax returns:

(a) From records which have been audited.

(b) From records which have not been audited.

Contesting assessments or prosecuting tax claims.

Preparing and rendering opinions on tax claims.

Acting as adviser, agent, or advocate in tax matters.

### 9. System Services:

System services may cover:

(a) General accounting systems:

Conducting surveys.

Devising and installing systems of account and of record.

(b) Cost systems:

Conducting surveys.

Devising and installing cost-finding and reporting systems.

### 10. Budgetary Services:

Budgetary services may consist of investigation and survey work, formulating budget policies, designing budget procedures, and offering counsel with reference to budget policies and procedures.

### 11. Opinions:

This class of service consists of preparing and rendering opinions having to do with accounting and financial matters.

### 12. Miscellaneous:

This class includes services not comprehended in t h e foregoing classes, such as acting as liquidating trustee, as advocate in the arbitration of commercial disputes, as arbitrator in commercial disputes, as umpire in accounting controversies involving accountants, or clients, or as comptroller, auditor, or bookkeeper, giving testimony in court and arbitration cases, interpreting financial data, rendering advice in accounting matters, preparing and recording bookkeeping entries, instructing bookkeepers, and checking statements, etc.

## SUMMARY

Much of this chapter has been devoted to a discussion of the different types of audits. The balance sheet audit is the most common type used. Its purpose is to show to those interested, the true financial position of the company at a given time and the change in financial condition resulting from the operations of the period. Such an audit is feasible only when the routine of business operations and accounting control are such as to reasonably assure a satisfactory accuracy in the financial records for the period covered.

Special types of audits are made for special purposes. Clients wishing an audit made should investigate the types of audits, the fitness of each type to their particular problems and the probable expense involved. Such a knowledge would aid materially in eliminating misunderstandings, often existent at the time of completion of an audit engagement, between the client and his auditor.

The scope of any audit will depend on the purposes of the audit, the condition of the books and records, and the adequacy of the internal check. In any audit, there are certain limitations upon the auditor which he should definitely realize, and the value of the engagement will in many cases depend on how well, with the means at his command, these limitations may be overcome. As audits vary, depending on the purpose for which they are made, the client should understand what the auditor is doing, and what may be fairly realized from the type of engagement for which he has contracted.

## AUDITING THEORY

1—1. Distinguish between auditing and accounting.

1—2. State briefly some of the most desirable qualifications of a professional auditor (a) from the standpoint of training, and (b) from the standpoint of experience.

1—3. How are the employees of professional accounting firms generally classified?

1—4. What factors are to be considered in determining the type of audit one should recommend to a client?

1—5. What is meant by an internal check?

1—6. What are the duties of an internal auditor?

1—7. Distinguish between a continuous and a periodic audit.

**1—8.** Distinguish between a balance sheet and a detailed audit.

**1—9.** What do you consider the major objectives of a balance sheet audit?

**1—10.** How is the position of an auditor affected if the system of a concern under audit is defective as to internal check?

**1—11.** Under what circumstances would you advise a client that a complete detailed audit should be made?

**1—12.** (a) What is the purpose of a cash audit?   (b) A system audit?

**1—13.** To what extent are the duties of an auditor affected by the plan of the accounting system and the condition of the records?

**1—14.** Explain how certified statements extending over a period of years might facilitate the sale of a business.

**1—15.** If you were consulted as to when would be the most appropriate time for a company to have its accounts audited, what in general, would be your recommendation?

**1—16.** The directors of a company authorize you to audit the company books. The factory employs from two hundred to three hundred men and sales are to a large number of diversified customers. The company is primarily managed and operated by the president and general manager. What type of an audit would you recommend and why?

**1—17.** Large corporations frequently employ internal auditors. Under such conditions would you deem it advisable to employ a certified public accountant to make periodical audits?                (C. P. A. Ind.)

**1—18.** The American Institute of Accountants requires applicants for membership to pass an examination. The following question appeared in one of these examinations: "In making detailed audits some auditors verify all postings and footings of general and subsidiary ledgers, even though controlling accounts are kept. State reasons for and against such procedure." Answer this question.*

**1—19.** How far are the duties of an accountant auditing the books of a company affected by the character and extent of the company's system of internal check?                (A. I. A.)

**1—20.** You receive the following letter: "We have never had our books audited, but are contemplating an audit now. Two of our friends have recommended you to us. Both have businesses similar to ours, but their advice as to the time required is very different. Do you make different kinds of audits? If so, what are the different kinds and under what circumstances do you recommend one kind and when another." Write a reply.                (A. I. A.)

---

*Many of the questions and problems used in this text were taken from C. P. A. Examinations held in the different states and from the examinations given annually by the American Institute of Accountants. These questions and problems are distinguished by using the abbreviations (C. P. A.) or (A. I. A.) following the question or problem.

# CHAPTER TWO

## AUDITING PROCEDURE

### THE AUDIT PROGRAM

**The Engagement.** It is important that the auditor have a proper understanding with his client as to the nature and scope of the audit to be made. Business men are sometimes willing to depend upon the judgment of the auditor as to the scope of the work and as a result in many cases the work has been started without a definite understanding of its nature and scope. This frequently leads later on to a misunderstanding and to dissatisfaction. It is not satisfactory to depend upon an oral understanding with the client. It is better to have a written agreement. Accountants as a rule use an engagement blank to record the terms of the engagement in detail. The form of engagement blank may vary, but it should show all facts in connection with the agreement made with the client, such as, type of audit, scope of audit, purpose of audit, date audit report must be submitted, terms, and such other information as may be a guide to the completion of the engagement. A form of engagement blank is shown in Illustration No. 1.

39

# ENGAGEMENT BLANK

Office:
9 W. Third Street
Cincinnati, Ohio

## Stevenson and Bennett

Telephone:
Main 2647

### Certified Public Accountants
### and Auditors

Cincinnati, Ohio, Dec. 20, 1937

1. Client The Blank Manufacturing Company ..
2. Official position...Board of Directors..........
3. Address....Indianapolis, Indiana...........
4. Conference....C. H. Bossard, Chairman ......
5. File No.....A245...................................
6. Telephone No.....Main 24.........................
7. Report to be addressed to.Mr. Bossard............
8. Account to be opened with.The Blank Mfg. Co...
9. Nature of engagement
   Examination of Financial Statements
10. Work to be done at..their office................
11. Nature of the business.manufacturing.............
12. When to be commenced.Jan. 17, 1938 .............
13. Probable time required..two weeks.................
14. Accountants required one senior; two juniors
15. Rates...regular ...................................

Engagement No........141...    Date completed..........

Assigned to staff ....A........    Report mailed............

(Signed) THE BLANK MANUFACTURING CO.
Per C. H. Bossard

STEVENSON AND BENNETT
Per M. D. Stevenson

Illustration No. 1.  Engagement Blank

**The Letter of Introduction.** In starting out on an engagement, one is sure to come in contact with a number of different persons. Naturally, he goes first to the client. He also needs to meet heads of departments and others in arranging to begin the work. It is, therefore, important that he have a letter of introduction. An auditor is engaged in professional work and the nature of his work and the liberties extended him are such that he should be properly introduced.

**Equipment.** In the way of equipment, an auditor needs journal, ledger, and analysis paper. Analysis paper may be secured with almost any number of columns. Fourteen column paper is well adapted to the use of the working sheet and is, therefore, preferable. He also needs black, blue, green, and red pencils, an eraser, a ruler, bank certificates in blank, time and expense report blanks, and a memorandum book.

**Audit Routine.** When an auditor reports to his client and is ready to begin work, the first thing he does is to prepare a program for the audit. Naturally the routine will vary depending upon the scope of the engagement, the nature of the business, the purpose of the audit, and the number of junior and senior accountants engaged in the audit. The work of each of the auditors must be carefully planned by the managing senior or the one in charge of the audit. The general program is somewhat as follows:

(1) (a) Obtain a list of the accounting records.

(b) Obtain a copy of the financial reports prepared at the end of the previous period.

(c) Obtain a trial balance as of the end of the period under audit.

(d) If the client is a partnership, obtain a copy of the partnership agreement, and if a corporation, obtain the minute books and charter.

(2) (a) Read the partnership agreement or corporation minutes and charter.

(b) Check the trial balance with the general ledger.

(c) Count the cash and verify the bank balances.

(3) Check and prepare a list of the securities owned.

(4) (a) Audit the receivable assets including accounts re-

ceivable, notes receivable, and any other receivable accounts including accrued accounts receivable.

(b) Prepare schedules of receivable accounts kept in subsidiary ledgers and check the total with the general ledger controlling accounts.

(c) Compute the interest accrued on notes receivable or any other interest bearing receivable items.

(5) Audit the inventories.

The scope of the inventory audit will depend upon the type of audit being made. In a balance sheet audit it will usually consist of checking the extensions and footings and making tests to determine accuracy of the count, listing, and prices.

(6) (a) Analyze the fixed asset accounts including tangible and intangible assets and check the valuation of all property included in the fixed assets.

(b) Ascertain if proper provision has been made for depreciation or depletion of the property owned.

(7) (a) Audit the accounts and notes payable including accrued accounts payable.

(b) Prepare schedules of accounts kept in subsidiary ledgers and check the total with the general ledger controlling accounts.

(c) Compute the interest accrued on notes payable or any other interest bearing payable items.

(8) Audit the fixed liabilities including the funded debts represented by bonds and mortgages outstanding.

(9) Audit the capital accounts.

In case of a corporation verify the outstanding capital stock by comparison of the stock ledger accounts with the stock certificate records.

(10) (a) Check footings of all books of account including the books of original entry and the ledgers.

(b) Test the postings from the books of original entry to the ledgers.

(c) Prepare schedules of any other accounts kept in subsidiary ledgers and check totals with general ledger controlling accounts.

Audit programs applicable to specific lines of business frequently are developed by accountants' organizations. For instance, the Society of Certified Public Accountants of New Jersey has adopted the following audit program designed to meet the requirements for an audit of New Jersey Building and Loan Associations. The committee in a statement, prefacing the program, said "Being essentially a program and not a treatise on the subject, audits will constitute a specialization of general audit procedure and not a limitation of it. Accordingly, a full and comprehensive knowledge and experience in auditing generally is a prerequisite to the intelligent use of this program. Skillful and careful application will dictate the extent of amplification and concentration which particular engagements may demand."

(A) INSTALLMENT SHAREHOLDERS' LEDGER (Roll Book)

1. Verify additions of monthly receipts.

2. Schedule monthly receipts and check to cash book.

3. Prove dues arrears.

4. Prove interest arrears.

5. Prove dues paid in advance.

6. Prove interest paid in advance.

7. Schedule and prove totals of dues arrears, interest arrears, dues advances, interest advances.

8. Prove monthly interest receipts.

9. Schedule shares by series, showing number of

(a) Shares at beginning.

(b) Shares issued in new series.

(c) Shares reinstated.

(d) Shares withdrawn.

(e) Shares matured.

(f) Shares lapsed.

(g) Shares end of year.

10. On above schedule 9 extend amount of dues, and prove total of dues.

11. Prove amount of insurance and taxes advanced for borrowers and schedule.

12. Check all journal entries and transfers between shareholders' accounts.

(B) CASH BOOK

1. Check receipts to deposits per bank statement.

2. Vouch paid checks, notes, and vouchers (watch distribution and checks not passed, through trustee's account).

3. Reconcile bank balance at beginning and end of audit period.

4. Verify cash book balance with check book.

5. Verify rate of interest and amount of interest charged by bank on loans.

6. Verify interest rebates by bank on payments made prior to due dates of notes.

7. Confirm bank balance by direct communication.

8. Confirm notes paid by direct communication.

9. Verify addition of all columns.

10. Prepare schedule of receipts and disbursements.

11. Verify rate and amount of premium charged on mortgage and share loans with minute book.

12. Check amounts advanced and amounts repaid on insurance and taxes for borrowers to borrowers' accounts.

13. Check all journal entries affecting shareholders' accounts to roll book.

14. Vouch and scrutinize all journal entries.

15. Check disbursements to minute book for authority of disbursements.

16. Schedule checks drawn which have been endorsed by and deposited to account of trustee for mortgage loans (to be used in auditing trustee's account).

(C) Paid-up Shares

1. Schedule and prove outstanding shares as to number and amount.

2. Schedule all shares paid off during the year, and examine and account for all certificates canceled, during year.

3. Verify amounts paid on shares withdrawn; also verify amount of dividends paid at time of withdrawal (check period covered as well as calculation).

4. Verify amount of dividends paid on paid-up shares for entire year.

5. Confirm by direct communication all outstanding accounts, as well as all accounts surrendered during the year.

(D) Installment Shares

1. Prepare schedule of certificates canceled and withdrawn during year.

2. Examine and account for all certificates canceled during year.

3. Verify amount dues paid on shares withdrawn during year.

4. Verify amount profits paid on shares withdrawn during year.

5. Verify by pass book audit or confirm by direct communication all outstanding accounts as well as all accounts surrendered by maturity, withdrawn or retired during the year.

(E) Bond and Mortgage Loans

1. Prepare schedule and prove total of mortgage loans outstanding at end of fiscal year.

2. Examine files to see if all necessary papers are on hand and if properly prepared and executed.

3. Examine minutes authorizing loans made and foreclosures commenced or consummated during the year.

4. Examine amount of each loan to determine if any are in excess of amount allowed by law.

5. Confirm amount of mortgages and status of all accounts by direct communication.

(F) Share Loans

1. Prepare schedule and prove total of share loans outstanding at end of fiscal year.

2. Examine files for presence of certificates and notes and if properly prepared and executed.

3. Determine if sufficient payments have been made by each shareholder to warrant the amount loaned, and if within the limit permitted by Building and Loan Act and the constitution and by-laws of the association.

4. Confirm amount of loan (or balance) and status of the account by direct communication.

### (G) REAL ESTATE OWNED

1. Prepare schedule and prove total of real estate owned.

2. Examine deed and/or certificate of counsel as to ownership of all real estate. (See if cost of association building is within legal limit.)

3. Check up on cost of real estate as carried on the books, verifying the amounts in detail of all real estate acquired during the year (examine bonds and mortgages of original owners).

4. Examine insurance policies for each property owned, and see if association is properly and sufficiently protected against fire, owner's liability, etc.

5. Audit rent income and verify expenses in connection with all real estate owned.

### (H) TRUSTEE'S ACCOUNT

1. Check deposits with bank statement.

2. Vouch disbursements with paid checks and vouchers.

3. Reconcile bank balances.

4. Prepare statement of receipts and disbursements, noting particularly receipt of cash by trustee from sources other than association, and from the schedule that was prepared from the association's cash book, trace all items to trustee's records.

5. Reconcile balance in bank with amounts still due or not yet paid on each individual account. (Total balances in detail accounts should agree with balances still in bank to be disbursed, or trustee's fees not yet drawn.)

6. Confirm balance by direct communication with the depository.

### (I) MISCELLANEOUS

1. Prepare schedule and prove total of lapsed shares outstanding at end of fiscal year; check up on shares lapsed during year, verifying amount credited to lapsed share account with shareholders' account; verify amounts paid on lapsed shares withdrawn during the year, examine canceled certificate and confirm accounts still open and accounts withdrawn during the year by direct communication.

2. On new mortgage loans—verify installments of dues and interest from date of first disbursement by the association.

3. Is an adequate system followed in checking up tax payments on real estate mortgaged by the association?

4. Examine officers' bonds and employees' bonds.

5. Examine liability and fire insurance policies.

6. Examine robbery and hold-up insurance policies and all other insurance policies that may be carried.

7. See if all officers and directors are shareholders as required by law.

8. Verify calculation of profits.

9. Verify distribution of book profits and withdrawal profits by series.

10. Calculate amounts of reserve required by law and determine if proper amounts have been set up.

11. Read the minutes of all directors' and shareholders' meetings held during the year, making note of the items that are to be verified in the books of account. Verify these items by tracing them into the books of account, being particularly careful to see that all acts of the officers have been either authorized or ratified.

12. Check accrued interest, and all other balance sheet items not mentioned elsewhere in this program.

(J) General Ledger

1. Check all entries and verify additions of all accounts.

2. Take off trial balance and extend working sheet.

3. Prepare statement of assets and liabilities, profit and loss statement, and all necessary schedules.

4. Check up retained copy of association's annual report to state department with statements prepared from the books.

5. Check up figures contained in printed report of association with statements prepared from the books.

(K) Report

Prepare a report which sets forth the scope, extent and results of the audit, giving full and explicit comments deemed necessary; comment on the manner of conducting the association so as to prevent the occurrence or recurrence of any improper conduct or practice; make recommendations for the improvement of the method of keeping the books, and of procedure and internal check.

The balance sheet should be set up in the accepted form, setting forth the assets and liabilities appearing on the books, together with the corrected figures where changes of importance have been made; this should be followed by detailed schedules of the items appearing on the balance sheet

## THE TRIAL BALANCE

**The Bookkeeper's Trial Balance.** There is no reason why an auditor should not accept a trial balance offered him by the head bookkeeper at the beginning of the audit, but that does not mean that he need not verify the items listed thereon. If he were to refuse the trial balance offered him, the chances are the bookkeeper would be offended and it might lead to his opposition instead of his cooperation during the audit. It would seem to be better practice, however, for the auditor to prepare his own trial balance even though he is furnished with one by the head bookkeeper or the client. Trial balances may be made of the subsidiary ledgers as well as of the general ledger, provided summary or control accounts are maintained in the subsidiary ledgers. Usually, however, no such accounts are maintained in the subsidiary ledger, therefore, the only way a trial balance can be taken is to check the list of accounts taken from the subsidiary ledger with the control account in the general ledger.

**The Auditor's Trial Balance.** The auditor will find that he has a splendid opportunity to become familiar with the details of the accounting system while preparing a trial balance. He cannot help, in going over all the accounts and making the necessary calculations to determine the correct balances, but build up in his mind a general knowledge of the organization as a whole.

Some bookkeepers and business men think that an auditor by some sort of magic should be able to detect all mechanical errors in bookkeeping and arrive at a correct trial balance in a few minutes time. However, the fact is that it is no part of an auditor's duty to locate an error or errors in a trial balance unless he has been employed specifically to do so. An auditor who accepts an engagement to perform an audit, and who on beginning his work finds that the books are not in balance, should report the matter to his client and lay the facts before him. He can, of course, undertake to do the necessary clerical work in order to locate the errors in the accounts so as to obtain a trial balance, but to do so without previous arrangement with the client is liable to result in difficulties when the bill for services is presented. Anyone who spends his time in ordinary clerical work is hardly to be considered a professional auditor and it would seem to be better to permit the bookkeeper to locate his own errors and obtain a trial balance before beginning the audit.

If the work is being done under a contract and the time necessary to do the work has been previously estimated, it would certainly be foolish to put in a lot of time finding ordinary clerical mistakes in bookkeeping, and to do so may result in a loss on the engagement. If the work is being done on a per diem basis, the auditor is apt to become involved in disagreeable discussions with the client because of the length of time spent in performing the ordinary clerical work of the bookkeeper. The books should be in balance before the auditor begins his work, and if they are not in balance, the bookkeeper should be given an opportunity to locate his own errors and obtain a trial balance, after which, the auditor may proceed with his work.

The trial balance is not a financial statement, neither is it a test as to the accuracy of the bookkeeping work. It is merely a list of the balances of the open accounts in the ledger. Therefore, it is nothing more than a surface indication that an equilibrium of debits and credits has been maintained.

**Procedure in Taking a Trial Balance.** First, prove each account by footing both sides of the account and subtracting the two footings so as to verify the balance. It does not matter whether this has been done by the bookkeeper previously or not. The auditor should make his own verification independent of that of the bookkeeper.

Second, every page in the ledger should be examined. Experience will prove that some bookkeepers have peculiar ideas with regard to the arrangement of their accounts, consequently blank pages may be found here and there throughout the ledger and unless every page is examined, accounts might be omitted.

Third, subsidiary and memorandum accounts may be found in the general ledger. For instance, one ledger may be used. It may be divided into sections; the first section may contain all the assets and liabilities together with controlling accounts for customers and creditors; the second section of the ledger may contain accounts with customers; and the third section, accounts with creditors. On the other hand, it is frequently found that subsidiary ledgers are kept, but there are no controlling accounts maintained in the general ledger. The bookkeeper when preparing his trial balance simply makes schedules from the subsidiary ledgers and uses the total of the schedules in his trial balance.

Fourth, some bookkeepers seem to have the idea that a cash account need not be kept in the general ledger simply because a cash book is kept. While it is poor practice to eliminate the cash account in the ledger, yet such will often be the case, consequently a trial balance cannot be obtained unless the cash balance is first obtained from the cash book and included in the trial balance. The only sound accounting theory is that a general ledger should balance independently of all the other books of account. Any procedure, contrary to these principles, is contrary to good accounting practice.

Fifth, the trial balance is usually taken after the posting has been done at the end of the period and before any adjustments have been made. The auditor will have to be on the lookout for items posted to the accounts after the bookkeeper completed his trial balance. This is sure to happen when an audit is made at a date later than the end of the period under audit.

## READING THE MINUTES

If the client is a corporation the auditor should ask for the minutes of the stockholders' and directors' meetings. Without a doubt the minutes should be read as early after the audit is begun as may be practical. They will give an insight into the organization that cannot be gained in any other way; consequently, the auditor will be prepared to do more intelligent work in completing the audit. He will know whom to consult in case any further information is desired because the minutes show who the officers are and what their duties and responsibilities are.

The articles of incorporation will usually be embodied in the minutes of the stockholders' meetings, but if not, the auditor should ask for a copy of the articles or for the certificate of incorporation or charter. The auditor should note in his working papers the exact name of the corporation, the date the certificate was filed, the authorized capital stock showing the kind of stock, the par value of each share and the number of shares, the names of the incorporators, and any other information likely to be of benefit in the preparation of the report. It is better to write down more than will ever be used than to find when making the report that certain information is necessary and that he failed to make note of it in his working papers. The importance of this statement will be understood when it is considered that frequently an audit is made in a distant city, while the report will be prepared in the office. The audit might be made in Seattle and the report might be written in Boston. Therefore, it would be quite embarrassing to learn that not all the information desired had been obtained.

The minutes of the stockholders' meetings should be examined with regard to election of officers, compensation of officers, bond of the treasurer, contracts with the manager and other employees, any special contracts that may exist, resolutions fixing the value of property purchased, the rates of depreciation, etc. The minutes of the board of directors should be examined for additional information.

An executive committee often exists in a corporation. It may be composed of three or more of the directors. Financial matters are usually looked after by this committee, and it often outlines the financial program and has authority to make appropriations, etc. The duties and responsibility of such a committee should be carefully noted.

In the case of a corporation the by-laws will often furnish additional information and should, undoubtedly, be read. One cannot become too well acquainted with the organization and its details. The auditor has a right to insist upon seeing the charter or minute books of a corporation. Should he be refused access to these records he cannot certify the reports without qualifying his certificate.

## DEVELOPMENT OF AUDITING PROCEDURE

During the past two decades, efforts have been made to formulate accounting principles and procedures which may be followed with some degree of uniformity by accountants in performing audits from which financial statements are to be prepared for credit purposes or for distribution in annual reports to stockholders. In 1917 the Federal Trade Commission, with the assistance of a committee appointed by the American Institute of Accountants, prepared and approved a memorandum on procedure. Later the Federal Reserve Board gave it tentative endorsement and in April, 1917, it was published in the Federal Reserve Bulletin. In 1918 it was reprinted for general distribution under the title of "Approved Methods for the Preparation of Balance Sheet Statements." This move was intended to standardize the forms of statements submitted to bankers for credit purposes. Accountants, bankers, and business men in general, realized the importance and value of standard procedure in the preparation of financial reports. Bankers were interested because the extension of credit is based largely on the financial statements presented by borrowers. Business men were interested because they had learned that oftentimes they were unable to obtain the desired credit because of inaccurate financial reports. Accountants were interested because they knew that inaccurate financial statements tended to discredit accountancy as a profession.

In 1929 a committee of the American Institute of Accountants prepared a revision of Approved Methods for the Preparation of Balance Sheet Statements under the title of "Verification of Financial Statements." The work of this committee was approved by the executive committee of the Institute and was printed for general distribution by order of the Federal Reserve Board.

In 1936 a committee of the American Institute of Accountants completed a revision of the material contained in the preceding bulletins by giving effect to the many changes in accounting concepts that had taken place since 1929. This was published
under the title of "Examination of Financial Statements by
Independent Public Accountants." The following is quoted
from the preface:

"Developments of accounting practice during recent years
have been in the direction of increased emphasis on accounting
principles and consistency in their application, and of fuller
disclosure of the basis on which the accounts are stated. These
developments have been accelerated by the prominence given to
such matters in regulations of the Securities and Exchange Commission dealing with financial statements and also in correspondence during the years 1932 to 1934 between the American Institute of Accountants and the Committee on Stock List of the
New York Stock Exchange."

**Scope of the Procedure.** The procedures advocated in
"Examination of Financial Statements" emphasizes the im-
practicability of setting forth "in any single program, procedures
which will fit the widely varying situations which will be encountered." The procedures suggested "will apply in most
cases but there are few cases where all of them will be used.
The particular program chosen is intended for an examination,
made for a report to stockholders or for bank-credit purposes, of
the statements of a small or moderate-sized manufacturing or
merchandising concern which has a reasonable system of internal
check and control.

"The scope of the examination and the extent of the detailed
checking must be determined by the independent public accountant in the light of the conditions in each individual company.
If there is little or no system of internal check, the client should
be advised that a more detailed examination than that outlined
hereafter is necessary if an unqualified report is to be furnished.
If there is an adequate system of internal check, certain parts
of the detailed procedure may be unnecessary.

"For the sake of simplicity, the procedure suggested is
submitted in the form of an audit program with such comments
as seem called for on matters of principle. The procedure will

16901

not necesssarily disclose defalcations nor every understatement of assets concealed in the records of operating transactions, or by manipulation of the accounts. Suggestions are made in the program as to the extent of information which should be given in the financial statements. While the final determination of this question rests with the company whose statements are the subject of examination, the accountant should use his influence to bring about adequate disclosure. If there is failure to disclose information which he believes to be material in the circumstances, his recourse is to comment on the matter in his report.

"It should be understood that all of the work outlined need not necessarily be done as of the closing date of the period covered by the examination. It is frequently desirable to do the detailed work on the inventories or receivables as of an earlier date and, where conditions warrant it, this is satisfactory."

Because of the importance of the procedures outlined in "Examination of Financial Statements" to the professional accountant and to the student of auditing, the procedures relating to the verification of the various balance sheet and profit and loss items have been included in this treatise.

## GENERAL INSTRUCTIONS FOR AN EXAMINATION OF FINANCIAL STATEMENTS

"1. The accountant should determine (a) whether accepted accounting practices have been followed during the period under examination and (b) whether they have been changed in any material respect since the previous period. If the accountant is not satisfied in either respect and the amounts involved are material, reference thereto should be made in his report.

"2. Compare the trial balances with the general ledger at the beginning and end of the period. Trace the items in the trial balances to the balance sheets. Determine that no 'contra' asset and liability have been improperly omitted from the balance sheets that the assets and liabilities have been grouped in the same manner at the beginning and end of the period. Review the general ledger to ascertain if any transactions recorded in accounts opened and closed during the period have a bearing on the financial position at the close of the period.

"3. A comparison of the balance sheets at the beginning and end of the period under review will usually reflect the major changes which have occurred during the period. This may assist in indicating special points that will require more than ordinary attention during the examination.

"4. Minutes of directors' and stockholders' meetings should be read and all matters contained therein affecting the accounts should be noted."

## SUMMARY

Those engaged in making an audit should be thoroughly familiar with the terms of the engagement so that there may be no misunderstanding as to the type of audit to be made or the character of work to be done. The auditor should possess the necessary equipment consisting of pencils, an eraser, ruler, and the proper stationery. Included in the stationery should be any special forms to be used in preparing reports and analysis or columnar paper to be used in the recording of the data gathered in completing the audit.

The auditor has a right to expect to find the general ledger in balance and will usually ask for the bookkeeper's trial balance as of the date of the close of the period under audit. If for any reason a trial balance is not available or cannot be obtained, the matter should be discussed with the client to determine whether the auditor is to prepare a trial balance from the general ledger, and in case he finds that the ledger is not in balance to make an audit necessary to locate and eliminate any errors in bookkeeping. Unless it was known that the general ledger accounts were not in balance and this was taken into consideration in the audit agreement, the work involved in putting the ledger in balance will be in addition to the work required in the regular audit, hence there must be a definite understanding in regard to the compensation for this extra work.

At the beginning of an audit the auditor should study the partnership agreement or read the corporation minutes to familiarize himself with the legal organization of the business and to gather such information as may be helpful in completing the audit. After the necessary preliminary information has been obtained, an audit program should be outlined which will serve as a guide in completing the audit. The senior in charge of the audit is responsible for preparing the audit program and for seeing that it is followed.

## AUDITING THEORY

**2—21.** (a) In making arrangements with a client for an audit, what points should be covered in the agreement?

(b) Is it necessary that the agreement be in writing and that it be signed by the client?

**2—22.** What equipment is needed by an auditor in performing the duties involved in completing a balance sheet audit?

**2—23.** If in reporting at the office of a client to begin a balance sheet audit, you find that the bookkeeper has not prepared a trial balance as of the date of the close of the period under audit, what recommendations would you make?

**2—24.** Prepare a general outline of an audit program for a balance sheet audit of a report to be submitted to a banker.

**2—25.** Explain what is meant by "an examination of financial statements."

**2—26.** In making an audit, should the auditor require to see the corporate minute book, and such other purely corporate records of a company? Give reasons for your answer.

(C. P. A. Ind.)

**2—27.** What is the general course for an accountant to follow when called upon to audit the books of any business?

(C. P. A. Mich.)

**2—28.** In commencing the audit of the accounts of a corporation, what would be your first step and what instructions might be given to the bookkeeper, showing the work that should be done before the audit commences?

(C. P. A. Mich.)

**2—29.** What attitude should an auditor take with respect to the refusal by the officers of a corporation to produce its minute book for inspection in a balance sheet audit which is being made for the first time, although the corporation has been in existence for ten years? Explain fully.

(A. I. A.)

**2—30.** In auditing the accounts of a corporation, for the first year of its existence, what records and documents should be examined in addition to the books of account and the vouchers?

(A. I. A.)

# CHAPTER THREE

## AUDIT WORKING PAPERS

1. Importance of Working Papers
2. What is Included in Working Papers
   (a) The Trial Balance
   (b) The Working Trial Balance
   (c) Forms of Working Trial Balances
      (1) Columnar Working Sheets
      (2) The Working Trial Balance in Two Sections
      (3) The Working Trial Balance in Four Sections
   (d) Schedules and Analyses
   (e) Adjusting Journal Entries
3. Preparation of Working Papers
   (a) Should Working Papers Be Written in Ink or Pencil
   (b) Arrangement of the Working Papers
   (c) Indexing the Working Papers
   (d) Filing the Working Papers
   (e) Importance of Understanding Audit Working Papers
4. Application of Principles
5. An Audit Case—First Installment

## IMPORTANCE OF AUDIT WORKING PAPERS

The subject of auditing may be discussed from at least three points of view, namely (1) auditing from the point of view of theory, technique, and procedure, (2) auditing from the point of view of the form, content, and arrangement of auditors' working papers, and (3) auditing in respect to the preparation of auditors' reports. Many separate volumes have been written on each of these three phases of the subject. The subject of audit working papers is so closely related to the discussion of auditing theory and practice that it seems logical, in a textbook on auditing, that a brief discussion should be presented on audit working papers before embarking on the detailed discussion of verification of the accounts.

Audit working papers serve several useful functions. They are used by the auditor in preparing his report. The report includes, generally, a balance sheet, a statement of profit and loss, a certificate, and comments on the audit. The working papers serve also as a permanent record of the audit, and later may be referred to for information not needed at the time the audit was completed. They also provide information which will be of assistance to the auditor at the time of making succeeding audits.

## WHAT IS INCLUDED IN WORKING PAPERS

Audit working papers comprise a collection of all the recorded information pertinent to an audit. The following items are generally included in a set of audit working papers: (1) a work sheet or working trial balance; (2) schedules or analyses; (3) adjusting journal entries for corrections in the bookkeeper's trial balance; (4) comments made by the auditor covering suggestions, criticisms, and matters for further inquiry which the auditor wishes to make; (5) a rough draft of the balance sheet and profit and loss statement prepared as a result of the audit; (6) a copy of the report made at the conclusion of the audit; and (7) miscellaneous papers, such as an audit program, excerpts from the minutes of the board of directors, etc.

**The Trial Balance.** In starting an audit, it is necessary for the auditor to have a trial balance of the general ledger. The accounts in the general ledger trial balance are to be verified by the auditor in part or in total, depending on the type of audit that is to be performed. The trial balance, therefore, becomes the center of all the auditor's activities.

**The Working Trial Balance.** The trial balance is set up in work sheet form for convenience in conducting the audit. The work sheet is generally referred to as a working trial balance. In writing the accounts in the working trial balance, it is best to arrange them as nearly as possible in the order in which they are to appear in the balance sheet and statement of profit and loss. Some auditors allow one or two lines between the accounts so that new account titles may be inserted if necessary to record adjustments or for convenience in recording two or more adjustments affecting the same account.

**Forms of Working Trial Balances.** There are several forms of working trial balances in use, at least three of which have wide usage. Opinions of accountants vary as to which form is preferable. Three types will be discussed and illustrated.

(1) *Columnar Work Sheets.* Accountants generally use a columnar work sheet as a means of summarizing the information needed in preparing statements at the close of a fiscal period. Eight, ten, twelve, or more columns may be used in compiling and classifying the desired information. Perhaps the simplest form of work sheet is an eight-column work sheet with headings provided for (a) Trial Balance, (b) Adjustments, (c) Profit and Loss, and (d) Balance Sheet. Usually it is found more satisfactory to provide two additional columns for an Adjusted Trial Balance, making ten columns in all. Of course, additional columns may be provided for listing the manufacturing accounts, trading accounts, or any other particular group of accounts which it is desired to classify or list separately.

An auditor's work sheet may differ somewhat from the bookkeeper's or accountant's work sheet. Usually the auditor prefers to include in his working trial balance, for comparative purposes, the adjusted trial balance from the audit of the previous year. In other words, the auditor's working trial balance usually provides a summary of information beginning with the auditor's adjusted trial balance taken at end of previous year and ending with an adjusted trial balance taken at close of year under audit, with a proper classification of the accounts into at least balance sheet and profit and loss columns. There is no such thing as a standard form of working trial balance and there is no limit to the number of columns which may be provided.

In Illustration No. 2 there is a ten-column working trial balance for The Waverly Supply Company. The first two money columns are devoted to the adjusted trial balance taken at the close of previous fiscal year. The next two money columns are used for recording the bookkeeper's trial balance taken at end of year under audit.

The next two money columns are devoted to recording the adjustments which the auditor deems necessary to a correct statement of the accounts. Following is a list of the journal entries which the auditor recommends be posted to the accounts:

(*Continued on page 59*)

## THE WAVERLY SUPPLY COMPANY
### Working Trial Balance

| Sched. No. | Account | Adjusted Trial Balance 12-31-36 Dr. | Cr. | Bookkeeper's Trial Balance 12-31-37 Dr. | Cr. | Auditor's Adjustments Dr. | Cr. | Profit and Loss 12-31-37 Dr. | Cr. | Balance Sheet 12-31-37 Dr. | Cr. |
|---|---|---|---|---|---|---|---|---|---|---|---|
| 1 | Cash | 1,100.00 | | 1,400.00 | | | | | | 1,400.00 | |
| 2 | Accounts Receivable | 4,800.00 | | 5,100.00 | | | | | | 5,100.00 | |
| 3 | Merchandise Inventory | 20,000.00 | | 20,238.00 | | (3) 200.00 | | | | 20,438.00 | |
| 4 | Furniture and Fixtures | 3,000.00 | | 3,100.00 | | | | | | 3,100.00 | |
| 4-a | Res. Depr. Furn. and Fix. | | 900.00 | | 900.00 | | (1) 310.00 | | | | 1,210.00 |
| 5 | Accounts Payable | | 600.00 | | 950.00 | | | | | | 950.00 |
| 6 | Accrued Federal Taxes | | 442.00 | | 480.00 | | (2) 140.00 | | | | 620.00 |
| 7 | Capital Stock | | 20,000.00 | | 20,000.00 | | | | | | 20,000.00 |
| 8 | Surplus | | 3,958.00 | | 3,558.00 | | | | | | 3,558.00 |
| 9 | Sales | | 80,500.00 | | 90,000.00 | | | | 90,000.00 | | |
| 10 | Cost of Sales | 67,708.00 | | 75,465.00 | | | (3) 200.00 | 75,265.00 | | | |
| 11 | Selling Expense | 6,000.00 | | 6,300.00 | | (1) 210.00 | | 6,510.00 | | | |
| 12 | General Expense | 3,500.00 | | 3,950.00 | | (1) 100.00 | | 4,050.00 | | | |
| 6 | Federal Taxes | 442.00 | | 480.00 | | (2) 140.00 | | 620.00 | | | |
| 13 | Purchase Discount | | 400.00 | | 485.00 | | | | 485.00 | | |
| 14 | Sales Discount | 250.00 | | 340.00 | | | | 340.00 | | | |
| | | 106,800.00 | 106,800.00 | 116,373.00 | 116,373.00 | 650.00 | 650.00 | 86,785.00 | 90,485.00 | 30,038.00 | 26,338.00 |
| | Net Income | | | | | | | 3,700.00 | | | 3,700.00 |
| | | | | | | | | 90,485.00 | 90,485.00 | 30,038.00 | 30,038.00 |

Illustration No. 2. Ten-Column Working Trial Balance

(1)

Selling Expense............................. $210.00
General Expense............................ 100.00
    Reserve for Depr. of Furn. and Fix.......     $310.00
        To record depreciation of furniture
and fixtures.

(2)

Federal Taxes.............................. 140.00
    Accrued Federal Taxes.................     140.00
        To record an increase in the amount of
accrued Federal taxes.

(3)

Merchandise Inventory..................... 200.00
    Cost of Sales..........................     200.00
        To record increase in Merchandise In-
ventory and to correct the Cost of Sales for
errors in computation of inventory.

The explanation following each of these journal entries will explain the purpose of the entry.

The next four money columns are devoted to a classification of the adjusted accounts. These columns provide the information needed in preparing a profit and loss statement and a balance sheet. Some accountants might list the balance sheet accounts first on the theory that the accountant usually prepares the balance sheet first. However, it seems best to list the profit and loss accounts first and the balance sheet accounts last since a certified balance sheet is usually the principal objective of an audit. Furthermore, the profit and loss accounts are temporary proprietorship accounts which are closed out at the end of the fiscal period leaving only the balance sheet accounts open in the general ledger. Sometimes the last two columns of a working trial balance are devoted to a post-closing trial balance, but since it would provide the same information as the balance sheet, nothing is gained by providing another pair of columns for a final trial balance.

(2) *The Working Trial Balance in Two Sections.* Many accountants prefer to have the working trial balance divided into sections segregating the balance sheet accounts from the profit and loss accounts, each section being independent of the other and balanced separately.

## THE WAVERLY SUPPLY COMPANY
### Working Trial Balance   (Sec. 1)

| Sched. No. | Balance Sheet Accounts | Adjusted Trial Balance 12-31-36 Dr | Cr | Bookkeeper's Trial Balance 12-31-37 Dr | Cr | Auditor's Adjustments Dr | Cr | Adjusted Balances 12-31-37 Dr | Cr |
|---|---|---|---|---|---|---|---|---|---|
| 1 | Cash | 1,100.00 | | 1,400.00 | | | | 1,400.00 | |
| 2 | Accounts Receivable | 4,800.00 | | 5,100.00 | | | | 5,100.00 | |
| 3 | Merchandise Inventory | 20,000.00 | | 20,238.00 | | (3) 200.00 | | 20,438.00 | |
| 4 | Furniture and Fixtures | 3,000.00 | | 3,100.00 | | | | 3,100.00 | |
| 4-a | Res. for Depr. of Furn. and Fix. | | 900.00 | | 900.00 | | (1) 310.00 | | 1,210.00 |
| 5 | Accounts Payable | | 600.00 | | 950.00 | | | | 950.00 |
| 6 | Accrued Federal Taxes | | 442.00 | | 480.00 | | (2) 140.00 | | 620.00 |
| 7 | Capital Stock | | 20,000.00 | | 20,000.00 | | | | 20,000.00 |
| 8 | Surplus | | 3,958.00 | | 3,558.00 | | | | 3,558.00 |
| | Balances from Sec. 2 | 3,000.00 | | 3,950.00 | | 250.00 | | 3,700.00 | |
| | | 28,900.00 | 28,900.00 | 29,838.00 | 29,838.00 | 450.00 | 450.00 | 30,038.00 | 30,038.00 |

## THE WAVERLY SUPPLY COMPANY
### Working Trial Balance   (Sec. 2)

| Sched. No. | Profit and Loss Accounts | Adjusted Trial Balance 12-31-36 Dr | Cr | Bookkeeper's Trial Balance 12-31-37 Dr | Cr | Auditor's Adjustments Dr | Cr | Adjusted Balances 12-31-37 Dr | Cr |
|---|---|---|---|---|---|---|---|---|---|
| 9 | Sales | | 80,500.00 | | 90,000.00 | | | | 90,000.00 |
| 10 | Cost of Sales | 67,708.00 | | 75,465.00 | | | (3) 200.00 | 75,265.00 | |
| 11 | Selling Expense | 6,000.00 | | 6,300.00 | | (1) 210.00 | | 6,510.00 | |
| 12 | General Expense | 3,500.00 | | 3,950.00 | | (1) 100.00 | | 4,050.00 | |
| 6 | Federal Taxes | 442.00 | | 480.00 | | (2) 140.00 | | 620.00 | |
| 13 | Purchase Discount | | 400.00 | | 485.00 | | | | 485.00 |
| 14 | Sales Discount | 250.00 | | 340.00 | | | | 340.00 | |
| | Balances to Sec. 1 | 3,000.00 | | 3,950.00 | | | 250.00 | 3,700.00 | |
| | | 80,900.00 | 80,900.00 | 90,485.00 | 90,485.00 | 450.00 | 450.00 | 90,485.00 | 90,485.00 |

**Illustration No. 3. Working Trial Balance in Two Sections**

Eight money columns are used in setting up this form of work sheet: two columns for the adjusted trial balance of the previous year, two columns for the bookkeeper's trial balance of the current year, two columns for the auditor's adjustments, and two columns for the adjusted balances. The adjusted balances in the balance sheet section comprise the accounts for the balance sheet. The adjusted balances in the profit and loss section comprise the accounts for the profit and loss statement.

In Illustration No. 3 there is shown a working trial balance divided into two sections. It is based on the same data as is used in Illustration No. 2, thus facilitating comparison to see what advantages are obtained through the use of such a working trial balance.

(3) *The Working Trial Balance in Four Sections.* Some accountants go one step further in sectionalizing the trial balance, and divide the balance sheet section into two parts, one for *assets* and the other for *liabilities*. The profit and loss section is likewise divided into two parts, the *income section* (profit and loss credits) and the *expense section* (profit and loss debits). This results in the trial balance being divided into four sections. In this manner, it is possible to have all of the accounts of a like nature grouped together.

The reserves for depreciation and for doubtful accounts may be recorded either in the asset section or in the liability section, whichever is preferred. If they are shown in the asset section, they should be recorded in "red" to indicate that they are credits. Some accountants prefer to list the reserves in the liability section with the balance sheet credits. Notes receivable discounted may also be listed either in the asset section or the liability section of the working trial balance. If it is listed in the asset section, it should be recorded in "red" to indicate a credit or deduction. If it is listed in the liability section, it is well to earmark the notes receivable account in the asset section as a means of referring to the fact that there are notes discounted outstanding on which the client is liable because of endorsement. Keep in mind the fact that notes receivable discounted may be shown on the balance sheet either as a deduction from notes receivable or as a contingent liability.

(*Continued on page 64*)

## THE WAVERLY SUPPLY COMPANY
### Working Trial Balance (Sec. 1)

| Sched. No. | Assets | Adjusted Balances 12-31-36 | Bookkeeper's Balances 12-31-37 | Auditor's Adjustments Dr. | Auditor's Adjustments Cr. | Adjusted Balances 12-31-37 |
|---|---|---|---|---|---|---|
| 1 | Cash | 1,100.00 | 1,400.00 | ...... | ...... | 1,400.00 |
| 2 | Accounts Receivable | 4,800.00 | 5,100.00 | ...... | ...... | 5,100.00 |
| 3 | Merchandise Inventory | 20,000.00 | 20,238.00 | ③ 200.00 | ...... | 20,438.00 |
| 4 | Furniture and Fixtures | 3,000.00 | 3,100.00 | ...... | ...... | 3,100.00 |
| | | 28,900.00 | 29,838.00 | 200.00 | | 30,038.00 |

## THE WAVERLY SUPPLY COMPANY
### Working Trial Balance (Sec. 2)

| Sched. No. | Liabilities | Adjusted Balances 12-31-36 | Bookkeeper's Balances 12-31-37 | Auditor's Adjustments Dr. | Auditor's Adjustments Cr. | Adjusted Balances 12-31-37 |
|---|---|---|---|---|---|---|
| 5 | Accounts Payable | 600.00 | 950.00 | ...... | ...... | 950.00 |
| 6 | Accrued Federal Taxes | 442.00 | 480.00 | ...... | ② 140.00 | 620.00 |
| 4-a | Reserve for Depreciation of Furniture and Fixtures | 900.00 | 900.00 | ...... | ① 310.00 | 1,210.00 |
| 7 | Capital Stock | 20,000.00 | 20,000.00 | ...... | ...... | 20,000.00 |
| 8 | Surplus | 3,958.00 | 3,558.00 | ...... | ...... | 3,558.00 |
| | Balances from Sec. 3 | 3,000.00 | 3,950.00 | 450.00 | 200.00 | 3,700.00 |
| | | 28,900.00 | 29,838.00 | 450.00 | 650.00 | 30,038.00 |

## THE WAVERLY SUPPLY COMPANY
### Working Trial Balance
(Sec. 3)

| Sched. No. | Profit and Loss Credits | Adjusted Balances 12-31-36 | Bookkeeper's Balances 12-31-37 | Auditor's Adjustments Dr. | Cr. | Adjusted Balances 12-31-37 |
|---|---|---|---|---|---|---|
| 9 | Sales | 80,500.00 | 90,000.00 | | | 90,000.00 |
| 10 | Purchase Discount | 400.00 | 485.00 | | | 485.00 |
| | Footings from Sec. 4 | 80,900.00 | 90,485.00 | 450.00 | 200.00 | 90,485.00 |
| | | 77,900.00 | 86,535.00 | | 200.00 | 86,785.00 |
| | Balances to Sec. 2 | 3,000.00 | 3,950.00 | 450.00 | 200.00 | 3,700.00 |

## THE WAVERLY SUPPLY COMPANY
### Working Trial Balance
(Sec. 4)

| Sched. No. | Profit and Loss Debits | Adjusted Balances 12-31-36 | Bookkeeper's Balances 12-31-37 | Auditor's Adjustments Dr. | Cr. | Adjusted Balances 12-31-37 |
|---|---|---|---|---|---|---|
| 11 | Cost of Sales | 67,708.00 | 75,465.00 | | (3) 200.00 | 75,265.00 |
| 12 | Selling Expense | 6,000.00 | 6,300.00 | (1) 210.00 | | 6,510.00 |
| 13 | General Expense | 3,500.00 | 3,950.00 | (1) 100.00 | | 4,050.00 |
| 6 | Federal Taxes | 442.00 | 480.00 | (2) 140.00 | | 620.00 |
| 14 | Sales Discount | 250.00 | 340.00 | | | 340.00 |
| | Footings to Sec. 3 | 77,900.00 | 86,535.00 | 450.00 | 200.00 | 86,785.00 |

Illustration No. 4.  Working Trial Balance in Four Sections

Where unissued capital stock appears in the trial balance, it may be listed either in the asset section or the liability section of the working trial balance. If it is listed in the liability section it should be recorded in "red" to indicate a debit or deduction. If listed among the assets, it should be earmarked to show that it should be listed on the balance sheet as a deduction from capital stock. Such accounts as notes receivable discounted and unissued capital stock are sometimes referred to as contra accounts meaning that they are to be treated as deductions from other accounts. That is, notes receivable discounted is a deduction from notes receivable and unissued capital stock is a deduction from capital stock.

In Illustration No. 4 there is shown a working trial balance in four sections. This also is based on the same data as is used in Illustrations Nos. 2 and 3. The subsequent use of the different forms of working sheets will not only reveal the purpose they serve, but will also indicate the advantages to be derived from the use of each form.

**Schedules and Analyses.** The auditor records on data sheets the pertinent facts concerning the verification of each item in the trial balance. These data sheets are referred to as schedules or analyses. It is best to use one or more separate sheets of stationery for each schedule prepared. The heading for each schedule should contain the following: the name of the company being audited, the name of the account to which the schedule relates, and the date of the audit. The size of the schedule page will depend on the nature and amount of material to be recorded. Columnar or analysis paper should be used in preparing the necessary schedules.

Several schedules may be necessary in connection with the verification of some accounts. For example, in verifying the cash account, a schedule is made of the amount of undeposited cash on hand. A second schedule is necessary for the bank reconciliation. Other cash schedules may be necessary, such as those for proof of cash, count of petty cash, and so forth.

Analyses are made of some of the accounts. In verifying the fixed asset accounts, for example, it is usually necessary to make an analysis of the charges and credits made during the audit period. If all entries made by the bookkeeper are supported by vouchers or other documentary evidence such as receipted bills or invoices, the auditor should have no difficulty in ascertaining that the entries have been properly recorded. Property that has been disposed of must also be verified to see that the retirement was properly recorded.

Each item in the balance sheet section of the working trial balance will usually be supported by one or more schedules or analyses. If the auditor has made a previous audit of the records and no changes have taken place in some of the accounts since the preceding audit, it will not be necessary to prepare schedules for these items. It will be sufficient to make notations on the working trial balance, stating that no changes have taken place in these accounts since the date of the previous audit.

**Adjusting Journal Entries.** The adjusting journal entries made by an auditor may be classified into several types. If the auditor discovers entries that have been made incorrectly in the ledger accounts, he may make the necessary adjusting entries. Entries of various types may have been omitted. For example, accrued and deferred income and expense items may not have been recorded at the close of the fiscal period. Depreciation and the allowance for uncollectible accounts may not have been provided for. If fixed assets have been sold during the fiscal period, the depreciation reserve may not have been cleared of the amount which was applicable to the property. Profits or losses on sales of securities may not have been recorded in the accounts. These and many other types of entries may be necessary in order to show the earnings and the financial condition correctly at the close of the audit period.

The adjusting journal entries are usually recorded on journal or analysis paper. The entries are drafted, generally, at the time each error or omission is discovered by the auditor, but they probably will not be posted to the working trial balance until the audit work is completed. The entries will then be posted to the working trial balance and the working trial balance will be totaled and balanced. If the accounts of the client are to be brought into accord with the auditor's report, it will be necessary for the bookkeeper to record the adjusting entries on his books. The auditor is fully justified in making such a recommendation. If the books are brought into accord with the auditor's report, it will simplify succeeding audits.

## PREPARATION OF WORKING PAPERS

**Should the Working Papers Be Written in Ink or in Pencil?** Opinions differ on this question. Some accountants insist that audit working papers should be recorded in ink. The working papers are the property of the auditor and are a permanent record of the audit. For this reason it is maintained that they should be written in ink. It is easier, however, to make changes in pencil figures, and if a good grade of pencil is used, the figures hold up well even after years of use. It is safe to say that the majority of auditors' working papers are written in pencil.

**Arrangement of the Working Papers.** The working papers of the auditor should be so arranged that they may be readily used for reference purposes. Most firms of public accountants adopt certain standards which they expect their employees to follow in the completion of audits. The working papers preferably should be of the same size so that they may be punched to fit a loose-leaf binder of standard size. Information in regard to more than one subject usually should not be recorded on the same sheet of paper. One or more sheets of paper should be devoted to the recording of the data gathered on each subject. For instance, it would be unwise to record the cash count and a list of securities on the same sheet of paper. Where an audit program or a definite schedule is being followed in the completion of an audit, the working papers should be assembled or arranged in the order of the schedule or program. Usually the working papers of all employees engaged on a particular audit are assembled and retained by the senior in charge until the audit is completed, when all of the working papers must be referred to the one who will prepare the final report for the client.

**Indexing the Working Papers.** If the working trial balance is divided into sections (i. e., separate sections for balance sheet and for profit and loss accounts, or separate sections for assets, liabilities, profit and loss debits, and profit and loss credits), it is a common practice to index the schedules to the working trial balance, since the accounts will usually be listed in the working trial balance approximately in the order in which they will appear in the statements. Space may be allowed along the left hand margin, or elsewhere on the page, for the schedule or analysis number. The schedules are usually indexed numerically or literally in the order in which the accounts appear in the working trial balance.

Some accountants find it advantageous to index the schedules to a balance sheet and profit and loss statement in addition to indexing them to the working trial balance. Accountants' working papers should be so arranged that when the balance sheet and statement of profit and loss are prepared in their final form, it will be possible to trace any item appearing in the statements back to the working trial balance and the supporting schedules.

If the working trial balance is divided into sections so that the balance sheet accounts are grouped together in one section and the profit and loss accounts in another, it is usually possible to trace the items into the completed balance sheet and profit and loss statement. In this case, it is probably more convenient to index the schedules to the accounts in the working trial balance than to attempt to index them to the balance sheet and profit and loss statement.

**Filing Working Papers.** The working papers should be filed in such a way as to be readily accessible in case they are wanted for reference. They may be filed either alphabetically or numerically. If filed by number, an alphabetical index file of clients will be used as a reference to determine the number under which the working papers are filed. In preparing the papers for filing, they may be placed in folders and inserted in large file envelopes. The envelopes containing the working papers are then filed until needed for subsequent engagements.

**Importance of Understanding Audit Working Papers.** It is well to state at this point that one who plans to seek a position as a junior accountant on an auditing staff should be thoroughly familiar with the mechanics of audit working papers. A beginning junior accountant can be of much greater value to his employer and, also, will stand a much better chance of making a favorable impression with the senior accountants for whom he works, if he understands the preparation of audit working papers. A senior accountant usually cannot take the time to teach a junior accountant matters which the junior accountant can and should find out for himself before seeking employment.

## APPLICATION OF PRINCIPLES

### AUDIT OF THE BLANK MANUFACTURING COMPANY

(*Beginning with this chapter and ending with Chapter 15, the principles developed in each chapter will be applied through the medium of an audit of the accounts of The Blank Manufacturing Company. The primary purpose of this is to illustrate audit procedure and to develop the working papers of the auditors engaged in making the audit. Instead of reproducing the handwriting of the auditors, the data compiled by them is printed in italics, as in Illustration No. 5, pages 72 to 74. This provides better illustrations which are more legible, hence easier to read.*)

Stevenson and Bennett, certified public accountants, were engaged by The Blank Manufacturing Company to make an audit classified as an "Examination of Financial Statements." The auditors' report was to be included in the company's annual report to stockholders. The company had been in active operation for two years but this audit represented the first annual audit of the company's books. The calendar year 1937 was the year under audit.

Mr. W. H. Merz, a senior accountant, and Mr. C. E. Shaw and Mr. J. I. King, junior accountants, were assigned to make the audit. They reported at the general office of The Blank Manufacturing Company on Monday morning, January 17, 1938, and were introduced to Mr. L. W. Shields, general manager, Mr. Harold Pond, chief accountant, and the heads of the various departments.

Mr. Merz requested and was supplied with the following by the chief accountant:

(a) A list of the books of account and records

(b) A trial balance of the general ledger accounts taken as of December 31, 1937

(c) Information regarding adjustments considered necessary by the chief accountant, but which have not been taken into account and which are not reflected in the trial balance.

Mr. Merz assigned Mr. Shaw to audit the cash and securities and Mr. King to audit the notes and accounts receivable, while he proceeded to examine the company's certificate of incorpora-

(*Continued on page 70*)

### Books of Account

(a) General Journal
(b) Purchases Book
 c) Purchases Returns Book
(d) Sales Book
(e) Sales Returns Book
(f) Cash Receipts Book
(g) Cash Payments Book
(h) Notes Receivable Book
(i) Notes Payable Book
(j) General Ledger
(k) Customers' Ledger
(l) Creditors' Ledger

### Data on Adjustments Compiled by Mr. Pond

1. The inventories as calculated by company employees at December 31, 1937, were as follows:

| | |
|---|---:|
| Raw Materials | $25,000.00 |
| Goods in Process | 30,000.00 |
| Finished Stock | 80,000.00 |

2. Accrued Salaries and Wages............ 6,311.20

3. Unexpired Insurance.................... 1,146.37

4. Accrued Interest on Marketable Securities.. 77.08

5. Accrued Interest on Sinking Fund Investment 160.42

6. Credits to the reserves for depreciation of fixed assets are to be made at the same rates as were used at the end of the preceding year.

7. Organization expense is to be written off at the rate of 10% per annum.

8. Bond discount is to be written off at the rate of 5% per annum.

9. It is estimated that approximately 2% of notes and accounts receivable will prove to be worthless.

10. During the year 1937, $25,150 was spent for advertising in a nation wide advertising campaign. The officers of the company wish to distribute this cost over a period of two years.

tion and to read the minutes of the stockholders' and board of directors' meetings. He also verified the footings and balances of the general ledger accounts.

In examining the company's certificate of incorporation and in reading the corporation minutes, and from other sources, Mr. Merz obtained the following information: (1) the company was organized and received its charter from the State of Indiana, July 15, 1935; (2) its plant and business offices are located in Indianapolis, Indiana; (3) on January 10, 1936, the first year of operation, the board of directors authorized that organization expenses amounting to $8,166.67 be written off over a period of ten years; (4) on January 15, 1936, an issue of 20-year bonds with a par value of $100,000 was sold to underwriters at a discount of $7,500. The bonds were issued to provide additional working capital for the company. The directors voted that this discount should be distributed over the life of the bonds by writing off 5% each year; (5) on July 1, 1937, the board of directors declared a dividend of 5% payable August 1, 1937, to stockholders of record July 15, 1937. This dividend amounted to $22,500. Cash equivalent to the amount of the dividend was withdrawn from the Merchants National Bank—Checking Account, and deposited in a special bank account on which dividend checks were issued. There remains in the dividend account $2,050 which represents the amount of dividends unclaimed. Checks to this amount were returned by the post office marked "Unclaimed." No further information of interest to the auditors was obtained from the minutes, as only routine business was transacted at the meetings of the stockholders and board of directors other than that indicated above. (The schedule prepared by Mr. Merz is reproduced in Chapter Fourteen. See Illustration No. 37.)

Mr. Merz plans to prepare a working trial balance in two sections with the following columnar arrangement:

(1) Bookkeeper's balances. Dr. and Cr.

(2) Auditor's adjustments. Dr. and Cr.

(3) Adjusted balances. Dr. and Cr.

Ordinary analysis paper is used in the preparation of the working trial balance. Illustration No. 5 shows the working trial balance after Mr. Merz copied the bookkeeper's trial balance

(*Continued on page 75*)

## THE BLANK MANUFACTURING COMPANY

### Trial Balance, December 31, 1937, Prepared by Mr. Pond

| | | |
|---|---:|---:|
| Petty Cash | $ 500.00 | |
| Merchants Bank—Checking Account | 20,179.76 | |
| Merchants Bank—Dividend Account | 2,050.00 | |
| Merchants Bank—Bond Interest Account | 2,500.00 | |
| Marketable Securities | 20,225.00 | |
| Notes Receivable—Trade Debtors | 7,145.72 | |
| Accounts Receivable—Trade Debtors | 81,687.00 | |
| Reserve for Doubtful Notes and Accounts | | $ 56.00 |
| Raw Materials Inventory | 37,310.50 | |
| Finished Goods Inventory | 15,000.00 | |
| Office Furniture (net) | 2,600.50 | |
| Delivery Trucks | 15,000.00 | |
| Reserve for Depr. of Delivery Trucks, 20% | | 3,000.00 |
| Tools and Implements (net) | 20,215.00 | |
| Machinery | 100,000.00 | |
| Reserve for Depreciation of Machinery, 6% | | 6,000.00 |
| Buildings | 150,000.00 | |
| Reserve for Depreciation of Buildings, 2½% | | 3,750.00 |
| Land | 140,000.00 | |
| Sinking Fund | 5,000.00 | |
| Prepaid Insurance | 4,997.34 | |
| Salary Advances to Employees | 980.00 | |
| Bond Discount | 7,125.00 | |
| Organization Expense | 7,350.00 | |
| Office Supplies | 510.00 | |
| Notes Payable | | 21,000.00 |
| Accounts Payable | | 39,462.00 |
| State U. C. Contributions Payable | | 1,609.41 |
| Dividend Payable—Unclaimed Checks | | 2,050.00 |
| Employer's Fed. Excise Tax Payable (O. A. B.) | | 957.23 |
| Employees' Income Tax Payable (O. A. B.) | | 957.23 |
| Employer's Fed. Excise Tax Payable (U. C.) | | 753.22 |
| First Mortgage, 5%, 20-Year Bonds | | 100,000.00 |
| Capital Stock, 50,000 shares, $10 par value | | 500,000.00 |
| Unissued Capital Stock | 50,000.00 | |
| Surplus | | 41,879.81 |
| Sinking Fund Reserve | | 2,750.00 |
| Dividend #1 | 22,500.00 | |
| Sales—Less Returns and Allowances | | 635,597.47 |
| Raw Material Purchases | 195,250.00 | |
| Freight In | 2,831.00 | |
| Factory Labor | 300,200.00 | |
| Property Taxes | 2,010.00 | |
| Capital Stock Tax | 650.00 | |
| Maintenance and Repairs | 13,471.00 | |
| Miscellaneous Factory Expenses | 615.00 | |
| Federal Social Security Excise Tax (O. A. B.) | 3,829.21 | |
| Federal Social Security Excise Tax (U. C.) | 753.22 | |
| State U. C. Contributions | 6,778.98 | |
| Garage Expense | 2,000.00 | |
| Delivery Salaries | 8,600.00 | |
| Salaries of Salesmen | 30,220.00 | |
| Advertising | 25,150.00 | |
| Office Salaries | 37,560.00 | |
| Office Expense | 12,875.00 | |
| Miscellaneous General Expense | 910.00 | |
| Dividends Received | | 450.00 |
| Rent Income | | 250.00 |
| Interest and Discount (net) | 734.81 | |
| Bond Interest | 2,708.33 | |
| Total | $1,360,522.37 | $1,360,522.37 |

## THE BLANK MANUFACTURING COMPANY

### Working Trial Balance, December 31, 1937

(Sec. 1)

| Sched. No. | Balance Sheet Accounts | Bookkeeper's Balances | Auditor's Adjustments | | Adjusted Balances | |
|---|---|---|---|---|---|---|
| | Petty Cash | 500.00 | | | | |
| | Merchants Bank—Checking Account | 20,179.76 | | | | |
| | Merchants Bank—Dividend Account | 2,050.00 | | | | |
| | Merchants Bank—Bond Int. Account | 2,500.00 | | | | |
| | Marketable Securities | 20,225.00 | | | | |
| | Notes Receivable—Trade Debtors | 7,145.72 | | | | |
| | Accounts Receivable—Trade Debtors | 81,687.00 | | | | |
| | Res. for Doubtful Notes and Accounts | 56.00 | | | | |
| | Raw Materials Inventory | 37,310.50 | | | | |
| | Goods in Process Inventory | | | | | |
| | Finished Goods Inventory | 15,000.00 | | | | |
| | Office Furniture (net) | 2,600.50 | | | | |
| | Delivery Trucks | 15,000.00 | | | | |
| | Res. for Depr. of Delivery Trucks, 20% | 3,000.00 | | | | |
| | Tools and Implements (net) | 20,215.00 | | | | |
| | Machinery | 100,000.00 | | | | |
| | Reserve for Depr. of Machinery, 6% | 6,000.00 | | | | |
| | Buildings | 150,000.00 | | | | |
| | Reserve for Depr. of Buildings, 2½% | 3,750.00 | | | | |
| | Land | 140,000.00 | | | | |
| | Sinking Fund | 5,500.00 | | | | |
| | Prepaid Insurance | 4,997.34 | | | | |
| | Salary Advances to Employees | 980.00 | | | | |
| | Bond Discount | 7,125.00 | 30.00 | | | |

| | | |
|---|---|---|
| Organization Expense | 7,350.00 | |
| Office Supplies | 510.00 | |
| Notes Payable | | 21,000.00 |
| Accounts Payable | | 39,462.00 |
| State U. C. Contributions Payable | | 1,609.41 |
| Dividend Payable—Unclaimed Checks | | 2,050.00 |
| Employer's Fed. Ex. Tax Pay. (O. A. B.) | | 957.23 |
| Employees' Income Tax Pay. (O. A. B.) | | 957.23 |
| Employer's Fed. Ex. Tax Pay. (U. C.) | | 753.22 |
| First Mortgage, 5%, 20-year bond | | 100,000.00 |
| Cap. Stock, 50,000 shares, $10 par value | | 500,000.00 |
| Unissued Capital Stock | 50,000.00 | |
| Surplus | | 41,879.81 |
| Sinking Fund Reserve | | 2,750.00 |
| Dividend # 1 | 22,500.00 | |
| | 713,375.82 | 724,224.90 |
| Balance from Section 2 | 10,849.08 | |
| | 724,224.90 | 724,224.90 |

Illustration No. 5.  Working Trial Balance

## THE BLANK MANUFACTURING COMPANY

### Working Trial Balance, December 31, 1937

(Sec. 2)

| Sched. No. | Profit and Loss Accounts | Bookkeeper's Balances | | Auditor's Adjustments | | Adjusted Balances | |
|---|---|---|---|---|---|---|---|
| | Sales—Less Returns and Allowances | | 635,597.47 | | | | |
| | Raw Material Purchases | 195,250.00 | | | | | |
| | Freight In | 2,831.00 | | | | | |
| | Factory Labor | 300,200.00 | | | | | |
| | Property Taxes | 2,010.00 | | | | | |
| | Capital Stock Tax | 650.00 | | | | | |
| | Maintenance and Repairs | 13,471.00 | | | | | |
| | Miscellaneous Factory Expenses | 615.00 | | | | | |
| | Fed. Social Security Excise Tax (O.A.B.) | 3,829.21 | | | | | |
| | Fed. Social Security Excise Tax (U.C.) | 753.22 | | | | | |
| | State U. C. Contributions | 6,778.98 | | | | | |
| | Garage Expense | 2,000.00 | | | | | |
| | Delivery Salaries | 8,600.00 | | | | | |
| | Salaries of Salesmen | 30,220.00 | | 30.00 | | | |
| | Advertising | 25,150.00 | | | | | |
| | Office Salaries | 37,560.00 | | | | | |
| | Office Expense | 12,875.00 | | | | | |
| | Miscellaneous General Expense | 910.00 | | | | | |
| | Dividends Received | | 450.00 | | | | |
| | Rent Income | | 250.00 | | | | |
| | Interest and Discount (net) | 734.81 | | | | | |
| | Bond Interest | 2,708.33 | | | | | |
| | | 647,146.55 | 636,297.47 | | | | |
| | Balance to Section 1 | | 10,849.08 | | | | |
| | | 647,146.55 | 647,146.55 | | | | |

and made an adjustment for an error of $30 in the debit foot-
ing of the account with salary advances to employees and an
error of the same amount in the credit footing of the account
with salaries of salesmen. When these errors were called to the
attention of the bookkeeper the following correcting entry was
drafted in journal form and posted to the accounts:

Salaries of Salesmen............................ $30.00
  Salary Advances to Employees.............           $30.00

As the audit progresses additional adjustments will be made
when necessary so that at the completion of the audit the working trial balance will provide a complete list of the adjusted
balances of all accounts as they should appear in the auditor's
report.

### SUMMARY

This brief discussion of audit working papers is presented
at the beginning of the text so that the reader will be acquainted
with the method followed in conducting an audit before studying
the chapters on auditing principles and procedure.

An audit could not be conducted without the use of working
papers. As each item in a trial balance is verified, it is necessary,
generally, to prepare one or more schedules, giving information
about the item verified. The schedule may be a reconciliation of
accounts, or a list of items comprising an account balance. It
may be an analysis of an account. In addition to schedules, there
may be letters of confirmation of bank balances, or of amounts
due from customers. Excerpts may be taken from the minutes
of the board of directors' and of stockholders' meetings. All of
this written information should be included in the audit working
papers.

Working papers are the papers upon which the auditor
compiles his data, analyses, computations, notes, schedules, and
records pertaining to an audit. From these papers is extracted
the material for the audit report which is submitted to the
client. The only media of connection between the records of the
client and the audit report are the working papers prepared on
the premises of the client by the auditor. They are the only
proof of the correctness of the records and of the correctness of
the audit report. The working papers serve the auditor as the
source of information for his remarks and advice in discussing

business matters with the client, in solving taxation problems with the Bureau of Internal Revenue, in defending his position from criticism, in defending himself in the event of legal action, in the preparation of his report, in the review of his report and his work by the principals or partners, and in serving as a guide for the next audit of the same client.

## AUDITING THEORY

**3—31.** Of what importance are audit working papers to an auditor?

**3—32.** What use may be made of audit working papers after an audit has been completed?

**3—33.** Name five types of records which would ordinarily be found in a set of audit working papers.

**3—34.** Distinguish between a trial balance and a working trial balance. Of what importance is a working trial balance in conducting an audit?

**3—35.** Describe three types of working trial balances, and mention any advantages you can think of in regard to each type.

**3—36.** Why are schedules and analyses used in conducting an audit?

**3—37.** Should audit working papers be written in ink or in pencil?

**3—38.** What is meant by indexing audit working papers? Why should audit working papers be indexed?

**3—39.** Should the auditor's adjustments be recorded on the books or is it sufficient that their effect be reflected in the auditor's report?

**3—40.** Describe a proper arrangement of audit working papers—
(a) During an audit.
(b) When ready for filing.

(A. I. A.)

## AUDITING PROBLEMS

**3—1.** The bookkeeper for Uptown Store, Inc. prepared an adjusted trial balance as of December 31, 1938.

An audit of the accounts disclosed that the following additional adjustments should be made:

(1) The petty cash fund had not been cleared of expense vouchers (Miscellaneous General Expense) amounting to $105 at December 31, 1938.

(2) Accrued interest on marketable securities and accrued interest on notes receivable amounting to $250 and $80, respectively, had not been recorded at December 31, 1938.

(3) The reserve for bad debts should be increased to 2½% of the accounts receivable.

(4) Provision is to be made for depreciation on the furniture and fixtures and the building at the following depreciation rates: furniture and fixtures, 10%; building, 3%.

## UPTOWN STORE, INC.
### Trial Balance, December 31, 1938

| | | |
|---|---:|---:|
| Petty Cash | $ 300.00 | |
| Farmers National Bank—Checking Account | 31,000.00 | |
| Marketable Securities | 22,000.00 | |
| Notes Receivable | 10,000.00 | |
| Accounts Receivable | 65,000.00 | |
| Reserve for Bad Debts | | $ 310.00 |
| Merchandise Inventory | 165,000.00 | |
| Furniture and Fixtures | 28,000.00 | |
| Reserve for Depr.—Furniture and Fixtures | | 1,410.00 |
| Building | 220,000.00 | |
| Reserve for Depr.—Building | | 36,000.00 |
| Land | 60,000.00 | |
| Office Supplies | 325.00 | |
| Prepaid Insurance | 720.00 | |
| Good Will | 50,000.00 | |
| Notes Payable | | 40,000.00 |
| Accounts Payable | | 61,000.00 |
| Capital Stock—Common | | 200,000.00 |
| Capital Stock—Preferred—5%, cum. | | 200,000.00 |
| Surplus | | 62,762.00 |
| Preferred Dividend #24 | 5,000.00 | |
| Sales | | 820,000.00 |
| Cost of Sales | 732,000.00 | |
| Sales Salaries | 20,500.00 | |
| Advertising | 2,450.00 | |
| Office Salaries | 9,975.00 | |
| Miscellaneous General Expense | 640.00 | |
| Taxes | 3,100.00 | |
| Interest Income | | 590.00 |
| Purchase Discount | | 6,200.00 |
| Interest Expense | 1,402.00 | |
| Sales Discount | 860.00 | |
| | $1,428,272.00 | $1,428,272.00 |

(5) The good will account was established during the year 1938, by action of the board of directors with a corresponding credit to the surplus account. The company's earnings during the past few years were larger in amount than the earnings of their competitors. It was, therefore, contended that the company was justified in setting up the good will account. (Debit surplus and credit good will to reverse entry made by bookkeeper.)

(6) A check of the unpaid invoice file disclosed accounts payable for the purchase of merchandise, amounting to $2,850, which were unentered at December 31, 1938. The merchandise had been received and was included in the inventory at December 31, 1938. (Debit cost of sales and credit accounts payable.)

(7) Accrued wages to employees amounting to $660 (sales salaries, $440; office salaries, $220) had not been recorded by the bookkeeper at the close of the period.

(8) Included in the notes payable were notes amounting to $20,000 due to the Farmers National Bank on which interest of $190 was prepaid at December 31, 1938.

(9) Accrued taxes, other than income taxes, amounting to $1,300 had not been recorded at the close of the period.

(10) The debit balance in the preferred dividend account indicates that a dividend was declared and paid during the period. The dividend account should, therefore, be closed into surplus.

REQUIRED: Prepare journal entries to record the above adjustments and post them to a working trial balance arranged in two sections as shown in Illustration No. 3.

3—2. The bookkeeper for Alexander Brothers, Inc. has prepared a trial balance as at December 31, 1938, before making adjustments for the following:

(1) Merchandise inventory, December 31, 1938, $50,000. (Clear inventories, purchases, and freight in through cost of sales account.)

(2) The reserve for bad debts should be maintained at 2% of the accounts receivable.

(3) Depreciation of fixed assets is to be provided for at the following rates: furniture and fixtures, 10% per annum; and store building, 2½% per annum.

(4) The balance in the marketable securities account represents an investment in the following bonds upon which the accrued interest has not been recorded at December 31, 1938:

New York Central, 5%, maturing in the year 2013, $5,000 par, cost, $3,800, interest payable April 1 and October 1.

Atchison T. and S. F., 4% maturing in the year 1958, $5,000 par, cost, $5,500, interest payable January 1 and July 1.

(5) Accrued interest on notes receivable amounted to $145.

(6) The prepaid insurance account has not been adjusted for expired insurance premiums. The following insurance policies were in operation during the year 1938:

| | Date | | | Total | Unexpired |
|---|---|---|---|---|---|
| Policy | From | To | Coverage | Premium | 1-1-38 |
| Atlantic #4673-W | 1-15-37 | 1-15-40 | Bldg. $90,000.00 | $720.00 | $490.00 |
| Gulf # 194-J | 7- 1-36 | 7- 1-39 | Furn. 10,000.00 | 80.00 | 40.00 |
| Southern # 91-M | 1- 1-38 | 1- 1-39 | Mdse. 40,000.00 | 120.00 | 120.00 |

(7) The following two notes were payable to the Travelers National Bank at December 31, 1938, for loans secured by discounting the company's own notes payable:

| | | | Interest | |
|---|---|---|---|---|
| Date of Note | Maturity Date | Amount | Rate | Amount Paid |
| 12- 1-38 | 3- 1-39 | $10,000.00 | 6% | $150.00 |
| 12-15-38 | 3-15-39 | 5,000.00 | 6% | 75.00 |

(8) Accrued sales and office salaries amounted to $400 and $220 respectively at December 31, 1938.

## ALEXANDER BROTHERS, INC.

### Trial Balance, December 31, 1938

| | | |
|---|---:|---:|
| Petty Cash | $ 100.00 | |
| Travelers National Bank—Checking Account | 16,000.00 | |
| Marketable Securities | 9,300.00 | |
| Notes Receivable | 16,500.00 | |
| Notes Receivable Discounted | | $ 2,000.00 |
| Accounts Receivable | 81,000.00 | |
| Reserve for Bad Debts | | 540.00 |
| Merchandise Inventory, December 31, 1937 | 61,000.00 | |
| Furniture and Fixtures | 19,000.00 | |
| Reserve for Depr.—Furniture and Fixtures | | 7,600.00 |
| Store Building | 110,000.00 | |
| Reserve for Depr.—Store Building | | 11,000.00 |
| Land | 16,000.00 | |
| Prepaid Insurance | 650.00 | |
| Prepaid Advertising | 90.00 | |
| Office Supplies | 210.00 | |
| Notes Payable to Bank | | 15,000.00 |
| Accounts Payable | | 44,000.00 |
| Unissued Capital Stock | 40,000.00 | |
| Capital Stock | | 200,000.00 |
| Surplus | | 46,921.00 |
| Dividend #12 | 4,000.00 | |
| Sales | | 290,000.00 |
| Sales Returns | 4,000.00 | |
| Purchases | 193,000.00 | |
| Freight In | 10,000.00 | |
| Selling Expense (control) | 24,000.00 | |
| General Expense (control) | 13,000.00 | |
| Interest Income | | 705.00 |
| Purchase Discounts | | 1,964.00 |
| Interest Expense | 430.00 | |
| Sales Discounts | 1,450.00 | |
| Total | $619,730.00 | $619,730.00 |

REQUIRED: (1) Prepare adjusting journal entries for the adjustment data above. (2) Prepare a four-section working trial balance similar to the one shown in Illustration No. 4.

## AUDITING PRACTICE
### An Audit Case (First Installment)

**Introduction.** An audit project is provided to supplement the discussion in each chapter beginning with this chapter and ending with Chapter Fifteen. The project is arranged in installments, an installment being presented at the end of each chapter to cover verification of items discussed in that chapter.

The project is designed to illustrate an entire audit engagement and is arranged so as to require the services of Mr. Ken B.

Swift, who is a senior accountant in the employ of Knight and Day, certified public accountants. Mr. Swift is to conduct the entire audit, index his working papers at the completion, and write a report covering the engagement.

If questions of principle or procedure arise he is to consult Mr. Knight or Mr. Day for their opinion. Each student in performing the audit work outlined in the project is to consider that he is Mr. Ken B. Swift and follow instructions accordingly.

The audit is designated as an "Examination of Financial Statements" and represents the regular annual audit of the Beverly Supply Company's records preparatory to the preparation of the management's annual report to the company's stockholders. It may be assumed that Knight and Day have performed the Beverly Supply Company's annual audit each year since the company's incorporation, December 20, 1932. The Beverly Supply Company is incorporated in the state of California and conducts most of its business in the city of Los Angeles. The current audit represents the sixth annual audit of the company's records.

**Working Trial Balance.** Ken B. Swift reports at the Beverly Supply Company's office at 8:30 on the morning of January 3, 1939 and is introduced to the company's bookkeeper and to other office employees. He is presented with the bookkeeper's trial balances of the general ledger and subsidiary ledgers, and with a list of the accounting records maintained by the company.

The student who is to perform the work of Mr. Swift is instructed to set up a working trial balance from the general ledger trial balance presented on page 81. It may be assumed that Mr. Swift checked the bookkeeper's trial balance with the ledger accounts to determine that the balances were in agreement.

Knight and Day have adopted a standard form of working trial balance that is used on all of their audit engagements. The working trial balance is in two sections, one section for balance sheet accounts and a second section for profit and loss accounts.

(*Continued on page 82*)

## BEVERLY SUPPLY COMPANY
### Trial Balance

| Ledger Accounts | Auditor's Adjusted Trial Balance 12-31-37 | | Bookkeeper's Trial Balance 12-31-38 | |
|---|---|---|---|---|
| Petty Cash..................... | 300.00 | ......... | 300.00 | ......... |
| Farmers' National Bank................ | 27,100.00 | ......... | 30,183.65 | ......... |
| Marketable Securities............... | 14,740.00 | ......... | 24,788.00 | ......... |
| Notes Receivable, Trade Debtors....... | 3,100.00 | ......... | 15,860.00 | ......... |
| Accrued Interest Receivable......... | 74.00 | ......... | ......... | ......... |
| Accounts Receivable, Trade Debtors .... | 7,670.00 | ......... | 6,925.90 | ......... |
| Res. for Doubtful Notes and Accounts... | ......... | 737.00 | ......... | 170.10 |
| Accounts Payable Debit Balances...... | 200.00 | ......... | ......... | ......... |
| Accrued Bond Interest Receivable...... | 45.00 | ......... | ......... | ......... |
| Merchandise Stock .................. | 55,000.00 | ......... | 61,500.00 | ......... |
| Furniture and Fixtures.............. | 16,900.00 | ......... | 17,922.50 | ......... |
| Reserve for Depr.—Furn. and Fix....... | ......... | 5,560.00 | ......... | 7,352.25 |
| Delivery Equipment.. ............... | 8,200.00 | ......... | 9,200.00 | ......... |
| Reserve for Depr.—Del. Equip.......... | ......... | 3,680.00 | ......... | 5,520.00 |
| Buildings....................... | 170,000.00 | ......... | 190,000.00 | ......... |
| Reserve for Depr.—Buildings.......... | ......... | 12,937.50 | ......... | 20,187.50 |
| Land........................... | 16,725.00 | ......... | 26,725.00 | ......... |
| Prepaid Insurance................. | 745.83 | ......... | 647.43 | ......... |
| Store and Office Supplies............. | 224.50 | ......... | 246.00 | ......... |
| Bond Discount and Expense........... | 2,220.00 | ......... | 2,100.00 | ......... |
| Notes Payable.................... | ......... | 18,000.00 | ......... | 30,000.00 |
| Accrued Interest Payable............. | ......... | 270.00 | ......... | ......... |
| Accounts Payable................. | ......... | 28,170.84 | ......... | 31,411.25 |
| Accounts Receivable Credit Balances.... | ......... | 190.00 | ......... | ......... |
| Employer's Fed. Ex. Tax Pay. (O.A.B.) | ......... | ......... | ......... | 82.00 |
| Employees' Income Tax Pay (O.A.B.).. | ......... | ......... | ......... | 82.00 |
| Employer's Fed. Excise Tax Pay. (U.C.) .. | ......... | ......... | ......... | 99.19 |
| State U. C. Contributions Payable...... | ......... | ......... | ......... | 189.00 |
| Accrued Salaries................... | ......... | 1,300.00 | ......... | ......... |
| Accrued Property Taxes Payable....... | ......... | 2,450.00 | ......... | ......... |
| Accrued Capital Stock Tax Payable.... | ......... | 150.00 | ......... | ......... |
| Serial Bonds Payable—5%........... | ......... | 95,000.00 | ......... | 90,000.00 |
| Accrued Interest on Bonds............. | ......... | 1,979.17 | ......... | ......... |
| Deferred Interest Income............. | ......... | 10.00 | ......... | ......... |
| Unissued Capital Stock..... | 50,000.00 | ......... | 50,000.00 | ......... |
| Capital Stock ($100 par)........... | ......... | 200,000.00 | ......... | 200,000.00 |
| Surplus......................... | ......... | 3,133.71 | ......... | 32,133.71 |
| Sales........................... | ......... | 251,014.45 | ......... | 298,291.19 |
| Sales Returns.................... | 2,400.00 | ......... | 3,050.00 | ......... |
| Cost of Sales..................... | 190,400.00 | ......... | 220,080.00 | ......... |
| Sales Salaries.................... | 14,000.00 | ......... | 14,200.00 | ......... |
| Advertising...................... | 6,000.00 | ......... | 5,820.00 | ......... |
| Delivery Salaries.................. | 5,100.00 | ......... | 5,250.00 | ......... |
| Bad Debts..... .................. | 590.00 | ......... | ......... | ......... |
| Depreciation of Delivery Equip......... | 1,640.00 | ......... | 1,840.00 | ......... |
| Office Salaries.................... | 4,500.00 | ......... | 4,420.00 | ......... |
| Administrative Salaries.............. | 10,000.00 | ......... | 10,492.00 | ......... |
| Miscellaneous Expense............... | 850.00 | ......... | 661.65 | ......... |
| Insurance Expense................. | 715.00 | ......... | 535.00 | ......... |
| Fed. Social Security Excise Tax (O.A.B.) | ......... | ......... | 317.70 | ......... |
| Fed. Social Security Excise Tax (U.C.).. | ......... | ......... | 99.19 | ......... |
| State U. C. Contributions............. | ......... | ......... | 892.67 | ......... |
| Store and Office Supplies Used........ | 90.00 | ......... | 193.00 | ......... |
| Depreciation of Furn. and Fix.......... | 1,690.00 | ......... | 1,792.25 | ......... |
| Depreciation of Buildings............ | 4,250.00 | ......... | 4,750.00 | ......... |
| Capital Stock Tax............. | 150.00 | ......... | 150.00 | ......... |
| Deferred Capital Stock Tax........... | 150.00 | ......... | ......... | ......... |
| Property Taxes.................... | 4,900.00 | ......... | 2,600.00 | ......... |
| Interest on Notes Receivable........... | ......... | 180.00 | ......... | 210.00 |
| Bond Interest Income................ | ......... | 242.50 | ......... | 154.58 |
| Dividends Received.................. | ......... | 970.00 | ......... | 1,045.00 |
| Interest on Notes Payable............ | 415.00 | ......... | 620.00 | ......... |
| Interest on Bonds Payable............ | 4,770.84 | ......... | 2,645.83 | ......... |
| Bond Dis. and Exp. Written Off......... | 120.00 | ......... | 120.00 | ......... |
| Total.......................... | 625,975.17 | 625,975.17 | 716,927.77 | 716,927.77 |

The balances of the profit and loss columns are forwarded to the balance sheet section to bring both sections into balance. The arrangement and columnar headings of the working trial balance should be the same as in Illustration No. 3.

The auditor's adjusted trial balance at December 31, 1937, and the bookkeeper's general ledger trial balance at December 31, 1938, are given on page 81.

# CHAPTER FOUR

## CASH

1. **Beginning the Audit**

2. **Verifying the Cash Balance**
   - (a) Counting the Cash
   - (b) Verifying the Bank Balance
   - (c) Reconciling the Bank Certificate
   - (d) Proving the Cash Balance
   - (e) Petty Cash Fund
   - (f) Special Cash Funds

3. **Verifying the Cash Records**
   - (a) Testing
   - (b) Proving the Footings
   - (c) Internal Check and Control
   - (d) Types of Internal Check

4. **Verifying the Cash Receipts Record**
   - (a) Extent of Verification
   - (b) Cash Audits

5. **Verifying the Cash Payments Record**
   - (a) Audit Procedure
   - (b) Examining the Paid Checks
   - (c) Kiting of Checks

6. **Auditing Procedure**

7. **Application of Principles**

8. **An Audit Case—Second Installment**

A complete verification of cash would involve a verification of the cash balance at the close of the fiscal period and a verification of the cash receipts and disbursements records for the period. Most audits do not involve a complete verification of the cash records. If a complete audit of cash is to be made, four questions confront the auditor which may be stated as follows:

(1) Was the cash balance shown to exist by the cash records actually on hand or on deposit in the concern's bank account at the close of the fiscal period?

(2) Was all the cash received during the fiscal period properly recorded in the cash receipts records, and correctly posted to the ledger accounts?

(3) Was all the cash recorded in the cash receipts record during the audit period deposited in the concern's bank account or otherwise accounted for?

(4) Were all the disbursements of cash correctly recorded and properly accounted for?

In a complete audit of cash, the auditor should investigate and provide a satisfactory answer to all of these questions. But, as a matter of fact, in very few audits is an attempt made to do so. The cash balance is verified in every audit, but it is neither necessary nor desirable in many audits to attempt to answer completely the other questions mentioned above.

The internal organization and financial control of many concerns may be such as to make a complete audit of the cash records unnecessary. A concern may maintain an auditing division which reviews the work of the employees in the cashier's and accounting departments. The duties of the various employees concerned with the receiving and recording of cash may be so arranged that it would be exceedingly difficult for a misappropriation of cash to occur and to remain undetected.

Most annual audits may be classified as "Examinations of Financial Statements" and are made for the purpose of preparing verified statements of financial condition rather than for the purpose of reviewing all the transactions of the year to see that they have been correctly recorded. In verifying the cash in such audits, the auditor is principally concerned with determining that the cash balance, consisting of cash on hand, in transit, or on deposit, is correctly stated.

### BEGINNING THE AUDIT

Most audits begin with a count of the cash on hand and a verification of the cash balance as shown by the record of receipts and disbursements. The fact that in most instances the auditor begins an engagement by counting the cash on hand is probably the result of early practice when most audits were simply cash audits made for the purpose of detecting fraud, misappropriation or embezzlement. An audit of cash may materially aid an auditor in familiarizing himself with the accounting methods, office routine, and business procedure.

While audits may begin with the verification of cash, care should be taken to see that all assets that may readily be converted into cash are audited at approximately the same time as cash. Therefore, cash, securities, and notes receivable should be verified simultaneously so that funds derived from one source may not be used to make up a shortage in another. For example, notes or securities may be sold to provide funds to make up a shortage of cash, or cash may be used after it has been verified to redeem notes or securities that have been fraudulently hypothecated.

**Cash Records.** Upon reporting for duty the auditor should immediately prepare a list of the cash records kept by his client which will include the general cash records, the petty cash records, any special cash records, and the bank records. Separate records may be kept for receipts and disbursements. There may or may not be a petty cash fund and other special funds. There may be one or more bank accounts. In addition to the original records of cash receipts and disbursements, there may be a general and other special cash accounts kept in the general ledger. Practice in regard to this is not uniform. In some cases no general cash account will be kept in the general ledger; a cash book serving the function of a cash account. Obviously, the auditor needs to obtain all this information before he may proceed intelligently with an audit of cash.

**Counting the Cash.** The cash should be counted at the close of business and on the last day of the period under audit if possible. However, it frequently happens that the audit takes place subsequent to the close of the accounting period, therefore, it is best to count the cash before business hours on the morning of the first day of the audit.

The cash to be counted consists usually of (1) the undeposited cash receipts of the last business day preceding the count, and (2) special cash funds maintained for the purpose of making change and for petty cash payments. All cash should be counted at approximately the same time to prevent substitution of amounts from one fund to another. Forms for a cash count are shown in Illustrations Nos. 8 and 9.

Some advocate that it is best to permit the person who is in charge of the cash to handle it and do the actual counting for

# THE BLANK MANUFACTURING CO.

## Indianapolis, Ind.

January 17, 1938.

The Merchants National Bank
100 Main Street
Cincinnati, Ohio

Gentlemen:

Our auditors, Stevenson and Bennett, Certified Public
Accountants, are now making the periodic audit of our books.
Will you kindly furnish them with the information requested
below, as of the close of business on January 15, 1938? An
addressed, stamped envelope, is enclosed for your convenience.

1. Balance in the checking account.

2. Balance in any special accounts now maintained with
you.

3. A statement of all notes held by you of which we are
the makers or endorsers.

4. A statement of any collateral which you hold.

5. A statement of any contingent items not stated in any
of the above.

Sincerely yours,

THE BLANK MANUFACTURING CO

*L. W. Shields*

LWS-DS

General Manager

Illustration No. 6.    Request for Bank Certificate

the reason that he is, as a rule, skilled in the handling of cash. Another reason is that if the auditor does not handle the cash in person, he avoids the possibility of becoming involved in any irregularities. In case the cashier or person in charge of cash is permitted to count it, the auditor must, of course, supervise the count with the greatest care.

In counting the cash, the auditor must ascertain that all customers' checks, produced as a part of the cash balance, have been properly entered in the cash book prior to the close of business on that date, and should note the dates and descriptions of such checks as well as the dates and descriptions of cash advances made and not recorded on the books. Any advances to employees should be carefully investigated, and if they are secured by personal checks the auditor should see that the checks are certified by the bank on which they are drawn before the close of the audit.

Any unusual cash items, such as I. O. U.'s, should be carefully listed for investigation. However, the auditor should not adopt an attitude with regard to such matters that will react against him. If an employee owes an item of a few cents because he could not make change, it is not necessary to take the matter up with the head of the department or the president of the company.

One will frequently find bad coins that have been taken in unknowingly. These, of course, must be taken into consideration, but it does not justify criticism or fault-finding. The auditor should not adopt the attitude of a detective.

**Verifying the Bank Balance.** Certificates must be obtained from the various banks in which accounts are maintained, as at the close of business, on the same day that the cash balance is counted. It is preferable that this be done on the last day of the fiscal period, otherwise on the first day of the audit. This is done by presenting to the banks a request signed by the depositor or his agent asking for a certificate showing the balance on deposit on a certain date and such other information as may be desired. This certificate should be mailed to the auditor, not to the depositor. A usual form of request is shown in Illustration No. 6. A bank certificate is shown in Illustration No. 11.

**Reconciling the Bank Certificate.** The items which should appear in the bank reconciliation are ascertained (1) by comparing the deposits entered in the cash book, or check book, with those appearing on the bank statement for the period immediately preceding the date of verification of cash, and (2) by comparing the canceled checks returned by the bank with the entries in the cash payments record. To these current differences should be added any items from the preceding month's reconciliation which have not been cleared through the bank, or have not been recorded in the cash book.

Where several banks are used as depositories, this becomes more complicated, but the general plan of procedure is the same. The list of checks outstanding, should be investigated before the audit is completed, when it will likely be found that most of them have been presented to the bank for payment. Any checks still outstanding should be investigated to ascertain why they have not been presented for payment.

Many forms of bank reconciliations are in use. The form shown in Illustration No. 7 has wide usage and has as its advantage the fact that it shows the available cash balance at the close of the period and also shows clearly the adjustments that need to be made to the cash book balance in order to arrive at the available cash balance.

This type of reconciliation will usually suffice for a business which has a well arranged accounting organization. Many small companies not only do not deposit all receipts daily, but they pay bills from the cash on hand, so that receipts do not equal deposits, nor do payments equal the total value of checks issued. The firm may make cash payments from the cash in the register, placing the bill or voucher in the drawer for a record of the transactions. The bookkeeper may then enter these cash payments in the cash book and make the proper charge to the vouchers payable each day. In case of such procedure, in order to reconcile deposits with receipts, the total receipts must be equal to the deposits plus the cash payments, and the total disbursements equal to total checks issued plus the cash payments.

**Proving the Cash Balance.** After the cash on hand has been counted and the balance on deposit in the bank has been reconciled, the total cash balance should be checked with the balance of the cash account or cash book. If a general cash ac-

### Bank

| | | |
|---|---:|---:|
| Balance per bank certificate (Date)............................................. | | $ 717.84 |
| Add: Undeposited cash receipts of December 31 (per schedule of count)......... | | 384.50 |
| | | $1,102.34 |
| Deduct Outstanding checks: | | |
| No. 346................................................... | $ 12.25 | |
| No. 378................................................... | 110.00 | |
| No. 379................................................... | 50.00 | |
| No. 380................................................... | 250.00 | |
| No. 390................................................... | 10.00 | 432.25 |
| Adjusted bank balance.................................................. | | $ 670.09 |

### Cash Book

| | |
|---|---:|
| Balance per cash book (Date)............................................. | $ 178.92 |
| Add: Collection of note................................................. | 500.00 |
| | $ 678.92 |
| Deduct: Bank "charge-back" of check returned N.S.F.—M. Keller.............. | 8.83 |
| Adjusted book balance.................................................. | $ 670.09 |

**Illustration No. 7. Bank Reconciliation**

count is kept in the general ledger the balance of this account should be compared with the cash receipts and disbursements records to see that they are in accord. Usually an audit is made some days after the close of the period. This necessitates the counting of cash on a later date and working back to the day desired. After the exact cash balance has been determined on the date of audit, add the disbursements and deduct the receipts and the balance for the date desired will be obtained. This should be compared with the cash book balance on the date at the close of the fiscal period.

To illustrate this procedure:

| | |
|---|---:|
| Balance per cash book, March 12, 1938.......... | $12,380.24 |
| Add: Disbursements, since December 31, 1937... | 6,205.18 |
| | $18,585.42 |
| Deduct: Receipts since December 31, 1937...... | 4,756.98 |
| Balance, December 31, 1937, end of period........ | $13,828.44 |

## PETTY CASH FUND

The petty cash fund should be counted simultaneously with the count of the undeposited cash receipts and with the verification of the securities and the notes receivable. The items in the fund should be listed, and the total of the cash, checks, expense vouchers, and I.O.U.'s which comprise the fund should equal the amount shown by the general ledger account to be in the fund. A petty cash count is shown in Illustration No. 8.

Where an audit is being made some time after the close of the fiscal period, the petty cash fund should be checked and the auditor should work back to the close of the period under audit. If it is found that expenses paid out of the petty cash fund have not all been recorded on the general books as at the close of the period, it may be necessary to make adjustments to record the expenses in the auditor's working papers. The auditor should also make a list of the items being carried in the cash fund, such as, receipts, checks, I. O. U.'s, etc. Unusual items should be discussed with the petty cashier and if the auditor is not satisfied with his explanation they should be reported to the proper authority which is usually the executive to whom the petty cashier is responsible.

The auditor should make a sufficient test of the petty cash fund and records to satisfy himself on the following points:

(1) That the petty cashier is properly recording all disbursements.

(2) That no invoices are being paid out of the petty cash fund which should be paid out of the general cash fund.

(3) That all funds entrusted to the petty cashier are being used for the purpose for which intended.

(4) That all disbursements for the period under audit are recorded on the general books.

If discrepancies are found in connection with any of the first three points, the auditor should report to the proper authority. If it is found that not all of the disbursements for the period have been recorded on the general books, it may be necessary for the auditor to make such entries in his working papers in order that they may be included in his report.

**Special Cash Funds.** In addition to the regular cash and petty cash accounts, many companies may have special funds set up for some specific purpose. For example, there may be pay roll funds with a special bank account for the funds. A fund may be set up for the purpose of advancing amounts to officers and employees who are traveling for the company, or funds may be provided for any other purpose which the officials of the company may see fit to provide. Such accounts may usually be verified through the regular channels, but may require special considerations from the auditor. For example, in the pay roll account there will often be unclaimed wages, which the auditor must set up as a liability, the funds provided therefor being carried as a part of the cash account until called for. The advances account may contain I.O.U.'s which should be presented as advances and not as cash, and so on, depending on the conditions surrounding the operations of the company's activities.

## VERIFYING THE CASH RECORDS

While most audits do not include in their scope the verification of the entries in the cash book, yet, for completeness of discussion, it is considered desirable to discuss briefly the audit work involved in auditing the cash book. The reader should keep in mind that there is a two-fold problem involved in an audit of cash. First, there is the problem of determining that the cash balance, shown to be on hand by the ledger accounts, actually is on hand as stated. Second, there is the problem of auditing the cash records to see that the transactions have been properly recorded, that the money columns have been correctly footed, and that the postings were made correctly.

**Proving the Footings.** The principle of testing may be used in connection with much of the audit procedure. It may be used particularly in the task of verifying the footings of the cash book and other books of original entry. If the cash book is to be audited for three months of the year, the money columns for the months selected should be footed. The work of footing the columns may be reduced from 20 to 40 per cent by adding the "dollar" columns only, omitting the "cents" columns. After the "dollar" column has been added, the amount necessary to carry to the "ten-dollar" column can be estimated with reasonable accuracy.

**Internal Check and Control.** The amount of checking necessary to verify cash and other records will depend somewhat upon the internal organization of the concern to be audited. The following quotation from the bulletin "Examination of Financial Statements" emphasizes the importance of this question: "An important factor to be considered by an accountant in formulating his (audit) program is the nature and extent of internal check and control in the organization under examination."

"The term 'internal check and control' is used to describe those measures and methods adopted within the organization itself to safeguard the cash and other assets of the company as well as to check the clerical accuracy of the bookkeeping. The safeguards will cover such matters as the handling of incoming mail and remittances, the proceeds of cash sales, the preparation and payment of pay rolls and the disbursement of funds generally, and the receipt and shipment of goods. These safeguards will frequently take the form of a definite segregation of duties or the utilization of mechanical devices. For example, the cashier will have no part in the entering of customers' accounts or the preparation of their statements, and neither he nor the ledger keeper will have authority to issue or approve credits to customers; the clerk recording the labor time and preparing the pay roll will not be permitted to handle the funds; approval and entry of vouchers will be made by others than the disbursing officer; and stock records and inventory control will be kept independent of both the shipping and receiving departments. The extent to which these and other measures are practicable will naturally vary with the size of the organization and the personnel employed."

**Types of Internal Check.** The following are some of the desirable policies followed to safeguard cash and to make misappropriations of funds difficult:

(1) Persons engaged in handling cash should not have access to the ledger accounts. This provision is made in order to eliminate the possibility that entries might be made in the accounts in an attempt to conceal a defalcation of cash.

(2) It is desirable to have incoming mail opened and cash received listed (in triplicate) by someone other than the cashier. After the cash has been listed, it will be turned over to the cashier together with a list of the funds received. The bookkeeping de-

partment will also receive a copy so that postings may be made to the customers' accounts.

(3) An imprest or petty cash fund should be used for the payment of small amounts not requiring the issuance of a check.

(4) Each day's cash receipts should be deposited in the bank intact on the next banking day following the receipt. No payments should be made from the daily receipts. Cash payments should be made from a petty cash fund, or by checks drawn on the concern's bank account.

(5) Deposit slips should be prepared in duplicate and receipted by the bank. The duplicate should be retained for reference.

(6) All checks should be signed by two or more officials authorized to sign checks.

(7) The monthly reconciliation of the bank account should be made by someone other than the cashier.

(8) Someone other than the bookkeeper or the cashier should be designated to approve all credits to customers and the write-off of uncollectible accounts.

(9) All employees should take a vacation. By so doing other employees will be doing the work of the one on vacation and any discrepancies in the records may be disclosed.

(10) The sales tickets should be numbered consecutively and all numbers and amounts accounted for.

Many other safeguards could be mentioned, but those given above will suffice to illustrate the methods followed.

### VERIFYING THE CASH RECEIPTS RECORDS

**Extent of Verification.** The cash receipts and disbursements records are not verified to any great extent in audits designated as balance sheet audits or examinations of financial statements. The auditor is concerned in these audits with the verification of the cash balance at the close of the period. The cash records are checked only as it may be necessary to verify the cash balance. The cash records are verified in detail, however, in audits designated as cash audits and in audits classified as detailed or complete audits. In this latter type of audit, it is intended that the entries in the books of original entry should be verified either completely or by the use of tests.

**Cash Audits.**  Audits limited in scope to include only the cash transactions (cash audits) are rarely performed except in connection with religious, fraternal, or charitable organizations which operate on a cash basis.  With this type of organization, it is the desire of the members or of the governing body to have the records audited to determine that all the cash received and cash paid out has been properly accounted for by the employees entrusted with the handling of cash.  In such audits all the recorded transactions may be scrutinized by the auditor and also a check be made to ascertain that all the cash received was recorded in the cash records and deposited in the organization's bank account.

**Audit Procedure.**  Most concerns deposit all cash receipts daily, and all payments are made by check with the exception of small items, which are usually cared for through a petty cash fund.  Where this is done and there is a reasonable system of internal check, the following procedure may be followed:

(1) The money columns of the cash receipts record should be footed for all twelve months, or for as many months as seem advisable if test checking is being used.  The totals should be cross footed and the amounts traced to the ledger accounts.

(2) Test checks should be made of the entries recording receipts from customers and from cash sales to see that there is a proper system of internal check in the recording of these items and that it is functioning properly.

(3) The totals of cash receipts by months should be compared or reconciled with the total deposits in the bank as shown by the pass book or bank statements.  This procedure is frequently referred to as "proving cash," and is done in order to prove that the cash receipts as recorded in the cash book have been deposited in the bank.  Of course this procedure is useless unless the footings of the cash book have been proved also.  An alternative to this procedure is to check each individual deposit recorded in the cash book with the amount recorded on the bank statement.

(4) The duplicate deposit slips for the last five or more days of the audit period should be compared item for item with the entries in the cash receipts records.  This comparison should be made to see that there are no items deposited in the bank that have not been recorded in the cash receipts record.

Unrecorded deposits might be made during the days imme-diately preceding the close of the period in order to repay funds previously borrowed so as to avoid showing a shortage at the balance sheet date. Also if there are two or more bank accounts, a check might be issued on one bank and deposited in a second bank without recording either the check or the deposit. Such a maneuver is referred to as "kiting" checks. A comparison of the duplicate deposit slips with the entries in the cash receipts record would disclose such a transaction.

A comparison of duplicate deposit slips might also disclose "lapping of cash receipts." A cashier can borrow comparatively large sums of money by withholding customers receipts of one date and giving the customers credit at a later date. This is done by using the funds received from other customers to credit the accounts of those whose funds were previously withheld. Where "lapping" is practiced, the customers eventually get credit for their payments, but not on the date on which the payments were made.

### VERIFYING THE CASH PAYMENTS RECORD

**Audit Procedure.** The amount of audit work that the auditor should perform in verifying the cash disbursements records will depend upon the type of audit that is being performed and the internal organization of the concern being audited. Generally the following procedure may be followed:

(1) The money columns of the cash disbursements records should be footed for the entire audit period or for such months as seem advisable if a test audit is being made. The column totals should be cross footed and the postings of the totals traced to the ledger accounts.

(2) The checks paid and returned by the bank should be compared with the entries in the cash disbursements records. (See the discussion on examining paid checks which follows.)

(3) The total cash payments by months as shown by the cash payments records should be compared with or reconciled to the total payments by months as shown by the bank statement and canceled checks.

(4) If cash discounts are allowed to customers, a test should be made of the accuracy of some of the items to determine whether the customer actually took the discount and whether

the amount shown in the discount column was correctly recorded. Funds may be extracted and be concealed by recording discounts for customers who have paid after the discount period, but who did not deduct the discount in making their remittance. The amount of discounts taken by customers may also be raised in amount and small sums of money extracted equal to the amounts by which the discounts were raised. If reference is made to the customers' accounts, or to the remittance stubs, the auditor can determine whether the customers were entitled to the discounts and whether they deducted them in making the remittances.

(5) One or more pay rolls should be audited. The pay roll should be footed, and the amounts traced to the general ledger accounts. The names on the pay roll should be checked against the personnel department's records or time clock cards to determine that the individuals named are actually in the employ of the concern being audited. If padding of the pay roll is suspected, the auditor should be present and supervise the paying of employees. If employees do not call to claim their pay envelopes, investigation should be made to determine that the individuals concerned are actually employees.

**Examining the Paid Checks.** If a cash audit or a detailed audit is being performed, the auditor should secure the bank statements and the canceled checks for each month of the audit period. The checks should be examined and compared with the entries in the cash disbursements record. The cash disbursements record may be a check register or a cash disbursements journal. In some cases only check book stubs may be maintained. In examining and comparing canceled checks, the following procedure should be followed:

(1) Compare the name of the payee and the amount of the check with the name and the amount recorded in the cash disbursements record. A check mark should be made after the amount of each item compared. Unchecked items should represent outstanding checks.

(2) Endorsements on the back of the check should be carefully scrutinized as checks may be issued to fictitious persons and the funds appropriated by the cashier or other employees. Two endorsements would generally appear on such checks. Checks with two or more endorsements should be examined carefully.

(3) Checks bearing the client's own endorsement stamp should also be investigated as checks may be issued and deposited to the client's account by the cashier to cover a cash shortage.

(4) The numbers of all checks should be accounted for as it would be possible for a cashier to issue a fraudulent check, not record it in the cash book, and extract and destroy the check when it was returned by the bank.

**Kiting of Checks.** If the concern being audited has two or more bank accounts, it is especially necessary for the auditor to determine that there have been no unrecorded checks issued during the five or ten days preceding the close of the audit period. An unrecorded check could be issued on one bank and deposited in another bank to cover a shortage in the latter account. The unrecorded check could be omitted from the cashier's bank reconciliation and not be disclosed to the auditor. A comparison of duplicate deposit slips for the last five or ten days of the fiscal period with the entries in the cash receipts records would disclose any items that were deposited which were not recorded in the cash receipts book. Likewise, if the auditor secured a bank statement and the canceled checks from the bank five or ten days after the close of the fiscal period after all checks outstanding at the closing date had cleared through the banks, any checks issued but not recorded would be discovered by comparing the checks returned by the bank with the entries in the cash disbursements record. If any checks which were deposited at the close of the period were returned by the banks on which they were drawn on account of insufficient funds or for other reasons, they would also be discovered by the auditor.

### AUDITING PROCEDURE APPLICABLE TO CASH

The American Institute of Accountants suggests the following procedure in auditing cash in connection with an "Examination of Financial Statements" for a small or moderate sized company maintaining a reasonable system of internal check and control:

"1. Count cash on hand and compare with the recorded cash balance. This count should be made at the same time as notes receivable and investments are inspected or taken under control. Precautions should be taken to guard against the possibility of a shortage in one of these assets being covered up by temporarily converting other negotiable assets or withdrawing funds from the bank.

"2. Ascertain when counting cash that all checks (other than those cashed for others) produced as part of the cash balance have been entered in the cash book prior to the close of the period. Note the dates and particulars of such checks and of all advances made from cash but not recorded on the books. Investigate closely advances to employees; if they are represented by personal checks see that these checks (and those cashed for persons outside the company) are deposited and paid before completion of the examination.

"3. See that all cash funds are cleared of material amounts representing disbursements prior to the date of the balance sheet.

"4. Obtain directly from all depositaries certificates as of the close of business on the closing date. Obtain reconciliation of the balances shown on the certificates with the balances shown by the cash book, check book stubs, or check registers, taking into consideration the outstanding checks, and other outstanding items.

"5. Compare the checks returned by banks, item by item, with the cash book for last month, or work backwards from the last day of the period under examination until all recently drawn outstanding checks have been covered. As this procedure will not disclose any outstanding checks which may not be recorded, a better confirmation may be provided by comparing the outstanding checks shown on the bank reconciliation with checks returned by the banks in the subsequent month. Make special inquiry to ascertain if there are any unpaid checks long outstanding. See that no checks are drawn for cash or other purposes at the end of the period but not entered until the next period.

"6. Ascertain that receipts shown in the cash book as deposited on the last day of the period, but not credited by the bank on that day, have actually been deposited as claimed.

"7. If currency and bank transactions are recorded together in the cash book and the cash is not counted until after the close of the period under review, reconcile the bank balances as at the date of the cash count as well as at the date of the balance sheet. Cash on hand, which forms only a part of the balance, may be correct at the date of the count, but it does not follow that the total cash balance (including bank balances) is correct.

"8. Check deposits shown on bank statements or pass books for the last two or three days of the period with the cash receipts book; determine that they were composed of bona fide receipts and that no check drawn by the company was deposited in a bank without being deducted, prior to the close of the period, from the balance at the bank on which the check was drawn. In certain instances such comparison may be extended to include a check of original deposit slips or authenticated copies thereof.

"9. Reconcile total deposits shown by the bank statements for at least one month with the total receipts shown by the cash book; also reconcile total disbursements shown by the bank statements with total checks drawn as recorded in the cash book for the same period.

"10. Trace to the cash book all checks outstanding at the beginning of the period that were not returned and checked in a previous examination.

"11. Funds subject to withdrawal restrictions should be so described on the balance sheet."

**Modifications of Program for Larger or Smaller Concerns.** "Where there are a great many bank accounts with a number of relatively small working funds which are reconciled periodically by employees independent of the cashier's department, it may not be necessary for the accountant to reconcile all the working funds but only to do so for the principal bank accounts, accepting copies of reconciliations signed by internal auditors for the remainder. On the other hand, where the company does not deposit all of its receipts daily it may be desirable for the accountant to check cash book footings in addition to the other steps described."

It has been mentioned that wherever there is an extensive system of internal check the accountant should determine the extent to which he would be justified in reducing the amount of the detailed checking which otherwise he might consider necessary. Only in a large organization is it usually possible to obtain the most satisfactory separation of functions and duties. In a very small organization or one having a highly restricted system of internal check and control, it will be necessary to make a more detailed examination than that heretofore outlined.

## APPLICATION OF PRINCIPLES

### AUDIT OF THE BLANK MANUFACTURING COMPANY (Continued)

As instructed, C. E. Shaw, one of the junior accountants, proceeded to count and audit the cash and securities, while J. I. King, the other junior accountant, audited the notes and accounts receivable. The count and examination of cash, securities, and notes receivable should be done at approximately the same time (simultaneously) so that there can be no substitution of funds derived from one source to make up deficiencies in another.

The discussion in this chapter is confined to the audit of cash. The details concerning the audit of securities and notes receivable will be presented in Chapters Five and Six respectively.

The working papers prepared by Mr. Shaw are shown in the accompanying illustrations and include the following:

(1) A copy of the letter to the bank requesting a confirmation of the cash balances as of the close of business January 15, 1938. (Illustration No. 6.)

(2) Count of the petty cash fund. (Illustration No. 8.)

(3) Count of the undeposited cash receipts of January 15, 1938. (Illustration No. 9.)

(4) Reconciliation of bank balances. (Illustration No. 10.)

(5) Certificate from Merchants National Bank confirming the bank balances. (Illustration No. 11.)

Mr. Shaw verified the footings of the cash receipts book and cash payments book for the first fifteen days of January. The totals for this period were as follows: cash receipts, $36,494.89; and cash payments, $31,402.08.

Other information noted by Mr. Shaw concerning the cash and cash records is as follows:

(1) The footings of the cash book were in ink.

(2) It was the custom of the company to make a deposit each day at noon.

(3) The cash on hand represented the receipts for Saturday, January 15, 1938, which were deposited at noon January 17, 1938.

(4) The cash and cash items listed in the cash count were entered in the cash receipts book as of January 15, 1938.

The student should study the working papers prepared by Mr. Shaw in connection with this audit and make sure that the procedure is understood. It may be well to read again the discussion relating to the audit of The Blank Manufacturing Company in Chapter Three. The working sheet illustrated in Chapter Three is used throughout the audit. The adjusting journal entries drafted by Mr. Shaw will be reflected thereon when the completed working sheet is illustrated at conclusion of the audit.

### THE BLANK MANUFACTURING COMPANY
### Petty Cash
### December 31, 1937

*Cash counted January 17, 1938, at 9:40 a. m. in the presence of I. M. Smartt, Cashier.*

| Denomination | Quantity | Amount | |
|---|---|---|---|
| Currency | | | |
| $10.00 | 5 | $50.00 | |
| 5.00 | 12 | 60.00 | |
| 1.00 | 52 | 52.00 | $162.00 |
| | | | |
| Coin | | | |
| $1.00 | 20 | $20.00 | |
| .50 | 31 | 15.50 | |
| .25 | 50 | 12.50 | |
| .10 | 100 | 10.00 | |
| .05 | 75 | 3.75 | |
| .01 | 205 | 2.05 | 63.80 |

Expense vouchers

| | |
|---|---|
| Vouchers dated December, 1937........................... | 180.00 |
| Vouchers bearing dates between January 1 and January 15, 1938...................................................... | 94.20 |
| Total...................................................... | $500.00 |

*Note:* No entry had been made at December 31, 1937, to reimburse the petty cash fund for the December expense vouchers. The December payments amounted to $180 and were chargeable to expense accounts as follows: Office Expense, $110, and Miscellaneous General Expense, $70. The following adjusting entry should be made:

| | |
|---|---|
| Office Expense................................... | $110.00 |
| Misc. General Expense......................... | 70.00 |
|     Merchants Bank—Checking Account............. | $180.00 |

C. E. Shaw
*(Junior Accountant)*                                   *(Schedule No. 1)*

**Illustration No. 8.  Count of Petty Cash**

## THE BLANK MANUFACTURING COMPANY
### Count of Undeposited Cash Receipts
### January 15, 1938

*Counted January 17, 1938, at 9:15 a. m. in the presence of I. M. Smartt, Cashier.*

| Denomination | Quantity | Amount | |
|---|---|---|---|
| Currency | | | |
| $20.00 | 35 | $700.00 | |
| 10.00 | 36 | 360.00 | |
| 5.00 | 40 | 200.00 | |
| 2.00 | 10 | 20.00 | |
| 1.00 | 80 | 80.00 | $1,360.00 |
| | | | |
| Coin | | | |
| $1.00 | 6 | $ 6.00 | |
| .50 | 35 | 17.50 | |
| .25 | 33 | 8.25 | |
| .10 | 23 | 2.30 | |
| .05 | 14 | .70 | |
| .01 | 41 | .41 | 35.16 |

| Checks | | | |
|---|---|---|---|
| Date | | | |
| 1-11-38 | C. P. McGerry | $ 75.29 | |
| 1-13-38 | P. E. Admire | 154.00 | |
| 1-14-38 | A. E. Mandeck | 23.93 | |
| 1-10-38 | G. W. Gerring | 87.60 | |
| 1- 6-38 | E. H. Lehman | 1.50 | |
| 1-15-38 | H. E. Biddinger | 123.90 | |
| 1- 8-38 | S. J. Musick | 156.00 | |
| 1- 8-38 | W. A. Wirtz | 321.80 | |
| 1-14-38 | C. W. Jones | 1,280.10 | |
| 1-12-38 | C. C. White | 1,347.86 | 3,571.98 |

| Money Orders | | | |
|---|---|---|---|
| P. O. money order—W. W. Ward | $ 1.60 | | |
| Express money order—J. E. Joiner | 2.96 | | 4.56 |

*Total Cash* .................................................. $ 4,971.70

*The above fund was deposited at noon, January 17, 1938, and the duplicate deposit slip and pass book were examined by me.*

C. E. Shaw
(*Junior Accountant*)                   (*Schedule No. 2*)

**Illustration No. 9. Count of Undeposited Cash**

### THE BLANK MANUFACTURING COMPANY
#### Reconciliation of Bank Account
#### as of January 15, 1938

#### Merchants National Bank—Checking Account

| | | |
|---|---|---|
| *Balances per bank certificate*.................... | | *$24,400.50* |
| *Add: Undeposited cash (see record of count)*...... | *$4,971.70* | |
| \**Check returned by bank N.S.F., not entered* | | |
| *in the cash book at January 15, 1938*...... | *17.76* | *4,989.46* |
| | | *$29,389.96* |

*Deduct outstanding checks:*

| No. | Date | Amount | | |
|---|---|---|---|---|
| 4527 | 12- 8-37 | $ 765.80 | | |
| 4597 | 1- 5-38 | 1,499.10 | | |
| 4599 | 1- 7-38 | 75.00 | | |
| 4670 | 1-10-38 | 985.00 | | |
| 4682 | 1-14-38 | 292.49 | | 3,617.39 |

| | |
|---|---|
| *Balance per cash book, 1-15-38*.......................... | *$25,772.57* |
| *Add disbursements, January 1 to 15*...................... | *31,402.08* |
| | *$57,174.65* |
| *Deduct receipts, January 1 to 15*........................ | *36,994.89* |
| *Balance per ledger account, 12-31-37*.................... | *$20,179.76* |

#### Adjusted Cash Balance

| | |
|---|---|
| *Balance per cash book, 12-31-37*......................... | *$20,162.00* |
| *Less amount to reimburse petty cash fund*............... | *180.00* |
| *Cash balance as adjusted, 12-31-37*...................... | *$19,982.00* |

#### Merchants National Bank—Dividend Account

*Balance per bank certificate*.............................. $ 2,050.00

*This balance represents the amount of dividend checks which were returned by the post office unclaimed. It is offset in the trial balance by a liability account, "Dividends Payable—Unclaimed Checks," for the same amount.*

#### Merchants National Bank—Bond Interest Account

*Balance per bank certificate*.............................. $ 2,500.00

\**Note: A bank debit memo for $17.76 was included in the canceled checks returned by the bank at close of business January 15, 1938. This was to cover a check returned by the bank on which it was drawn on account of "Not Sufficient Funds." Since the returned check had not been recorded by the cashier, the following adjusting entry should be made:*

> *Accounts Receivable—Trade Debtors.  $17.76*
> *  Merchants Bank—Checking Acct...        $17.76*

C. E. Shaw
*(Junior Accountant)*                              *(Schedule No. 3)*

**Illustration No. 10.  Reconciliation of Bank Balances**

# THE MERCHANTS NATIONAL BANK

## Indianapolis, Ind.

January 18, 1938

Stevenson and Bennett
Certified Public Accountants
9 West Third Street
Cincinnati, Ohio

Gentlemen:

In compliance with the request of Mr. L. W. Shields, general manager of The Blank Manufacturing Co., we hereby certify that The Blank Manufacturing Co. is carrying the following accounts with us and that the balance credited to their accounts as at the close of business January 15, 1938, is as stated.

| Accounts | Balance |
|---|---|
| General checking account | $24,400.50 |
| Dividend account. | 2,050.00 |
| Bond interest account | 2,500.00 |
| Total | $28,950.50 |

At the close of business, December 31, 1937, the company was not obligated or indebted to us as maker or endorser on loans or contracts with the exception of the following notes which were discounted and bear the endorsement of the company:

| Date | Amount | When Discounted | When Due | Name of Maker |
|---|---|---|---|---|
| 10/30/37 | $4,275.00 | 12/1/37 | 1/30/38 | Alberts & Blackmar |
| 11/18/37 | 1,485.28 | 12/1/37 | 2/18/38 | R. O. Elmeier & Co. |

Respectfully submitted,

THE MERCHANTS NATIONAL BANK

W. H. Wilson
Auditor

WHW/DS

**Illustration No. 11. Bank Certificate**

## SUMMARY

When the audit engagement calls for making a detailed audit of cash it will be necessary to check all receipts and disbursements. In verifying the record of receipts it will be necessary to check the receipts as recorded in the cash book with the sales records. In verifying the record of disbursements it will be necessary to check the disbursements as recorded in the cash book with the vouchers which support or provide evidence of disbursements. Strictly speaking, there should be a voucher of some sort for every disbursement made. The auditor must use every precaution to assure himself that all receipts and disbursements have been properly recorded and accounted for. He should also assure himself that all disbursements were properly authorized. Pay rolls must be carefully examined to make sure that they have not been padded.

If the audit engagement calls for a balance sheet or partial audit, it may only be necessary to count the cash on hand and obtain a certificate from the bank showing the amount on deposit. The bank certificate should then be reconciled with the records to ascertain the true cash balance. The record of receipts and disbursements should be tested in order that the auditor may satisfy himself as to the probable accuracy of the cash balance. The extent to which the verification of receipts and disbursements need be made will depend upon the extent of the internal check.

If one of the primary purposes of the audit is to detect fraud or embezzlement, it will usually be necessary to make a detailed audit which may extend far beyond a mere checking of the cash receipts and disbursements. In any event, such tests should be made as will satisfy the auditor that the cash balance is correct and that he may safely certify that it is correctly stated in the balance sheet. It must be remembered, however, that a balance sheet audit may not be sufficient to disclose fraud or embezzlement although it frequently will be sufficient to indicate evidence of discrepancies in the handling of cash. When such discrepancies are revealed they should be reported to the proper officials with the recommendation that a detailed audit of cash be made. Before making such recommendations the auditor must ascertain beyond a doubt that such discrepancies exist, for otherwise he may get himself into rather serious trouble.

## AUDITING THEORY

**4—41.** Prepare an outline of a specific audit program for verification of the cash balance, assuming the audit is to be made thirty days after the close of the audit period.

**4—42.** In a balance sheet audit made some two or three weeks after the date of the balance sheet, would you consider it necessary to count the cash and how would you verify the bank balance? State exactly how you would proceed, giving your reasons for each step.

**4—43.** Outline a method of routine for handling cash received through the mail for articles shipped to customers out of town.

**4—44.** In organizing the routine of a large department store, how would you assure that all receipts were properly accounted for?

**4—45.** In an audit, if

(a) cash is received but not properly accounted for,

(b) cash is paid for goods that were never delivered, and

(c) cash is paid for wages that were never earned,

all with fraudulent intent, state concisely what methods you would employ to prevent such happenings in the future.

**4—46.** You have been informed that during a period covered by a balance sheet audit, which you have made, a defalcation was going on in the petty cash which was not discovered by you. State what you would do and draft a letter to the board of directors explaining your position.

**4—47.** In making a balance sheet audit for a corporation where cash funds are carried at thirty branches, you are led to believe that the firm is inflating its cash balance. Detail all steps you would take to verify the correct amount of the cash, and indicate what steps would lead to discovery of the manipulations.

**4—48.** Outline a possible routine for verifying the accuracy of disbursements for capital expenditures.

**4—49.** If, in an examination of the accounts of a merchant, the balance shown in the bank, or the balance as certified by the banker, agreed with the balance as disclosed on the merchant's cash book, would you consider any further examination necessary? (C. P. A. Ind.)

**4—50.** The cashier of a firm had disappeared. The cash book is left written up and in balance, the custom being to deposit any cash balance in the bank each day. What course would you pursue to ascertain whether there were any defalcations? (C. P. A. Mich.)

**4—51.** If the actual cash on hand at the date of the balance sheet had not been verified by the auditor on the day of balancing, what method should be employed to prove the correctness before signing or certifying the statements? (C. P. A. New York.)

**4—52.** You are required to make a detailed cash audit for the three-year period ended October 31, 1938. You find a disbursement for "Rent October, 1935, $1,000" on November 6, 1935. You are told the receipt is missing and the duplicate cannot be obtained. You are shown as a voucher, a check dated November 6, 1935, payable to the landlord or order for $1,000, endorsed with a rubber stamp and marked by the client's bankers "paid."

State, with your reasons, whether you would accept this as sufficient evidence that the payment was made as recorded and, if not, what course you would adopt.                                                       (A. I. A.)

**4—53.** In the audit of the books and accounts of the U. S. Corporation for the fiscal year ended June 30, 1938, you find that the cash book consists of a loose-leaf record, typewritten in duplicate. The original sheets which comprise the treasurer's records are given to you for purposes of the audit. The duplicate payment sheets go to the accounts payable department, and the duplicate receivable sheets to the accounts receivable department. State specifically how you would ascertain in your verification of cash that these cash records were real.                                                    (A. I. A.)

## AUDITING PROBLEMS

**4—3.** The result of your count of the "Cash on Hand" at a large agency on January 1, 1939, discloses:

| | | |
|---|---:|---:|
| Bills............................................... | | $1,979.00 |
| Coins.............................................. | | 484.19 |
| Cash items supported by properly signed vouchers: | | |
| January 14, 1936, Sub-agent Jones....... | $200.00 | |
| July 20, 1937, Sub-agent Thomas........ | 140.00 | |
| August 20, 1937, Sub-agent Vincent...... | 75.00 | |
| September 30, 1938, Sub-agent Nelson... | 230.00 | 645.00 |
| Cash balance as per general ledger............... | | $3,108.19 |

Does this count complete your duty as an auditor?  If you consider that further steps are necessary, state what you would do.   (C. P. A. La.)

**4—4.** Fraud is suspected on the part of the cashier of a general trading concern and you are asked to check the transactions recorded by him as shown by the cash book. The books had been audited to December 31, 1938, and the fact established that there was an overdraft of $10.32 after all checks drawn had been presented and paid by the bank. The cash book for the month of January, 1939, shows the following receipts and disbursements:

### Receipts

| | | | |
|---|---|---|---:|
| Jan. | 4 | Collections from customers | $ 2,818.62 |
| | 7 | " | 1,147.33 |
| | 10 | " | 1,064.87 |
| | 13 | " | 1,232.55 |
| | 17 | " | 1,463.24 |
| | 24 | " | 2,417.14 |
| | 26 | " | 1,283.84 |
| | 29 | " | 1,543.62 |
| | 31 | " | 1,054.27 |

Total receipts per cash book.................... $14,025.48

### Disbursements

| | | | |
|---|---|---|---:|
| Jan. | 3 | Overdraft on Bank | $ 10.32 |
| | 3 | Sundry checks | 2,153.27 |
| | 7 | " | 1,427.83 |
| | 11 | " | 926.84 |
| | 15 | " | 853.87 |
| | 19 | " | 428.32 |
| | 24 | " | 647.83 |
| | 29 | " | 2,437.38 |
| | 31 | Balance as shown by cash book | 5,139.82 |

$14,025.48

Cash on hand undeposited amounted to $56.33.

A petty cash fund is operated on the Imprest System.

The deposits in the bank for the month of January, as shown by the bank pass book, after having it balanced at the close of business January 31, amounted to $13,854.37, and the checks returned by the bank for the same period totaled $8,832.34. There were checks outstanding at the time of balancing, January 31, amounting to $53.27.

Prepare a statement showing the results of your investigation. Your solution should show total amount of the discrepancy.　　　(C. P. A. Ohio)

4—5. A commission consisting of three members, A, B, and C, are sent on a special mission and on their return an expense account is turned in by the chairman, A, as follows:

Expenses—

| | | |
|---|---:|---:|
| 3 R. R. Tickets @ $15.50 ............... | $46.50 | |
| 1 Cash Fare.......................... | 15.75 | |
| Sleeping Car......................... | 9.00 | |
| Hotel, etc........................... | 37.50 | |
| To B for incidentals................... | 15.00 | |
| To C " " ................... | 12.00 | |
| To A " " ................... | 9.50 | $145.25 |

Refunds—

| | | | |
|---|---|---:|---:|
| 1 R. R. ticket returned for redemption | | $15.50 | |
| Cash returned by B to A | | 5.30 | |
| " " " C to A | | 3.70 | |
| " " " A to balance | | 30.25 | 54.75 |

$200.00

Cash advanced to A.............................. $200.00

Was the account correct? If not, what amount of money should A have returned? Explain fully.                    (C. P. A. Mich.)

4—6. A concern which you are auditing has several branches, each of which carries a large cash fund on the Imprest System. In counting this fund in one office, where your working papers indicate that there should be $12,000 you find $9,000 made up as follows:

| | |
|---|---:|
| Receipts for expenditures | $4,700.00 |
| Cash in bank per cashier's check book | 2,100.00 |
| Cash in drawer | 860.00 |
| Various I. O. U.'s | 140.00 |
| Various checks in drawer | 1,200.00 |

These checks include one for $380 signed by the cashier, one for $500 signed by the branch manager, the others being personal checks the drawers of which you do not know. State fully what you will do with regard to each of the items. How will you show them on your balance sheet? Which, if any, would you take up with the officers of the concern and why?

(A. I. A.)

## AUDITING PRACTICE

### An Audit Case (Second Installment)

Before setting up the working trial balance on January 3, Ken B. Swift counted the cash and examined the securities and notes receivable. While these three items are verified at approximately the same time (simultaneously) only the cash will be discussed in this installment.

The audit work in connection with the examination of securities and notes will be presented in the third and fourth installments.

In conducting the audit of the Beverly Supply Company, Mr. Swift was instructed to follow the usual audit procedure applicable to an "Examination of Financial Statements." The procedure outlined in steps 1 to 9, pages 97 to 99, is especially appropriate to the audit of cash in this engagement.

## Cash Receipts

| DATE | ACCOUNT CREDITED | ACCT. NO. | AMOUNT |
|------|------------------|-----------|--------|
| Dec. 28 | Brought Forward................... | | 22,714.65 |
| 28 | Cash Sales......................... | 300 | 140.00 |
| 28 | Interest Income.................... | 860 | 60.00 |
| 28 | I. M. Short........................ | 2 | 35.00 |
| 29 | Cash Sales......................... | 300 | 205.00 |
| 29 | K. L. Johnson...................... | 2 | 10.00 |
| 29 | M. N. Kahn........................ | 2 | 420.00 |
| 29 | D. V. Lyons........................ | 2 | 30.00 |
| 30 | Cash Sales......................... | 300 | 300.00 |
| 30 | R. F. Crane........................ | 2 | 80.00 |
| 30 | M. P. Forbes....................... | 2 | 60.00 |
| 30 | C. H. Jones........................ | 2 | 40.00 |
| 31 | Cash Sales......................... | 300 | 270.35 |
| 31 | A. B. Black........................ | 2 | 25.00 |
| 31 | C. D. Brown....................... | 2 | 50.00 |
| 31 | E. F. Green........................ | 2 | 75.00 |
| 31 | G. H. Orange...................... | 2 | 100.00 |
| 31 | I. J. White........................ | 2 | 125.00 |
| | | | |
| | Total........................ | | 24,740.00 |
| Jan. 1 | Balance $30,183.65 | | |

Following is a narrative of the information obtained by Mr. Swift in connection with his audit of the cash records of the Beverly Supply Company:

1. The last page of the cash receipts record and the cash disbursements record for December, 1938, are shown at the top of this and the opposite pages.

2. Following is the cashier's bank reconciliation at November 30, 1938:

| | |
|---|---|
| Balance per bank statement....................... | $21,945.65 |
| Add undeposited cash............................ | 480.00 |
| | $22,425.65 |
| Deduct outstanding checks (per schedule)........... | 563.00 |
| Balance per cash book............................ | $21,862.65 |

## Cash Disbursements

| DATE | PAYEE | CHECK No. | AMOUNT |
|---|---|---|---|
| Dec. 6 | E. F. Anderson & Co. | 801 | 2,400.00 |
| 6 | Bohm Supply Co. | 802 | 1,907.30 |
| 6 | Pay roll Account | 803 | 1,400.00 |
| 10 | K. L. Davis | 804 | 410.00 |
| 11 | City Water Dept. | 805 | 5.00 |
| 15 | Citrus Power Co. | 806 | 25.20 |
| 18 | D. V. Boyce & Co. | 807 | 100.00 |
| 20 | C. M. Gower | 808 | 3,000.00 |
| 20 | Pay roll Account | 809 | 1,400.00 |
| 24 | Atlantic Insurance Co. | 810 | 520.00 |
| 27 | Acme Corporation | 811 | 3,500.00 |
| 27 | So. Pac. R. R. | 812 | 160.00 |
| 28 | O. P. Franklin | 813 | 1.50 |
| 30 | The Chronicle | 814 | 90.00 |
| 30 | S. T. Hansen | 815 | 700.00 |
| 30 | Barton Furniture Co. | 816 | 780.00 |
| 31 | Dartmouth Supply Co. | 817 | 20.00 |
| | Total | | 16,419.00 |

### List of Outstanding Checks

| | |
|---|---|
| #340 | $ 25.00 |
| #784 | 100.00 |
| #791 | 80.00 |
| #793 | 125.00 |
| #794 | 10.00 |
| #795 | 5.50 |
| #796 | 50.00 |
| #797 | 70.00 |
| #798 | 35.00 |
| #799 | 32.50 |
| #800 | 30.00 |
| Total | $563.00 |

3. The bank statement received by Mr. Swift as of the close of business December 31 shows a balance of $30,567.30 and was accompanied by the following canceled checks and debit memo:

| #784—$100.00 | #800—$  30.00 | #807—$  100.00 |
| #791—  80.00 | #801—  2,400.00 | #808—  3,000.00 |
| #793—  125.00 | #802—  1,907.30 | #809—  1,400.00 |
| #794—  10.00 | #803—  1,400.00 | #810—  520.00 |
| #795—  5.50 | #804—  410.00 | #811—  3,500.00 |
| #796—  50.00 | #805—  5.00 | #816—  780.00 |
| #797—  70.00 | #806—  25.20 | |

Debit memo—$35 (check of I. M. Short, a customer, deposited 12–28–38 returned by bank marked N.S.F.)

4. The following cash and cash items comprise the undeposited cash receipts of December 31, which was counted by Mr. Swift at 9:30 a. m., January 3.

Currency and Coin:

Ten dollar bills—11; five dollar bills—25; one dollar bills—12; half dollars—11; quarters—24; dimes—90; nickels—42; pennies—75.

Checks:

| A. B. Black | (dated Dec. 30) | $ 25.00 |
| C. D. Brown | (dated Dec. 29) | 50.00 |
| E. F. Green | (dated Dec. 31) | 75.00 |
| G. H. Orange | (dated Dec. 31) | 100.00 |
| I. J. White | (dated Dec. 28) | 125.00 |

5. The count of the petty cash fund at 10:30 a. m., January 3, disclosed the following items:

Currency and Coin:

Five dollar bills—8; one dollar bills—22; half dollars—50; quarters—48; dimes—60; nickels—80; pennies—30.

Checks:

R. S. Edwards (an employee) Dated Dec. 1, 1938...... $ 50.00
Frank T. Collins (the cashier) Dated Jan. 15, 1939......   100.00

Expense Vouchers (chargeable to miscellaneous expense).....   40.70

6. Mr. Swift totaled the deposits and canceled checks by months for the twelve months as shown by the bank statements, and made a comparison of these figures with the monthly totals of receipts and disbursements as shown in the cash book. The receipts and disbursements per books and per bank are shown in the following tabulation. It is desirable to reconcile the receipts and disbursements as shown by the cash book with those shown by the bank statement to determine that recorded receipts have been deposited and that all disbursements have been recorded. Mr. Swift also tested the cash book footings to determine their accuracy.

## Receipts

|  | Books | Bank | Bank Under* |
|---|---|---|---|
| January..................... | 27,500 | 27,900 | 400 |
| February.................... | 21,110 | 20,980 | 130* |
| March....................... | 20,450 | 20,960 | 510 |
| April....................... | 26,990 | 26,870 | 120* |
| May......................... | 22,140 | 20,030 | 2,110* |
| June........................ | 28,890 | 29,200 | 310 |
| July........................ | 29,500 | 29,650 | 150 |
| August...................... | 27,800 | 27,350 | 450* |
| September................... | 20,250 | 20,390 | 140 |
| October..................... | 21,580 | 21,480 | 100* |
| November.................... | 22,325 | 22,300 | 25* |
| December.................... | 24,740 | 26,930 | 2,190 |
| Total.................... | 293,275 | 294,040 | 765 |

## Disbursements

|  | Books | Bank | Bank Under* |
|---|---|---|---|
| January..................... | 28,900 | 29,486 | 586 |
| February.................... | 17,560 | 17,270 | 290* |
| March....................... | 17,945 | 18,650 | 705 |
| April....................... | 20,280 | 19,750 | 530* |
| May......................... | 19,775 | 19,270 | 505* |
| June........................ | 28,648 | 28,900 | 252 |
| July........................ | 18,120 | 18,485 | 365 |
| August...................... | 27,690 | 27,410 | 280* |
| September .................. | 27,978 | 27,660 | 318* |
| October..................... | 18,790 | 19,120 | 330 |
| November.................... | 17,670 | 18,110 | 440 |
| December.................... | 16,419 | 15,903 | 516* |
| Total.................... | 259,775 | 260,014 | 239 |

The bank reconciliation at December 31, 1937 (the preceding year) showed undeposited cash receipts of $1,410.35 and outstanding checks amounting to $1,268.00. In comparing the bank deposits for the year with the cash book receipts, it is necessary, of course, to eliminate receipts of the preceding year which were deposited during the year under audit.

The total cash receipts for the year as shown by the monthly totals in the cash receipts book, may be reconciled with the total deposits made at the bank (as shown by the monthly bank statements) by the following procedure:

### Reconciliation of Receipts Totals

| | |
|---|---:|
| Total deposits in bank.............................. | $294,040.00 |
| Less: Undeposited cash 12-31-37 (included in January deposits)................................. | 1,410.35 |
| | $292,629.65 |
| Add: Undeposited cash 12-31-38 (not deposited in 1938)......................................... | 645.35 |
| Total receipts per monthly totals of cash book.... | $293,275.00 |

The yearly disbursements totals may likewise be reconciled by adding and subtracting the differences, outstanding checks, bank charge-backs, etc.

7. Duplicate deposit slips (secured from the bank by Mr. Swift) for the cash receipts of December 29 and 30, deposited December 30 and 31, are as follows:

## FARMERS' NATIONAL BANK

December 30, 1938

| | | |
|---|---|---:|
| Currency, | | $ 180.00 |
| Gold, | | |
| Silver, | | 25.00 |
| | | |
| Checks, | | $ 205.00 |
| | 16-212 | 10.00 |
| | 16-180 | 420.00 |
| | 15- 30 | 30.00 |
| | 16-266 | 2,000.00 |
| | Total | $2,665.00 |

DEPOSITOR'S NAME:

Beverly Supply Company

## FARMERS' NATIONAL BANK

December 31, 1938

| | |
|---|---|
| Currency, | $255.00 |
| Gold, | |
| Silver, | 45.00 |
| | |
| Checks, | $300.00 |
| 12- 1 | 80.00 |
| 16- 29 | 60.00 |
| 16-201 | 40.00 |
| Total | $480.00 |

**DEPOSITOR'S NAME:**

Beverly Supply Company

8. Mr. Swift also received a bank statement for the pay roll account together with the canceled checks for the past two pay rolls. No balance remained in the account at 12–31–38, as all checks had been cashed and charged against the account.

9. A bank confirmation was received from the Farmers' National Bank. (See page 116.)

### INSTRUCTIONS

1. Read and study the auditing procedure suggested for the verification of cash in an "Examination of Financial Statements."

2. Study the forms of schedules shown in the illustrative set of audit working papers for The Blank Manufacturing Company. See Illustrations Nos. 8, 9, 10, and 11 all of which relate to the verification of cash.

3. Perform the audit work suggested for verification of cash in so far as the procedure applies to this audit.

4. Prepare a letter addressed to the Farmers' National Bank to confirm the cash balance at December 31, 1938, and to confirm other items that you think should be verified by correspondence with the bank.

---

# FARMERS' NATIONAL BANK

## Los Angeles, California

January 4, 1939

Knight™and Day
Certified Public Accountants
Los Angeles, California

Dear Sirs:

At the close of business December 31, 1938, the following
balances were on our books to the credit of the Beverly Supply
Company:

General checking account_____$30,567.30
Payroll account_____no balance
Bond interest account_____no balance

At the close of business December 31, 1938, the Beverly
Supply Company was indebted to us on unsecured notes evidencing
loans as follows:

Note dated 11-16-38 maturing 2-14-39 @ 6% $15,000.00
Note dated 12-1-38  maturing 1-30-39 @ 6%  10,000.00

The Company was also contingently indebted to us on the
following notes which bear their endorsement:

Note maturing 1-14-39@ 6% $  400.00 I. M. Painter (Maker)
Note maturing 3-3-39 @ 6% 1,600.00 O. K. Presser (  "  )

Sincerely yours,

Farmers' National Bank

JHM/VL                    J. H. M. Loan Officer

---

5. Prepare working papers (schedules) in proper form for
the following: (a) petty cash count; (b) count of undeposited
cash; (c) bank reconciliation at December 31, 1938; (d) proof or
reconciliation of total cash receipts per books with total deposits
in the bank during the year; (e) reconciliation of total cash disbursements per books with the total disbursements per bank
statements for the year.

6. Prepare adjusting journal entries wherever necessary.
These entries need not be posted to the working trial balance
until after the audit has been completed.

7. Start a memorandum sheet for comments which you
think should be included in the audit report to be written at the
completion of the audit.

# CHAPTER FIVE

## SECURITIES

1. Investments
   - (a) Speculative and Non-Speculative
   - (b) Temporary
   - (c) Permanent

2. Types of Investments
   - (a) Call Loans
   - (b) Marketable Securities
   - (c) Mortgages
   - (d) Investments in Securities of Subsidiary Companies
   - (e) Sinking Fund Investments

3. Examining Securities

4. Valuation of Securities
   - (a) Types of Valuation
   - (b) Temporary Investments
   - (c) Permanent Investments

5. Auditing Procedure

6. Application of Principles

7. An Audit Case—Third Installment

## INVESTMENTS

Securities may be one of the important items in a balance sheet. Individuals, partnerships, and corporations may invest surplus funds in marketable securities temporarily. Permanent investments may be made in the securities of affiliated companies. Investments may be either speculative or non-speculative. When securities are purchased for temporary holding in anticipation of an increase in the market value, it is generally looked upon as a speculative investment, but when securities are purchased as a permanent investment with a view to obtaining a fixed income, the investment is generally considered non-speculative.

**Speculative and Non-Speculative Investments.** Securities may be purchased outright or on a margin basis. If purchased outright, payment is made in full. If purchased on a margin, payment is made in part and the securities are pledged as collateral security with the broker or bank through which the securities are purchased. When securities are purchased either outright or on a margin, with the expectation of selling at any time when the market price is favorable, the investment is made not because of income the securities will produce, but because of the expectation of realizing a profit through resale. These securities in a sense become the stock-in-trade of the investor and like any other stock-in-trade should be recorded at cost. The cost should include the brokerage and any other expenses incurred in connection with the purchase.

Non-speculative investments may consist of marketable securities in which surplus funds are invested for the purpose of obtaining a temporary income, or they may consist of securities in which funds are invested permanently, the intention being to hold the securities until maturity.

**Temporary Investments.** Securities purchased as a temporary investment should be recorded at cost regardless of whether they represent a speculative or non-speculative investment. To record such securities at par value would result in a profit or loss being recorded at the time of the purchase as the discount or premium could not be amortized or distributed over the life of the securities because it is not known how long the securities will be held. To record the discount or premium as a profit or loss at the time of the purchase of the securities would obviously be incorrect and unsound.

**Permanent Investments.** The term "permanent investments" is usually applied to investments in stocks of subsidiary companies, but in every-day usage the term may include investments in special funds such as sinking funds, endowment funds, and trust funds where it is the intention to retain the securities for long periods of time. Investments included in sinking funds, trust funds, and endowment funds should be considered permanent only so long as the securities receive a high investment rating. The values of securities in these funds should be watched closely and changes should be made whenever reliable investment information indicates that the conditions underlying the security back of the investment have changed and there is likelihood that the securities may take a permanent drop in value.

Securities purchased as a permanent investment may be recorded either at cost or par value. Practice varies but the usual custom is to record the securities at cost price. If bonds are recorded at par value it is necessary to amortize or distribute the discount or premium over the remaining life of the securities. In other words, if bonds are purchased at a discount and are recorded at par value, the discount should be recorded separately and should be distributed over the remaining life of the securities by making an annual credit to interest or profit and loss and a debit to the discount account. If the securities were purchased at a premium and recorded at par value, the premium should be recorded separately and should then be distributed over the remaining life of the securities by making an annual credit to the premium account and a debit to interest or profit and loss. The adjustment is usually through the interest account, hence any discount or premium paid on securities purchased as a permanent investment to be held until maturity, represents an adjustment of the income on the investment.

## TYPES OF INVESTMENTS

**Call Loans.** Call loans are demand loans which are made to brokers. Such loans are usually made by banks to brokers dealing in securities listed on the New York Stock Exchange, or other exchanges. Of course, there is nothing to prevent business firms from loaning surplus funds to brokers at the call money rate and accepting securities as collateral. Such loans are sometimes referred to as bootleggers' loans on the ground that when loans are made direct by business or industrial firms they are infringing upon a practice which is generally looked upon as a part of the banking business. Nevertheless in recent years, particularly in 1929 when call loan rates in New York averaged more than 10% a month, the balance sheets of many industrial concerns showed that call loans amounting to millions of dollars had been made. This was due to the fact that many firms found that they could derive a higher income through loaning funds to brokers than they could from the usual operations of their business. During this period there was a shortage of funds available for stock market operations, hence interest rates were abnormally high. In periods where there is an abundance of funds in the call money market the interest rates are generally so low as not to be attractive to industrial concerns.

If in auditing securities it is found that surplus funds have been loaned to brokers in the form of demand loans it will be necessary to check the securities held as collateral to ascertain if their market value is sufficient to protect the loan. If such loans are made in the New York call money market it will be found that the securities may be in the possession of a New York bank or brokerage house, in which case the auditor may have to accept a certificate of collateral holdings, to which reference should be made in his audit report.

**Marketable Securities.** Surplus funds are frequently invested in marketable securities for the purpose of realizing a temporary income. It is not often that such funds will be used for speculation. The securities listed under this classification generally consist of stocks and bonds which are listed on the various exchanges and which have a readily determinable market value. These securities may be listed on the balance sheet as quick assets along with or immediately following cash or they may be listed with the investments following the inventories. Practice is not uniform.

**Mortgages.** Mortgages will be frequently found among the securities owned. Where mortgages are owned there are usually notes evidencing the amount of the debt. Both should be examined carefully, the mortgage being checked to see if it is legally recorded and the note being checked to see if it is properly accounted for. The auditor may find the note recorded under notes receivable with no record of the mortgage or he may find the mortgage recorded with no record of the note. Ordinarily, mortgages are recorded as such, but in any event there should be a proper cross reference. In other words, if the note is recorded it should be indicated that it is secured by a mortgage, and if the mortgage is recorded it should be indicated that it is supported by a note.

Occasionally, especially on second mortgages, there may be some doubt as to the value of the paper. The auditor may make several tests as to possible values in most cases. Tax duplicates, prior liens on properties, delinquent tax lists, appraisals as in the case of building and loan companies, and other means are often at his command for comparisons of values. Where payments of interest and principal are delinquent, the auditor should determine what action has been taken, what is the probable value of the mortgage, and what is the probability of loss.

Where mortgages are owned against improved real estate, insurance policies should be examined. In such cases the insurance policies should be held by the holder of the mortgage, and the amount of the insurance carried, type, and the period in force should be determined. The insurance policies should always be sufficient to protect the value of the mortgage in case of loss.

Payments received to apply on the principal of a mortgage should be endorsed on the mortgage itself. Evidences of such payments will usually be found in the accounts, but sometimes the auditor will find that the payments have not been properly endorsed on the mortgage.

**Investments in Securities of Subsidiary Companies.** In view of the present day tendency toward large business units, it is not uncommon to find large amounts invested in the securities of subsidiary companies. Through these investments, companies may be controlled and affiliation of interests maintained. The investments may include common stocks, preferred stocks and bonds. Such securities are generally shown as a separate caption in the balance sheet, or under the heading of investments. In either case they are usually shown between the current and fixed asset sections.

**Sinking Fund Investments.** Funds deposited with a sinking fund trustee or held in a special fund for the future redemption of bonds or other funded debt, may be invested in securities with a view to realizing an income. The income derived from the investment of a sinking fund in securities should be treated as an addition to the fund. The income may be recorded, however, as either sinking fund income or general income. The auditor should obtain sufficient information in regard to this to permit an intelligent classification of the income in his report. The auditor should also make a careful investigation to ascertain that the sinking fund trustee is not exceeding his authority in the investment of funds entrusted to his care. It is customary to list the sinking fund as a separate caption in the balance sheet, or it may be listed together with other permanent investments under the heading of investments and be shown between the current and the fixed asset sections on the balance sheet.

In many cases a reserve for sinking fund will be found set up on the books. It may be and usually is listed in the capital section of the balance sheet as an appropriation of surplus.

## EXAMINING SECURITIES

Securities should be verified simultaneously with the verification of cash and notes receivable in order that there may be no substitution of funds derived from one source to make up shortages in another. The securities are usually kept in a safe deposit box at a bank or trust company. The examination should be made in the presence of the client or one or more of his representatives. A representative having access to the safe deposit box should accompany the auditor to the bank and should be present at all times during the examination of the securities.

The auditor should obtain a list of securities from the client against which he may check the securities as they are examined. If a list has not been prepared, the auditor should prepare one as the examination is being made.

In examining bonds it is essential that the auditor record their exact description including the interest rate and the maturity date. Railroads and public utility companies frequently have several bond issues outstanding whose interest rates and descriptions are similar, but whose market prices vary considerably in amount due to factors such as the type of security back of the bonds, or the remoteness of the maturity date. It is advisable to note the dates of the coupons on the bonds to see that they are all intact and none are missing.

## VALUATION OF SECURITIES

**Types of Valuation.** Securities may be valued at cost, book value, par value, or market value. When valued at cost, brokerage and other expenses incurred in connection with the purchase of securities should be included in the cost. Book value is the value at which securities are recorded on the books. It may represent cost, par, or market value. Par value represents the value specified on the face of the security. Some securities have no par value. Much of the common and preferred stock being issued at present has no par value. Market value is based upon the selling price of the securities. In other words, it is the price at which securities may be bought or sold at a given time.

**Temporary Investments.** The methods of valuing securities vary with different companies. The variation may depend upon whether the securities are temporary, marketable securities, or permanent investments in allied, affiliated, or subsidiary companies.

Irrespective of how the securities may be valued on the books of the company, the auditor should determine their market quotations if possible in order that a comparison may be made between the market values and those shown by the books. A reserve for shrinkage in value should be provided if the market figures are materially lower in amount than the values carried on the books. If the securities are listed on a security exchange, the market price is the closing quotation on the last day of the fiscal period. Official quotations of stock exchanges may be secured which list the high, low, and closing quotations for the day's trading. If the securities are not listed on a security exchange, it is generally possible to get bid and ask quotations from brokerage houses or from the daily newspapers. The bid quotation may be used, or if a wide discrepancy exists between the bid and ask prices, it is customary to use the mid-point or average of the two quotations. If no quotations are available, it may be possible to examine recent financial statements of the companies whose securities are being valued. The book values per share of stock as shown by these statements may be the only ones determinable, and under such circumstances, the book values may be used in lieu of any other quotations. If book values are used, this fact should be noted on the balance sheet.

Many accountants favor stating the temporary investments in marketable securities at their market value. If this represents an increase over cost the difference will represent a nonoperating profit. If it represents a decrease from cost it will represent a nonoperating loss. There is some objection to the use of market value in listing securities on the balance sheet, in that it results in the inclusion of gain or loss which is often based upon merely a temporary fluctuation in market values, and which in no sense can be considered as an earned gain or loss until such time as the securities may be sold. In no event should securities be listed at a value exceeding market value. If the securities are recorded at cost and the market value has declined below cost, a reserve should be set up for the difference and this reserve should be listed as a deduction from securities on the balance sheet, so that the asset value will be the net amount based upon current market values.

**Permanent Investments.** Securities representing a permanent investment are commonly listed at cost, but in some cases, are listed at market value. It seems preferable to use cost so as to avoid giving effect to mere fluctuations in market value. Such securities are usually held for income purposes rather than their appreciation in value and it is more conservative to carry them at cost. When permanent investments consist of securities of affiliated or subsidiary companies, book values are commonly used so as to give effect to changes in values resulting from the operations of affiliated or subsidiary companies. Originally such securities are recorded at cost, but subsequently the profits or earnings of affiliated or subsidiary companies applicable to the securities held may be recorded by charging the investment account and crediting an income account. Any losses in earnings may be taken up on the books of the holding* company by charging a loss account and crediting the investment account. Further adjustments in the book value of investments may be made as a result of dividends being declared and paid by affiliated or subsidiary companies so that the account with investments in securities of affiliated or subsidiary companies merely represents the book value of such securities.

In the preparation of audit reports care should be used to prevent any overstatement of the values of the investments. It may be necessary to analyze the statements of the affiliated and subsidiary companies to verify the book value of the securities of such companies. Should it be found that the book value is excessive it should be adjusted to a sound value basis.

---

*A holding company is a company controlling the operations of affiliated or subsidiary companies through ownership of securities. Before a holding company can control the operations of a subsidiary company it must own a controlling interest in the voting capital stock. A holding company may be an operating company deriving its income partly from operations and partly from the interest and dividends on securities of subsidiary companies, or merely a financial organization deriving its entire income from the interest and dividends on securities of subsidiary companies.

## AUDITING PROCEDURE APPLICABLE TO SECURITIES
### In an "Examination of Financial Statements"

"1. Obtain or prepare a list of securities owned showing particulars such as:

> Description of security (give interest rate of bonds)
> Denomination of bonds or par value of shares
> Number of shares and face value of bonds
> Cost of securities and amount at which carried on the books
> Interest and dividends received during period under examination
> Market quotations, if available
> Location of securities, and if hypothecated, with whom and for what purpose.

"2. Compare this list with the corresponding ledger accounts and ascertain the basis on which the securities are carried on the books.

"3. Examine the securities listed or obtain confirmation from the holders if any are held by depositaries or others for safekeeping or as collateral. Make this examination of securities as close to the date of the balance sheet as possible (see also Par. 1 under Cash). It is more satisfactory to inspect the actual securities than to account for their disposition subsequent to the date of the balance sheet.

"4. See that certificates of stock and registered bonds are made out in the name of the company or, if they are in the names of others, that they are so endorsed as to be transferable to the company or are accompanied by powers of attorney.

"5. Examine coupons on bonds to ascertain that unmatured coupons are intact.

"6. Confirm with transfer agents the ownership of certificates out for transfer.

"7. Ascertain that the totals of dividends and interest received by the company as shown by the list (Par. 1) have been duly recorded, and that the income from securities shown in the profit and loss account is correctly reported.

"8. Examine brokers' advices in support of the purchase and sale prices of securities bought and sold through them.

"9. Confirm the cash-surrender value of life insurance policies of which the company is the beneficiary and any policy loans by reference to the insurance policies or by correspondence with the insurance companies.

"10. Examine mortgages and, if important in comparison with total assets, obtain confirmation.

"11. The amount of securities that are considered to be readily convertible into cash and in which surplus funds of the company have been invested temporarily should be shown on the balance sheet under current assets. Where stocks and bonds represent control of or a material interest in other enterprises and have a value to the company aside from their dividend or interest return, they are more in the nature of permanent investments to be shown below the current assets in the balance sheet. Securities not readily marketable should be excluded from current assets.

"12. If the total market value of securities included under current assets is less than the total book value by any material amount, a reserve for the shrinkage in value should be provided. If cost prices are used the quoted market values should be shown on the balance sheet.

"13. If examination of available data, including market quotations or, in their absence, balance sheets and income accounts supplemented by information and explanations from responsible officials, indicates that there has been a substantial shrinkage in value of securities held for investment since their acquisition, appropriate reserves should be provided or the facts should be disclosed in the financial statements.

"14. When corporations have acquired their own stocks, such stocks should preferably be deducted from the capital stock or from surplus or from the total of the two at either par or cost as the laws of the state of incorporation and other relevant circumstances require. If acquired and held for a specific purpose, however, such temporary holdings may be treated as assets, but they should be shown as a separate item and not under current assets.

"15. If any securities owned by the company have been hypothecated, this fact should be stated on the balance sheet."

## APPLICATION OF PRINCIPLES
## AUDIT OF THE BLANK MANUFACTURING COMPANY (Continued)

**Marketable Securities.** Immediately after completing the count of the petty cash fund and the undeposited cash receipts as of January 15, 1938, Mr. Shaw accompanied Mr. I. M. Smartt, the cashier, to the vault of the Merchants National Bank for examination of the securities contained in the company's safe deposit box. Reference to the trial balance (page 71) shows accounts with marketable securities and sinking fund, both of which should be verified.

The marketable securities consisted of the following at December 31, 1937: U. S. Treasury, 3¼% bonds, $5,000 par; Canadian Pacific R. R., 5% bonds, $2,000 par; American Telephone Company, common stock, 50 shares; and U. S. Steel Corporation, common stock, 100 shares.

After examining the securities at the bank, C. E. Shaw proceeded with the detailed verification of the marketable securities. He performed the audit procedure recommended by the American Institute of Accountants for the verification of securities. In this connection he prepared a schedule (Illustration No. 12) showing the list of securities, together with pertinent facts concerning them.

**Sinking Fund Investments.** Verification of the sinking fund revealed that at December 31, 1937, the fund consisted of two deposits, each for $2,750, which had been made with the Merchants National Bank, the trustee. The first deposit was made December 30, 1936, and the second deposit was made December 31, 1937. The amount in the fund at December 31, 1937, totaled $5,500. The bond indenture provides for annual contributions to the fund of $2,750. The president of the Merchants National Bank was authorized to invest the funds in real estate first mortgages, paying not less than 6% interest, with the provision that the amount of the mortgage is in no event to exceed two-thirds of the appraised value of the real estate. In discussing the matter with representatives of the bank, it was found that the first installment to the fund made December 30, 1936, amounting to $2,750, had been loaned to Harrison G. Matthews. A first mortgage was obtained dated January 15, 1937, with interest at 6%, payable annually. The mortgage was secured by property having an assessed valuation,

## THE BLANK MANUFACTURING COMPANY
### Marketable Securities—December 31, 1937

| Description | Int. Date | No. of Shares or Face Value | Value 12-31-37 | | | Date of Last Coupon | Income Received | | Accrued Income |
|---|---|---|---|---|---|---|---|---|---|
| | | | Book | Market Quot. | Market Value | | Interest | Dividends | |
| *Bonds* | | | | | | | | | |
| U. S. Treasury 3¼% '41 | J-D | 5,000 | 5,200.00 | 106-26 | 5,340.63 | 12-1-37 | 135.42 | | 27.08 |
| Canadian Pacific 5% '44 | J-J | 2,000 | 2,225.00 | 113⅞ | 2,277.50 | 7-1-37 | 50.00 | | 50.00 |
| Total Bonds | | | 7,425.00 | | 7,618.13 | | 185.42 | | *77.08 |
| *Stocks* | | | | | | | | | |
| Am. Tel. and Tel. (100 par) | | 50 | 7,300.00 | 182¼ | 9,112.50 | | | 450.00 | |
| U. S. Steel, com. (100 par) | | 100 | 5,500.00 | 122½ | 12,250.00 | | | | |
| Total Stocks | | | 12,800.00 | | 21,362.50 | | | 450.00 | |
| Total | | | 20,225.00 | | 28,980.63 | | 185.42 | 450.00 | 77.08 |

The above securities were examined at the Merchants National Bank at 10:45 a. m., January 17, 1938, in the presence of I. M. Smartt, cashier. The securities were all made out in the name of The Blank Manufacturing Company and contained no endorsements.

*The following adjusting entry should be made to record the interest accrued on bonds to December 31, 1937:

Accrued Interest Receivable.............. 77.08

Interest and Discount.................. 77.08

C. E. Shaw

(Junior Accountant)

(Schedule No. 4)

for tax purposes, of $10,000. The accrued interest on the mortgage at December 31, 1937, amounted to $160.42. The second installment to the fund had not been invested at the date of the audit.

The audit schedule prepared by Mr. Shaw in verifying the sinking fund is shown in Illustration No. 13.

### THE BLANK MANUFACTURING COMPANY
#### Sinking Fund—December 31, 1937

| | |
|---|---:|
| Cash........................................................ | $2,750.00 |
| Real estate mortgage, 6%................................. | $2,750.00 |
| Accrued interest on mortgage........................... | 160.42 |
| Adjusted balance......................................... | $5,660.42 |

*The bond indenture provides for the establishment of a sinking fund to be maintained by annual contributions on December 31 of each year of $2,750. The funds are to be invested in first real estate mortgages paying not less than 6% interest. The amount of the mortgage is in no event to exceed two-thirds of the appraised value of the real estate.*

*The amount in the fund represents the first two installments, which were paid on December 30, 1936, and December 31, 1937. The Merchants National Bank is named as trustee, and the president of the bank is authorized to make the investments.*

*The entire amount of the first installment was invested in a first mortgage dated January 15, 1937, with interest at 6%, payable annually. The mortgagor is Harrison J. Mathews, who pledged property valued at $10,000 (valuation for tax purposes) as security for the loan.*

*The mortgage, together with a fire insurance policy payable to the bank as trustee, was examined at the Merchants National Bank.*

*The accrued interest receivable (on the mortgage) at December 31, 1937, is $160.42, representing interest on $2,750 @ 6% for 350 days. The following adjusting journal entry is required to record the interest accrued on sinking fund investments:*

> *Sinking Fund ..............................$160.42*
> *      Sinking Fund Income................... $160.42*
>           *To record interest accrued on sinking*
>       *fund investments at December 31, 1937.*

*C. E. Shaw*                                    *(Schedule No. 5)*
*(Junior Accountant)*

### Illustration No. 13. Verification of Sinking Fund

## SUMMARY

The procedure in auditing securities is somewhat similar to cash. The securities should be examined and listed on the first day of the audit. The auditor should inspect all securities carefully and should record all of the data which may be needed for the subsequent verification of security values. In verifying security values reference should be made to legal records, corporation records, and market quotations. Pledged securities or those not in the possession of the client should be verified through correspondence with the holders.

A clear distinction should be made between temporary and permanent investments. Temporary investments consisting of call loans and marketable securities should be treated as current assets, while permanent investments in the securities of other companies should be treated as fixed assets. In listing securities at cost, care should be taken to make certain that the cost does not exceed present market values. Where the cost does exceed the market value of the securities the auditor should recommend that a reserve equal to the difference be set up and be deducted from the cost of the securities on the balance sheet. Where investments in the securities of subsidiary companies are listed at book value, the auditor should satisfy himself that the book values represent sound values not in excess of cost or market value whichever is the lower. In these times when corporations commonly have large investments in call loans, marketable securities and investments in the securities of affiliated and subsidiary companies, the auditing of securities has become a very important part of a balance sheet audit and needs to be given very close and careful attention.

## AUDITING THEORY

**5—54.** Distinguish between the following securities:

(a) Notes receivable
(b) Mortgages
(c) U. S. Treasury bonds
(d) Industrial bonds
(e) Common stock.

**5—55.** How should U. S. Treasury bonds be valued and how should they be classified in the balance sheet?

**5—56.** (a) If in completing an audit you find that your client has invested surplus funds in marketable securities and the market value of the securities has declined to the extent of 25% of their original cost, how would you deal with the situation?

(b) In case the market value of the securities had increased to the extent of 25% of the original cost, what would you recommend?

**5—57.** How may the market value of the following securities be ascertained:

(a) U. S. Treasury bonds
(b) Stocks listed on the New York Stock Exchange
(c) Unlisted stocks.

**5—58.** In auditing securities what data should be recorded in the working papers of the auditor?

(C. P. A. Ohio)

**5—59.** In auditing a trust company's accounts, you find that the company is co-trustee for a number of estates. The securities are locked in a safe deposit box that cannot be opened without the assistance of the absent trustee, who will be away for several months. What precautions should be taken to safeguard the integrity of your audit?

(C. P. A. New York)

**5—60.** A concern has established a sinking fund for the retirement of a mortgage. An investment has been made in bonds the present market value of which is below cost. Would you inventory them at market value or at book value?

(C. P. A. Mich.)

**5—61.** In auditing the securities of a corporation about two months subsequent to the date of the balance sheet which you are asked to certify, how would you proceed?

(A. I. A.)

**5—62.** In auditing the books of a corporation you find record of the ownership of stocks and bonds, some of which are on hand, some are deposited with bankers or others for safekeeping, and others are lodged as security for loans. State what kind of evidence you would require in each case, specifying particularly in the case of stocks and registered bonds, if not registered in the name of the corporation, what you consider necessary to protect your client's interests.

(A. I. A.)

## AUDITING PROBLEMS

**5—7.** In completing an audit of the accounts of Mr. Walter Brady, an attorney, you find investments in securities as follows:

10 shares Goodyear Rubber Co., no-par common stock, purchased January 15, 1929, at 134½, commission, $2.50.

March 15, 1929, exercised right to subscribe to 3 shares of the Goodyear Rubber Co., no-par common stock, at 80.

March 22, 1929, purchased 12 shares of Goodyear Rubber Co., no-par common stock, at 142½, commission, $5.

March 25, 1929, purchased 25 shares of Goodyear Rubber Co., no-par common stock, at 137⅜, commission, $7.25.

April 23, 1929, purchased 25 shares of Pillsbury Flour Mills, no-par common stock, at 52¾, commission, $6.

April 24, 1929, purchased 25 shares Engineers Public Service, no-par common stock, at 54⅜, commission, $4.25.

May 24, 1929, exercised right to subscribe to 6 shares of Engineers Public Service, no-par common stock, at 42½.

June 13, 1929, purchased 25 shares of Engineers Public Service, no-par common stock, at 53, commission, $6.

June 13, 1929, received 48/100 shares of Engineers Public Service, no-par common stock as a stock dividend. Market value 53.

(a) Assuming that you were the auditor, prepare a work sheet showing your analysis of the account and the valuation placed upon the securities, stating both cost and present market values.

(b) State how you would classify and list these securities on a balance sheet which you are to certify without qualification.

**5—8.** The Oak Furniture Co. placed $50,000 of its surplus funds in the hands of a broker, giving him instructions to invest it in U. S. 4% bonds. A few days later the company received notice from the broker to the effect that he had purchased forty-nine $1,000 bonds, paying 101⅜ plus a commission of ⅛.

(a) Draft journal entries to record, (1) the transfer of the funds to the broker, (2) the purchase of the bonds by the broker, and (3) the return of the unexpended balance by the broker.

(b) Assuming that these bonds were quoted at 99 on the last day of the audit period, how would you value the bonds for balance sheet purposes?

(c) Also state how the bonds should be classified on the balance sheet.

**5—9.** At December 31, 1930, the "Investments" account on the general ledger of the X Company showed a balance of $83,400 made up as follows:

| Company | No. Shares Common | Cost | |
|---|---|---|---|
| | | Date | Amount |
| U. S. Steel Corporation.......... | 100 | Apr.  7, 1930 | $19,800.00 |
| General Motors Corporation...... | 100 | Apr. 10, 1930 | 5,400.00 |
| X Company.................... | 200 | Apr. 14, 1930 | 10,000.00 |
| Y Company.................... | 600 | Apr. 18, 1930 | 42,000.00 |
| Z Company.................... | 100 | Apr. 21, 1930 | 6,200.00 |
| | | | $83,400.00 |

At this same date, a "Reserve for Loss on Investments" account was carried. This account had a credit balance of $36,900, constituted as follows:

| | |
|---|---:|
| U. S. Steel Corporation | $ 6,900.00 |
| General Motors Corporation | 1,900.00 |
| X Company | 1,000.00 |
| Y Company | 24,000.00 |
| Z Company | 3,100.00 |
| | $36,900.00 |

The market prices of three of these stocks were:

| | December 31 | |
|---|---:|---:|
| | 1930 | 1931 |
| U. S. Steel Corporation | 139 | 40 |
| General Motors Corporation | 35 | 22 |
| X Company | 45 | 20 |

No market quotations of the stocks of the Y and Z companies were available.

The common stock of X Company consists of 100,000 shares of $10 par value. Its books, before adjustment, show an operating surplus of $3,000,000 at December 31, 1930, and $2,800,000 at December 31, 1931, indicating a loss from operations for the year 1931 of $200,000.

The Y Company has 1,000 shares of no-par common stock issued and outstanding. On the books of this company, the common stock is carried at $10,000 and the earned-surplus account shows a credit balance of $20,000 at December 31, 1930, and $15,000 at December 31, 1931.

Statements of the Z Company indicate that its capital stock outstanding consists of 10,000 shares of $10 par value, and that its surplus at December 31, 1930, was $210,000, and at December 31, 1931, $180,000.

On May 12, 1931, the X Company sold 100 shares of its treasury stock for $3,500, and on August 31, 1931, purchased 500 shares of its outstanding stock for $15,000. On October 31, 1931, it purchased 100 shares of the American Telephone and Telegraph Company for $13,700. The market price of this stock on December 31, 1931, was $120 a share. On December 21, 1931, it sold the 100 shares of General Motors Corporation for $2,300. All these transactions were charged or credited to the "Investments" account.

Indicate exactly how you would show the transactions, with their respective balances, in preparing the balance sheet as of December 31, 1931, and also in the related statements of surplus and profit and loss.

(A. I. A.)

## AUDITING PRACTICE
### An Audit Case (Third installment)

January 3, after Ken B. Swift had completed his count of the petty cash fund and the undeposited cash receipts of December 31, 1938, he accompanied Frank T. Collins, the cashier, to the company's safe deposit box at the Farmers' National Bank, where he proceeded to examine and count the investments. The securities count disclosed the stocks and bonds listed in the

(Continued on page 135)

## Schedule of Stocks and Bonds

| Company | Par Value | No. Shares or Face Value | Cost | Div. or Int. Date | Rate Per Yr. | High | Low | Close | Bid | Ask |
|---|---|---|---|---|---|---|---|---|---|---|
| **Stocks:** | | | | | | | | | | |
| Am. Tel. & Tel...... | $100 | 100 shares | $9,800 | Q. 1/15 | $9.00 | 190⅛ | 186 | 188¾ | | |
| Chase National Bank. | | 50 shares | 1,700 | 2/1-8/1 | 1.40 | | | | 48⅞ | 52⅜ |
| Standard Oil of Calif.. | N. P. | 100 shares | 4,700 | Q. 3/15 | @1.00 | 35 | 33⅞ | 34½ | 507 | 527 |
| Sun Life Assurance Co. | $100 | 10 shares | 5,010 | (None since 1932) | | | | | | |
| Beverly Supply Co.... | $100 | 15 shares | donated | | | | | | | |
| **Bonds:** | | | | | | | | | | |
| Goodrich 6½ '47...... | $100 | 1 M | 1,078 | 1/1-7/1 | 6½ | 108¼ | 107⅞ | 108 | | |
| So. Pac. R. R. 4½ '69 | $100 | 2 M | 1,400 | 5/1-11/1 | 4½ | 98 | 97¾ | 97¾ | | |

accompanying schedule, all made out in the name of the Beverly Supply Company and bearing no endorsements.

Bond coupons, not yet matured, were all intact on the bonds.

The account with marketable securities contained entries during the year as follows:

### Marketable Securities

| Date | Items | Debit | Credit | Balance |
|---|---|---|---|---|
| 1-1-38 | Balance<br>A. T. & S. F. R. R. 4½ '62 2M (Interest Dates 3/1-9/1) (acquired 4-15-37).............. | 1,840 | | |
| | So. Pac. R. R. 4½ '69 2M (acquired 7-10-37).............. | 1,400 | | |
| | Chase National Bank 50 shares (acquired 7-10-37).............. | 1,700 | | |
| | Am. Tel. & Tel. 100 shares (acquired 7-10-37).............. | 9,800 | | 14,740 |
| 2-1-38 | Goodrich 6½ '47 1M @ 107⅞...... | 1,078 | | 15,818 |
| 4-15-38 | Standard Oil of Cal. 100 shares @ 47 | 4,700 | | 20,518 |
| 7-2-38 | Sun Life Assurance Co. 10 shares @ 507 | 5,010 | | 25,528 |
| 8-1-38 | A. T. & S. F. 4½ '62 2M @ 112¼ .. | | 2,240 | 23,288 |
| 12-20-38 | Beverly Supply Co. 15 shares (donated) | 1,500 | | 24,788 |

The accounts with bond interest income and dividends received are shown below.

### Bond Interest Income

| Date | Items | Debit | Credit | Balance |
|---|---|---|---|---|
| 1-1-38 | (S. P. R. R. $15; A. T. & S. F. $30)..... | 45.00 | | 45.00 |
| 2-1-38 | Goodrich—accrued at date of purchase | 5.42 | | 50.42 |
| 3-1-38 | A. T. & S. F.—semi-annual interest . | | 45.00 | 5.42 |
| 5-1-38 | S. P. R. R.—semi-annual interest.... | | 45.00 | 39.58 |
| 7-1-38 | Goodrich—semi-annual interest..... | | 32.50 | 72.08 |
| 8-1-38 | A. T. & S. F.—accrued at date of sale | | 37.50 | 109.58 |
| 11-1-38 | S. P. R. R.—semi-annual interest.... | | 45.00 | 154.58 |

### Dividends Received

| Date | Items | Debit | Credit | Balance |
|---|---|---|---|---|
| 1-15-38 | A. T. & T......................... | | 225.00 | 225.00 |
| 2-1-38 | Chase National................... | | 35.00 | 260.00 |
| 4-1-38 | A. T. & T......................... | | 225.00 | 485.00 |
| 6-15-38 | Standard Oil of Calif............... | | 25.00 | 510.00 |
| 7-1-38 | A. T. & T......................... | | 225.00 | 735.00 |
| 8-1-38 | Chase National................... | | 35.00 | 770.00 |
| 9-15-38 | Standard Oil of Calif............... | | 25.00 | 795.00 |
| 10-1-38 | A. T. & T......................... | | 225.00 | 1020.00 |
| 12-15-38 | Standard Oil of Calif............... | | 25.00 | 1045.00 |

The list of marketable securities shows that there is included 15 shares of the capital stock of the Beverly Supply Company which represents treasury stock. It also shows that bonds of the A. T. & S. F. Railroad, with a face value of $2,000, were purchased on April 15, 1937 for $1,840 and were sold on August 1, 1938 for $2,240, the entire selling price being credited to the account with marketable securities.

## INSTRUCTIONS

1. Read and study the auditing procedure suggested for the verification of securities in an "Examination of Financial Statements."

2. Study the form of schedule shown in the illustrative set of audit working papers for The Blank Manufacturing Company. See Illustration No. 12 which relates to the verification of securities.

3. Perform the audit work suggested for verifying securities in so far as the procedure applies to this audit.

4. Prepare a schedule of the securities owned by the Beverly Supply Company on December 31, 1938. Compute the interest income that should have been received on bonds and the dividends received on stocks and see that these amounts agree with the balances shown in the ledger accounts.

5. Prepare adjusting journal entries, where necessary, to adjust the account balances.

# CHAPTER SIX

## RECEIVABLES

1. Notes Receivable
   - (a) Trade Customer's Notes
   - (b) Other Notes
   - (c) Discounted Notes
   - (d) Past Due Notes
   - (e) Acceptances Receivable
   - (f) Auditing Procedure

2. Accounts Receivable
   - (a) Confirming Accounts
   - (b) Aging Accounts
   - (c) Accounts Having Credit Balances
   - (d) Assigned Accounts
   - (e) Installment Accounts
   - (f) Consignment Accounts
   - (g) Capital Stock Subscriptions
   - (h) Intercompany Accounts
   - (i) Advances to Employees
   - (j) Accruals Receivable
   - (k) Auditing Procedure

3. Reserves
   - (a) Reserve for Bad Debts
   - (b) Other Reserves

4. Application of Principles

5. An Audit Case—Fourth Installment

Receivables may consist of accounts receivable, notes receivable, trade acceptances receivable, drafts receivable, mortgages receivable, and accruals, such as interest, commisssions, salaries, bonuses, dividends, etc. Accounts and notes receivable may represent amounts due from employees, trade customers, and others. It is customary to record receivables separately according to type or origin. Accounts receivable representing amounts due from employees should be listed on the balance sheet separate from accounts receivable representing amounts due from trade customers. This also applies to notes receivable.

Accrued interest receivable may be analyzed so as to show separately the amount of interest accrued on accounts receivable, notes receivable, mortgages receivable, and other receivables.

Before an auditor is prepared to verify receivables properly, he should familiarize himself with the internal organization of the firm. He also needs to become familiar with the marketing methods as well as the accounting procedure in recording sales, returns, collections, discounts, allowances, and rebates.

Methods of distribution and policies of price quotations should be determined. Prices may be quoted f.o.b. factory, home office, branch offices, or depositories located at various points. Where shipments are prepaid, and the company sells f.o.b. point of origin, such charges for transportation should be added to the customers' accounts, as a part of the selling price. If prices are quoted f.o.b. point of destination, the transportation charges represent an expense of doing business and cannot be charged to the customer. Knowing the policy of the firm, the auditor may check the adequacy of the practices of the firm in a general way, while lacking such knowledge he may be handicapped in auditing the receivable accounts.

Knowledge of the terms of credit allowed by the company, and the trade in general, is often advantageous to the auditor, for he is able at a glance in many cases, to draw conclusions as to the liquidity of a balance from a casual examination of a customer's account. In addition to a general knowledge of the credit policy and the terms of credit which the company provides, the bad debt experience of the firm for the past few years, as well as for the industry as a whole, may provide the auditor with valuable information.

The marketing conditions existing, as well as the financial condition of the territories in which the company markets its products, may be of considerable importance, and should be studied by the auditor. A depression in one industry may result in slow collections, involving comparatively large collection expenses over a period of years, though the accounts themselves may be very good, even though long overdue in so far as the original terms were concerned. In other words, the general factors as they affect receivables should be thoroughly understood prior to verification of the amount due from customers on notes or open accounts.

## NOTES RECEIVABLE

Notes receivable should be verified simultaneously with the verification of cash and securities so that no substitutions may be made of funds derived from one source to make up deficiencies in another. Notes and securities may readily be converted into cash. Funds derived from either source could be used to make up a shortage in cash. Likewise, cash could be used after the auditor had completed his examination to redeem either notes or securities which had been pledged as security for an unauthorized loan.

**Trade Customers' Notes.** Notes receivable are written evidences of debt, usually arising from sales with long terms of credit, or from accounts receivable which were not paid at maturity. There are many types of businesses in which goods are sold on notes running from six months to several years. These enterprises will include such companies as farm implement companies, piano and radio dealers, and real estate agencies. The usual practice with such concerns is to sell the merchandise with a down payment and provision for payment in the future, either on a straight note or on the installment plan. On the other hand, notes often arise from overdue accounts receivable, in which the customers, not able to meet the usual terms of the company, request or agree to sign notes for a specified period with interest. Such a note is usually more liquid than the open account in that it represents a written acknowledgment of a debt, and usually may be discounted.

Most concerns maintain a notes receivable register or journal in which usually the following data are recorded:

1. Date
2. Maker
3. Payee
4. Where payable
5. Amount
6. When due
7. Rate of interest
8. Remarks

Other information may also be recorded but the above is the essential information which will usually be found recorded in either a notes receivable register or journal. At the beginning of an audit the client usually will furnish a trial balance with a list of the notes receivable on hand. However, the auditor should ask to see the notes and should prepare an independent list, recording the date, amount, interest rate, when payable, and the name of the maker. He should also observe if any partial payments have been endorsed on the back of the notes. In many cases the sum of the notes on hand at the time of the audit will not agree with the list furnished by the client or with the amount of the notes receivable shown on the trial balance. The audit may be made at some time subsequent to the date of the trial balance. In the meantime additional notes may have been received, notes may have been discounted, and notes may have been paid. Adjustment should be made for these changes in working back to the date of the trial balance.

**Other Notes.** Notes received from customers which arise from ordinary sales are usually classified as trade customers' notes, and should be listed on the balance sheet separately from other notes. Notes received from officials or employees of a company are usually the result of accommodation loans and such receivables always should be listed separately from the ordinary trade customers' notes receivable.

**Discounted Notes.** Notes discounted at the bank are still the contingent property of the company, and a contingent liability exists for payment thereof in case the maker fails to make payment at maturity. Such items should be traced through the note records and should be verified through correspondence with the banks concerned.

**Past Due Notes.** Overdue notes need careful scrutiny by the auditor. He may often rely on the aid of the client's staff in valuing such papers for statement purposes. If the client maintains a credit department, the personnel of that department may be of considerable service in deciding the value of any such paper. Dun and Bradstreet's and other credit agency reports may be of value in determing probable value of doubtful notes. Where a note originated from sales, the value thereof, if considered doubtful, should be charged back to accounts receivable, and the allowance for bad debts, when the note is finally proved bad, should be charged therefor.

**Acceptances Receivable.** A trade acceptance is usually a non-interest bearing instrument, evidencing an agreement to pay at the stated time for value received. The trade acceptance is usually more advantageous to the merchant or manufacturer, in that it provides the usual terms of sale to the buyer, and still permits the seller of the merchandise to discount the paper, and hence finance with considerably less capital than would be necessary were he forced to carry his customers on open account for thirty or sixty days.

A time draft after it has been accepted by the drawee, is similar to a note and is usually recorded in the same manner as notes receivable, hence, will be included with notes receivable on the balance sheet. Trade acceptances may also be included with notes receivable though many consider it advisable to list trade acceptances receivable separately on the balance sheet.

### AUDITING PROCEDURE APPLICABLE TO NOTES RECEIVABLE
#### In An "Examination of Financial Statements"

"1. Prepare a list of notes receivable at the end of the period, showing dates, makers' names, due dates, amounts, and interest rates, as shown by the book records.

"2. Examine outstanding notes and compare with the notes receivable record or with the list (see also Par. 1 under Cash). Check dates and due dates. Trace into the books of the company cash received for notes matured since the close of the period and therefore not presented for examination; when notes are in the hands of attorneys or banks for collection, obtain confirmation from the holders. If notes have been discounted obtain acknowledgement from the discounting banks.

"3. Give consideration to the probable value of the notes, particularly of renewed notes, and to the adequacy of the reserve provided. Ascertain the value of any collateral security for notes. The notes may be worth no more than the collateral, especially as collateral is usually required from debtors of doubtful standing.

"4. The best verification of notes receivable is written confirmation by the debtor that the notes are bona fide obligations, although such confirmation is not usually considered necessary in the case of companies having an adequate system of internal check. When this course is followed, mail personally the requests for confirmation in envelopes bearing the accountant's return address and enclose return envelopes addressed to the accountant.

"5. Notes, including installment notes, of a material amount maturing later than one year from the date of the balance sheet should be shown separately thereon unless trade practice warrants a different treatment. Balance sheets of businesses whose sales are largely installment sales should show the notes receivable in some detail.

"6. Notes from stockholders, directors, officers, and employees and also notes arising from transactions outside the ordinary business of the company should be shown separately on the balance sheet.

"7. Notes of affiliated concerns should not be included with customers' notes on the balance sheet even though received in respect of transactions in the ordinary course of business. They may be shown as current assets, investments, or otherwise as the circumstances justify; inclusion as current assets is allowable only if the debtor company has a satisfactory margin of current assets over current liabilities including such notes.

"8. The balance sheet should carry a footnote under 'contingent liabilities' showing amount of unmatured discounted notes (see Par. 2 above).

### Modifications of Audit Program for Larger or Smaller Concerns

"Large installment companies may have thousands of notes receivable which are controlled by a satisfactory internal check. In such cases it may not be necessary or desirable for the accountant to examine every note or installment account, but a reasonable test may be sufficient. On the other hand, if the company is small and has been accustomed to discount its notes receivable, special inquiry from all banks in which the company has maintained balances during the period may be necessary to determine the full contingent liability."

It has been mentioned that wherever there is an extensive system of internal check the accountant should determine the extent to which he would be justified in reducing the amount of the detailed checking which otherwise he might consider necessary, but that only in a large organization is it usually possible to obtain the most satisfactory separation of functions and duties.

In a very small organization or one having a highly restricted system of internal check and control, it will be necessary to make a more detailed examination than that heretofore outlined.

## ACCOUNTS RECEIVABLE

Accounts receivable may be roughly classified as follows:
(a) Trade customers' accounts
  1. Open
  2. Installment
(b) Consignment accounts
(c) Stock subscriptions
(d) Intercompany accounts
(e) Advances to employees
(f) Accruals receivable

As in the case of notes receivable, the client's staff should prepare a list of the accounts receivable prior to the start of the audit.

Such a list frequently consists of adding machine tapes on which the balances of the individual accounts are listed and totaled. It is necessary for the auditor to compare the amounts on the list with the balance of each individual account in the subsidiary ledger and to foot the list of accounts. It is necessary to foot the list of accounts even though the amounts appear on adding machine tapes. The total on an adding machine tape may not be the actual total of the items appearing on the tape. The carriage of the adding machine may have been dropped back, or the tape removed, and fictitious figures inserted in the machine but not recorded on the tape. Any desired total may be printed on the tape by this method which would make the subsidiary ledger figures appear to balance with the controlling account.

Sometimes receivables will be grouped to include some or all of the different types of receivables as stated above. Accounts receivable for balance sheet purposes should include only customers' balances resulting from bona fide sales. In case other types of receivables are included, the auditor usually segregates them into the different groupings according to the nature and origin of the accounts.

**Confirming Accounts.** There are various ways of verifying customers' accounts. One of the easiest methods is to supervise the sending of the monthly bills during the audit, placing on each bill a stamp reading somewhat as follows:

| |
|---|
| If any errors please notify<br>our auditors<br>Stevenson and Bennett<br>9 W. Third Street<br>Cincinnati, Ohio |

In this type of confirmation, the customer responds only when a difference exists between his balance and that shown by the statement. This method of confirming balances is frequently referred to as a negative one. A second procedure, referred to as a positive method, is to send two copies of the monthly statement to each debtor, one of which he is asked to sign and return to the auditors, noting thereon any differences that may exist.

When accounts are confirmed, the auditor should prepare a list of the accounts and their balances. The statements prepared by the bookkeepers should be compared with the auditors' list as to names, addresses, and amounts. The statements should be mailed in envelopes bearing the auditors return address, so that any statements not delivered by the post office department will be returned to the auditor and not to the office of the client. If there are any fictitious accounts, the letters will be returned unopened.

It is frequently necessary for the auditor to send out second and third requests for confirmations, as many customers will neglect to return the confirmation blanks when the first requests are sent out.

An alternative to confirming all the accounts receivable would be to confirm accounts having comparatively large balances, or to select accounts at random and to confirm a certain percentage of the total accounts, thus utilizing the principle of testing as may be done in connection with other phases of the audit.

As a whole, confirming accounts receivable is not resorted to with any frequency, due to the psychology of the procedure and the natural hostility of the client to such a procedure in connection with his customers.

**Aging Accounts Receivable.** The purpose of an audit of customers' accounts is threefold. The auditor wishes to assure himself that the accounts represent actual values resulting from bona fide sales, that the accounts are active and being paid, and that the amount of each account is correct.

All three of these purposes may usually be satisfied through an examination of the records. The auditor may check from the shipping papers to the sales register to assure himself that the sales are actually being recorded. He may check the postings from the sales records to the ledgers and vice versa, to ascertain whether this routine is being properly followed. He may examine the ledger accounts to determine whether such accounts are active. In doing this the usual practice is to "age" the accounts. That is, if the usual credit terms are 2/10 n/30, the auditor may classify, or have classified, all the accounts in columnar form as follows: (1) accounts not yet due; (2) accounts less than thirty days past due; (3) accounts thirty to sixty days past due; (4) accounts sixty to ninety days past due; and (5) accounts over ninety days past due. It may be easier to classify the accounts by months rather than by days. When this is done, the entries in each customer's account, representing amounts unpaid, are totaled by months and entered on a columnar working sheet under column headings corresponding to monthly billing dates. An aging schedule is shown in Illustration No. 15.

**Accounts Having Credit Balances.** In an audit of customers' accounts, credit balances may be found in some accounts. These balances should be carefully checked and the cause thereof determined. In case of an erroneous posting, one account may show a credit balance, the debit balance of the other account being overstated accordingly. Occasionally a customer may overpay, or there may be some adjustment which has not been entered in the ledger. In case of bona fide credit balances the total of the credit balances should be shown as a current liability in the balance sheet either as accounts payable or as accounts receivable—credit balances. An adjusting journal entry may be made for balance sheet purposes reclassifying the credit balances as follows:

```
Accounts Receivable.......................... xxx.xx
    Accounts Receivable—Credit Balance .....        xxx.xx
```

This entry should not be recorded on the client's books. It is made for the auditors' working papers as an aid in preparing the balance sheet.

**Assigned Accounts.** Some companies, especially those having financial difficulties, make assignments of receivables to financial houses, in order to realize thereon as quickly as possible. Any assigned receivable, of course, has the contingent liability of the endorser, and the total receivables should be verified, and the assigned portion carried as an offset. Verification of assigned receivables may usually be made through correspondence with the assignee.

**Installment Accounts.** The verification of other types of receivables varies widely. Sales on an installment basis in the past ten years have increased enormously. With this increase has come considerable improvement in accounting procedures and forms. It is sufficient to say here that most up-to-date systems of accounting for installment sales are so planned that the amount of the original sale, the periodic installment, the last installment paid, and all similar information, may be readily ascertained from the installment account register. Here again, the activity of the account is a vital point to the auditor. Where the accounts are being paid regularly and are up-to-date, there is little likelihood of their being bad or fictitious. Those accounts which are overdue, foreclosed, or which include special features out of the ordinary, should be investigated as the circumstances may warrant.

**Consignment Accounts.** Some companies forward merchandise to their selling agents on consignment. Such shipments remain the property of the consignor, the consignee simply acting as the agent of the shipper in making the sale. In accounting for such shipments, a common procedure is to charge accounts receivable and credit the consignment sales account. Such accounts are really not receivables at all and should be omitted therefrom. The auditor should reverse the entries therefor and charge merchandise for the proper value to include the item in the inventory, for the goods are still the property of the shipper and should be retained in his inventory at the proper valuation.

**Capital Stock Subscriptions.** Another frequent source of charges to receivables arises from the sale of capital stock or other securities to employees, customers, or others on a deferred payment plan. Usually under such contracts the capital stock or security issued remains in the hands of the company until the subscription is paid. In such cases the subscriptions receivable are usually bona fide current assets and should be so shown, provided the payments are being maintained and the procedures are regular. However, such assets are not the result of sales of merchandise, and hence are not similar to customers' accounts, and should not be grouped therewith. Such amounts may be checked against the subscription cards and registers, and the terms of the contracts being known, the verification of the payment of the deferred payments involves a check of the accounts against the cash records. Such amounts when audited should be carried as current assets but under a separate heading which will properly differentiate them from customers' balances.

**Intercompany Accounts.** A third type of miscellaneous receivables frequently found is that of intercompany items, arising either through merchandising transactions between companies or through loans on open account, which are carried as current receivables and payables by the individual companies concerned. Due to the affiliation of the different companies, such receivables are not assets due from debtors in the ordinary sense of the word and should not be so carried. Where such items are the result of merchandise transactions, they may usually be carried as "Due from Subsidiary or Affiliated Companies," while advances or loans to affiliated concerns on open account may preferably be carried under "Advances to Affiliated Companies."

**Advances to Employees.** Quite often the auditor finds in the receivable accounts advances to officers and employees. Such items may simply be loans for temporary purposes, or they may represent more permanent items which will be repaid from profit sharing, or items which in some other manner will liquidate themselves. Such accounts should be carefully scrutinized by the auditor, to determine if they have been duly authorized by the proper officials, their status, and likelihood of current payment. In any case, such accounts should not be included with the trade accounts receivable but should be stated separately.

**Accruals Receivable.** The interest accrued on notes receivable, mortgages, bonds, and other securities represents receivables similar to accounts receivable although they are usually listed separately among the current assets. Rent accrued on property leased also represents an accrued account receivable even though the rent may not be due until some time subsequent to the close of the period. There may be a number of other accruals representing accounts receivable such as royalties, commissions, wages, fees, etc. All accrued accounts receivable represent current assets which are usually itemized under the heading of "Accrued Assets" on the balance sheet.

## RESERVES

Receivables should be stated in the financial statement at their realizable value. As the usual procedure in stating receivables is to carry them at their gross value in the accounts, reserves must be set up to care for any estimated shrinkage in order properly to state such value.

**Reserve for Bad Debts.** The number and amount of such reserves vary widely. Most companies sell their merchandise on credit and as a result must provide for losses through bad debts. The amount of these provisions will vary as between companies and industries, depending on many factors, as general business conditions, credit policies, and condition of the territory or territories served. It is the business of the auditor to determine what amount is needed for bad debts which may occur, and to see that this provision is made. Several factors may be of use in judging the adequacy of the reserves set up. The auditor may go over the accounts with the proper officials of the company and determine, from the correspondence and by conference with the credit manager, what accounts are likely to prove good, bad, or doubtful. Financial services are also at his command. This element of the investigation naturally results, of course, from the aging of receivables as previously discussed.

Another criterion of the adequacy of the bad debt reserve may be obtained from the past experience of the company. Many concerns find that a certain percentage of total credit sales prove bad over a period of time, and as a result make a practice of setting aside such a sum. If this is done, the auditor should check the adequacy thereof against the condition of the accounts. In verifying the balances of the accounts, the auditor will often find accounts being paid currently, though a certain invoice is being consistently ignored. Such a situation immediately should place him on guard for a disputed amount, amount in process of settlement, or some difficulty which should be properly checked.

The auditor should investigate the procedure in writing off bad debts, and should see that a proper routine is followed for handling such items, and that the proper authority is existent for all write-offs.

It is seldom that separate reserves are provided for loss on accounts receivable and notes receivable, but sometimes this is done. It really makes no difference so long as an ample reserve is provided for the anticipated loss on doubtful accounts and notes receivable. If separate reserves are maintained they should be deducted separately from the notes receivable and accounts receivable accounts respectively on the balance sheet. Where a single reserve is maintained for losses on both notes and accounts receivable, the reserve should be deducted from the sum of the receivable accounts on the balance sheet.

**Other Reserves.** There are other reserves against receivables which may be found in many cases, and which are of considerable importance. Chemical and cement companies, for example, may ship their product in containers which remain the property of the consignor, though the customer is billed therefor until the return of the container. In such companies the consignor may have several thousands of dollars of charges in receivables representing the billed value of containers. The larger percentage of these charges will never be realized, the containers being returned instead. In such a case a reserve should be set up for the estimated amount of charges which will not be paid. Other illustrations are numerous. Firms granting cash discounts for payment of bills within a certain time will require a reserve for such items which their experience shows will never be paid, or the custom of a company may be to allow a certain amount on shipments for freight to customers, the total being charged to the customers' accounts until the net amount is paid.

## AUDITING PROCEDURE APPLICABLE TO
## ACCOUNTS RECEIVABLE

### In An "Examination of Financial Statements"

"1. Obtain lists of customers' balances open at the end of the period, with the amounts classified according to age. Foot these lists and compare them in detail with the customers' accounts in the ledgers. Note on the lists any amounts paid since closing.

"2. If separate ledgers are kept, reconcile the total of the lists of outstanding accounts with the controlling account in the general ledger. In this reconciliation credit balances in the customers' ledgers will be offset against the total of debit balances but on the balance sheet such credit balances should be included among the liabilities. (Similarly any debit balances in the accounts payable ledgers should be appropriately classified.)

"3. Examine the composition of outstanding balances. A customer may be making regular payments on his current account while old items, perhaps in dispute, are carried forward. Discuss disputed items and accounts that are past due with the credit department or with some responsible officer, and make such inquiries as are deemed necessary in order to form an opinion of the worth of the accounts and of the sufficiency of the reserve for bad and doubtful accounts. In the balance sheet the reserve should be shown as a deduction from the corresponding assets.

"4. When bad debts have been written off, see that the action has been approved by responsible authority.

"5. Inquire into the practice regarding the granting of trade discounts and so-called cash discounts if greater than 2 per cent and regarding freight allowed by the company. If such prospective allowances have not been deducted from accounts receivable, an appropriate reserve is required. Make inquiries as to customers' claims for reduction in prices and for allowances on account of defective material in order to ascertain that sufficient reserves have been established.

"6. Make inquiries to determine that goods consigned to customers or agents, or goods under order from customers for future delivery, title to which has not yet passed to customers, have not been included in accounts receivable. Such merchandise should be carried in the inventory on the usual basis of pricing.

"7. The best verification of accounts receivable is to communicate directly with the debtor regarding the existence of the debt, and this course may be taken after arrangement with the client. While such confirmation is frequently considered unnecessary in the case of companies having an adequate system of internal check, it is one of the most effective means of disclosing irregularities. If it is to be undertaken, mail personally the requests for confirmation, after comparing them with the lists of outstanding accounts, in envelopes bearing the accountant's return address and enclose return envelopes addressed to the accountant.

"8. If accounts of a material amount, including installment sales accounts, mature later than one year from the date of the balance sheet they should be shown separately thereon unless it is impracticable to segregate the proportion maturing beyond a year or trade practice warrants a different treatment. In that event the balance sheet should carry an explanatory note.

"9. Accounts receivable from stockholders, directors, officers, and employees, unless for ordinary and current trade purchases of merchandise, should be shown separately on the balance sheet. Deposits as security or guaranties and any other extraordinary items should also be shown separately.

"10. Accounts receivable from affiliated concerns, even though arising from transactions in the ordinary course of business, should be shown separately on the balance sheet. Accounts with affiliated companies may be shown as current assets, investments, or otherwise as the circumstances justify. They may properly be included as current assets only if the debtor company has a satisfactory margin of current assets over current liabilities including such accounts.

"11. The amount of any accounts receivable that have been hypothecated or assigned should be so shown on the balance sheet."

## Modifications of Program for Larger or Smaller Concerns

"If there are large numbers of customers and the customers' ledgers are kept by employees who do not have access to incoming cash or cashiers' records, who do not mail out the monthly statements nor initiate credits for returned goods or allowances, a relatively limited test of the individual customers' accounts may suffice. A more saisfactory check may thus be provided than would be obtained by a detailed examination of the accounts receivable of a company having inadequate internal control."

It has been mentioned that wherever there is an extensive system of internal check the accountant should determine the extent to which he would be justified in reducing the amount of the detailed checking which otherwise he might consider necessary, but that only in a large organization is it usually possible to obtain the most satisfactory separation of functions and duties. In a very small organization or one having a highly restricted system of internal check and control, it will be necessary to make a more detailed examination than that heretofore outlined.

## APPLICATION OF PRINCIPLES

### AUDIT OF THE BLANK MANUFACTURING COMPANY (Continued)

**Notes Receivable.** While C. E. Shaw, one of the junior accountants, audited the cash and securities, J. I. King, the other junior accountant, prepared a list of the notes receivable (Illustration No. 14) and performed the audit routine suggested by the American Institute of Accountants for the verification of notes receivable.

**Accounts Receivable.** Mr. Shaw next proceeded with the verification of the accounts receivable as follows:

(1) A transcript of the sales ledger controlling account in the general ledger was made showing a balance of $81,704.76.

(2) The schedule of accounts receivable furnished by Mr. Pond, the chief accountant, was checked with the sales ledger and it was found that the total of all the accounts with debit balances amounted to $84,739.26, while the total of those accounts which had credit balances amounted to $3,034.50.

(3) Mr. King ascertained that the terms on which goods are sold are net 30 days, no cash discount being allowed. Trade discounts are all deducted from the invoices and no record of these discounts is kept.

(4) He next prepared an aging schedule of the accounts receivable, which showed the accounts classified by billing dates as follows: December, 1937, $72,897.80; November, 1937,

*(Continued on page 155)*

## THE BLANK MANUFACTURING COMPANY

### Notes Receivable—December 31, 1937

| MAKER | ENDORSEMENT | DATE OF NOTE | MATURITY DATE | AMOUNT | INTEREST RATE | INTEREST ACCRUED | COLLATERAL HELD AS SECURITY | REMARKS |
|---|---|---|---|---|---|---|---|---|
| J. B. Olds | none | 11- 1-37 | 2- 1-38 | 845.72 | 6% | 8.46 | none | Paid 1-10-38 |
| Robert Burns | none | 9-25-37 | 1-25-38 | 3,200.00 | 6% | 51.73 | none | Cash book, page 391 |
| The Oilor Co. | J. Oilander | 12-10-37 | 1-10-38 | 1,000.00 | 6% | 3.50 | none | Protested 11-22-37 |
| J. A. Hewes & Co. | J. A. Hewes | 8-22-37 | 11-22-37 | 600.00 | 6% | 13.10 | none | Note of officer |
| L. W. Shields | none | 12-24-37 | 6-24-38 | 1,500.00 | 5% | 1.46 | none | |
| Total | | | | 7,145.72 | | 78.25 | | |
| Discounted Notes | | | | | | | | |
| Alberts & Blackman | | 10-30-37 | 1-30-38 | 4,275.00 | | | | Discounted 12-1-37 at Merchants Bank |
| R. O. Elmeier & Co. | | 11-18-37 | 2-18-38 | 1,485.28 | | | | Discounted 12-1-37 at Merchants Bank |
| Total | | | | 5,760.28 | | | | |

The above notes were examined 1-17-38, 9:30 a. m. Mr. Shields, the general manager, believes all the notes are collectible. His own personal note was authorized by the board of directors.

J. I. King
(Junior Accountant)

(Schedule No. 6)

Illustration No. 14. Analysis of Notes Receivable

## THE BLANK MANUFACTURING COMPANY
### Accounts Receivable—Trade Debtors
### Aging Schedule—December 31, 1937

| NAME | LEDGER BALANCE | SALES MADE DURING | | | | COLLECTED IN JANUARY (TO JAN. 17) | CONFIRMED |
| --- | --- | --- | --- | --- | --- | --- | --- |
| | | DECEMBER | NOVEMBER | OCTOBER | PRIOR TO OCTOBER | | |
| Forwarded from preceding pages. | *2,234.50 | *2,234.50 | | | | | |
| Richards, J. B. | 71,326.50 | 61,375.04 | 7,481.46 | 1,630.00 | 840.00 | 30,500.00 | |
| Sanford Corporation | *800.00 | *800.00 | | | | | √ |
| Sneed and Cohen, Inc. | 2,910.00 | 1,690.00 | 842.00 | 378.00 | | 2,910.00 | √ |
| Thomas, Leslie R. | 1,500.00 | 1,500.00 | | | | | |
| Vinson and White | 980.00 | 640.00 | 340.00 | | | 980.00 | √ |
| Well, I. N. | 6,400.00 | 6,400.00 | | | | | |
| Young, Earl M. | 330.00 | | 110.00 | 150.00 | 70.00 | 330.00 | √ |
| | 1,275.00 | 1,275.00 | | | | | |
| Total    Credits | *3,034.50 | *3,034.50 | | | | | |
| Total    Debits | 84,721.50 | 72,880.04 | 8,773.46 | 2,158.00 | 910.00 | 34,720.00 | |

*Credit Balances

| | LEDGER BALANCE | DECEMBER |
| --- | --- | --- |
| Ledger balance | 81,687.00 | 69,845.54 |
| Add Check returned N.S.F. | 17.76 | 17.76 |
| Total | 81,704.76 | 69,863.30 |
| Add Credit balances | 3,034.50 | 3,034.50 |
| Adjusted balance | 84,739.26 | 72,897.80 |

*The above schedule was prepared from the customers' ledger and all collections during January were traced to the cash book. The December 31 accounts, remaining uncollected at 1–17–38, were confirmed by correspondence with the debtors. Negative confirmations were used and only minor differences were reported in the replies received. Mr. J. D. Crenshaw, the credit manager, considers all of the accounts to be collectible. However, the reserve for bad debts is to be maintained at 2% of the accounts receivable.*

*(Schedule No. 7)*

J. I. King
(Junior Accountant)

Illustration No. 15.   Analysis of Accounts Receivable

$8,773.46; October, 1937, $2,158.00; prior to October, 1937, $910.00. (See Illustration No. 15.) After this was completed, those accounts more than 30 days past due were taken up with the credit manager and carefully analyzed.

(5) It was ascertained that at the beginning of the year, January 1, 1937, the total of accounts receivable amounted to $51,200. A reserve for bad debts amounting to 2% of accounts receivable was set up at that time. During the year accounts amounting to $968 were found to be worthless and were charged off by debiting the reserve account. These were found to have been duly authorized.

(6) No accounts were found to be hypothecated or assigned.

(7) No accounts from directors, officers, or employees were found to be included in the accounts receivable; also there were no deposits, guarantees, or any extraordinary items included. The credit balances noted in connection with a few of the customers' accounts were found to represent overpayments, allowances on merchandise returned, and other allowances on account of claims.

### THE BLANK MANUFACTURING COMPANY
#### Audit of Notes and Accounts Receivable
#### Adjusting Journal Entries

| | | |
|---|---:|---:|
| *Accrued Interest Receivable*...................... $ | 78.25 | |
| *Interest and Discount*....................... | | $    78.25 |
| *To record accrued interest on notes receivable at December 31, 1937.* | | |
| *Notes Receivable—Officers*..................... | 1,500.00 | |
| *Notes Receivable—Trade Debtors*........... | | 1,500.00 |
| *To show the notes of officers separately for balance sheet purposes.* | | |
| *Accounts Receivable—Trade Debtors*............ | 3,034.50 | |
| *Customers' Overpayments*.................. | | 3,034.50 |
| *To properly classify accounts receivable in the working trial balance and to facilitate showing accounts with credit balances as a liability on the balance sheet.* | | |
| *Loss on Bad Debts*............................. | 1,952.91 | |
| *Reserve for Doubtful Notes and Accounts*.... | | 1,952.91 |
| *To increase the reserve for doubtful notes and accounts to 2% of the amount of the notes and accounts receivable on hand at December 31, 1937.* | | |

**Illustration No. 16.  Adjusting Entries**

(8) With the consent of the client, statements were made out and mailed to all customers in envelopes bearing the auditors' return address. By means of a rubber stamp the following notice appeared on each statement:

> Please examine this account immediately. If incorrect, address Stevenson and Bennett, Certified Public Accountants, 9 West Third Street, Cincinnati, Ohio.

Only minor differences were reported in the replies received.

## SUMMARY

Receivables may consist of notes receivable, accounts receivable, mortgages receivable, or any other accounts representing amounts due or accrued. Receivables constitute current assets which rank next to cash and marketable securities in the order in which they should be listed on a balance sheet. The receivables should be classified so as to show separately accounts representing trade customers and accounts with officers and employees. In a balance sheet audit, the auditor should satisfy himself that all receivable accounts are bona fide and that they are collectible.

Usually it is advisable to verify the accuracy of the receivable accounts through correspondence with the debtors. Statements may be sent to all customers with a request that in case of an error in the amount due as shown by the statement, the customer should correspond direct with the auditor. However, in the case of notes receivable, and other negotiable instruments, the client may object to corresponding with the debtor, in which case the auditor may be able to satisfy himself as to the correctness of the accounts through analysis of the transactions in connection with which the receivables were obtained. However, in the event of doubt or of suspicion the auditor should insist upon a confirmation of the receivables by the maker or debtor.

As an aid to testing the adequacy of the reserve for doubtful accounts, the notes receivable should be examined to see if any are past due and the accounts receivable should be aged by preparing a list of the accounts showing separately first, those not due; second, those not more than thirty days past due, and third, those over thirty days past due. The past experience of the company should be considered and in the case of questionable accounts it may be advisable to obtain reports through credit agencies. At best, the reserve for doubtful accounts is an estimate of the amount which it is expected to lose on receivable accounts and past experience is usually the best guide in determining what amount should be added to the reserve for the current period. Since the receivables may constitute a considerable portion of the current assets, it is important that they be carefully audited in order to prevent a misstatement of the financial condition of the concern whose accounts are being examined.

## AUDITING THEORY

**6—63.** Prepare an outline of a specific audit program for verification of the receivable accounts for a firm engaged in the real estate business, assuming that the audit is to be started on the last day of the audit period.

**6—64.** Name at least five different types of receivables which may be found in the accounts of a business enterprise.

**6—65.** Why is it of the utmost importance that the auditor thoroughly acquaint himself with the sales, shipping, and bookkeeping routine prior to checking receivables?

**6—66.** (a) What is the difference between a note and a trade acceptance? (b) How should trade acceptances be listed on a balance sheet?

**6—67.** How should the following be handled in preparing a balance sheet to be certified:

(a) Dishonored notes
(b) Notes receivable discounted
(c) Credit balances in customers' accounts
(d) Advances to officers and employees
(e) Receivables due from affiliated companies?

**6—68.** In an audit of the accounts of a firm selling merchandise on the installment plan, in what manner would you determine the validity and value of the accounts receivable?

**6—69.** Lay out your method of providing an adequate reserve against bad debts. What conditions might prompt you to make inquiries as to a possible default of any item in an account?

**6—70.** A corporation has a controlling account in the general ledger for accounts receivable. The balance of the controlling account is $80,000. The debit balances of the individual accounts total $100,000, and the credit balances total $20,000. Is a statement correct which uses the controlling account balance as an asset? If not, what would you do? Give reasons.

(C. P. A. Mich.)

**6—71.** Indicate what would guide you in examining and criticising accounts receivable carried on the branch office books of a business. What would you require before

(a) Accepting the debits as good, or
(b) Writing off those you were told were bad?

(A. I. A.)

**6—72.** You have completed an audit of Corporation A and have discovered that its financial condition was verging on bankruptcy. Later, you are required to audit the accounts of Corporation X and you ascertain that this concern has on its books, considered as a good account receivable, a substantial amount charged to Corporation A for merchandise sold. What would be your attitude with regard to the accounts receivable of Corporation X?

(A. I. A.)

**6—73.** In auditing the books of the Moving Picture Producing Company you find the total balance due from customers as shown by the controlling account in the general ledger is less than half the total debit balances shown by the list you have taken from the customers' ledger. What does this indicate? How should the facts be shown on the balance sheet?

(A. I. A.)

## AUDITING PROBLEMS

**6—10.** As a junior accountant you are assigned to audit the accounts receivable balance, the amount of which appears on the trial balance of The Rising Sun Manufacturing Co. as $42,675.80. The bookkeeper has provided you with a list of the accounts the total of which is in agreement with the accounts receivable controlling account in the general ledger. Since a balance sheet audit is being made, you are not required to make a detailed audit of all the individual accounts with customers, but you are instructed to make a sufficient test of the accounts receivable to satisfy yourself that the amount appearing in the trial balance is correct beyond any reasonable doubt. You ascertain that a bookkeeping machine is used in posting to the individual accounts receivable. One of the accounts included in the list prepared by the bookkeeper is with the Anderson Supply Co. According to the list, the amount due from the Anderson Supply Co. on December 31, 1938, was $105.58. Upon request, you are given the ledger sheet for this account. (See page 159.) Audit the account and answer the following questions:

(a) What is the balance as of December 31, 1938?
(b) On what terms does your client sell the Anderson Supply Co.?
(c) What invoices remain unpaid in full or in part, on December 31, 1938?
(d) How do you account for the fact that the Anderson Supply Co. was given credit for only $16.68 for the C. O. D. shipment of October 28 when the shipment was returned on November 29?
(e) Are there any other items in this account which you would question?

NAME   Anderson Supply Co.

ADDRESS   Anderson, Ind.

| BALANCE | DATE | FOLIO | MEMO. | REMARKS | CHARGES | CREDITS |
|---|---|---|---|---|---|---|
| 1.28 | Jan. 1–38 | 567 | J/E | Loss on A/R | | 1.28 |
| .00 | May 2–38 | 826 | COD | | 105.56 | |
| 105.56 | Sep. 19–38 | 512 | | | | 105.56 |
| .00 | Sep. 28–38 | 847 | COD | | 116.22 | |
| 116.22 | Oct. 2–38 | 102 | COD | | 106.64 | |
| 222.86 | Oct. 7–38 | 110 | COD | | 18.92 | |
| 241.78 | Oct. 14–38 | 557 | | | | 222.86 |
| 18.92 | Oct. 14–38 | 563 | | | | 18.92 |
| .00 | Oct. 20–38 | 121 | | | | |
| 19.94 | Oct. 28–38 | 125 | COD | | 19.94 | |
| 123.22 | Nov. 4–38 | 130 | COD | | 103.28 | |
| 147.72 | Nov. 5–38 | 607 | COD | | 24.50 | |
| 44.44 | Nov. 14–38 | 138 | COD | | 102.32 | |
| 146.76 | Nov. 15–38 | 313 | RET | | | 103.28 |
| 130.08 | Nov. 29–38 | 642 | | | | 16.68 |
| 105.58 | Nov. 30–38 | | | | | 24.50 |

NAME   Asheville Can Co.

ADDRESS   Asheville, N. Car.

| BALANCE | DATE | FOLIO | MEMO. | REMARKS | CHARGES | CREDITS |
|---|---|---|---|---|---|---|
| 66.60 | May 15-38 | 515 | | | 66.60 | |
| 81.95 | May 27-38 | 518 | | | 15.35 | |
| 71.45 | June 1-38 | 51 | RET | | | 10.50 |
| 363.11 | Aug. 14-38 | 531 | | 9/1 DATING | 291.66 | |
| 375.35 | Sep. 16-38 | 582 | | | 12.24 | |
| 477.02 | Oct. 6-38 | 614 | | | 101.67 | |
| 492.29 | Oct. 7-38 | 616 | | | 15.27 | |
| 129.18 | Oct. 18-38 | 52 | J/E | | | 363.11 |
| 140.00 | Nov. 1-38 | 626 | | | 10.82 | |
| 250.15 | Dec. 2-38 | 653 | | | 110.15 | |
| 359.29 | Dec. 6-38 | 655 | | | 109.14 | |
| 245.38 | Dec. 15-38 | 19 | | | | 113.91 |
| 398.78 | Dec. 31-38 | 665 | | | 153.40 | |

**6—11.** Upon request, you are also given the ledger sheet for The Asheville Can Co. (See page 160) which, according to the list prepared by the bookkeeper, had a balance of $398.78 on December 31, 1938. Audit the account to see if the balance agrees with the amount shown on the list prepared by the bookkeeper and answer the following questions:

(a) What invoices remain unpaid on December 31, 1938?

(b) State what further information may be needed to verify the balance of this account.

(c) Explain the relation of the following entry in the general journal to the ledger account.

### October 18, 1938

| | | |
|---|---|---|
| Notes Receivable | $250.00 | |
| Cash | 113.11 | |
| Asheville Can Co. | | $363.11 |

(d) The Rising Sun Manufacturing Company's sales to The Asheville Can Co. have been made on a basis of terms net thirty days. What additional information would you need in determining whether or not this account should be classified as a doubtful account?

(e) Would you deem it advisable to audit any additional customers' accounts before certifying the total amount of accounts receivable as being correct?

**6—12.** During the course of an audit of the books of a company manufacturing and installing large units of electrical machinery, you find an account receivable of $100,000 due on contract No. 100. Upon a further examination of this account and contract, you find the following conditions:

The total amount of the contract is $200,000 and by reason of certain concessions the customer agreed to pay one-half upon signing the contract and one-half upon completion of the installation. You find that at December 31, 1938, the contract has been signed, $100,000 has been received, but work on the contract has not been commenced. The following entries appear on the books:

| | | |
|---|---|---|
| Accounts receivable | $200,000.00 | |
| Sales | | $200,000.00 |
| Cost of sales (estimated) | 120,000.00 | |
| Reserve for construction costs | | 120,000.00 |
| Cash | 100,000.00 | |
| Accounts receivable | | 100,000.00 |

The officers of the company advance the explanation that, inasmuch as conservative estimates show that the contract will net a profit of $80,000 and having received $100,000 in cash, they are correct in taking up all profit. What would you do under these conditions?

(A. I. A.)

## AUDITING PRACTICE

### An Audit Case (Fourth Installment)

On January 4, Ken B. Swift proceeds to verify the notes and accounts receivable. The notes submitted for examination, all of which were made out to the Beverly Supply Company as payee, were as follows:

| Maker | Date | Maturity | Rate | Amount | Remarks |
|---|---|---|---|---|---|
| R. M. Carpenter.... | 11– 1–38 | 1–30–39 | 6% | $   840.00 | |
| C. D. Cook......... | 8– 1–38 | 12– 1–38 | 6% | 1,500.00 | |
| T. M. Mason....... | 12– 1–38 | 5– 1–40 | 6% | 1,000.00 | |
| I. S. Plumber....... | 12– 1–38 | 1–30–39 | 6% | 2,020.00 | (Interest included in face of note) |
| D. B. Beverly....... | 9–15–38 | 4–15–39 | 4% | 10,000.00 | (D. B. Beverly is president of Bev. Supply Co.) |
| O. M. Shoemaker... | 12–16–38 | 2–14–39 | 6% | 500.00 | |

Memoranda in the note file indicated the following notes, discounted at the Farmers' National Bank at 6% interest, were outstanding at 12-31-38:

| Maker | Date | Maturity | Rate | Amount | Remarks |
|---|---|---|---|---|---|
| I. M. Painter....... | 11–15–38 | 1–14–39 | 6% | $   400 00 | Discounted 11–18–38 |
| O. K. Presser....... | 12– 2–38 | 3– 3–39 | 6% | 1,600.00 | Discounted 12– 4 38 |

The above notes are in agreement with the items listed in the note register and in the notes receivable account in the general ledger. All are unsecured and contain no endorsements.

S. M. Dollar, the credit manager, states that all of the above notes are collectible. C. D. Cook has agreed to pay his note on January 31, 1939.

Mr. Swift has been asked to prepare, as part of the audit engagement, a schedule aging the accounts receivable. The aging schedule is to contain money column headings as follows: Ledger Balance; December; November; October; September; Prior to September; Remarks.

Customers are granted a thirty-day credit period within which to pay their accounts. No cash discounts are allowed. Some customers are permitted to purchase merchandise on terms of sixty and ninety-day trade acceptances.

As part of the program of verification Mr. Swift reviewed the accounts and notes receivable with S. M. Dollar, the credit manager. The credit manager expressed the opinion that all the accounts and notes were collectible, with the exception of the account with Fleece M. Cloud, which is doubtful of collection.

It was decided to add to the reserve for doubtful notes and accounts an amount sufficient to bring the balance of the reserve up to 10% of the amount of the notes and accounts receivable at December 31, 1938, excluding any consignment accounts that might be carried as accounts receivable and excluding notes and accounts of officers or employees of the company.

The accounts with accounts receivable control and reserve for doubtful notes and accounts appeared on the general ledger of the Beverly Supply Company as follows:

### Accounts Receivable Control

| Date | Items | Debit | Credit | Balance |
|------|-------|-------|--------|---------|
| 1- 1-38 | Balance.................... | 7,670.00 | .......... | 7,670.00 |
| 6-30-38 | Sales on account to June 30.............. | 9,400.00 | .......... | 17,070.00 |
| 6-30-38 | Cash received on account to June 30........ | .......... | 11,070.00 | 6,000.00 |
| 7-31-38 | Sales on account..................... | 1,961.00 | .......... | 7,961.00 |
| 7-31-38 | Cash received...................... | .......... | 1,000.00 | 6,961.00 |
| 8- 5-38 | Credit memo — T. F. Lyon.................. | .......... | 25.00 | 6,936.00 |
| 8-31-38 | Sales on account..................... | 966.40 | .......... | 7,902.40 |
| 8-31-38 | Cash received....................... | .......... | 1,370.00 | 6,532.40 |
| 9-30-38 | Sales on account..................... | 715.65 | .......... | 7,248.05 |
| 9-30-38 | Cash received....................... | .......... | 858.40 | 6,389.65 |
| 10-31-38 | Sales on account..................... | 1,517.60 | .......... | 7,907.25 |
| 10-31-38 | Cash received....................... | .......... | 1,267.40 | 6,639.85 |
| 11-30-38 | Sales on account..................... | 1,866.05 | .......... | 8,505.90 |
| 11-30-38 | Cash received....................... | .......... | 1,138.00 | 7,367.90 |
| 12- 8-38 | Credit memo—D. R. Field.... | .......... | 90.00 | 7,277.90 |
| 12- 9-38 | Credit memo—Brook C. Trout.... | .......... | 120.00 | 7,157.90 |
| 12-15-38 | Note receivable—O. M. Shoemaker........ | .......... | 500.00 | 6,657.90 |
| 12-31-38 | Sales on account..................... | 3,244.00 | .......... | 9,901.90 |
| 12-31-38 | Cash received..................... | .......... | 2,976.00 | 6,925.90 |

### Reserve for Doubtful Notes and Accounts

| Date | Items | Debit | Credit | Balance |
|------|-------|-------|--------|---------|
| 1- 1-38 | Balance................... | .......... | 737.00 | 737.00 |
| 8-15-38 | C. D. Flint—uncollectible.................. | 300.00 | .......... | 437.00 |
| 11-30-38 | K. T. Ash—uncollectible.................. | 266.90 | .......... | 170.10 |

The accounts charged to the reserve for doubtful accounts during the year were investigated and appear to be uncollectible.

The accounts in the accounts receivable ledger having balances at December 31, 1938, are shown on pages 164 and 165. The consignment to C. T. House on December 28 was billed at the cost price. The offsetting credit was to the sales account. None of the consigned merchandise had been sold at December 31, 1938.

## Mark C. Anthony

| 1938 | | | 1938 | | |
|---|---|---|---|---|---|
| 7/1 | Bal. | 600.00 | 7/18 | Cash | 600.00 |
| 7/21 | Inv. | 100.00 | 8/20 | Cash | 100.00 |
| 9/20 | Inv. | 28.00 | 11/8 | Cash | 28.00 |
| 11/4 | Inv. | 40.00 | | | *728.00* |
| 12/9 | Inv. | 200.00 | | | |
| | *240.00* | *968.00* | | | |

## C. C. Brooks

| 1938 | | | 1938 | | |
|---|---|---|---|---|---|
| 7/1 | Bal. | 1120.00 | 7/10 | Cash | 1120.00 |
| 8/30 | Inv. | 75.50 | 9/30 | Cash | 50.00 |
| 9/15 | Inv. | 125.00 | | | *1170.00* |
| 10/1 | Inv. | 250.00 | | | |
| 11/9 | Inv. | 130.05 | | | |
| 12/5 | Inv. | 418.20 | | | |
| | *948.75* | *2118.75* | | | |

## Fleece M. Cloud

| 1938 | | |
|---|---|---|
| 7/28 | Inv. | 360.00 |
| 8/20 | Inv. | 236.50 |
| | | *596.50* |

## A. D. Farmer

| 1938 | | | 1938 | | |
|---|---|---|---|---|---|
| 7/1 | Bal. | 250.00 | 9/10 | Cash | 250.00 |
| 10/3 | Inv. | 100.00 | 12/9 | Cash | 100.00 |
| 11/8 | Inv. | 265.00 | | | *350.00* |
| | *265.00* | *615.00* | | | |

## D. R. Field

| 1938 | | | 1938 | | |
|---|---|---|---|---|---|
| 9/18 | Inv. | 261.00 | 10/2 | Cash | 261.00 |
| 11/9 | Inv. | 390.00 | 12/2 | Cash | 390.00 |
| | | *651.00* | 12/8 | C/M | 90.00 |
| | | | | *90.00* | *741.00* |

## W. T. Hale (Employee)

| 1938 | | |
|---|---|---|
| 10/5 | Mdse. | 150.00 |
| 11/1 | Mdse. | 60.00 |
| | | *210.00* |

## I. M. Hills

| 1938 | | | 1938 | | |
|---|---|---|---|---|---|
| 7/1 | Bal. | 3433.50 | 7/15 | Cash | 3433.50 |
| 7/10 | Inv. | 890.00 | 8/5 | Cash | 670.00 |
| 9/26 | Inv. | 112.40 | 10/9 | Cash | 112.40 |
| 10/7 | Inv. | 717.60 | | | *4215.90* |
| 12/5 | Inv. | 850.00 | | | |
| | *1787.60* | *6003.50* | | | |

## C. T. House, Consignee

| 1938 | | |
|---|---|---|
| 12/28 | Inv. | 950.00 |

## H. I. Knave

| 1938 | | | 1938 | | |
|---|---|---|---|---|---|
| 8/24 | Inv. | 8.40 | 9/9 | Cash | 8.40 |
| 9/18 | Inv. | 38.00 | 10/3 | Cash | 38.00 |
| 11/3 | Inv. | 46.00 | 12/8 | Cash | 46.00 |
| 12/9 | Inv. | 25.00 | | | *92.40* |
| | *25.00* | *117.40* | | | |

## T. F. Lyon

| 1938 | | | 1938 | | |
|---|---|---|---|---|---|
| 9/20 | Inv. | 61.25 | 8/5 | C/M | 25.00 |
| 11/26 | Inv. | 110.00 | | | |
| 12/5 | Inv. | 290.80 | | | |
| | *437.05* | *462.05* | | | |

## E. C. Street (Employee)

| 1938 | | | 1938 | | |
|---|---|---|---|---|---|
| 9/29 | Mdse. | 10.00 | 11/3 | Cash | 10.00 |
| 11/8 | Mdse. | 180.00 | | | |
| 12/5 | Mdse. | 135.00 | | | |
| | *315.00* | *325.00* | | | |

## O. M. Shoemaker

| 1938 | | | 1938 | | |
|---|---|---|---|---|---|
| 7/1 | Bal. | 596.50 | 8/10 | Cash | 596.50 |
| 7/15 | Inv. | 250.00 | 12/2 | Cash | 200.00 |
| 8/28 | Inv. | 340.00 | 12/15 | Note | 500.00 |
| 10/6 | Inv. | 110.00 | | | *1296.50* |
| 12/16 | Inv. | 375.00 | | | |
| | *375.00* | *1671.50* | | | |

## Brook C. Trout

| 1938 | | | 1938 | | |
|---|---|---|---|---|---|
| 7/31 | Inv. | 181.00 | 10/6 | Cash | 256.00 |
| 8/28 | Inv. | 75.00 | 12/4 | Cash | 240.00 |
| 11/6 | Inv. | 240.00 | 12/9 | C/M | 120.00 |
| | | *496.00* | | *120.00* | *616.00* |

## D. T. Tyler

| 1938 | | | 1938 | | |
|---|---|---|---|---|---|
| 7/29 | Inv. | 180.00 | 10/5 | Cash | 100.00 |
| 8/16 | Inv. | 231.00 | | | |
| 9/21 | Inv. | 80.00 | | | |
| 10/7 | Inv. | 190.00 | | | |
| 11/5 | Inv. | 405.00 | | | |
| | *986.00* | *1086.00* | | | |

The accounts which were credited from the cash receipts record during the last few days of December for the balance due and which were in balance, are not reproduced. In other words, all accounts which were in balance as of December 31 are omitted from this list of accounts receivable. This explains why there are no accounts for customers named on the last page of the cash receipts record for December, which is reproduced on page 110.

## INSTRUCTIONS

1. Read and study the auditing procedure suggested for the verification of notes and accounts receivable in an "Examination of Financial Statements."

2. Study the form of schedules shown in the illustrative set of audit working papers for The Blank Manufacturing Company. See Illustrations Nos. 14 and 15.

3. Perform the audit work suggested for verification of notes and accounts receivable in so far as the procedure applies to this audit.

4. Prepare schedules of notes receivable and accounts receivable as of December 31, 1938.

5. Prepare an analysis of accounts receivable and of the reserve for doubtful notes and accounts showing the adjusted balance of each account as of December 31, 1938.

6. Draft adjusting journal entries, where necessary, to adjust the account balances. No adjustment need be made on account of the deferred interest on discounted notes as the amount is too small to warrant adjustment.

# CHAPTER SEVEN

## INVENTORIES

1. Accounting for Inventories
   - (a) Types of Inventories
   - (b) Importance of Inventory Records
   - (c) Goods Not Possessed
   - (d) Goods in Transit
   - (e) Goods Pledged

2. Bases of Valuation
   - (a) Cost
   - (b) Cost or Market Price, Whichever is the Lower
   - (c) Retail Method

3. Kinds of Goods
   - (a) Raw Material
   - (b) Goods in Process
   - (c) Finished Goods

4. Responsibility of Auditor
   - (a) Verification of Quantities
   - (b) Clerical Accuracy of Inventory
   - (c) Verification of Prices

5. Auditing Procedure

6. Application of Principles

7. An Audit Case—Fifth Installment

The inventory is frequently one of the largest items in the balance sheet and from the point of view of its relation to the profit and loss statement may be considered one of the most important items. A serious misstatement of the value of the inventory not only materially affects the amount of the current assets but increases or decreases the net profit for the period. The accuracy of any inventory depends in part upon the accuracy of the quantities, the prices, and the computations involved in its valuation. A misstatement of any one of the three elements distorts the value of the inventory. An auditor can usually verify the prices and the computations, but is seldom able to verify the quantities unless he was present at the time the inventory was taken. However, there is much the auditor can do to ascertain that the inventory quantities seem reasonable. More will be stated on this point in a later section of the chapter.

## ACCOUNTING FOR INVENTORIES

**Types of Inventories.** Three types of inventories may be encountered in statements. A brief discussion of the three types of inventories is presented below:

(1) Physical Inventory. A physical inventory is one in which the quantities are determined by actual count, weight, or measurement of the items in stock. After the count has been completed, the items are priced on a basis of unit costs. The value of each item in the inventory is determined by multiplying the quantity by the unit price. The total value of the inventory is determined by totaling the values of the individual items in the inventory.

(2) Continuous Inventory. A stock record of all goods purchased, issued, or sold may be kept so that at any time the records will show the quantity and value of the goods in stock.

If proper care is used in keeping the stock records, a book inventory will provide information regarding the value of the goods in stock which may be used as the basis of interim reports, and which will provide the management with current information that may safely be used as a guide in the management of the business. However, in the preparation of annual reports the book inventory should not be used without verification through an actual count of the goods in stock, or through sufficient testing to insure reasonable accuracy of the book inventory. Regardless of how carefully the stock records may be kept or the extent to which an internal check is maintained, there may be discrepancies between the stock records and a physical inventory. These discrepancies may not be the result of errors in recording purchases and sales, but may be the result of loss resulting from the theft of goods, spoiled goods, or deterioration of goods in stock.

(3) Estimated Inventory. In the event that a continuous or book inventory is not maintained, and it is inconvenient or impossible to take a physical inventory, as in the case of fire, the inventory may be estimated. The usual method of estimating the value of the inventory is to ascertain the average percentage

of gross trading profit over a period of years based upon sales. The amount of the gross trading profit may then be ascertained by multiplying the net sales by the rate of gross profit. After computing the amount of the gross profit it is only necessary to deduct this amount from the net sales to find the cost of the goods sold. The cost of the goods on hand at the beginning of the period, plus the cost of the goods purchased during the period, less the cost of the goods sold, will be the estimated value of the goods on hand at the end of the period covered by the report.

Of course, this method assumes that the percentage of gross trading profit for the current period is approximately the same as for previous periods. In other words, the use of this method will provide accurate results only when operations are maintained on a normal basis. In an abnormal year the percentage of gross trading profit would not be a reliable guide for the computation of inventory values. The use of an estimated inventory is advisable only under conditions which do not justify the taking of a physical inventory or in case it is impossible to make an actual count of the goods in stock, as in the event of a flood, fire, or other disaster which may have resulted in complete or partial destruction of goods.

**Importance of Inventory Records.** There is a growing tendency on the part of manufacturing and trading concerns to keep a merchandise stock record, commonly known as a "running" or "going" inventory. Every business firm keeps a record of cash regardless of what other records are kept. It is difficult to understand why it isn't just as important to keep an accurate record of merchandise as it is of cash. Without a doubt, the loss from thefts and misappropriation of merchandise amount to more in a year than embezzlements of cash amount to in a decade. It is a well known fact that merchandise, worth millions of dollars, is carried away annually by employees and others because they know the loss may never be discovered. In the face of these facts, it would seem to be very important that an accurate record of goods on hand be kept whether the business is a trading or a manufacturing concern. Without the waste of time, labor, and delay incident to stocktaking, the manufacturer or trader should, at all times, know exactly how he stands concerning the amount and value of all stock on hand.

If a separate stock ledger is kept, then it will be necessary to maintain a controlling account in the general ledger, the same as for any other subsidiary ledger. The accounts in the stock ledger will usually show on the debit side quantities purchased, cost per unit, and amount purchased; on the credit side quantities sold, cost per unit, and amount sold. A balance column may be provided so that there may be shown quantities on hand, cost per unit, and total amount or value at cost price.

**Goods Not Possessed.** Goods owned may not always be in the possession of the owner. They may be out on consignment, they may be stored in warehouses, or they may be in the possession of customers to whom they have been sold on an installment basis under an agreement whereby title remains with the seller until payment is made in full. All goods owned whether actually possessed or not, should be included in the inventory and should be valued on the same basis as goods possessed. The auditor may be forced to verify the goods not possessed by checking the client's records by correspondence with the consignee or other holders of the goods, and by examination of the warehouse receipts. It is also well to obtain an inventory certificate from each warehouse in which goods may be stored.

**Goods in Transit.** Usually there are some goods in transit at the end of a financial period. The proper method of accounting for goods in transit revolves around the question of ownership. Merchandise may be purchased f.o.b. destination or f.o.b. point from which shipment is made. Where goods are purchased f.o.b. the destination, such goods belong to the shipper until delivered, hence the goods belong in the shipper's inventory and not in that of the buyer. On the other hand, goods purchased f.o.b. origin, are the goods of the buyer as soon as delivered to the common carrier. In transit items may be listed on the balance sheet in several ways. Some organizations place them in the inventories, provided title has passed to the client. Others use an "In Transit" item in the balance sheet, and show the liability therefor under "Unaudited Vouchers" or some similar account. The latter method, carrying such items as deferred charges or items until such time as they may be received, checked in, and the verification of the invoice made, has much in its favor. The former method places a valuation on the inventories which have not been verified, the only basis for which may be the invoice of the shipment and the purchase order. Conservative practice will probably keep such items out of the inventory accounts, provided they are of sufficient importance to affect the value of that account to any great degree.

**Goods Pledged.** Some companies, especially those in need of capital, may pledge a part of their inventory for the purpose of obtaining adequate working capital. In such cases the goods are usually covered by a trust or warehouse receipt, and as the goods are taken from storage and placed on the floor, the owner thereof must make certain payments as per the agreement in force between the parties concerned.

Pledged merchandise is not eligible, of course, for use in obtaining further credit. As a result, it is advisable to divide the merchandise accounts, where pledged goods exist, into pledged and unpledged goods. Usually where goods are pledged to secure loans the contract calls for a specific margin of safety as between the value of the loan and of the merchandise pledged. Such a contract should be carefully scrutinized by the auditor, and he should assure himself that the terms thereof are being properly adhered to.

## BASES OF VALUATION

The following are the most commonly used bases for valuing inventories:

(a) Cost
(b) Cost or market price, whichever is the lower
(c) Retail price

**The Cost Method.** When the cost price is used it is customary to use it uniformly, regardless of the market value of the goods. However, care should be taken not to include any goods which have become unsalable because of deterioration, damage, changes in style, or other factors which are common to many types of business. Only such goods as are in salable condition should be included in the inventory regardless of the basis of valuation. Any goods that have become worthless should be written off in the event a continuous inventory is maintained and should not be included in a physical inventory. If this plan is followed the value of such goods will be charged against the current period which should stand the loss. This will be reflected in the trading or manufacturing statement where the cost of goods sold is computed. It is sound accounting to use the cost price of all goods as a basis for inventory valuation. Under this method profits are not taken in advance of the sale of the goods and losses are not anticipated, but are accounted for in the period in which the goods are sold. In a business where market values do not fluctuate widely, the cost price may be used safely from year to year for inventory valuation.

Some firms follow a custom of labeling the goods so as to show the cost after they are placed in stock. If this plan is followed it will be a simple matter to ascertain the cost of all goods in stock at any time. Where the goods are not labeled as to cost price, it may be necessary to use either the average invoice prices for the period, or to use the latest invoice prices. The usual procedure is to use the latest or most recent invoice prices. This is on the assumption that goods first purchased are first to be sold, whereas the goods in stock are the last to be purchased hence the most recent invoice prices should apply.

### The Cost or Market, Whichever is Lower Method.

The inventory basis most generally used by professional accountants is "The cost or market price, whichever is the lower." This may be an arbitrary method and it may seem unreasonable, but nevertheless, it is generally accepted by accountants, bankers, and the Bureau of Internal Revenue of the Treasury Department (for income tax purposes) and may therefore be considered as a safe method to use. Under this method goods will be valued at cost when the cost price is less than the market value, and will be valued at the market price when the cost price is more than the market value. This method of inventorying, results in the current period being charged with any loss resulting from a decline in the market value of the goods to a point below the cost price. In other words, it results in taking a loss in the period in which the market value declines rather than in the period in which the goods are sold. On the other hand, an increase in the market value above the cost price of the goods does not result in the current period being credited for the gain as it would not be sound accounting practice to take a profit on goods which had

not been sold. Profits must be accounted for when realized
through actual sales, but losses may be accounted for when they
have accrued regardless of whether or not the goods have been
sold.

**The Retail Method.** The retail method of valuing inventories has increased in popularity in recent years, until today
it is apparently the most popular method in certain lines of
business, especially among department stores, chain stores, and
branch stores. For several years, the Bureau of Internal Revenue
refused to recognize the retail method for tax purposes which
tended to hinder its spread and development, but it may now
be so used, provided accurate and adequate records are maintained, the basis is used consistently, and the method is plainly
stated on the return.

Under the retail method of valuation, retail prices are used
throughout all inventory work. In general, this method is based
on the formula that the inventory at the beginning of the period
(at retail prices) plus the purchases for the period (at retail
prices), adjusted by mark-ups, mark-downs, cancellations, and
stock shortages, less the sales (at retail prices), gives the inventory
at the end of the period (at retail prices).

Having computed the inventory at retail prices, and from
previous calculations based on the mark-ups and mark-downs,
and cancellations of both during the period, and knowing the net
percentage of mark-up, the accountant may determine the value,
at cost or market price. It should be noted here that the retail
method of valuing inventories, does not disturb the customary
method of valuing inventories in commercial concerns at cost
or market, whichever is lower. The retail method is simply a
procedure by which cost or market may be obtained easier,
quicker, and cheaper than under the other methods of inventorying.

The leading advantages of the retail method of inventorying
may be summarized as follows:

(1) It is an aid to management allowing accurate budgetary
control, control of mark-downs, and mark-ups, and permits the
accurate forecasting of future inventories, purchases, and financial
requirements.

(2) It permits orderly comparisons between cost and retail values, with resulting operating records instead of having to depend upon the memory and guesswork of executives.

(3) It may be used to give accurate data of stocks on hand at any time with little effort; as it permits statistical data to be easily computed and calculated from stated prices.

(4) It reduces labor costs of marking, costing, etc., in that no prices or information need be placed on merchandise other than sales prices.

(5) Permits a more flexible merchandise control, through elimination of marking, etc., which speeds up the stock movement.

(6) Greatly simplifies the taking of the physical inventories, in that much of the work connected therewith may be done in the office, codes and similar devices being eliminated.

The accuracy of the retail method depends to a great extent on the internal machinery set up to care for the control and recording of mark-ups, mark-downs, and cancellations. Without proper support to the buyers, and control between the statistical division and the marking group, this method of control will usually fall down.

As a result, where the retail method is in use, the auditor may well spend considerable time determining the method and procedures of controlling such items, the degree of internal check on such factors, and the experience of the concern over a period of years as to losses incurred in the inventories through various causes.

## KINDS OF GOODS

Goods carried in stock may be classified as follows:

(a) Raw materials
(b) Goods in process
(c) Finished goods.

In a merchandising business all goods carried in stock may be finished goods which are purchased ready for sale. In a manufacturing business or in any business where goods are produced or where they are not acquired ready for sale, they may be classified into three groups. Goods or materials purchased from which other goods are to be made are generally known as raw materials. Goods in process of being changed or manufactured into different or finished goods may be known as goods in process or goods in progress of manufacture. The goods fully manufactured are known as finished goods.

It will readily be seen that in any manufacturing business there is likely to be goods on hand in all three stages, that is, in the new material stage, in the process stage, and in the fully manufactured stage. The basis for valuation of raw materials, goods in process, and finished goods for a manufacturing concern need not vary from the basis used in valuing the inventory of finished goods for a merchandising concern. Where conditions within an industry are such that it would be impractical to use cost or market price, whichever is the lower, of the raw materials and goods in process, the cost price basis should be used. If it is practical to use the cost or market price, whichever is the lower, then the proper price should be applied to all goods regardless of their stage of completion. In other words, it would be unreasonable to use one basis for inventorying the value of raw materials in stock, and a different basis for inventorying finished goods in stock. If the market price of raw materials has declined below cost then it is probable that the market price of finished goods may also have declined below cost, hence it may be advisable to inventory both at market price in order that the current period may be charged with the loss arising from the decline in the market values of the goods in stock to a point below actual cost of the goods.

There are many variable factors in accounting for the cost of goods manufactured and the auditor needs to be well versed in the principles of cost accounting. He also should be familiar with the practices adopted and used uniformly by many of the trade associations. Without such knowledge it will be difficult to determine the accuracy of cost values of goods manufactured or in process of being manufactured. Of course, no particular difficulty will be encountered in ascertaining the cost of raw materials, as the same policy may be followed as in ascertaining the cost of the finished goods handled by a merchant. In other words, the invoice prices of materials purchased may be used. Where the materials in stock cannot be identified in relation to the actual invoice prices, the latest invoice prices may be used.

If standard costs are used in recording the cost of goods manufactured, care must be taken to see that in no case the standard cost exceeds the actual cost and in case the market price has declined below cost, then care must be used to see that the standard cost in no case exceeds the market price of the goods fully manufactured.

## RESPONSIBILITY OF THE AUDITOR

The responsibility of the auditor in relation to inventory valuations is not clearly established from a legal viewpoint. Where the auditor does not take nor supervise the taking of a physical inventory, it is customary for him to accept a certificate of inventory from an official of the firm. The auditor who accepts a certificate of inventory without any verification, is certainly negligent and is avoiding the responsibility which he should assume regardless of whether or not there may be any legal responsibility involved. There is evidence of gross negligence on the part of the auditor in a case such as the following:

A firm of public accountants had annually audited and certified to the statement of a large industrial concern which maintained manufacturing plants in several different cities. After the concern had apparently prospered over a period of years, bankers were induced to underwrite a large issue of bonds and stockholders were given the right to subscribe to additional stock at what appeared to be an attractive price. Subsequently an employee of one of the branch factories wrote one of the bankers involved in the underwriting agreement, to the effect that he believed the inventory had been grossly overstated in the concern's financial statements. The bank immediately took action in the courts and obtained an injunction to prevent the concern from using any of the funds which had been obtained from the sale of the bonds to the bankers, pending the result of an audit to see if fraud had been committed. In due time, the auditors employed by the bankers reported a discrepancy of at least $300,000 in the inventory valuation. In the final proceedings it was found that this discrepancy was extended to nearly $1,000,000.

The accountants who had certified to the original statement escaped legal liability on the ground that they had accepted an inventory certificate signed by the president of the firm. The president was found guilty of having committed fraud in connection with the sale of the bonds and the firm was ordered by the court to return the entire proceeds of the bond issue to the bankers. While the bankers escaped loss, the stockholders suffered a loss which clearly may be attributed to the negligence on the part of the accountants. It is unfortunate that there has not been established some means of protection from loss resulting from negligence or carelessness on the part of accountants who certify financial statements to be used in connection with the sale of securities. Even though an auditor may not be legally liable under such cases, there is certainly a moral responsibility which the auditor should not seek to avoid. If steps are taken to verify the inventories taken without the supervision of the auditor, the public may be saved millions of dollars annually.

The auditor should at least hold himself responsible for the following:

(a) Testing the accuracy of the quantities, and verification of quality and condition of items in the inventory.

(b) Verifying the clerical accuracy of the listings, extensions, and footings.

(c) Verification of inventory prices.

**Verification of Quantities, Quality, Etc.** The auditor should make sufficient investigation of the methods used in preparing the inventory to substantiate the fact that the inventory was taken in a reliable manner. Copies of the original inventory instructions should be examined if they are available. The original inventory cards or sheets used in taking the inventory should be secured and tests made by comparing the description and quantities on the original inventory record with the corresponding items on the typed inventory sheets. If perpetual inventory records are maintained, comparisons may be made of the quantities in these records with those appearing in the completed inventory as a test of the reasonableness of the inventory quantities.

The auditor cannot assume complete responsibility for the quantities in the inventory unless he was on hand to supervise the taking of the count. Where the auditor supervises the taking of an inventory, company employees should place tags on all the items to be counted and record the quantities of the items on the tags. The auditor and his staff can then test count the inventory items and extract the tags on which are listed the quantities. If the tags are prepared in two sections, the quantities should be recorded on both sections. The inventory cards can then be severed and the auditor may retain one copy and the client's employees the other. After the inventory has been prepared in final form, the auditor can test the quantities appearing in the completed inventory with the quantities recorded on inventory cards retained by him, to see that the quantities were correctly listed in the inventory prepared by the employees of the company.

Investigation should be made to determine that no obsolete or unsalable stock is included in the inventory except at realizable figures. A certificate should be obtained from responsible officers of the company attesting to the fact that the quantities were determined by actual count, weight or measurement, and that proper allowance has been made for damaged, obsolete, or unsalable stock.

**Clerical Accuracy of Inventory.** While the auditor may not be expected to assume complete responsibility for the inventory quantities, he must assume responsibility for its clerical accuracy.

The arithmetical computations of all large amounts should be checked and sufficient tests should be made of the remainder of the inventory to indicate that the inventory has been accurately prepared. The auditor should be alert to detect errors in extensions due to misplaced decimal points and to errors due to extensions where items are priced in dozens, gross, and hundredweight. If some quotations are expressed as unit prices and others as prices per dozen or per gross, care must be taken to see that the proper values are determined. All footings should be proved, and if the inventory is divided into sections, the totals of each section should be verified and the amounts traced into the summary and the summary footed.

**Verification of Prices.** A substantial portion of the inventory prices should be tested by the auditor to see that the inventory is correctly valued. The prices of all large amounts should be verified. Prices may be obtained from invoices of the most recent purchases, or market quotations frequently may be secured from published quotations in catalogues, trade journals, daily newspapers, and from other published price lists. The auditor should prepare a pricing schedule on which may be listed items in the inventory that are tested. The schedule should give a description of the inventory items, their unit price, and value as shown by the inventory list. To these data should be added the information obtained from recent invoices, such as the name of the vendor, the date of recent purchase, the unit price, and the value if the unit price differs materially from the amount shown in the inventory. A column may be included for the amount of the inventory reduction if errors are discovered.

## AUDITING PROCEDURE APPLICABLE TO INVENTORIES
### In an "Examination of Financial Statements"

"1. The accountant's examination of inventories falls naturally into three main divisions:

"(a)  Accuracy of computations, footings, and recapitulations.

"(b)  Basis of pricing.

"(c)  Quantities, quality, and condition.

"2. The responsibility of the accountant in the first two cases is clear: check the inventories sufficiently to be satisfied as to the substantial accuracy of the clerical work performed and that the goods are valued in accordance with the usual commercial practice—that is, at cost or market, whichever is lower or on some other reasonable basis which is accepted as sound accounting practice in the particular trade or business.

"3. The duties and responsibilities of the accountant in the case of quantities, quality, and condition of stock vary with the circumstances; but he must rely principally for information as to quantities, quality, and condition upon the responsible officers and employees of the company. In the case of a business which does not call for technical knowledge and presents no substantial difficulties, the accountant, by special arrangement with his client, may be justified in assuming a greater degree of responsibility than in cases where expert knowledge is essential. Make reasonable inquiries and tests to ascertain that quantities have been carefully determined and that quality and condition have received due consideration.

"4. Obtain copies of company's inventory instructions and determine how complete the physical stocktaking has been or whether there has been substantial reliance on book inventories. In the latter case inquire how frequently they have been tested by physical inventories throughout the period. If the accountant can discuss the situation before the actual stocktaking, it is desirable that he do so and ascertain the methods to be followed.

"5. Obtain original stock sheets if they are in existence. Test the final inventory sheets by comparison with the originals and with tickets, cards or other means used in recording the original count.

"6. See that inventory sheets are signed or initialed by the persons responsible respectively for taking the stock, determining the prices, and making the calculations and footings. Obtain from a responsible official a clear and detailed statement in writing as to the method followed in taking stock and pricing it and as to the quantity, quality, and condition and the accuracy of the inventory as a whole.

"7. Test the accuracy of the footings and extensions, especially of the larger items.

"8. Make a test comparison of the inventories with the stock records, if these are maintained, in support of quantities, prices and values. Any material discrepancy should be satisfactorily explained.

"9. See that goods which are not owned but are on consignment from others have not been included in the inventory.

"10. See that goods set aside for shipment, the title to which has passed to customers, have not been included in the inventory.

"11. Whenever a cost system is not adequately controlled by the financial accounting, special attention is required. There is always a possibility that orders may have been completed, billed, and shipped but not have been taken out of the work-in-process records. This is the case especially where such reliance is placed on work-in-process records that a physical inventory is not taken at the end of the period to check their accuracy. In such cases compare sales for the month preceding the close of the fiscal period with the orders in process shown by the inventory to see that goods which have been shipped are not erroneously included in the inventory.

"12. See that no machinery or other material which has been charged to plant or property account is included in the inventory.

"13. Make inquiries and tests to ascertain that purchase invoices for stock included in the inventory have been entered on the books. Look for post-dated invoices and give special attention to goods in transit.

"14. If it is customary in the particular business to receive deliveries under purchase contracts which are not promptly billed, confirm the quantities delivered by communication with the contractor.

"15. Ascertain that inventories are stated at cost or market prices, whichever are the lower at the date of the balance sheet, or determine that any other basis which has been adopted is in accordance with sound accounting practice in the particular trade or business. Deduct trade discounts in determining inventory cost prices. Cash discounts may or may not be deducted, depending upon the practice of the trade and of the particular company. Market prices may be determined by obtaining current quotations, consulting trade journals, and by comparison with recent purchases. Replacement costs should be considered and also selling prices, less shipping and selling expenses.

"16. In the case of raw materials and merchandise purchased make a test comparison of cost prices used with purchase invoices or other sources of information. A general examination and test of the cost system in force is the best means of checking the cost of the work in process and finished goods. See that no selling expenses, interest charges, or administrative expenses are included in the factory overhead cost (except so far as administrative expenses apply to production); that any interdepartmental profits and, in the case of consolidated statements, intercompany profits, are eliminated from the inventories; and that the factory overhead cost is equitably distributed over the various departments, shops, and commodities. Ascertain whether overhead allocation is based on actual production or normal capacity. Normal capacity is preferable.

"17. If duties, freight, insurance, and other direct charges have been added, the amounts should be tested to ascertain that they are proper.

"18. Give consideration to the possibility that obsolete, excessive, or damaged stock may be included in the inventories at greater than realizable values; make test of detailed stock records to determine if the quantities are reasonable in relation to average consumption and purchases; and discuss with responsible officials.

"19. Make inquiry to ascertain if the company has discontinued the manufacture of any of its products during the year; if so the inventory of such products or parts thereof should be carefully scrutinized and provision made for anticipated losses.

"20. In the case of part shipments or uncompleted contracts it is preferable not to take up profits except in cases where the informaton available clearly indicates that a partial profit has been realized after making provision for possible losses and contingencies. Ascertain from the contracts the selling prices for contract work in progress and if it is apparent that there will be a loss on the completed contract, provisions should be made for the estimated loss.

"21. Check the inventory total by the 'gross profit test,' comparing the percentage of gross profit with that of previous years. In a business in which the average gross profit has been fairly constant, this test is satisfactory; if the rate of gross profit is not maintained and the discrepancy can not be explained by a rise or fall in the cost of production or in the selling price, the difference may be due to errors in the inventories.

"22. Ascertain that the inventories at the beginning and at the end of the period are stated on the same basis, determined generally in the same manner, or if not, the approximate effect on the operating results.

"23. Advance payments on account of purchase contracts for future delivery should preferably be shown in the balance sheet under a separate heading.

"24. If stocks have been hypothecated, that fact and the book value of the stocks hypothecated should be stated on the balance sheet."

### Modifications of Audit Program for Larger or Smaller Concerns

"Many large companies maintain comprehensive continuous inventory records which are subject to periodic and independent physical stocktaking. In such cases the accountant should use his best judgment in determinng the extent of the examination required, but the various points mentioned in the program regarding inventories given above should be considered."

## APPLICATION OF PRINCIPLES
### AUDIT OF THE BLANK MANUFACTURING COMPANY (Continued)

C. E. Shaw, one of the junior accountants in the employ of Stevenson and Bennett, verified the inventories. He referred to the audit procedure recommended by the American Institute of Accountants for verifying inventories and gave consideration to each of the steps enumerated therein wherever they applied to the conditions found in the audit.

**Raw Materials.** The inventory was checked as to extensions and footings. Also, tests were made by actual count of some of the items listed. Prices of raw materials and finished goods were verified by examination of recent invoices, price catalogues, and by comparison with inventory cards and cost records. An inventory pricing schedule was prepared in connection with the verification of the raw materials. (Illustration No. 17.) In verifying the prices of the raw materials inventory, errors totaling $2,085 were ascertained by Mr. Shaw. It was not necessary to make an adjusting journal entry to correct the errors as the inventory had not been recorded. Corrections were made in the inventory records and on Mr. Shaw's working papers.

**Goods in Process.** The goods in process were valued at the actual cost of the raw materials consumed, plus the direct labor cost and the factory overhead expenses applicable to the incompleted work. An item of $4,980.20, representing the accrued factory pay roll, had not been included in the value of the goods in process, as valued at $27,894.80. The value of the goods in process was, therefore, increased to $32,875. No adjusting journal entry was needed to reflect this change, as the inventories had not been recorded on the books.

**Finished Goods.** In arriving at the value of the finished goods, the factory overhead costs were added to the costs of direct material and direct labor as determined by an analysis of the accounts. The computations made by employees of the company were checked and appeared to be reasonable. No selling expenses, interest charges, or administrative expenses were included in the factory overhead cost.

A certificate of inventory (Illustration No. 18) was obtained from the company, signed by Harold Pond, chief accountant,

(Continued on page 186)

## THE BLANK MANUFACTURING COMPANY
### Pricing Schedule—Raw Materials Inventory
#### December 31, 1937

| Item No. | Quantity | Unit Price | Amount | Market Price | Corrected Value | Inventory Reduction |
|---|---|---|---|---|---|---|
| Bro't For'd | ......... | ...... | 23,556.00 | ........ | .......... | 1,124.00 |
| #4207 | 75 | .20 | 15.00 | .21 | .......... | .......... |
| 4209 | 210 | 1.25 | 262.50 | 1.25 | .......... | .......... |
| 4210 | 90 | 6.00 | 540.00 | 4.00 | 360.00 | 180.00 |
| 4211 | 100 | 15.00 | 1,500.00 | 8.00 | 800.00 | 700.00 |
| 4215 | 82 | .30 | 24.60 | .35 | .......... | .......... |
| 4216 | 30 | .74 | 22.20 | .74 | .......... | .......... |
| 4217 | 40 | .88 | 35.20 | .90 | .......... | .......... |
| 4218 | 820 | .05 | 41.00 | .05 | .......... | .......... |
| 4231 | 55 | 1.00 | 55.00 | 1.00 | .......... | .......... |
| 4232 | 34 | 2.25 | 76.50 | 2.25 | .......... | .......... |
| 4233 | 270 | 3.10 | 837.00 | 2.80 | 756.00 | 81.00 |
| 4234 | 1000 | .12 | 120.00 | .12 | .......... | .......... |
| ........... | .......... | ...... | 27,085.00 | ........ | .......... | 2,085.00 |
| Less reduct | ions..... | ...... | 2,085.00 | ........ | .......... | .......... |
| Corrected i | nventory | value | 25,000.00 | ........ | .......... | .......... |

Due to the comparatively small size of the raw materials inventory, the prices of all the inventory items were checked. Where the values stated were higher than the current market price at 12–31–37, the corrected values were computed and the inventory reduction noted.

Computations and extensions were checked on all items over $10, and the footings were verified completely.

The original cards used in taking the inventory were obtained and checked against the typed inventory sheets. No differences were noted as to quantities. Tests were also made by comparing quantities in the inventory with those shown by the perpetual inventory records.

D. W. Owen, the stock clerk who participated in the taking of the inventory, states there is no obsolete or unsalable material included in the inventory, and that all the material is unencumbered property of the company.

### Inventory Summary
| | |
|---|---|
| Raw materials......................... | $ 25,000.00 |
| Goods in process...................... | 32,875.00 |
| Finished goods........................ | 80,000.00 |
| Total.............................. | $137,875.00 |

C. E. Shaw
(Junior Accountant)                                                    (Schedule No. 8)

**Illustration No. 17. Inventory Pricing Schedule**

# THE BLANK MANUFACTURING CO.

## INDIANAPOLIS, IND.

January 18, 1938.

Stevenson and Bennett
Certified Public Accountants
9 West Third Street
Cincinnati, Ohio

Gentlemen:

      This is to certify that on December 31, 1937, our
inventories were as follows:

          (a) Raw Material.............$25,000.00
          (b) Goods in Process......... 32,875.00
          (c) Finished Goods........... 80,000.00

      These inventories are the unencumbered property of
the company and were taken under our supervision as follows:

      (a) The inventories of raw materials, goods in
process, and finished goods were taken by actual weight, count,
and measurement except certain goods in process of manufacture
which were not subject to physical count, the value of which
was conservatively estimated.

      (b) Cost or market price, whichever was the lower, on
December 31, 1937, was used in pricing all items. Deductions
were made for obsolete and damaged stock.

      (c) Incoming materials and supplies in transit
billed f.o.b. point of shipment, were included in the inventory.

      (d) Outgoing goods billed but not shipped, were not
included in the inventory.

      (e) Extensions have all been carefully checked.

                Sincerely yours,

                *Harold Pond*
                Chief Accountant

                *D. W. Owen*
                Stock Clerk

HP/DS

**Illustration No. 18. Certificate of Inventory**

### THE BLANK MANUFACTURING COMPANY

#### Audit of Inventories

#### Adjusting Journal Entries

| | | |
|---|---|---|
| *Raw Materials Inventory* | *$25,000.00* | |
| *Goods in Process Inventory* | *32,875.00* | |
| *Finished Goods Inventory* | *80,000.00* | |
| *Profit and Loss* | | *$137,875.00* |

*To record inventories as of December 31, 1937.*

| | | |
|---|---|---|
| *Profit and Loss* | *52,310.50* | |
| *Raw Materials Inventory* | | *37,310.50* |
| *Finished Goods Inventory* | | *15,000.00* |

*To transfer inventories at beginning of period to the profit and loss section of the working trial balance. There was no inventory of goods in process on hand at beginning of period under audit.*

**Illustration No. 19. Adjusting Entries**

and D. W. Owen, stock clerk, showing the following inventories as of December 31, 1937:

| | |
|---|---|
| Raw Materials | $25,000.00 |
| Goods in Process | 32,875.00 |
| Finished Goods | 80,000.00 |

#### SUMMARY

Inventories may constitute one of the principal assets on a balance sheet and may be one of the principal factors in computing the profits for a given period. It is obviously important that great care be used in counting and valuing the inventory of goods on hand at the end of a fiscal period. Under ordinary circumstances a physical inventory should be insisted upon. If a book inventory is kept and there is any discrepancy between the records and the physical inventory, the records should be adjusted so that they will conform to the physical inventory. Proper steps should also be taken to eliminate any discrepancies which are found to be the result of carelessness or due to the lack of an efficient method of internal check. Discrepancies in the inventory which point to the possibility of fraud or theft, should be carefully analyzed and should be reported to the management. Certificates of inventory should not be accepted without testing to determine general accuracy in counting the goods and in computing the value of the goods.

Inventory cost factors may include purchase prices, transportation cost, labor cost, and manufacturing expenses. In the case of raw materials, the cost factors will include the purchase price and the transportation inward cost. In the case of goods in process of being manufactured, the cost factors will include the raw material cost, plus the direct labor, and overhead or manufacturing expenses incurred up to the date of the inventory. In the case of finished goods, the cost factors will include either the purchase price of the goods plus transportation inward cost, or raw material cost plus direct labor cost and overhead or manufacturing expenses incurred in manufacturing the goods.

## AUDITING THEORY

7—74. Distinguish between a physical and a continuous inventory.

7—75. Under what circumstances may a physical inventory be dispensed with?

7—76. Explain how the gross trading profit test may be used as a means for verifying the correctness of a physical inventory.

7—77. Why is the proper valuation of the inventory of such great importance in an audit?

7—78. What is meant by "Cost or market price, whichever is the lower" when applied to inventory valuation?

7—79. If an inventory is taken at market price which is lower than cost, how will the loss representing the difference between the market price and the cost be shown in the statement of profit and loss?

7—80. In connection with an audit, an inventory is submitted to you certified by the general manager. Would you accept and use the inventory in your report without verification? If not, what steps would you take to confirm the correctness of the inventory?

7—81. What duties and responsibilities has an auditor in connection with inventories of goods on hand?

(C. P. A. Ore.)

7—82. Is the common old-fashioned method of adding the inventory of merchandise on hand to the credit side of the merchandise account before closing the books, theoretically correct? Explain fully.

(C. P. A. Mich.)

7—83. A manufacturing company purchased a large stock of material during the year at low prices. At the time of the annual inventory, values had abnormally increased. At what value, in your opinion, should the inventory be stated on the balance sheet, and how should the gain in values be accounted for?

(C. P. A. Mich.)

7—84. Assume that an inventory had been taken promptly at November 30 and there was every reason to believe that the inventory had been accurately taken. At December 31 the inventory was very large, owing to heavy purchases in December. Explain the steps that an auditor might justifiably take to verify the inventory at December 31 without counting the many items.

(C. P. A. Ohio)

7—85. Why is it essential that any hypothecation of assets, or any liens existing thereon, be disclosed in a balance sheet? Indicate the steps you would take to ascertain whether or not any part of the inventory of a manufacturer has been pledged to secure loans or advances.

(A. I. A.)

## AUDITING PROBLEMS

7—13. Explain whether or not the following items should be included in taking an inventory:

(a) Outgoing goods in transit to branch office

(b) Outgoing goods in transit to depository to be sold on consignment

(c) Outgoing goods in transit to customer sold on terms f. o. b. destination

(d) Goods stored in a public warehouse

(e) Incoming goods in transit purchased f. o. b. destination

(f) Goods ordered from manufacturer but not received, the invoice having been received and recorded

(g) Insured goods damaged by fire

(h) Goods received but not recorded due to the fact that no invoice has been received from shipper

(i) Goods billed to customer, the sale having been recorded but shipment not having been made.

7—14. In a certain department store at the end of each fiscal year an amount between 4% and 5% of the inventory is set aside by debiting profit and loss and crediting an account with reserve for depreciation of merchandise. The inventory has always been taken at cost which at the present time is lower than the market price, and those articles that were old or damaged in any way were taken at less than cost in proportion to the damage. During the last three years this policy has been followed and the store now has an amount of nearly 15% of the merchandise on hand credited to the reserve for depreciation of merchandise. It has been the custom in making a balance sheet to deduct this reserve from the total amount of the inventory treating the difference as a current asset.

(a) Is it proper to deduct a reserve for depreciation from the inventory if the inventory is taken at cost less the damaged goods?

(b) Would it not be better to call the reserve a reserve for working capital or a reserve for anticipated decline in inventory values, and treat it as a division of the surplus account?

**7—15.** At the close of the year 1934, a concern suffered a loss in its inventory value of approximately one-third, or $750,000. At December 31, 1938, the same concern deemed it prudent to establish a reserve for inventory in the sum of $500,000. The items on the inventory were priced in detail at cost or market, whichever was lower. State how you would show the reserve on the balance sheet, and what account you would charge for the amount of the reserve.

**7—16.** You are asked to certify to the balance sheet of a certain company. Upon investigation, you find that the inventories have been priced at cost, although the market prices at the close of the audit period were 10% lower on iron and 5% higher on wood. At the date of your audit the market on iron had risen to 5% above cost, and the market on wood had fallen to 15% below cost. What recommendation would you make as to the disposition of these items before certifying to the balance sheet?

(C. P. A. Ill.)

**7—17.** It is generally conceded that merchandise inventories should be calculated on a basis of "cost" prices, but in practice there are found many differences in the method of determining the cost price. State whether the following items should be added to or subtracted from invoice prices in determining cost for inventory purposes:

(a) Cash discounts
(b) Trade discounts
(c) Freight inward (on goods bought)
(d) Freight outward (on goods sold)
(e) Drayage and handling (inward)
(f) Packing and drayage (outward)
(g) Purchase rebates on account of goods damaged in transit.

(C. P. A. Fla.)

**7—18.** A company in the retail grocery business operates a chain of stores. Sales are made on a cash basis. The balance sheet shows that the principal assets are inventory and cash. The inventory represents 90% of the total assets. Would that condition suggest to you the need for any special consideration as to the extent of the auditor's examination of the inventory?

(A. I. A.)

## AUDITING PRACTICE

### An Audit Case (Fifth Installment)

On January 5, Ken B. Swift proceeds to verify the merchandise inventory, prepared by company employees as of December 31, 1938. Typed inventory sheets were submitted to Mr. Swift showing the quantity, the unit price, and the extended amount of each inventory item. The storekeeper assured him that the count was accurate and that the inventory items were priced at cost or market price, whichever was lower.

It is Mr. Swift's duty to use every means possible to substantiate the accuracy of the inventory. In an "Examination of Financial Statements," the suggested procedure in verifying inventories is outlined on pages 179 to 182. Mr. Swift believes that steps 7, 9, 13, 15, 18, and 21 of the procedure are especially applicable to this audit.

The general ledger accounts for merchandise stock and cost of sales are illustrated in summary form below.

### Merchandise Stock

| Date | Items | Debit | Credit | Balance |
|---|---|---|---|---|
| 1- 1–38 | Inventory............................. | 55,000.00 | .......... | .......... |
| 12–31–38 | Purchases—Summary of monthly totals... | 226,580.00 | .......... | .......... |
| 12–31–38 | Cost of sales—Summary of monthly entries | ......... | 220,080.00 | 61,500.00 |

### Cost of Sales

| Date | Items | Debit | Credit | Balance |
|---|---|---|---|---|
| 12–31–38 | Summary of monthly entries............ | 220,080.00 | .......... | 220,080.00 |

The following data represent the last page of the inventory submitted to Mr. Swift for verification. Only one page is given, as that is sufficient to illustrate the procedure of verification. It may be assumed that the items on the preceding inventory pages were correctly priced and extended.

### Merchandise Inventory 12-31-38

| Item (Description Omitted) | Quantity | Price | Amount |
|---|---|---|---|
| Brought forward |  |  | $52,843.75 |
| # 12789 | 20 units | $ 1.00 unit | 20.00 |
| 12790 | 300 " | .50 " | 150.00 |
| 1 | 79 " | 1.50 " | 118.50 |
| 2 | 185 " | 8.00 " | 1,480.00 |
| 3 | 20 doz. | 10.00 doz. | 200.00 |
| 4 | 40 units | 9.00 " | 360.00 |
| 5 | 6 gross | 15.00 gross | 90.00 |
| 6 | 10 units | .25 unit | 2.50 |
| 7 | 15 " | .90 " | 13.50 |
| 8 | 45 doz. | 5.00 " | 2,700.00 |
| 9 | 108 units | 1.00 doz. | 9.00 |
| 12800 | 2000 " | .10 unit | 200.00 |
| 1 | 23 " | 20.00 " | 560.00 |
| 2 | 94 " | .50 " | 470.00 |
| 3 | 1440 " | .20 gross | 288.00 |
| 4 | 22 " | 1.00 unit | 22.00 |
| 5 | 57 " | .50 " | 28.50 |
| 6 | 50 doz. | 10.00 doz. | 500.00 |
| 7 | 100 units | .10 unit | 100.00 |
| 8 | 60 cwt. | .07 lb. | 42.00 |
| 9 | 95 units | .70 unit | 66.50 |
| 12810 | 30 " | 3.50 " | 105.00 |
| 1 | 15 " | .25 " | 3.75 |
| 2 | 70 " | .10 " | 7.00 |
| 3 | 80 " | 1.50 " | 120.00 |
| Total |  |  | $61,500.00 |

The market prices of the inventory items, as determined by recent purchase invoices and published quotations, were as follows at 12–31–38:

| | | |
|---|---|---|
| #12789—$ 1.01 | #12798—$ 5.10 | #12806—$8.00 doz. |
| 12790— .50 | 9— 1.00 doz. | 7— .10 |
| 1— 1.20 | 12800— .12 | 8— .07 lb. |
| 2— 6.00 | 1— 15.00 | 9— .70 |
| 3— 10.50 doz. | 2— .50 | 12810— 4.50 |
| 4— 9.00 doz. | 3— .20 gross | 1— .26 |
| 5— 16.00 gross | 4— 1.50 | 2— .15 |
| 6— .24 | 5— .60 | 3— 1.40 |
| 7— .90 | | |

Investigation disclosed that inventory item #12790, above, represented merchandise received on consignment 12–28–38. No sales of the consigned goods had been made at the date of the inventory.

## INSTRUCTIONS

1. Read and study carefully the auditing procedure suggested for the verification of inventories in an "Examination of Financial Statements."

2. Prepare an inventory pricing schedule similar to the one shown in the illustrative set of audit working papers. (See Illustration No. 17.)

3. Perform the audit work suggested for verifying inventories in so far as this procedure applies to the information provided in this audit.

4. Prepare adjusting journal entries, where necessary, to adjust the account balances.

# CHAPTER EIGHT

## FIXED ASSETS

1. **Tangible Assets**
   - (a) Land
   - (b) Buildings
   - (c) Machinery and Equipment
   - (d) Tools and Implements
   - (e) Patterns, Dies, Drawings, Electrotypes, etc.
   - (f) Furniture and Fixtures
   - (g) Automobiles and Trucks
   - (h) Wasting Assets

2. **Intangible Assets**
   - (a) Good Will
   - (b) Patents
   - (c) Copyrights
   - (d) Trade-marks
   - (e) Franchises

3. **Reserves**
   - (a) For Depreciation
   - (b) For Depletion

4. **Insurance**
   - (a) Co-insurance
   - (b) Inventory Provisions
   - (c) Three-fourths Value
   - (d) Pro Rata Distribution

5. **Auditing Procedure**

6. **Application of Principles**

7. **An Audit Case—Sixth Installment**

The fixed assets of a business differ from the current assets in the purpose which they serve. The current assets consist primarily of cash, receivables, and stock-in-trade, while the fixed assets consist of the property used in operating the business.

In verifying current assets, the auditor is concerned primarily with the balances on hand at the balance sheet date. The changes that occurred during the year are not verified in detail except in audits designated as complete audits. With fixed assets, the auditor is concerned with all changes that took place during the audit period regardless of the type of audit that is being performed. All entries of any substantial amount which either increase or decrease the value of fixed assets must be verified. If the auditor is auditing the accounts for the first time, the balance at the beginning of the period should also be verified. It is customary for the auditor to prepare a schedule of the changes in each of the fixed asset accounts and to verify the entries by examining vouchers, receipted invoices, contracts, or other evidence proving that the entries in the account represent bona fide transactions.

Entries recording reduction in the value of fixed assets must be investigated as well as those increasing the value thereof. If equipment is sold or traded in on new equipment, the auditor should see that the transaction has been recorded correctly. The asset account should be cleared of the cost of the equipment, and the reserve for depreciation should be cleared of the amount of the depreciation applicable to the equipment disposed of. An apparent gain or loss may be realized in the trade-in of old equipment for new equipment, but under the Federal income tax regulations such gain or loss is not recognized. The regulations provide that, "No gain or loss is recognized if a taxpayer exchanges property held for productive use in his trade or business, together with cash, for other property of like kind for the same use, such as a truck for a new truck or a passenger automobile for a new passenger automobile to be used for a like purpose."

Applying the regulations, a transaction involving an exchange of old equipment for new equipment would be recorded by debiting the equipment account for the value of the new equipment purchased; by debiting the reserve for depreciation account for the amount of the depreciation applicable to the equipment traded in; by crediting the equipment account for the cost of the old equipment traded in, and by crediting cash for the difference paid in cash. The value of the new equipment is the book value of the old equipment plus the amount paid in cash or other property. Thus, if an automobile used for business purposes has a book value of $350 and is traded for a new car, $400 difference being paid in cash, the transaction is recorded as follows:

| | | |
|---|---|---|
| Automobile (New Car) | $750.00 | |
| Automobile (Old Car) | | $350.00 |
| Cash | | 400.00 |

In the foregoing entry it was assumed that the depreciation had been credited directly to the automobile account so that the account showed the book value of the car traded in. If a separate reserve for depreciation account were maintained and $450 of the reserve applied to the old car, which cost originally $800, the transaction should be recorded as follows:

| | | |
|---|---|---|
| Automobile (New Car)..................... | $750.00 | |
| Reserve for Depreciation................... | 450.00 | |
|    Automobile (Old Car) ................. | | $800.00 |
|    Cash................................. | | 400.00 |

It will be observed that under this method of recording such transactions, the amount of the trade-in allowance is not reflected in the entry. Neither is the purchase price or delivered price of the new car reflected in the entry. The new car is simply recorded at its cost and its cost is found by adding the amount of cash paid to the book value of the car traded in. The book value is the difference between the original cost of the car and the amount of depreciation provided in the reserve account.

### TANGIBLE ASSETS

Fixed assets may be tangible or intangible. Tangible assets usually consist of land, buildings, machinery and equipment, and furniture and fixtures. Intangible assets may consist of good will, patents, copyrights, trade-marks, and assets of like nature. The tangible fixed assets are generally used in operating a business. Expenditures for fixed assets should be recorded at cost at the time of purchase. The cost is subsequently charged into operations over the life of the assets. If this cost is not properly distributed as the assets are consumed through their use, it will result in an incorrect statement of operating profits.

**Land.** Land used in the operation of a business should be recorded separately from the land representing outside investments. The procedure in accounting for land used in the operation of a mercantile or industrial business differs considerably from procedure in accounting for land acquired for resale at a profit. In other words, it is necessary to distinguish between land acquired for business use and land acquired as an investment or speculation.

Land acquired for use in the operation of a business should always be recorded separately from the buildings which may be located thereon. The principal reason for this is that the buildings are subject to depreciation which must be treated as an operating cost while it is not customary to take into consideration any depreciation on land in ascertaining the operating costs of a business. In cases where an auditor finds land and buildings recorded in a single real estate account, he should recommend a segregation of the land and buildings with a specific value on each. This will facilitate the computation of depreciation of buildings apart from the land.

Land is, in a sense, the most permanent asset of a business. The land account should be charged with (a) the original cost, (b) the expenses incident to the purchase, such as, cost of investigating the title, recording the deed, commissions paid, and any other expenses which represent an addition to the purchase price, and (c) the cost of subsequent improvements which increase the value of the land, such as fencing, draining, grading, building approaches, laying of sidewalks, and assessments for sewers, street improvements, etc. It is not infrequent that the auditor will find that assessments for improvements have been included with the taxes and were charged off as current operating expenses. However, such costs should be charged to the land account.

When land is sold, the land account should be credited with the cost price, while the difference between the cost and the selling price should be recorded separately as a loss or gain. Under this procedure the balance of the land account will always represent the original cost plus the cost of improvements of the land owned. The auditor must analyze all charges to the land account to make sure that no revenue expenditures are capitalized. Interest on money borrowed for improvement purposes is sometimes charged to the land account, but it seems better to treat the interest cost as a financial expense. Certainly the land is no more valuable because of the interest paid on money borrowed for improvement purposes than it would be if the owner was able to make the improvements without the necessity of borrowing funds for that purpose.

Land may increase or decrease in value, but it is inadvisable to attempt to give effect to such increase or decrease in value in the accounting reports until such time as the land may actually be disposed of. The increase or decrease in the value of land can be measured only through estimates of market value based upon appraisals or the known market values of adjacent land. If for any reason it is desired to set up appraised values of land and such values are higher than cost, the difference should be credited to surplus arising from appreciation of land. If, on the other hand, such appraised values are lower than cost, the difference should be charged to loss arising from depreciation of land. Appreciation will be encountered more often than depreciation in the value of land.

Land acquired as an investment should be recorded at cost, including any expenses incurred in the purchase thereof. Up to this point there is no difference in the accounting for land purchased as an investment as compared with land purchased for use with the operation of a business. However, subsequent costs incurred in improving the land preparatory to resale are usually capitalized. Such costs will include the building of streets, the laying of sidewalks, the planting of trees, the installation of sewers, water, gas, and electricity, and the cost of subdividing the property into lots. In other words, all costs incurred in the development of a subdivision by a real estate firm may be added to the original cost of the land. This may even include the interest on money borrowed for improvement purposes, but should be limited to the period of construction or improvement. In other words, interest charges on money borrowed to purchase land or to make improvements thereon, should not be charged to the property account after completion of the improvements because to do so will result in an increasing valuation which might readily become an unreasonable value before the property could be sold. Many authorities oppose the capitalization of any part of the interest cost but the consensus of opinion seems to be in favor of capitalizing the interest on money borrowed for improvement purposes during the period of improvement or construction with no further charges for interest after the property has been put in condition for sale.

The taxes paid on land purchased as an investment are frequently capitalized during the period of development, but when the development has been completed and the property is offered for sale in the form of lots or otherwise, any further taxes paid should not be capitalized. To do so would result in an increasing value being placed upon the property the same as if interest were capitalized.

Following the development of property and its subdivision into lots, it is customary to apportion the total cost among the lots on a basis of the appraised selling value of the lots. It is necessary to apportion the cost to the lots on some basis if the profit on individual lots sold is to be computed. Otherwise, it would not be possible to compute the profit until all the lots in the subdivision had been sold.

**Buildings.** Buildings may be acquired through the purchase of real estate, in which case separate values should be placed upon the buildings and land, the basis of valuation being cost. In the preparation of annual reports thereafter, the buildings should be valued at cost plus additions and improvements less the depreciation. For balance sheet purposes, the buildings are generally listed at cost with the reserve for depreciation being deducted. The difference is extended as the net book value of the buildings.

Buildings may be constructed under contract or may be constructed by the firm itself. Buildings constructed under contract should be capitalized at actual cost whether they are built under a straight contract or a "cost plus" contract. Buildings constructed by the firm itself should likewise be recorded at actual cost. This will include the architect fees, expenses incurred in connection with permits and licenses, insurance, material, labor, all direct construction expenses, and a reasonable proportion of overhead expenses or burden. The auditor should be careful in analyzing the accounts with buildings constructed by the firm itself to see that only a normal amount of overhead is included in the cost. Since the construction of buildings is likely to be undertaken during a slack period in the business, there may be a tendency to charge into the building account a considerable amount of overhead which is really attributable to the slack period or unusual conditions in the business which have no bearing upon the building costs. Where interest is paid on money borrowed for construction purposes, it is frequently charged to the building account, but it is permissible to capitalize the interest cost for the period of construction only. After the building is completed there should be no further capitalizing of interest paid on the money borrowed for building purposes, for the building will not continue to increase in value as the interest continues to be paid on the money borrowed.

In an audit of the building account the auditor should prepare working papers in which different buildings are segregated. These working papers should show the book values at the beginning of the period under audit, the cost of additions or deductions during the period, and the balance at the end of the period. These beginning and ending balances should be checked with the value of the building account on the balance sheet as of both dates and should be in agreement with the account on the books. If a subsidiary building ledger is maintained, it should be checked with the controlling account in the general ledger to see that they agree. All additions and deductions during the period should be carefully verified to be sure that they have been properly accounted for, due care being used to distinguish between capital and revenue expenditures.

The ownership of land and buildings may be verified through an examination of property tax receipts and insurance policies. The property tax receipts give the name of the owner and a description of the property subject to tax. It may be necessary to refer to a city engineer's map to ascertain the location of the property described on the tax bill. The description on the tax bill usually gives the lot, block, and tract number, but does not give the street address. If the auditor has any reason to doubt the client's ownership of the property, he should have a search of title made by a title insurance and trust company.

**Machinery and Equipment.** A summary account for machinery and equipment may be kept in the general ledger with detailed accounts in a subsidiary ledger or separate accounts for each machine or other property may be kept in the general ledger. The auditor should ascertain this information before proceeding with a verification of the value of such assets. A summary account with machinery may be charged for the following items:

(a) The cost of machinery purchased

(b) The cost of machinery manufactured by the concern itself

(c) Cost of installation

(d) The cost of additions or alterations which actually increase the value or efficiency of the machinery in use

(e) The cost of new parts purchased.

Where machinery is purchased as part of a plant, it may be necessary to place an estimated value on machinery, which should, of course, be based upon the total purchase price. In recording the cost of additions or alterations to machinery, items should not be capitalized which represent alterations made necessary by a mere change in product or a cost incurred in moving and reinstalling machinery to permit of more economical operation. If such costs are large they may be treated as deferred expenses to be charged off over a period of years in which the most benefit will be derived.

The accounting for the cost of new parts purchased will depend upon the policy followed in determining rates of depreciation. In other words, the rate of depreciation may be such as to cover the replacement of parts. If the cost of new parts is charged to the machinery account, the cost of the worn parts being replaced must be credited to the machinery account at the same time being charged to the reserve account. The principal argument in charging the cost to the machinery account is the fact that the cost of the new parts may be higher or lower than the original parts, and if the cost of the old parts being replaced is credited to the account at the same time the cost of the new parts is debited to the account, the machinery account will at all times represent the actual cost of machinery in operation. In the case of machinery built or manufactured by the concern itself, the cost should include the cost of material and labor, plus the freight and cartage inward and a proper proportion of overhead expenses. It is customary, also, to capitalize the cost of experiments or research made in determining a desirable type of machine plus the cost of designs and patterns. Any machines or parts exchanged, discarded, destroyed, or otherwise disposed of, should be credited to the machinery account at the same time being charged to the reserve account at cost price.

The installation cost may include the building of foundations and the moving of the machinery into place. The balance of the machinery account should represent the actual cost of machinery in use. The book value will be the difference between this cost and the amount of the reserve for depreciation. Obsolescence is often an important factor in the valuation of machinery. New and improved models of machinery are continually being placed upon the market in every industry. It is often one of the most important elements in the depreciation of machinery and should be given due consideration by the auditor.

**Tools and Implements.**    There are several different methods for recording the value of tools.  It is always best, if the value of tools on hand is to be considered a fixed asset, to take a physical inventory at the end of the period under audit before preparing the statements.  Tools are so often lost, misplaced, or stolen, and they are used up so rapidly, that it is difficult to determine their actual value in any other manner.

One method is to charge the tools and implements account with the cost of all tools purchased and at the end of the year to take a physical inventory and make an adjusting entry crediting the asset account with the cost value of all tools used up or missing and charging the proper operating expense account.  If this is done, no reserve for depreciation need be set up.

Another method is to charge the account with tools as above, but to issue all tools to the workmen and at certain times require them to submit all tools for inspection.  At this time all tools worn out, broken, or worthless are charged to expense and new tools are issued to the workmen.  Any tools missing or otherwise unaccounted for are charged to the workmen and deducted from their wages.  In either case the account with tools would be credited with the cost price of the tools worn out, broken, worthless, or missing and the balance of the account would show the cost of tools on hand and in use.  No reserve for depreciation is necessary, but it is necessary to require the workmen to submit all tools for inspection before preparing the statements.

**Patterns, Dies, Drawings, Electrotypes, etc.**  In many businesses the cost of patterns, dies, drawings, electros, etc., may represent an important item.  Such items have but little scrap value, hence they should be carried as an asset only when they are to be used for repeat orders or for special jobs.  Many firms charge their cost against the original job or order, thereby eliminating them from any further valuation.  However, such items may have a value beyond the first job.  For instance, a book may be printed from electrotypes and the electrotypes may be held indefinitely for the purpose of reprinting future editions of the same book.  The auditor encounters much difficulty in valuing such items as patterns, dies, drawings, electrotypes, engravings, etc., for it may be difficult for him to determine the extent to which they may be used in the future. However, care should be taken to see that they are not overvalued. It will be better to err on the side of undervaluation than to overvalue such assets. In many cases it is doubtful if such assets should be valued at more than their scrap value.

**Furniture and Fixtures.** Usually a summary account is kept with furniture and fixtures. However, separate accounts should be kept for the furniture used in different departments or offices because the depreciation is an expense chargeable to the different departments or offices. In general the summary account with furniture and fixtures should be charged with the cost of all office equipment, including desks, safes, office appliances, fixtures, etc. However, it should not be charged with the cost of supplies and other expense items. A reasonable amount of depreciation should be charged off periodically. Many accountants will set up a reserve for depreciation on furniture and fixtures, while others favor crediting depreciation directly to the furniture and fixtures account, thereby writing down its book value to its estimated value.

The auditor should prepare a schedule showing the changes which were recorded in the furniture and fixtures account during the period under audit. Vouchers should be examined to verify all the larger amounts of all additions to the account. Retirements should be investigated to see that the transactions were properly recorded, and that the asset account was credited for the cost price and the reserve account cleared of the depreciation relating to the asset disposed of.

**Automobiles and Trucks.** The accounting for automobiles and trucks involves a number of problems. The auditor should satisfy himself that all cars included in the account are actually in operation and are owned by the company. An examination of the registration certificates issued by the State Department of Motor Vehicles is fairly conclusive evidence of ownership if the certificates are made out in the name of the client. The certificates list the name of the owner and give a description of the car, including the make, type, motor number, and other pertinent information.

The cars should be recorded at cost and adequate depreciation should be provided for. The determination of reasonable depreciation rates may be difficult, but usually they may be determined on a basis of past experience. The same rate may not apply to all cars, particularly where cars of different makes and costs are operated. The cost of upkeep of cars including replacement of tires, ordinarily should not be capitalized but should be charged to expense. The auditor's work will be facilitated if detailed records are kept covering the costs and maintenance of each car or truck.

**Wasting Assets.** Wasting assets consist of assets which are consumed through marketing instead of through use, such as mines and timber. Wasting assets are usually estimated as to quantity of commercial content upon the purchase or discovery of the valuable properties contained. On the basis of this estimate, depletion is usually calculable through dividing the total cost by the estimated barrels of oil, tons of mineral, or thousand board feet of lumber, thus obtaining the cost per estimated unit of product to be obtained. On the basis of this calculation and the number of units consumed during any given period, the periodic charge for depletion may be obtained. Such a charge closely resembles the charge for depreciation, and is usually handled much the same way, being charged to operations in order to properly state the profits for the period, and being credited to a reserve in order to state the net value of the asset involved.

The problem of the auditor in connection with wasting assets is to determine that the proper depletion charges are made, that they are adequate, and that the company's policies are properly carried out. He should examine the engineer's reports on quantity of materials recoverable, the rate per unit set, the basis of valuing the asset concerned, and the adequacy of the reserve to date. In the case of wasting assets the auditor often may find buildings, machinery, and equipment in use which will outlast the life of the mine. In such a case, if the value is too small to make it profitable to move such items, the depreciation should be based not on the life of the property, but rather on either the length of life of the mine or wasting asset, as its value is existent only in so far as the values of the mines, wells, or other wasting assets make it profitable to use such machinery, buildings, etc.

## INTANGIBLE ASSETS

Intangible assets include good will, patents, copyrights, trade-marks, franchises, etc. These assets often may be found grouped under a summary account. In such cases, the auditor should analyze the account, segregating the different items for purposes of verification.

The theory of accounting for intangibles has undergone a radical change in the past twenty years, a large part of which is probably due to the increasing use of no par stocks for financing companies whose assets include a large aggregate of intangible items. Intangible values usually have arisen through the purchase of properties with payment in stocks and other securities, the net tangible values of which were not equal in value to the par values of the securities exchanged. Such being the case, the securities were entered on the books at their par value and the difference between the net tangible asset value, and the par value of the securities concerned, was considered an intangible asset, usually good will.

As a result of the experiences immediately after the war, and the growth of no par stock issues, this practice is decidedly on the wane. The tendency of modern finance is to present the values, where possible, and for balance sheet purposes, at tangible values only. Many times the intangible values accruing to a company may be of more value than the tangible values, but such values are usually not the result of specific financial transactions and to properly value and state them in a financial statement involves difficulties which, in our present state of technique and knowledge, appear insurmountable.

Again, with the use of stated values, possibilities of stating no par value securities at nominal values, the tendency is not only to eliminate intangibles when purchased but even to eliminate such values which have been recognized on the books for years. As a result many corporations have, in the past few years, written off large sums of good will and other intangible values, changing their par issues formerly outstanding to no par issues, and stating the latter issues for balance sheet purposes at a very nominal sum. For instance, at one time good will was valued on the books of the Jewel Tea Company at $12,000,000 and the company had 120,000 shares of stock outstanding at a par value of $100 per share. Later the value of the good will was written down to $1 and the capital stock was changed to no par value with 120,000 shares outstanding at a stated value of $1 per share.

It is the duty of the auditor to verify the existence and values of the intangible items, and to see that they are properly stated in the light of current methods and general practice. Intangibles may be purchased for cash, for stock, or they may be developed through inventions, advertising and similar expedients. The method of carrying them on the financial statements is usually one of the following:

(a) Cost, when purchased for cash
(b) Nominal value
(c) At the difference of par values of securities exchanged and the net tangible assets received in exchange therefor.

In so far as the method of valuing good will and other intangibles in the books and accounts does not violate good accounting practice, the auditor will usually do well to carry such values to his audited statements. This does not mean that he should fail to verify the values and the existence thereof. It is one of the cardinal rules of conservative accounting practice that good will should not be recognized unless paid for. In the first audit, such principles should be checked against the actual transactions in order to determine that they are being properly recognized.

**Good Will.**  Good will is usually considered to represent the value of the excess earning capacity of a property over and above a fair rate of return for the industry or line of endeavor concerned. In other words, if a rate of return is earned by a business over a period of fifteen years, and a fair rate for such a type of business was 10%, the excess earning capacity would in case of purchase, be capitalized on some equitable basis, and the amount paid therefor would represent good will. Obviously, the value of the good will is the difference between the total value paid for an enterprise and the value of the sum of the assets received, taken individually.

In the past it has been argued that good will, unless the excess earning capacity has definitely ceased to exist, should not be written off the books. On the other hand, some argue that it should be written off over a period of a few years. The tendency of the better managed companies at the present time appears to be to write such values down to a nominal figure as soon as possible, and due to several factors affecting corporation procedures, this tendency bids fair to continue. Such action, however, should be a result of the vote of the directors, and should be written down through a charge to surplus, not operating expenses, as such a charge has nothing to do with the cost of producing the product, whatever that product may be.

**Patents.** Patents may be purchased from others or they may be developed and obtained through the efforts of the concern itself. Where patents are purchased, they are usually placed on the books at the purchase price and written off over their life. Where they are secured by the company itself, they may be handled in two ways. The costs of developing and securing the device and patent may be capitalized, or the costs may be charged directly to operating expenses as incurred. If capitalized, the value should be written off over the life of the patent which originally is seventeen years. Where patents are carried at a nominal value, or at no value at all, the management usually maintains a laboratory, proving ground, patent office, and other necessary equipment and personnel with very little change in cost from year to year. Their theory is that charging such costs currently to operations permits carrying the financial statement on a tangible basis and more equitably distributes the costs of development.*

**Copyrights.** Copyrights are exclusive rights granted by the government to reproduce, publish, and sell the matter and form of a literary or artistic work. Copyrights are granted for a period of twenty-eight years and are renewable for a further period of the same term. Copyrights are usually found in the publishing

---

*A good example of conservative practice in handling patents is illustrated by the practice of the National Cash Register Company. The company develops to a large extent its own patented devices and has consistently charged all expenditures therefor for some years to operating expenses. During the year 1926, the company purchased of the Remington Cash Register Company, Inc., a general license in the use of patents formerly in litigation. This item was capitalized and written off over a period of three years, as follows:

| | |
|---|---|
| 1926..................................... | $116,665.59 |
| 1927..................................... | $200,000.00 |
| 1928..................................... | Remainder |

business, and apply to books, articles, etc. Although applicable to a twenty-eight year period, most copyrights cease to have much value after a period of two or three years, due to the large factor of obsolescence connected with such properties. The same accounting principles, and the same auditing procedure, are applicable to the valuation of copyrights as apply to patents, though copyrights usually become obsolete much faster. The useful life of copyrights should be the basis of amortization and the auditor should continually be on the watch for obsolete copyrights included in the account.

**Trade-marks.** A trade-mark consists of some distinguishing symbol or mark which distinguishes the goods of a certain manufacturer, wholesaler, or merchant from those of another. A trade-mark may be registered, securing the exclusive right to use such a device for a period of thirty years subject to renewal. Examples are numerous, as the device used by the Radio-Victor Corporation of America, "His Master's Voice"; the Lion head on Monarch food products; and the symbol of Fisk tires, "Time to Retire," and many others.

Trade-marks, as other intangibles, should be carried at cost less their amortized value if not carried at a nominal value. The costs of most trade-marks are exceedingly small, unless purchased, in which case the cost of the idea may have involved considerable expenditure. The auditor should verify the charges to determine that they are proper capital expenditures, and survey the policies of the company as to write-downs and the proper handling of obsolete items.

**Franchises.** A franchise is a right granted to a corporation to use property for a period of time. A franchise may be perpetual as in the case of many power and other utility company agreements or it may be for a limited period of time. The value of franchises should be stated at cost less amortization over the life of the right, if limited in time. Perpetual franchises are not subject to amortization, though they may often, also, be written off gradually over a period of years.

### RESERVES

In connection with an audit of the fixed assets, various reserves may be encountered. These are sometimes referred to as valuation accounts and include such accounts as reserves for depreciation and reserves for depletion. Reserves for depreciation generally apply to those assets which are subject to wear and tear through use in the operation of a business. Reserves for depletion generally apply to the wasting assets which are consumed as they are sold, such as, mines and timber. There should be specific reserves for each asset which is subject to depreciation or depletion, except those assets which are inventoried periodically or with regard to which the depreciation is recorded by crediting the asset accounts directly. General reserves and contingent reserves if justified at all, should not be confused with reserves for depreciation or depletion.

It is the auditor's duty to determine within satisfactory limits the adequacy of the reserves set up and the adequacy of the charges for the period under consideration. The auditor will usually encounter little difficulty in determining the depreciation policy of the enterprise concerned. With the present mass of information as to the proper rates to apply to different types of buildings, machines, fixtures, and so on, he will usually find it a comparatively simple problem to determine the adequacy of the charges and the reserves set up. There are many ways of figuring depreciation and charging it to the product. The method used will be of little importance in a balance sheet audit in so long as the amounts set aside and charged to operations are sufficient to adequately care for decreases in value and to present a fair statement of the period's financial operations.

## INSURANCE

In connection with an audit of fixed assets the auditor should examine the insurance policies, determine that the properties are properly insured, the amount carried is adequate, and that the insurance policies are in the name of the company, as well as in its possession. Where improved real estate is mortgaged, the insurance policies will be made payable to the mortgagee and usually will be in the possession thereof. This will give the auditor just one more check on any outstanding indebtedness against the properties. Insurance policies are of various kinds and types, such as fire, flood, windstorm, occupancy, etc. The needs of the company should be carefully analyzed, and the auditor may frequently make valuable suggestions as to the proper amount and distribution of the policies. Where co-insurance is existent the policies should be carefully scrutinized, for such policies are many times misunderstood by the insured.

**Co-insurance.** The standard co-insurance clause for use in either fire or windstorm policies reads as follows:

"In consideration of the rate and/or form under which this policy is written, it is expressly stipulated and made a condition of this contract that the insured shall at all times maintain contributing insurance on each item of property insured by this policy to the extent of at least .... % of the actual cash value at the time of the loss, and that failing to do so, the insured shall to the extent of such deficit bear his, her, or their proportion of any loss."

The co-insurance clause requires that the insured carry insurance equal to 50, 60, 70, 80, 90, or 100% of the value of the property. The 80% clause is probably more extensively used although the present tendency is toward an even higher percentage of valuation. In the following discussion, the 80% clause is used for illustrative purposes.

The object of the co-insurance clause is to require every man to carry a fair amount of insurance, and provides as a penalty for his failure to do so, that he shall pay the same proportion on partial losses for which he is under-insured that he would pay should he meet with a total loss and be under-insured.

The majority of losses are partial, and companies knowing this, make their rates with a view of meeting partial losses. Hence, if the insured carries but little insurance as compared to the value of the property, any small fire would result in a total loss so far as the insurance is concerned. In order to equalize rates so that every man shall pay a premium in proportion to the indemnity afforded, and to induce him to carry a greater amount of insurance, a lower rate is offered him, based on his agreement to insure to at least 80% of the value of the property.

The following examples will illustrate the application of the 80% co-insurance clause:

Example A:

Value of Property Insured................$10,000.00
Insurance Carried (80%)................   8,000.00
Loss....................................   6,000.00

In this case the insurance company's liability is $6,000 which is the entire amount of the loss. Had the loss amounted to $8,000 the insurance company would have been liable for the full amount of the loss. However, had the loss amounted to $9,000 the insurance company would have been liable for only $8,000 which is the limit of its liability, for it represents the full amount of the insurance carried.

This example illustrates the fact that the co-insurance clause does not affect an insurer either in a partial or total loss, when insurance is carried to the amount of 80% or more of the value of the property. In such cases the insurance company will pay the entire amount of the loss not exceeding, of course, the amount of the policy. This is an important item for many persons have an idea that where co-insurance is in effect the insured can never collect more than 80% of any loss.

Example B:

Value of Property Insured................$10,000.00
Insurance Carried (60%).................  6,000.00
Loss...................................  8,000.00

In this case the insurance company's liability is $6,000 which is the total amount of the insurance carried. Under no circumstances is the insurance company liable for more than the amount of the insurance carried at the time the loss occurs.

This example illustrates the fact that the co-insurance clause does not affect the insurer when the loss equals or exceeds 80% of the value of the property even though the property is insured for less than 80% or, in other words, is under-insured.

Example C:

Value of Property Insured................$10,000.00
Insurance Carried (70%).................  7,000.00
Loss...................................  5,000.00

Under these conditions the insured becomes a co-insurer to the amount of the difference between 80% of the value of the property insured and the actual insurance carried at the time of the fire. In other words, the insurance company must stand seven-eighths of the loss or $4,375 and the insured one-eighth of the loss or $625.

In this case it will be seen that the insured was affected by the co-insurance clause, due to the fact that both the amount of the insurance carried and the amount of the loss fell below 80% of the value of the property insured.

**Inventory Provisions.** Sometimes a clause is inserted in fire and windstorm insurance policies waiving inventory or appraisement. Such a waiver provides that in the adjustment of any loss which does not exceed 2% of the total insurance carried it shall not be a part of compliance with the conditions of a co-insurance clause to inventory and/or appraise the undamaged property. Of course, the insured must always submit proof of the loss sustained, but in the event of a comparatively small loss it might work a considerable hardship upon the insured to require that an inventory or appraisal of undamaged property be taken in ascertaining the amount of the loss. In other words, where the loss does not exceed 2% of the insurance carried and it can be proved without taking an inventory or having the undamaged property appraised, this requirement may be waived.

In unprotected country districts, a clause is inserted in fire insurance policies covering merchandise or stock-in-trade, requiring:

(1) That the insured under this policy shall take an inventory of the stock and other personal property hereby insured at least once every twelve months during the term of this policy, and unless such inventory has been taken within one year prior to the date of this policy, one shall be taken in detail within thirty days thereafter;

(2) That the insured shall keep a set of books showing a complete record of business transacted, including all purchases and sales both for cash and credit;

(3) That the insured shall keep such books and inventory securely locked in a fireproof safe at night, and at all times when the store mentioned in the policy is not actually open for business, or in some secure place not exposed to a fire which would destroy the building where such business is carried on;

(4) That in case of loss the insured shall produce such books and last inventory.

This emphasizes the importance of an auditor taking proper steps to protect the insurance interests of a client whose place of business may be located in an unprotected district or where it is found that the insurance policies contain an inventory and iron safe clause.

**Three-Fourths Value.** In unprotected districts clauses are sometimes inserted in fire insurance policies covering merchandise or stock-in-trade, which provide that in the event of loss the insurance company shall not be liable for an amount greater than three-fourths of the actual cash value of the property covered by the policy at the time of such loss. This clause also provides that the total insurance permitted is limited to three-fourths of the cash value of the property covered. The three-fourths value clause should not be confused with the co-insurance clause as it is an entirely different provision and has no relation whatever to co-insurance. It simply limits the amount of insurance to be carried and also limits the amount of loss for which the insurance company will be liable in relation to the value of the property covered by insurance. The use of this clause is optional. It results in a lower rate due to the fact that the insured actually carries 25% of the insurance himself.

**Pro Rata Distribution.** Where an insurance policy is issued covering two or more buildings or fire divisions, a pro rata distribution clause may be inserted in the policy which provides as follows:

"It is a condition of this policy that the amount insured hereunder shall attach in or on each building, shed, and other structure and (or) place, in that proportion of the amount hereby insured that the value of the property covered by this policy in or on each said building, shed, and other structure and (or) place, bears to the value of all the property described herein."

This clause is often used in conjunction with the co-insurance clause. In such case the 80% co-insurance clause used in conjunction with the pro rata distribution clause is equivalent to the 90% co-insurance clause and the 90% co-insurance clause used in conjunction with the pro rata distribution clause is equivalent to the 100% co-insurance clause.

There are many other clauses which may be inserted in insurance policies with which the auditor will be concerned in case he is engaged to make an audit as a basis for settlement of loss resulting from fire or other casualty covered by insurance. In

such an engagement the auditor should first acquaint himself with
the provisions of the policies in effect. It is then his duty to make
such an investigation as is necessary to ascertain the true value
of the property destroyed or damaged.

The insurance company is not liable beyond the actual cash
value of the property at the time any loss or damage occurs. The
loss or damage shall be ascertained or estimated as to such actual
cash value with proper deduction for depreciation however
caused, and shall in no event exceed what it would then cost the
insured to repair or replace the same with material of like kind
and quality. In case the insured and the insurance company
disagree as to the amount of the loss, it shall be ascertained by
two competent and disinterested appraisers, the insured and the
insurance company each selecting one, and the two so chosen
selecting a competent and disinterested umpire. The amount
of the loss having been determined, the sum for which the insurance company is liable is payable sixty days after due notice,
ascertainment, estimate, and satisfactory proof of the loss have
been received by the company in accord with the terms of the
policy.

The auditor should bear in mind the fact that he may be
called upon to act as a witness in behalf of his client and therefore he should keep all of his working papers and be prepared to
give expert testimony regarding the amount of the loss sustained
by his client.

### AUDITING PROCEDURE APPLICABLE TO PROPERTY, PLANT, AND EQUIPMENT

#### In an "Examination of Financial Statements"

"1. Summarize the accounts grouped under the heading
property, plant, and equipment (such as land, buildings, plant,
and machinery) so as to show balances at the beginning of the
period, a summary of changes during the period and the balances
at the end of the period.

"2. See that the total of the balances at the beginning of the
period agrees with the total property, plant, and equipment as
stated in the balance sheet at that date; and that the balances at
the end of the period agree with the amount shown on the balance
sheet at the latter date. Property, plant, and equipment are usually carried at cost but if any other basis is used it should be

stated on the balance sheet as concisely as the material facts will permit. If appraisal figures are used, the date of appraisal should be given.

"3. The accountant should satisfy himself as to the propriety of capitalizing the additions to property, plant, and equipment during the period. Examine authorizations for expenditures made during the period; if costs of additions to property, plant, and equipment have exceeded the amounts authorized ascertain the reasons. Authorizations should indicate the accounts to which expenditures are to be charged, should bear the approval of a responsible official, and should show the nature of the work.

"4. When authorizations do not specify whether the work is a repair, a replacement, or an actual addition or where there are no formal authorizations, use whatever means may be available to ascertain the character of the work. Determine that amounts capitalized represent real additions or improvements.

"5. Examine the methods of distributing the pay roll and material and supply charges in sufficient detail to determine that the charges to construction jobs are reasonable. This applies to construction work done by the company's own employees. Examine invoices and other evidence for construction work by outside contractors; ascertain that liability for installments owed for construction work in progress has been taken up on the books.

"6. While it may be considered permissible in the case of construction work done by the company's own employees to capitalize a portion of the overhead cost, e.g., time of superintendent and his clerical force employed on construction work, etc. (but not general administrative expenses) such charges should be carefully scrutinized, inasmuch as it is possible that the overhead charges of a plant may not be decreased to any great extent when additions are not under way; consequently, the absorption of part of these charges in property accounts when construction is in progress may reduce the operating cost below that of periods in which no such work is being done, and may unduly affect comparisons between years.

"7. For purchases of real estate examine vouchers in support of payments made. Title deeds bearing endorsement of public recording officials are supporting evidence of such purchases. Verification of present title and search for encumbrances of record are legal matters which are not within the province of the accountant.

"8. In the case of leasehold property examine the leases, noting their terms. See that improvements, etc. on such property are being written off over a period not in excess of either the duration of the lease or the estimated life of the improvements.

"9. Ascertain the methods used in providing reserves for depreciation of buildings, machinery, and other equipment and also for depletion of natural resources. Investigate charges against the reserves. If the accountant is in doubt as to the adequacy of the current provision or the accumulated reserve shown on the balance sheet he should make suitable comment in his report.

"10. Make inquiries to determine that proper record is made when property is sold, abandoned, destroyed by fire, or otherwise put out of service. Any loss not provided for by depreciation or recoverable through insurance, salvage, or otherwise should be written off.

"11. Many of the foregoing suggestions apply only to property additions during the period under review. In addition, it is well to obtain general information relative to the composition of real estate, building, and machinery accounts to ascertain the principal property represented and the manner in which the accounts have been built up for some years past, if not from the inception of the business.

"12. Construction work in progress and material on hand at the end of the fiscal period which is designated for use in construction should be shown on the balance sheet under the heading property, plant, and equipment and not as part of the inventories."

### Modifications of Audit Program for Larger or Smaller Concerns

"Many companies maintain separate plant records which are controlled on the general books. If all capital additions are budgeted and authorized in advance and later checked and approved in the controller's department, the vouching of the larger items may be all that is necessary. In the case of companies without adequate detailed records, a more extensive examination is required. It is not the accountant's function to determine that every minor charge is justified. He should acquaint himself with the policies of the company with regard to capital additions, replacements, and repair charges and should satisfy himself that the total amount capitalized is reasonable, that plant units ascertained to have been abandoned are removed from the asset account, and that the depreciation reserves are being accumulated on some consistent and accepted basis."

### Intangible Assets

"Intangible assets such as patents, trade-marks, franchises, and good will should, if practicable, be shown separately in the balance sheet. Ascertain the basis on which they are carried in the accounts and the company's policy as to amortization of them."

It has been mentioned that wherever there is an extensive system of internal check the accountant should determine the extent to which he would be justified in reducing the amount of the detailed checking which otherwise he might consider necessary, but that only in a large organization is it usually possible to obtain the most satisfactory separation of functions and duties. In a very small organization or one having a highly restricted system of internal check and control, it will be necessary to make a more detailed examination than that heretofore outlined.

### APPLICATION OF PRINCIPLES

### AUDIT OF THE BLANK MANUFACTURING COMPANY (Continued)

W. H. Merz, the senior accountant in the employ of Stevenson and Bennett, made an analysis of the fixed asset accounts to determine whether all charges to the accounts represented actual capital disbursements and that adequate reserves for depreciation had been set up. The following information was obtained in analyzing the accounts:

**Land.** The amount charged to the land account, $140,000 represents the actual cost of the land at the time of its purchase, August 5, 1935. The deed was examined and found to be properly recorded. No changes were made in the land account since the date of purchase.

**Buildings.** Building operations were begun immediately after the purchase of the land and the book value as set up represents the actual contract price of the buildings when completed,

January 10, 1936. No changes have been recorded in the account since that date. The building contract and supporting documents were examined by Mr. Merz, also the insurance policies and the past year's tax receipts. The buildings account shows a debit of $150,000, the cost at the time of completion. An allowance for depreciation amounting to 2½% is to be provided for annually. The reserve for depreciation on buildings account shows a credit of $3,750, the depreciation for 1936, to which should be added the current year's provision for depreciation of $3,750.

**Machinery.** The book value of machinery amounting to $100,000 represents the original cost price of all machinery, including installation. An item amounting to $215 was found to have been posted to tools and implements, but it should have been charged to the machinery account, as it represented the cost of a new machine purchased December 15, 1937. Provision for depreciation amounting to 6% is to be set up annually. Purchase contracts and receipted invoices were examined in verifying the amounts expended for machinery.

**Tools and Implements.** The tools and implements account shows a debit balance of $20,215. Mr. Merz examined purchase invoices and other vouchers supporting entries in this account. An entry on December 15, 1937, for $215, represented the cost of a new machine which was posted to this account in error. It should have been posted to the machinery account.

No reserve for depreciation of tools and implements has been set up. The practice has been to credit the asset account with the amount of the estimated depreciation which was arrived at after a physical inventory and appraisal. On December 31, 1937, a physical inventory was taken under the supervision of the department foremen. Further investigation shows that the balance of the account represents the actual cost value less estimated depreciation of all tools considered at that date, either in the hands of the workmen or undistributed. The estimated value of tools consumed during the year, amounting to $6,500, was charged to maintenance and repairs at December 31, 1937.

**Delivery Trucks.** The delivery truck account shows a debit balance of $15,000, which represents the cost price of

## THE BLANK MANUFACTURING COMPANY
### Fixed Assets and Reserves for Depreciation
### December 31, 1937

| Fixed Assets | Balance 12-31-36 | Additions | Retirements | Balance 12-31-37 | Remarks |
|---|---|---|---|---|---|
| Office Furniture (net) | 2,600.50 | .... | 260.05 | 2,340.45 | .... |
| Delivery Trucks | 15,000.00 | .... | .... | 15,000.00 | .... |
| Tools and Implements (net) | 21,250.00 | 5,250.00 | 6,500.00 | 20,000.00 | .... |
| Machinery | 100,000.00 | 215.00 | .... | 100,215.00 | .... |
| Buildings | 150,000.00 | .... | .... | 150,000.00 | .... |
| Land | 140,000.00 | .... | .... | 140,000.00 | .... |
| Total | 428,850.50 | 5,465.00 | 6,760.05 | 427,555.45 | .... |

| Reserves for Depreciation | Rate | Balance 12-31-36 | Debit | Credit | Balance 12-31-37 | Remarks |
|---|---|---|---|---|---|---|
| Delivery Trucks | 20% | 3,000.00 | .... | 3,000.00 | 6,000.00 | .... |
| Machinery | 6% | 6,000.00 | .... | 6,000.00 | 12,000.00 | .... |
| Buildings | 2½% | 3,750.00 | .... | 3,750.00 | 7,500.00 | .... |

*Note:* No reserves for depreciation are maintained in connection with the office furniture and tools and implements accounts. The credits to these accounts in the retirement column above represent depreciation for the year at rates of 10% of the remaining value in the account for office furniture, and an inventory and appraisal method for tools and implements. The amounts provided for depreciation seem adequate. Through error tools and implements was charged for $215 on December 15, 1937 when the charge should have been made to the machinery account. No changes were made in the property accounts during the year except as noted above. The vouchers were examined for all additions to the property accounts.

*W. H. Merz*
*(Senior Accountant)*

*(Schedule No. 9)*

Illustration No. 20. Analysis of Fixed Assets

the equipment purchased January 1, 1936. No additions or retirements have been made since that time. Mr. Merz examined purchase contracts and State of Indiana registration certificates, evidencing ownership of the trucks included in the account. The reserve for depreciation shows a credit balance of $3,000, the amount of the entry made at December 31, 1936, for one year's depreciation at 20% per annum.

**Office Furniture.** The office furniture account was found to have a debit balance of $2,600.50. No reserve for depreciation has been set up, the practice being to credit the office furniture account annually with the estimated amount of depreciation. Depreciation, amounting to $260.05, has been calculated at 10% of the remaining balance of the account.

Mr. Merz made a schedule showing a summary of the changes in the property accounts and in the reserves for depreciation during the year 1937. (See Illustration No. 20.)

### THE BLANK MANUFACTURING COMPANY
#### Audit of Fixed Assets
#### Adjusting Journal Entries

| | | |
|---|---:|---:|
| *Machinery* .......................................... | *$ 215.00* | |
| *Tools and Implements* ...................... | | *$  215.00* |
| *To transfer the cost of a machine amounting to $215 from the tools and implements account to the machinery account.* | | |
| *Depreciation—Office Furniture* ................... | *260.05* | |
| *Depreciation—Delivery Trucks* .................. | *3,000.00* | |
| *Depreciation—Machinery* ....................... | *6,000.00* | |
| *Depreciation—Buildings* ........................ | *3,750.00* | |
| *Office Furniture* ............................. | | *260.05* |
| *Reserve for Depreciation—Delivery Trucks* .... | | *3,000.00* |
| *Reserve for Depreciation—Machinery* ......... | | *6,000.00* |
| *Reserve for Depreciation—Buildings* .......... | | *3,750.00* |
| *To record the depreciation of fixed assets for the period ending December 31, 1937.* | | |

*W. H. Merz*

*(Senior Accountant)*

**Illustration No. 21.  Adjusting Entries**

## AUDITING THEORY

**8—86.** How should cash discounts on new machinery purchased be treated?

**8—87.** You are employed to audit the accounts and records of a clothing manufacturer in whose balance sheet appears an item of good will amounting to $10,000,000. Outline your procedure.

**8—88.** If the value placed upon good will is based upon actual costs, would you consider it proper to write it off in its entirety in one year, or would it be better to write it off on a periodical basis?

**8—89.** The General Fuel Corporation leases a corner lot for 49 years and erects a $400,000 building thereon. How would you compute the depreciation on this property?

**8—90.** An alteration to existing equipment is made in a factory. State what you would do with the cost of such alteration.

(C. P. A. Ind.)

**8—91.** Auditing the yearly results of a large engineering company you find that the machinery and tools, which had been regularly depreciated for a number of years, have, during the year under audit, been appraised by a reputable appraising company, and have been revalued at a larger sum than the debit balances in the books. How would you dispose of the increased value due to the appraisal?

(C. P. A. Ind.)

**8—92.** A company purchased several machines and, in order to install them to the best advantage, old machines which are to remain in use were moved to make room for them. The machines were large and had to be taken apart before they could be moved. To what account should the cost of moving be charged and why?

(C. P. A. Pa.)

**8—93.** Mention under what circumstances, if any, reconstruction or rehabilitation expenses of a street railway company may properly be charged to property accounts.

(C. P. A. Ind.)

**8—94.** A company used its own material and laborers' services in the erection of an addition to its own plant. These additions to the capital account were charged at market prices, the profit being absorbed in current trading profits. Do you consider this method correct? Explain fully the principles involved.

(C. P. A. Nebr.)

**8—95.** A concern needs an addition to its plant. Not having enough ready capital, the money was borrowed and when the interest was paid it was charged to the plant account on the theory that it was not an expense in the ordinary conduct of the business and should, therefore, not be charged to the regular interest and discount account but might with propriety be charged as a part of the cost of the addition. Is the theory sound?

(C. P. A. Mich.)

8—96. A company purchased land and on this land was a building which the company had to pull down before constructing a new building. During the demolishing of the building, a workman was killed which cost the company $2,500. To what account should the compensation in respect of this accident be charged and why?

(C. P. A. Pa.)

8—97. What would you do in auditing the accounts of a corporation for the first time with regard to items appearing on the balance sheet under the headings "Land" and "Buildings"?

(A. I. A.)

## AUDITING PROBLEMS

8—19. The machinery account of The Highland Moulding Co. contains the following debits:

(a) Purchase of two machines, type A, including freight.... $8,000.00
(b) Cost of removing a disused machine, type B, to make
　　　room for new machine........................... 160.00
(c) Cost of installation of two new machines.............. 280.00
(d) Alterations to four type C machines, necessitated by
　　　change in product................................ 640.00
(e) Cost of moving two machines from Building A to Building
　　　B, to permit of more economical operation, including
　　　reinstallation.................................... 270.00

Analyze this account and submit a report containing your recommendation as to the proper treatment of each of the above items.

8—20. As auditor for the Maysville Roofing Co. you find that the company is occupying property, the lease on which has forty years to run from the beginning of the current audit period. This lease is carried on the books at its original cost of $50,000. It was acquired ten years previously and is considered to have a realizable value of about $100,000. Three years previous to the period covered by the current audit in January, $40,000 was spent in remodeling the building and this cost was charged against the current operations. No depreciation has ever been set up on the buildings and no part of the cost of the lease has been written off. State how you would determine the proper valuation of the leasehold for balance sheet purposes, and what would be your recommendation with regard to the handling of depreciation on the building? Draft the necessary journal entries to correct the accounts and to reflect the true profit for the current period.

8—21. A machine was constructed and charged to the machinery account nine years ago, together with other machines made at the same time, but a separate cost of each unit of machinery was not kept. According to regular practice, still in force, a credit was set up, in a reserve account, for depreciation of machinery at the rate of 10% on the total machinery account. At the end of nine years, this machine was sold for $1,000 and you can secure no more accurate information as to cost than the engineer's opinion that the item sold must have cost somewhere between $10,000 and $15,000 to construct. A new machine was purchased for $15,000 to replace the old one sold. What entries should appear on the books to record the sale of the old machine and the purchase of the new, assuming that it was finally decided to accept a value of $15,000 as the original cost of the old machine?

8—22. The National Tile Co. employs you to audit its accounts as a means of establishing the amount of loss sustained by fire. Upon reporting for duty you ask for the insurance policy and you find that it contains the following clause: "This company shall not be liable for a greater proportion of any loss or damage to the property described herein than the sum hereby insured bears to eighty per cent (80%) of the actual cash value of said property at the time such loss shall happen, nor for more than the proportion which this policy bears to the total insurance thereon." Your audit reveals that the actual value of the property at time of the fire amounted to $10,000.

(a) If the loss amounted to $8,000 and the insurance carried amounted to $9,000 at the time of the fire, what amount can be recovered from the insurance company?

(b) If the loss amounted to $5,000 and the insurance carried amounted to $8,000 at the time of the fire, what amount can be recovered from the insurance company?

(c) If the loss amounted to $4,000 and the insurance carried amounted to $5,000 at the time of the fire, what amount can be recovered from the insurance company?

(d) If the loss amounted to $9,000 and the insurance carried amounted to $5,000 at the time of the fire, what amount can be recovered from the insurance company?

8—23. The A. B. Land Co. buys a tract of land and makes improvements thereon (streets, sidewalks, water, and sewer connections, etc.) at a total cost of $50,000, its entire capital. To keep the property restricted it does not sell its lots but disposes of them all in its first year on ninety-nine-year leases for flat sums aggregating $100,000, and a nominal rental of $10 a year per lot to cover water and other service charges. Current expenses just consumed the nominal rentals for the first year. After paying a dividend of $90,000 the company's balance sheet at the close of the first year appeared as follows:

### Balance Sheet

| ASSETS | | LIABILITIES | |
|---|---|---|---|
| Land and improvements. | $50,000.00 | Capital stock | $50,000.00 |
| Cash | 10,000.00 | Surplus | 10,000.00 |
| | $60,000.00 | | $60,000.00 |

Is this correct accounting procedure or not? Give reasons.

(A. I. A.)

## AUDITING PRACTICE

### An Audit Case (Sixth Installment)

After verifying the current assets, Ken B. Swift proceeds with the examination of the fixed asset accounts on January 6. In view of the fact that the accounts were audited at December 31, 1937, by the firm of Knight and Day, it is necessary to verify only the entries made in the accounts during the year 1938. The following are the fixed asset accounts as they appear at December 31, 1938:

### Furniture and Fixtures (depreciation rate 10%)

| Date | Items | Debit | Credit | Balance |
|------|-------|-------|--------|---------|
| 1- 1-38 | Balance.................................. | 16,900.00 | ........ | 16,900.00 |
| 4- 1-38 | Cabinets................................ | 370.00 | ........ | 17,270.00 |
| 7- 5-38 | Carpets................................ | 500.00 | ........ | 17,770.00 |
| 9-30-38 | Desks................................. | 280.00 | ........ | ........... |
| 9-30-38 | Desks—traded in on new ones; cost $300.00; allowance $127.50; depreciation taken to 1-1-38, $150.00........................ | ........ | 127.50 | 17,922.50 |

### Reserve for Depreciation—Furniture and Fixtures

| Date | Items | Debit | Credit | Balance |
|------|-------|-------|--------|---------|
| 1- 1-38 | Balance................................ | ........ | 5,560.00 | 5,560.00 |
| 12-31-38 | Depreciation—1938..................... | ........ | 1,792.25 | 7,352 25 |

### Delivery Equipment (depreciation rate 20%)

| Date | Items | Debit | Credit | Balance |
|------|-------|-------|--------|---------|
| 1- 1-38 | Balance.............................. | 8,200.00 | ........ | 8,200.00 |
| 4- 1-38 | Plymouth Truck...................... | 1,200.00 | ........ | ........... |
| 4- 1-38 | Chevrolet Truck (purchased 1-10-34) cost $980; allowance $200; depreciation taken to 1-1-38, $784........................ | ........ | 200.00 | 9,200.00 |

### Reserve for Depreciation—Delivery Equipment

| Date | Items | Debit | Credit | Balance |
|------|-------|-------|--------|---------|
| 1- 1-38 | Balance................................ | ........ | 3,680.00 | 3,680.00 |
| 12-31-38 | Depreciation—1938.................... | ........ | 1,840.00 | 5,520.00 |

### Buildings (depreciation rate 2½%)

| Date | Items | Debit | Credit | Balance |
|------|-------|-------|--------|---------|
| 1-10-33 | Cost by purchase...................... | 75,000.00 | ........ | 75,000.00 |
| 7- 5-36 | Warehouse and additions per contract...... | 95,000.00 | ........ | 170,000.00 |
| 1- 5-38 | Write-up from appraisal................. | 20,000.00 | ........ | 190,000.00 |

### Reserve for Depreciation—Buildings

| Date | Items | Debit | Credit | Balance |
|------|-------|-------|--------|---------|
| 1- 1-38 | Balance—Depreciation from 1-1-33 to 12-31-37 @ 2½%.............................. | .......... | 12,937.50 | 12,937.50 |
| 1- 5-38 | Five years depreciation on write-up, $20,000 @ 2½% per year..................... | .......... | 2,500.00 | 15,437.50 |
| 12-31-38 | Depreciation, 1938...................... | .......... | 4,750.00 | 20,187.50 |

### Land

| Date | Items | Debit | Credit | Balance |
|------|-------|-------|--------|---------|
| 1- 1-38 | Balance................................ | 16,725.00 | ......... | 16,725.00 |
| 1- 5-38 | Write-up from appraisal................ | 10,000.00 | ......... | 26,725.00 |

The only entries made in the land and buildings accounts during the year were those made to record an increase in value which was shown to exist as the result of an appraisal made by the firm of Johnson, Johnson, and Johnson, appraisal engineers. The appraisal was completed December 20, 1937. The following journal entry, approved by the board of directors, was made to record the appraised values on the books:

### January 5, 1938

| | | |
|---|---|---|
| Buildings..................................... | $20,000.00 | |
| Land......................................... | 10,000.00 | |
|   Reserve for Depreciation—Buildings........ | | $ 2,500.00 |
|   Surplus................................... | | 27,500.00 |

Receipted invoices and sales contracts were produced by the bookkeeper as evidence of the propriety of the debit entries in the furniture and fixtures and the delivery equipment accounts. Certificates, evidencing ownership of the delivery trucks, were also examined, including the certificate for the Plymouth truck purchased during the year.

### INSTRUCTIONS

1. Read and study the audit procedure suggested for the verification of fixed assets (property, plant, and equipment) in an "Examination of Financial Statements."

2. Prepare a schedule showing in detail the additions to and deductions from the property accounts and a second schedule showing a summary of the property accounts and the reserves for depreciation. The latter schedule should be similar to the one shown in the illustrative set of audit working papers. (Illustration No. 20.)

3. Prepare adjusting journal entries, where necessary, to adjust the account balances.

# CHAPTER NINE

## DEFERRED ITEMS

1. **Deferred Charges to Operations**
   - (a) **Insurance**
   - (b) **Interest**
   - (c) **Discount on Bonds**
   - (d) **Discount on Capital Stock**
   - (e) **Experimental Expenses**
   - (f) **Organization Expenses**
   - (g) **Advertising**
   - (h) **Other Deferred Charges**

2. **Deferred Credits to Income**
   - (a) **Interest**
   - (b) **Rent**
   - (c) **Installment Sales**
   - (d) **Other Deferred Credits**

3. **Auditing Procedure**

4. **Application of Principles**

5. **An Audit Case—Seventh Installment**

It is the duty of an auditor to see that the period covered by his report is charged only with expenses and costs applicable to that period, and that it is credited only for income earned during the period. Expenses may be incurred which are not entirely applicable to that period. Materials and supplies may be consumed which were purchased in a previous period. Income may be obtained which was earned in a previous period or which will not be earned until a later period. In other words, expenses may be incurred and income may be collected in one period while they may be in whole or in part applicable to a preceding or succeeding period. Expenses incurred and income collected in advance of the period to which they apply are known as deferred items. Those items representing charges against future operations are called deferred expenses or deferred assets. Those items representing credits to the profits of a future period are known as deferred credits to income.

### DEFERRED CHARGES TO OPERATIONS

Expenses may be divided into two classes: First, those which are consumed before being paid for; Second, those which are paid for in advance of consumption. Expenditures for materials already used and for services already consumed should be charged directly to the proper expense account. No portion of such expenses should be deferred. It is only necessary to make sure that the cost of such expenses has been recorded, and if not, the accrued portion of the expenses applicable to the period should be recorded by charging the proper expense accounts and crediting the accrued liability account. When materials are purchased or services contracted for, payment being made in advance of the actual use or consumption of such materials and services, it is necessary to treat the unused or unconsumed portion of such materials and expenses as deferred charges to operations. Such expenditures may be charged originally to either expense or asset accounts. In either case proper adjustment should be made at the end of the period to charge the period with all expenses applicable to the period and to defer all expenses which are applicable to a future period.

**Insurance.** Insurance policies may be of various types. Most companies will carry fire, theft, use and occupancy, liability insurance of various types, and frequently life insurance on the principal officers of the company. Other insurance such as windstorm, sprinkler, elevator, and plate glass insurance may be carried. Such policies may be in force for periods of from one to five years, and several policies may be effective on one property. It is usually advisable for the auditor to prepare working papers covering the principal points on insurance, such as, the policy number, name of insuring company, the date of the policy, amount of premium paid, period of coverage, unexpired portion, unexpired premium, properties covered, and any other information needed. This information should be obtained from the policies themselves if available; if on mortgaged property, the information may be obtained from the mortgagee. In case an insurance register is maintained, the information should be checked against the information shown on the register. The auditor should assure himself that the unexpired insurance set up on the books is in agreement with the unexpired portion as shown by his working papers. An insurance policy schedule is shown in Illustration No. 22.

When examining and recording insurance information, the auditor may well classify the types of insurance carried, thus facilitating judgment as to the adequacy of the insurance carried, the existence of liens if any, and other properties or liabilities not stated in the records. Many companies carry co-insurance policies which should be carefully checked as to adequacy. The auditor may often offer valuable suggestions as to the proper insurance program for his client.

In recent years many companies have adopted the policy of taking out insurance on the lives of the principal executives as indemnity for the possible loss of profits as a result of the death of such individuals. Such policies carry what are known as cash surrender and loan values. A fire insurance policy may run for five years, the total premium amounting to $500. The policy furnishes only one thing, protection in case of the occurrence of the contingency insured. A life insurance policy on the other hand, involves two elements, the protection element and a property element. Where such policies exist that portion of the policy paid annually which is added to the cash surrender value, should be added to the insurance policy value, while the difference between this amount and the premium paid should be charged to operating expense. The surrender value of life insurance policies does not involve a deferred charge as it is not chargeable to future operations. Such amounts should be presented under a separate heading on the balance sheet, and the auditor should obtain certification of the values shown from the insurance company which issued the policies.

**Interest.** Prepaid interest cost applicable to a future period should always be treated as a deferred charge. The interest may be paid in advance on notes receivable discounted and on notes payable, hence both items should be examined with a view to determining what amount of prepaid interest should be deferred. Sometimes interest is included in the face of notes payable. This is equivalent to a prepayment of interest, and when the maturity of the notes extends beyond the audit period, the portion applicable to a future period should be deferred.

**Discount on Bonds.** Bonds under present methods of finance are usually sold to bankers at a discount, allowing the latter to resell to the public at approximately par and make a profit out of the transaction. In addition to the discount taken most issues of bonds involve legal, printing, and other expenses which reduce the net amount obtainable from the securities. Not all these costs are costs of the period in which they are incurred, but rather they are a part of the cost of capital for the period in which that capital is used, and hence should not be charged directly to expense, but should be deferred and distributed over the life of the bonds. That is, when a twenty-year bond issue is sold at a discount of $100 on a $1,000 bond, the discount should be charged proportionately over the twenty years and not charged to expense or surplus in the year incurred.

The auditor should examine the ledger account to see that the bond discount and expense is being amortized properly and that the entries are recorded in the accounts correctly. (For further discussion of bond discount, see Chapter XI.)

**Discount on Capital Stock.** Discount on capital stock is occasionally found carried as a deferred charge to operations. This should be discouraged, though some corporations adopt such a policy and write off such items against the following two or three years' net profits, or against surplus rather than charge the discount against the surplus account as of the date of the sale of the stock.

Strictly speaking, such items are valuation items against overstated capital stock values. They should be written off against the surplus account as soon as possible after being incurred. Where set up on the books the auditor should determine whether they are bona fide discounts.

**Experimental Expenses.** Experimental expenses incurred for the purpose of improving one's products are sometimes set up as a deferred item in the balance sheet on the theory that such costs are costs of the product to be sold in the future and not current charges. In the development of mechanical and other devices, large amounts are often expended to put a new improvement or a product on the market. Such expenditures may often be made several periods prior to the marketing of the commodity. Where this occurs, and the experimentation is an unusual item, it is usually considered legitimate to spread the cost over a period of three to five years, charging such periods on the theory that the return from the work involved is obtained during that time to a great extent. Care should be taken that these amounts do not include losses or costs of unproductive work. The larger corporations, employing technical staffs the year round, usually adopt the policy of charging experimental expense items to current operations, on the theory that the costs are periodic, fluctuate little from period to period, and that such a policy presents a more nearly accurate as well as conservative statement of operating conditions.

**Organization Expenses.** Organization expenses include such items as incorporation fees, attorneys' fees, cost of engraving and printing stock certificates, underwriting expenses, and other expenses incidental to the organization of a company. Generally speaking, all expenses incurred in the organization of a corporation up to the time of actual operation constitute proper charges to organization expense. Theoretically, such costs are applicable to the life of a corporation. If the corporation is incorporated under a perpetual charter, such items should remain as capital charges. On the other hand, though operating under perpetual charter, practically, most corporations do not enjoy continued existence for any great span of life. The larger part of our important corporations of today have been in operation under their present charters less than thirty years. Due to the vicissitudes of operation, a more conservative policy as concerns industrial and commercial companies has therefore developed, and the auditor should recommend that organization expenses be written off periodically.

The usual procedure in writing off organization expenses is to charge surplus rather than current profits. This procedure is based upon the theory that organization expenses represent capital rather than revenue expenditures. The undistributed portion of the cost, therefore, represents a deferred charge to surplus rather than a deferred charge to expense, although usually organization expenses are classified along with other deferred charges to operations, no attempt being made to distinguish between deferred charges to operations and deferred charges to surplus or capital.

**Advertising.** Frequently corporations will engage in a large advertising campaign, expending thousands of dollars in an endeavor to place a product successfully on the market. The returns from such an expenditure ordinarily will be realized in subsequent periods, and at least a part of such costs reasonably may be deferred. The auditor should determine the advertising policy of the concern, and should assure himself that such items are not ordinary advertising expenses deferred in order to avoid making an unfavorable financial showing for the period. Advertising expenses in local newspapers and for current operations should not be deferred and the auditor must assure himself that those expenditures which are deferred are of an extraordinary nature.

**Other Deferred Charges.** Prepaid rent may be found in those concerns which lease part of their plant or equipment. Rent is usually paid in advance monthly, quarterly, or semi-annually. The auditor should examine the lease and determine the correct status of the rent account, deferring any items applicable to future periods.

Where a company is occupying property under lease, it frequently finds it necessary to alter and remodel the premises to suit its needs. Such alteration and remodeling costs are a part of the cost of the lease and should be spread over the life of the lease, representing a part of the annual occupancy cost. They may be charged to a leasehold improvements account and be carried among the fixed assets, or they may be treated as deferred charges, depending on the circumstances. In either event, the auditor should verify the expenditures to assure himself that the funds were properly expended for such purposes, and that the proper periodic charges are being made to expense to amortize the cost at the expiration of the lease.

### DEFERRED CREDITS TO INCOME

Income may be collected in advance of rendering service, or goods may be paid for in advance of delivery. Where income is recorded before it is earned, any unearned portion not applicable to the period under audit should be deferred for credit to the period in which it is earned. Interest, rent, and fees are typical of the types of income which are commonly collected in advance. The extensive marketing of merchandise on an installment sales basis has resulted in the establishment of a procedure in accounting whereby the earned profit is based upon collections actually received during the period. That proportion of profit based upon the deferred installments is treated as a deferred income. Deferred credits to income are just the opposite of deferred charges to operations and should be so classified on the balance sheet. It is customary to list the deferred charges last among the assets and the deferred credits last among the liabilities on the balance sheet.

**Interest.** Interest collected in advance should be analyzed and that portion applicable to a future period should be treated as a deferred credit to income. Deferred credits are just the opposite of deferred charges, hence an auditor is just as likely to find that his client has collected interest in advance as he is to find that his client has paid interest in advance. In other words, interest paid in advance will represent a deferred charge on the books of one party to the transaction, and a deferred credit on the books of the other party to the transaction. In both cases, it is necessary to make a proper adjustment of the interest accounts in order that the operating statement may show the true operating result for the period.

**Rent.** Rent collected in advance should be analyzed to ascertain what portion will be applicable to a future period and this portion should be deferred. Rent is usually payable in advance, hence any portion applicable to a future period will represent a deferred charge to operations on the part of the tenant and a deferred credit to income on the part of the landlord.

**Installment Sales.** Where merchandise or other property is sold on an installment or deferred payment plan, the installment sales may be segregated from ordinary sales and the profits accounted for in such manner that the current period will be credited only with the profits applicable to the collections for the period. Profits applicable to deferred payments are then deferred. The usual procedure in accounting for deferred profits on installment sales is as follows: At the end of the period the gross profit to be realized on the total installment sales is determined and this rate is applied to the collections received during the year, to find the gross profit realized. The difference between the gross profit to be realized and the gross profit applicable to the collections from installment sales is then treated as a deferred profit applicable to installment accounts receivable. The deferred profits on installment sales is then classified along with other deferred credits on the balance sheet.

The following journal entries may be made to record the deferred profit on installment sales assuming that equipment costing $960 was sold for $1,600 and that cash collections during the period were $600.

(1)

| | | |
|---|---|---|
| Installment Sales................................. | $1,600.00 | |
| Cost of Sales (or purchases)..................... | | $960.00 |
| Gross Profit on Installment Sales................ | | 640.00 |

   To close the installment sales and cost of sales accounts, and to set up the gross profit on installment sales.

(2)

| | | |
|---|---|---|
| Gross Profit on Installment Sales.................... | $ 400.00 | |
| Deferred Profit on Installment Sales............. | | $400.00 |

   To defer the unrealized portion of gross profit on installment sales. (The gross profit ratio is 40% of sales, hence 40% of the amount collected during the period represents an earned profit. If $400 of gross profit on installment sales is deferred, the balance, or $240 will represent the earned profit for the current period.)

**Other Deferred Credits.** Attorneys frequently collect retainers' fees in advance. Insurance companies collect premiums in advance. Telephone companies collect in advance for services to be rendered. Bonds may be purchased at a discount as a permanent investment and it may be desirable to distribute the discount over the remaining life of the bonds. Schools may collect tuition in advance. In all such cases, that portion of income collected during the period, the earning of which applies to a future period, should be deferred as a credit to income in the period in which it is earned.

## AUDITING PROCEDURE APPLICABLE TO DEFERRED CHARGES
### In an "Examination of Financial Statements"

"1. Under this caption are included unexpired insurance, prepaid interest, taxes, royalties, and other prepaid expenses and also bond discount, development, and organization expenses and other deferred items unamortized.

"2. Check the mathematical accuracy and ascertain that they are proper amounts to carry forward as a charge to future operations. Whenever possible obtain documentary evidence in support of the items carried forward; for example, in the case of unexpired insurance examine the policies to ascertain dates of expiration, the amount of the premiums and the proportion to be carried forward; in case of prepaid royalties examine the agreements or contracts. Any adjustment of premiums for compensation insurance should be based upon the actual, not the predetermined, pay roll.

"3. Make inquiries to determine the company's policy as to amortization of deferred charges, such as whether bond discount is being amortized on a straight-line basis or bond-outstanding method or otherwise. If development and similar expenditures are deferred, they should be written off over a reasonable period having regard to the character of the expenditures.

"4. As prepaid expenses and deferred charges may be considered to include two classes of items which differ somewhat in their nature different treatment is sometimes accorded them. Prepaid expenses, as representing those items which eventually will be included in manufacturing or other operating expenses may, if desired, be set up as a separate item under deferred charges or may be included as a separate caption on the balance sheet."

## APPLICATION OF PRINCIPLES

### AUDIT OF THE BLANK MANUFACTURING COMPANY (Continued)

In the audit of The Blank Manufacturing Company by Stevenson and Bennett, C. E. Shaw, junior accountant, audited the deferred charges and prepared adjustments as follows:

**Insurance.** Mr. Shaw examined the insurance policies and verified the amount of the expired and unexpired premiums at December 31, 1937. In this connection he prepared an audit schedule on which was listed the insurance policies and the amounts of the expired and unexpired insurance premiums. (Illustration No. 22.) He also drafted the adjusting entries required to record the expired insurance. The balance of the prepaid insurance account represents a deferred charge which will appear in the balance sheet as an asset.

**Office Supplies.** The office supplies inventory, amounting to $280, was taken by company employees at December 31, 1937. Mr. Shaw checked the computations of the larger items and proved the footings. The amount of the inventory seemed reasonable. Since the office supplies account appears in the asset section of the general ledger, it was necessary for Mr. Shaw to make an adjusting entry debiting office supplies used and crediting office supplies for the cost of the supplies consumed during the year. After posting this entry, the balance of the office supplies account will represent a deferred charge and should be classified as an asset in the balance sheet.

**Prepaid Advertising.** Mr. Shaw, with the approval of Mr. Merz, arranged to defer half of the cost of the 1937 advertising campaign, amounting to $25,150. It was decided to distribute the cost over a two-year period. An adjusting journal entry was drafted debiting prepaid advertising and crediting advertising for one-half of the cost of the 1937 advertising campaign. After this entry is posted, the balance of the advertising account will represent an operating expense, while the amount charged to prepaid advertising will represent a deferred charge which will be listed as an asset in the balance sheet.

**Organization Expense.** Of the organization expense, 10% or $816.67, was written off in accordance with the policy previously established. The amount written off was charged to surplus rather than to current profits. It represents an adjustment of capital and has no bearing upon the current earnings. In drafting an adjusting entry to write off 10% of organization expenses, it was necessary to debit surplus and credit organization expense for the reason that organization expenses do not constitute an allowable deduction in a Federal income tax return and should not be treated as a charge against current profits.

**Bond Discount.** The bond discount is being amortized over the twenty-year life of the bonds, hence, 5% or $375 should be written off annually. In drafting the adjusting entries required to write off 5% of bond discount, it is necessary to decide whether to charge profit and loss or bond interest. He decided that since the discount is being written off on a straight-line basis,

(Continued on page 237)

## THE BLANK MANUFACTURING COMPANY
### Analysis of Insurance
### December 31, 1937

| COMPANY | POLICY No. | Coverage AMOUNT | Coverage PROPERTY | Period Covered FROM | Period Covered TO | TOTAL PREMIUM PAID | PREPAID 12-31-37 | EXPIRED 1937 | REMARKS |
|---|---|---|---|---|---|---|---|---|---|
| Apex...... | H-753 | 60,000.00 | Building | 8- 1-35 | 8- 1-38 | 420.00 | 81.67 | 140.00 | 80% co-ins. clause |
| Gulf...... | 10,531 | 60,000.00 | Building | 11- 1-35 | 11- 1-40 | 540.00 | 306.00 | 108.00 | 80% co-ins. clause |
| Southern... | E-79 | 80,000.00 | Equipment | 1-15-36 | 1-15-39 | 480.00 | 166.67 | 160.00 | 80% co-ins. clause |
| Occidental | M-628 | 10,000.00 | Trucks | 3- 1-37 | 3- 1-38 | 540.00 | ...... | 90.00 | |
| Occidental | R-1227 | 10,000.00 | Trucks | 3- 1-37 | 3- 1-38 | 540.00 | 90.00 | 450.00 | |
| Continental | D-941 | 30,000.00 | Mdse. | 3- 1-36 | 3- 1-37 | 90.00 | ...... | 15.00 | |
| Continental | H-348 | 70,000.00 | Mdse. | 3- 1-37 | 3- 1-38 | 210.00 | 35.00 | 175.00 | |
| Pacific Ins. | A-1946 | Pay roll | Work.Comp. | 3- 1-36 | 3- 1-37 | 1,908.00 | ...... | 318.00 | |
| Pacific Ins. | C-273 | Pay roll | Work.Comp. | 3- 1-37 | 3- 1-38 | 2,862.00 | 477.00 | 2,385.00 | |
| Total..... | | | | | | 7,590.00 | 1,156.34 | 3,841.00 | |

### Insurance Expense

| | |
|---|---|
| Prepaid insurance 12-31-36 ........ | 1,385.34 |
| Premiums paid during 1937 ........ | 3,612.00 |
| Total............................ | 4,997.34 |
| Less unexpired 12-31-37 ......... | 1,156.34 |
| Expired during 1937............. | 3,841.00 |

### Distribution of Expired Premiums

| | |
|---|---|
| Manufacturing expense............ | 2,420.00 |
| Administrative expense........... | 1,421.00 |
| Total........................... | 3,841.00 |

All of the policies were examined, with the exception of those which had expired within the year. The amount of insurance carried seems adequate.

C. E. Shaw
*(Junior Accountant)*

**Illustration No. 22. Analysis of Insurance**

*(Schedule No. 10)*

## THE BLANK MANUFACTURING COMPANY
### Deferred Charges—December 31, 1937

#### Office Supplies

*Balance per ledger account, December 31, 1937* . . . . . . . . . . . $    510.00
*Less inventory, December 31, 1937* . . . . . . . . . . . . . . . . . . . . . . .      280.00

*Office Supplies Used* . . . . . . . . . . . . . . . . . . . . . . . . . . . . . . . . . . . $    230.00

> *The inventory sheets were examined, the prices of the ledger items were tested, and the footings were proved.*

#### Prepaid Advertising

*Advertising cost per ledger account* . . . . . . . . . . . . . . . . . . . . . . $25,150.00
*Less amount charged to this year's expense* . . . . . . . . . . . . . . .  12,575.00

*Prepaid advertising, December 31, 1937* . . . . . . . . . . . . . . . . . . $12,575.00

> *It is the desire of the management that one-half of the cost of the advertising campaign carried on during 1937, be distributed over a two-year period.  As the benefits of the advertising campaign may easily extend over the two-year period, an adjusting journal entry was made to defer half of the amount as shown above.*

#### Organization Expense

*Balance per ledger account, January 1, 1937* . . . . . . . . . . . . . . $ 7,350.00
*Less 1/10 of $8,166.65, to be charged to surplus* . . . . . . . . . . .      816.67

*Balance as adjusted, December 31, 1937* . . . . . . . . . . . . . . . . . . $ 6,533.33

> *The organization expense is being written off over a ten-year period by an annual debit to surplus.  The above write-off is the second installment.*

#### Bond Discount

*Balance per ledger account, January 1, 1937* . . . . . . . . . . . . . . $ 7,125.00
*Less 1/20 of $7,500, the original discount* . . . . . . . . . . . . . . . . .      375.00

*Balance as adjusted, December 31, 1937* . . . . . . . . . . . . . . . . . . $ 6,750.00

> *The bond discount, amounting to $7,500 at date of issue, is being written off on a straight-line basis over the twenty-year life of the bonds.*

#### Salary Advances to Salesmen

> *The salary advances to salesmen amounted to $950 at December 31, 1937.  The vouchers bearing the signature of the employees and the approval of Mr. L. W. Shields, general manager, were examined by me.*

C. E. Shaw
(*Junior Accountant*)                                    (*Schedule No. 11*)

**Illustration No. 23.  Analysis of Deferred Charges**

## THE BLANK MANUFACTURING COMPANY

### Audit of Deferred Items
### Adjusting Journal Entries

| | | |
|---|---:|---:|
| *Expired Insurance—Manufacturing*........... | *$ 2,420.00* | |
| *Expired Insurance—Administrative*............ | *1,421.00* | |
| *Prepaid Insurance*........................ | | *$ 3,841.00* |
| *To record the insurance expired during the year ended December 31, 1937.* | | |
| *Office Supplies Used*........................ | *230.00* | |
| *Office Supplies*........................... | | *230.00* |
| *To record the cost of office supplies consumed during the year ended December 31, 1937.* | | |
| *Prepaid Advertising*........................ | *12,575.00* | |
| *Advertising*.............................. | | *12,575.00* |
| *To defer one-half of the advertising expense incurred during 1937.* | | |
| *Surplus*.................................. | *816.67* | |
| *Organization Expense*..................... | | *816.67* |
| *To charge off 10% of organization expense.* | | |
| *Bond Discount Written Off*................... | *375.00* | |
| *Bond Discount*........................... | | *375.00* |
| *To record the amount of bond discount written off for the year ended December 31, 1937.* | | |

*C. E. Shaw*
*(Junior Accountant)*

### Illustration No. 24. Adjusting Entries

(*Continued from page 234*)

it was better to treat it as a charge to profit and loss, hence, an account with bond discount written off is debited and bond discount is credited. In closing the accounts, the account with bond discount written off will, of course, be closed into profit and loss.

The working papers prepared in connection with the verification of deferred charges are shown in Illustrations Nos. 22, 23, and 24.

**Deferred Credits to Income.** No adjustments were necessary to record deferred credits to income.

### SUMMARY

Deferred items may consist of either charges to operations or credits to income. They arise from the fact that expenses may be paid in advance and income may be collected in advance.

Sound accounting involves proper adjustment of expense and income accounts, to insure the current period being charged only for those costs and expenses applicable to the period and being credited only for those gains and profits earned during the period. Familiarity with the nature of the business in which the client is engaged, will usually aid an auditor in determining what expense and income accounts are likely to require adjustment in order that all deferred items may be properly stated in the balance sheet, and that expense and income may be properly stated in the profit and loss statement. Deferred items should never be confused with accrued items. Accrued receivable accounts usually represent current assets, while deferred charges to operations do not constitute current assets and usually have no realization value to a liquidating concern. Accrued accounts payable represent current liabilities while deferred credits to income should not be classified as current liabilities because usually they do not involve a liability for payment in cash on the part of the client, but rather represent a liability to render service or to perform a contract for which payment has been received in advance.

## AUDITING THEORY

**9—98.** Explain why it is necessary to make adjustments for deferred items at the end of the fiscal period.

**9—99.** State which of the following items represent deferred charges to operations:

    (a) Unexpired insurance
    (b) Interest accrued on notes receivable
    (c) Prepaid interest on notes receivable discounted
    (d) Prepaid interest on notes payable
    (e) Unamortized bond discount
    (f) Organization expenses.

**9—100.** Under what conditions would it be proper to transfer a part of the cost of advertising?

**9—101.** In amortizing bond discount should the amount written off be charged to surplus, profit and loss, or interest cost?

**9—102.** You are consulted by a client as to the advisability of writing off organization expenses which have been carried on the books for a number of years at the original amount. What would be your advice in the matter and how would you advise writing off the organization expenses?

**9—103.** What are organization expenses? How are they to be treated in accounts? At what point do expenses cease to be organization expenses and become operating expenses?

(A. I. A.)

**9—104.** To what extent may the "Organization Expenses" of a corporation be regarded as a permanent asset and how should this account accordingly be dealt with?

(C. P. A. Me.)

**9—105.** State your views of a proper differentiation between (a) capital expenditure and operating expense, (b) current income and deferred income, and (c) deferred charges and deferred assets.

(A. I. A.)

**9—106.** (a) Is the deficiency in the early years of a corporation's activities (whether an actual loss or a deficiency between the earnings and the normal rate of return) similar to organization expenses?

(b) How should such deficiencies be treated in the accounts?

(c) To what extent is such a deficiency similar to interest paid during construction?

(d) May the deficiencies representing the difference between actual earnings and normal rate of return be capitalized, in the strict sense of having capital stock issued to a corresponding sum?

(A. I. A.)

## AUDITING PROBLEMS

**9—24.** In completing an audit you find that adjustments need to be made to record deferred items as follows:

(a) Insurance paid during the year amounted to $1,150 of which one-half has expired.

(b) Stationery purchased during the year amounted to $1,200 of which there remained on hand at the end of the year stationery which cost $300.

(c) On January 2 of the current year an issue of 20-year bonds was sold at a discount of $6,000. It is desired to defer this discount, charging it off over the life of the bonds on a straight-line basis.

(d) In forming a corporation, two years ago, organization expenses were incurred amounting to $7,500, which are to be distributed equally and written off over a period of five years.

(e) Thirty days before the close of the fiscal period $10,000 was borrowed from the Merchants National Bank on a sixty-day note, the interest at 6% being paid in advance and charged to interest cost.

(f) Property is rented for $500 a month, the rent being paid in advance on the 15th of each month.

(g) A piano store sold a piano for $1,400, a down payment of $400 being made and the balance to be paid in ten equal monthly installments of $100 each. The piano cost the dealer $840. At the end of the fiscal period the dealer had collected four monthly payments in addition to the down payment and it is desired to defer that part of the gross profit which is applicable to future collections.

Draft the required adjusting entries in journal form, assuming that the fiscal period ends on December 31 of the current year.

9—25. The bookkeeper for The Michigan Manufacturing Co., due to illness, has been unable to prepare the balance sheet, profit and loss statement, and manufacturing statement for the year ended December 31, 1938. You are therefore employed to prepare these statements. Upon reporting for duty, you are given the following list of adjusting journal entries and trial balance prepared by the bookkeeper:

## ADJUSTING ENTRIES
### December 31, 1938

| | | |
|---|---|---|
| Material Purchases.............................. | $27,214.41 | |
| Inventory of Mfg. Materials, Beginning of Period | | $27,214.41 |
| To close the beginning inventory into the material purchases account. | | |
| Inventory of Mfg. Materials, End of Period........ | 51,358.58 | |
| Material Purchases......................... | | 51,358.58 |
| To record inventory at end of period. | | |
| Interest Earned................................ | 134.83 | |
| Accrued Interest Payable................... | | 134.83 |
| To record interest accrued on notes payable. | | |
| Accrued Taxes................................. | 376.75 | |
| Accrued Taxes Payable...................... | | 376.75 |
| To record accrued taxes. | | |
| Labor......................................... | 487.66 | |
| Accrued Pay Roll........................... | | 487.66 |
| To record accrued pay roll. | | |
| Miscellaneous Factory Supplies Consumed......... | 200.00 | |
| Miscellaneous Factory Supplies.............. | | 200.00 |
| To record factory supplies on hand at end of period. | | |
| Fuel.......................................... | 2,202.62 | |
| Deferred Fuel.............................. | | 2,202.62 |
| To record fuel on hand at end of period. | | |
| Insurance..................................... | 1,720.18 | |
| Unexpired Insurance........................ | | 1,720.18 |
| To record insurance unexpired at end of period. | | |
| Loss on Bad Debts............................. | 8,068.60 | |
| Reserve for Loss on Bad Debts.............. | | 8,068.60 |
| To provide reserve for loss on bad debts. | | |

(Continued on page 242)

## THE MICHIGAN MFG. CO.
### Trial Balance, December 31, 1938

| | | |
|---|---:|---:|
| Cash on Hand and in Bank | $ 430.15 | |
| Notes Receivable | 7,907.62 | |
| Customers' Accounts Receivable | 20,797.80 | |
| Land | 10,000.00 | |
| Buildings | 25,333.83 | |
| Machinery and Equipment | 13,800.42 | |
| Auto Truck | 1,790.40 | |
| Inventory of Manufacturing Materials— Beginning of Period | 27,214.41 | |
| Material Purchases | 106,634.12 | |
| Miscellaneous Factory Supplies | 1,631.09 | |
| Productive Labor | 63,842.23 | |
| Freight, Express and Cartage "In" | 1,734.70 | |
| Delivery Expense | 1,694.11 | |
| Miscellaneous Nonproductive Labor | 1,993.50 | |
| Fuel | 5,554.82 | |
| Insurance | 3,872.32 | |
| Repairs to Machinery | 507.73 | |
| Taxes | 140.53 | |
| Advertising | 378.58 | |
| Discount Allowed to Customers | 3,362.19 | |
| Loss on Auto Truck | 475.00 | |
| Postage | 264.42 | |
| Salaries | 6,170.00 | |
| Stationery and Office Supplies | 296.02 | |
| Miscellaneous Main Office Expense | 241.08 | |
| Interest Cost | 3,386.80 | |
| Power Machinery Co. | | $ 727.77 |
| Notes Payable | | 22,344.81 |
| Accounts Payable | | 9,511.89 |
| Reserve for Bad Debts | | 1,059.51 |
| Capital Stock | | 85,000.00 |
| Sales | | 187,540.38 |
| Discounts Earned on Purchases | | 2,081.59 |
| Interest Earned | | 463.17 |
| Miscellaneous Earnings | | 724.75 |
| | $309,453.87 | $309,453.87 |

Inventory of Manufacturing Materials at close of year, $51,358.58; Factory Supplies on Hand, $200.00; Fuel, $2,202.62; Unexpired Insurance, $1,720.18; Accrued Interest on Notes Payable, $134.83; Accrued Taxes, $376.75; Accrued Pay Roll, $487.66; Add to Reserve for Loss on Bad Debts an amount sufficient to provide for Accounts Receivable doubtful of collection, $9,128.11; Depreciation of Machinery and Equipment, 10%; Depreciation of Buildings, 5%. Insurance, taxes, and the depreciation of buildings are to be distributed on a basis of ¼ to general operating and ¾ to manufacturing cost.

Res. for Depr. of Machinery and Equipment....... $ 1,234.49
Res. for Depr. of Buildings........................ 1,266.69
  Depreciation................................                   $ 2,501.18
        To set up reserve for depreciation at the
  rate of 10% on machinery and 5% on buildings.

These adjusting entries had not been recorded on the books of the company and you are limited in your engagement to the preparation of a balance sheet, profit and loss statement, and manufacturing statement from the information given. Audit the adjusting journal entries prepared by the bookkeeper. If the bookkeeper has erred in preparing any of these entries, draft and post the proper adjusting entries, and prepare a balance sheet and profit and loss statement.

## AUDITING PRACTICE

### An Audit Case (Seventh Installment)

The last group of asset accounts to be verified by Ken B. Swift are the accounts with deferred charges which include prepaid insurance, office supplies, and bond discount and expense. The following information should be considered in auditing these items:

#### Prepaid Insurance

The information contained in the insurance policy register indicates that the policies listed below were in effect during the year. Mr. Swift examined the insurance policies now in operation and found them to be in agreement with the information shown in the register. No mortgage clauses were attached to the policies.

| Policy* | Coverage | | Period Covered | | Premium Paid |
|---------|----------|--------|--------|--------|---------|
|  | Amount | Property | From | To |  |
| 1 | $10,000.00 | Furniture and Fixtures......... | 10–15–36 | 10–15–39 | $ 60.00 |
| 2 | 60,000.00 | Building..................... | 4– 1–37 | 4– 1–40 | 360.00 |
| 3 | 80,000.00 | Building..................... | 4– 1–37 | 4– 1–40 | 480.00 |
| 4 | 40,000.00 | Merchandise................. | 7– 1–37 | 7– 1–38 | 160.00 |
| 5 | 40,000.00 | Merchandise................. | 7– 1–38 | 7– 1–39 | 160.00 |
| 6 | ............ | Automobiles................. | 1– 1–38 | 1– 1–39 | 210.00 |
| 7 | ............ | Workmen's Compensation...... | 1– 1–38 | 1– 1–39 | 66.60 |

*Names of the insurance companies and the policy numbers are purposely omitted in this schedule.

Insurance premiums paid for workmen's compensation insurance are based on the amount of wages paid, with rates varying from $0.08 per $100.00 for office workers to $1.84 per $100.00 for deliverymen.

The entries recorded in the prepaid insurance account during the year were as follows:

### Prepaid Insurance

| Date | Items | Debit | Credit | Balance |
|------|-------|-------|--------|---------|
| 1- 1-38 | Balance.............................. | $745.83 | .......... | $ 745.83 |
| 1-10-38 | Automobile Insurance.................. | 210.00 | .......... | 955.83 |
| 1-18-38 | Workmen's Compensation.............. | 66.60 | .......... | 1,022.43 |
| 7- 8-38 | Merchandise Policy................... | 160.00 | .......... | 1,182.43 |
| 12-31-38 | Total of monthly credits............. | .......... | $535.00 | 647.43 |

The total of monthly credits represents the total expense resulting from insurance expired during the year. A comparison should be made of the amount of insurance carried with the approximate value of the property insured to see that the concern is carrying an adequate amount of insurance.

### Store and Office Supplies

The account with store and office supplies appeared as follows at December 31, 1938:

### Store and Office Supplies

| Date | Items | Debit | Credit | Balance |
|------|-------|-------|--------|---------|
| 1- 1-38 | Balance.............................. | $224.50 | .......... | $224.50 |
| 4-20-38 | Invoice............................. | 80.50 | .......... | 305.00 |
| 8- 6-38 | Invoice............................. | 134.00 | .......... | 439.00 |
| 12-31-38 | Supplies used—1938 ................. | .......... | $193.00 | 246.00 |

The store and office supplies inventory, prepared by company employees as of the close of business December 31, 1938, contained inventory items totaling $246. Mr. Swift tested the prices and computations of the larger items and found them to be correct except for minor differences too small to be adjusted.

### Bond Discount and Expense

The information concerning bond discount and expense is presented in the ninth installment which is devoted to an audit of the fixed liabilities.

**INSTRUCTIONS**

1. Read and study the auditing procedure suggested for the verification of deferred charges in an "Examination of Financial Statements."

2. Prepare schedules for prepaid insurance and store and office supplies similar to those shown in the illustrative set of audit working papers.

3. Perform the audit work suggested for verifying deferred charges.

4. Prepare the required journal entries to adjust the account balances.

# CHAPTER TEN

## CURRENT LIABILITIES

Current liabilities may consist of notes payable, accounts payable, dividends payable, and accruals. Notes and accounts payable may represent obligations to trade creditors, banks, or others. Dividends payable represent an obligation to stockholders arising from the distribution of profits. It is customary to record payables separately according to type or origin. The different types of payables should be listed as separate items on the balance sheet. The payable accounts usually include all of the current liabilities. The current liabilities are usually recognized as those obligations that mature within a comparatively short period of time—at least in the succeeding fiscal period. Those obligations, the maturity of which extends beyond the succeeding period, are generally looked upon as fixed liabilities. The current liabilities may be divided into secured and unsecured liabilities. In making a balance sheet audit for credit purposes, an accountant is more concerned with the current liabilities than with the fixed liabilities. Banks do not extend credit to merchandising or trading concerns with a view to furnishing additional capital, but rather to enable them to carry a large stock-in-trade during a busy season or to enable them to discount their accounts payable at a time when the company's quick assets are composed largely of inventories and receivable accounts. Banks usually advance money on short time or demand loans, hence the current assets of the borrowing company should be such that sufficient funds may be realized to liquidate maturing liabilities within the credit period.

## NOTES PAYABLE

Notes, time drafts, and acceptances payable are usually listed as one item, although in some cases it will be found that they are recorded in separate accounts. Notes and time drafts are usually interest bearing obligations, while acceptances are usually non-interest bearing obligations. A note frequently is given in settlement of an account payable, for the purpose of delaying cash disbursements beyond the period covered under the original terms of the credit sale. Acceptances on the other hand are the result of business transactions, and are more acceptable to the seller as they may be discounted readily, thereby enabling him to obtain cash from his transactions instead of waiting thirty to sixty days for the payment of the open account payable.

In auditing notes and acceptances payable, the auditor should be furnished with a schedule of notes, showing the maker, amount due, date of maturity, and interest accrued. This schedule should be drawn from the records and should be ready for verification. The auditor should check this list against the note records. The usual practice in companies where notes and acceptances payable are issued to any extent, is to maintain a notes payable register. These records will be compared by the auditor, who usually will prepare a schedule showing the dates of the instruments, the dates due, to whom payable, where payable, the interest accrued to the date of the audit, and any other information which may be pertinent to the engagement at hand. If the paper is endorsed, collateral deposited to secure payment, or the notes renewed, such information should be stated. The total of all notes shown by the schedules should agree with the notes payable account in the general ledger.

Notes payable to banks should be verified by correspondence with the payees. Trade loans made to purchase merchandise or equipment may be traced through the purchase records as to merchandise or property received in exchange. Loans from officers or employees should be examined and verified. Where notes have been given to banks and company officials, the authorization of the board of directors or finance committee should be obtained from the minutes.

. Notes which have been paid should be examined. The canceled notes are the best vouchers for such disbursements. Where securities have been deposited as collateral to secure notes payable, the depository should confirm their existence in writing.

## AUDITING PROCEDURE APPLICABLE TO NOTES PAYABLE

### In an "Examination of Financial Statements"

"1. Obtain or prepare a schedule showing the dates and amounts of notes payable, interest rates, due dates, names of payees, collateral, endorsers, and interest accrued to the date of the balance sheet.

"2. See that the schedule agrees with the notes payable book and with the balance of the notes payable account in the ledger.

"3. Confirm notes payable by obtaining from all banks in which the company maintains balances and from all note brokers with whom the company transacts business, statements of notes and drafts discounted or sold and not paid prior to the date of the balance sheet and details of collateral held, endorsements, etc. Check the schedule with these statements. Confirm other notes payable recorded on the books, if important in amount.

"4. See that there is an adequate control of notes payable and ascertain, preferably by examination of the canceled notes, that notes paid during the period have been properly discharged. An analysis of the interest account may provide additional information regarding interest-bearing liabilities.

"5. Hypothecation of any of the company's current assets or investments as collateral for notes payable or other liability should be noted on the balance sheet.

"6. Notes payable to affiliated companies and to stockholders, directors, officers, and employees should be shown separately on the balance sheet."

## ACCOUNTS PAYABLE

**Accounts with Trade Creditors.** The caption, "accounts payable," usually includes all merchandise accounts due within one year. The client's staff should prepare for the auditor a detailed list of the amounts due to creditors. The auditor should compare the amounts in the list with the balances in the ledger accounts, and reconcile the total of the individual accounts with the balance of the general ledger control account. The list of accounts should be footed by the auditor to determine that the footings are correct. If the list includes balances due to officers, employees, or affiliated companies, such balances should be segregated and shown separately in the balance sheet. Any omission of book items from the list of balances, or vice versa, should be carefully scrutinized and the book and list balances checked for any apparent errors. When checking the list balances with the ledger balances, the auditor should scrutinize the dates of the items, to determine that they are recent and specific transactions. Payables outstanding for any length of time after the regular terms of payment for such transactions have expired should be investigated, and items in dispute should be examined.

Where records are properly maintained, and purchase and voucher records are available for inspection, the verification of accounts payable is usually readily made. The auditor should assure himself that the proper routines are adequately performed, and that the necessary internal checks are available and in operation. He should check the receiving records for the past few days of the period under audit with the voucher and inventory records, in order to insure that the goods received at the end of the period are properly accounted for. If such goods were received and included in the inventory, but not included in the payables, profits for the period will be overstated, and payables on the balance sheet will be understated. The auditor should also check the entries for the first few weeks of the succeeding period to determine whether the entries for purchases and payables are the result of the receipt of goods during the past or present period.

Where a voucher system is not in use, and methods of accounting are not adequate, the verification of accounts payable may be more difficult. Frequently unpaid invoices are not recorded until payment is made. These unpaid invoices should be obtained and examined along with cash disbursements, immediately after the close of the period. If the ordinary credit terms are usually thirty days, vouchers paid for that period immediately after the fiscal closing should be analyzed to determine which were applicable to the different financial periods.

**Accounts with Officers and Employees.** Where accounts payable are due to officers, employees, or affiliated companies it is usually considered better practice to state such items in the financial statements separately. The auditor should determine their source and verify the amounts. Where they are the result of bonus or extra-payment agreements, these agreements should be examined and the mathematical calculations should be verified. Payables due officers or affiliated companies may often be included in accounts payable when they are mere advances to the corporation concerned. As these items are not the result of purchase transactions, separate captions may more properly be used for balance sheet purposes.

Some auditors, in verifying accounts payable, advocate circularizing the creditors, asking them to verify the balances as shown by the books. This practice is hardly feasible in most cases. Clients resent such procedure, and it is not necessary in most engagements. Where the auditor is engaged on an audit the first few days of a fiscal period, he may find it advisable to compare the monthly statements with the book balances, as a check on accuracy of the routines of the office and the values stated on the books.

**Dividends Payable.** When dividends are declared by the directors, they become a current liability until such time as they are paid. In recording the declaration of dividends it is customary to debit surplus and credit dividends payable. It should be remembered, however, that dividends are not payable until declared by the board of directors. Sometimes no entry is made until the dividends are paid and then they are charged to dividends paid and credited to cash. When this is done the dividends paid account must be closed into surplus or undivided profits at end of year.

The dividends on many preferred stock issues are cumulative. Such securities are entitled to a stated rate of return prior to the payment of dividends on the junior stock, and if not paid at any given period, the portion unpaid must be declared and paid before any declaration of dividends may be paid to the holders of the junior stock. Dividends do not accrue as does interest, hence they are not liabilities until declared. They do represent, however, rights against the surplus of the corporation and it is customary to show the amount of cumulative dividends in arrears in a footnote to the balance sheet.

**Merchandise Received on Consignment.** Where merchandise is received on consignment, the auditor should examine all contracts and records, and determine what liability, if any, exists in connection therewith. Where merchandise received on consignment has been sold, the liability should be shown in the balance sheet.

**Contracts for Future Delivery.** In some lines of industry, business enterprises make commitments on contracts for merchandise purchases covering a comparatively long period of time. Where this condition is existent, the auditor should examine the contracts, and if any liability exists it should be stated. In times of fluctuating prices, such a contract may be highly advantageous or dangerous, depending on the trend of prices. In some cases, such contracts are based on sales contracts so that any change in one item is offset by the other.

**Goods in Transit.** Goods in transit should be verified by the auditor. Where goods are purchased f. o. b. destination, the title belonging to the vendor, no liability exists on the part of the purchaser until the goods are received. On the other hand, if merchandise is purchased f. o. b. point of origin, the railroad or other common carrier is the agent of the purchaser, and title passes to the purchaser upon delivery of the goods to the common carrier. Such being the case, provision should be made for the liability involved.

## AUDITING PROCEDURE APPLICABLE TO ACCOUNTS PAYABLE

### In an "Examination of Financial Statements"

"1. Obtain a list of the recorded accounts payable and make appropriate check with the ledger accounts or with open items in the voucher register, according to the system in use. Reconcile the total with the controlling account in the general ledger. Investigate any large balances which do not represent specific or recent items. Obtain confirmation from the creditor if any account appears to be irregular. If there are accounts in dispute, large enough to affect substantially the total of current liabilities, investigate the causes of dispute.

"2. The following procedures are helpful in determining that all liabilities are included in the accounts:

"(a) Review vouchers entered in the voucher register and/ or payments shown by the cash book subsequent to the date of the balance sheet to ascertain whether any of them are applicable to the period under review.

"(b) Examine bills on file not vouchered or entered to ascertain if any of them belong to the period under review.

"(c) Make a test examination of the monthly statements received from creditors having large balances.

"(d) Examine receiving records for the last day of the period for the purpose of ascertaining that the corresponding liabilities are included.

"3. Inquire if any goods have been received on consignment, and if so examine the pertinent records and ascertain that liability has been set up for all such goods sold.

"4. As an additional precaution against the omission of liabilities obtain in writing from a responsible official of the company (1) a statement that all outstanding liabilities for purchases and expenses have been included in the accounts and (2) a summary of any liabilites for legal claims, infringements of patents, claims for damages, etc. not included in the accounts. It is advisable to obtain the signature of the president or other senior officer to this statement as only a senior officer of the company may know the extent of such obligations.

"5. Liabilities to affiliated companies and advances by stockholders, directors, officers, and employees if material in amount should be shown separately on the balance sheet."

### ACCRUALS PAYABLE

There are any number of expenses in connection with a going business which become liabilities as of the date of the balance sheet, but are not payable until the following period. Such items are expenses of one period payable in the succeeding month, quarter, or year. They arise usually due to the difference between date of payment and the date of their being incurred as expenses. They may be definite liabilities, or liabilities the amounts of which are still undetermined. The leading types of accounts involved may be summarized as follows:

(a) Salaries and wages

(b) Interest

(c) Commissions

(d) Royalties

(e) Taxes

The staff of the client should prepare schedules of all accruals and should enter such items in the books and records prior to closing the books. The auditor's duty then becomes one of verifying the accruals.

**Salaries and Wages.** Salaries and wages accrued may be found in any balance sheet unless the date of the statement happens to coincide with the time of meeting the pay roll. The latter case is the exception, not the rule. Salaries are usually paid every two weeks, or every month. In case the date of the balance sheet falls between that of pay roll dates, wages and salaries accrued will be existent. The auditor may check the amount shown with that shown on former reports and with the pay roll data. In many large organizations, pay rolls are made out by groups of employees, each group being paid on different days, thus allowing the clerical work of the pay roll division to be spread over the period. The records of the pay roll division, by classes of employees, may be checked against the schedule of such items as prepared by the staff, and will usually provide an adequate verification of such records.

**Interest.** Interest accrued can usually be verified through a comparison of the schedule presented as against the schedules of notes, mortgages, and bonds payable which the auditor prepares in verifying the principal amounts concerned. In his working trial balance for such liabilities, he usually provides a column for accrued interest, and this total should compare with the total stated in the schedule presented by the client's staff. If this procedure has not been adopted, the auditor should check the accruals presented against the interest bearing securities outstanding, providing a check against the principal amounts outstanding, as well as against the accruals.

**Commissions.** In many organizations commissions to salesmen are withheld until receipts for sales have been received, or for a certain period after the sale. In other cases a part of the commission may be paid and the remainder accrued for a period. Accrued commissions may best be checked against the sales records of the salesmen concerned, and the procedure in handling commissions should be determined either from the proper sales officials or from the contracts between the company and the salesmen. In some cases, especially in the wholesale grocery line, commissions may vary on different lines of goods. In such cases the computation of the accruals will require detailed checking and verification.

**Royalties.** Royalties may be accrued on the basis of production or of sales. Contracts permitting the use of machines or patents should be examined to determine the terms of the licenses and the clerical accuracy of the royalties should be verified.

**Taxes.** Accrued taxes payable should, of course, be shown on the balance sheet as a current liability. This applies to taxes assessed against either real or personal property, but unpaid at the date as of which a balance sheet is being prepared. Thus, if a balance sheet is prepared as of December 31, one-half of the real property tax having been paid on December 20, the other half represents an accrued liability which should appear on the balance sheet. State and local laws vary widely in their provisions as to the assessment and collection of property taxes and the auditor must familiarize himself with such laws before he can hope to account for such taxes properly.

Federal and state income taxes applicable to the period governed by the auditor's report should be shown as a liability, if unpaid at the close of the period. Usually income taxes are payable sometime after the close of the taxable period. Before the balance sheet and profit and loss statement can be prepared and certified it is necessary to compute the income tax liability. The provisions of the Federal and state laws will govern the computation of such taxes. The usual method of recording the income tax liability is to debit income taxes and credit income taxes payable. Sometimes the taxes are estimated and shown on the balance sheet as a reserve in which case the amount of the reserve should be verified and the auditor should satisfy himself that the amount is adequate.

Pay roll taxes imposed under the Federal Social Security Act, the Carriers' Taxing Act, the Railroad Unemployment Insurance Act, and under the State Unemployment Compensation Acts, should be treated as a liability if accrued but unpaid at the close of the period under audit. The employer is liable for any taxes which he is required to withhold from the wages paid to his employees and any amounts which have been withheld, but which have not been paid to the proper governmental agency at the date of the balance sheet must be listed thereon as a liability. The additional taxes imposed on the employer but unpaid at the date of the balance sheet must also be shown as a liability. The auditor should know that in some cases the pay roll taxes are based on wages actually or constructively paid with respect to employment during the calendar year, while in other cases the taxes are based on wages payable with respect to employment during the calendar year regardless of the time of actual payment. In other words, some of the pay roll taxes are imposed on wages *paid* while other pay roll taxes are imposed on a basis of wages *payable.* In any case the employer's liability on account of any pay roll taxes imposed on him, whether or not withheld from the employees wages, constitute a liability if not paid at the date of the balance sheet.

Other taxes may constitute a liability and it is the duty of the auditor to make sure that the balance sheet reflects the client's liability for all taxes payable to the Federal, state, or local governments. The increasing tax burden in recent years has made this a very important item and it is not sufficient for the auditor to satisfy himself as to the client's liability for property, income, and pay roll taxes. He must also check to determine the client's liability for capital stock taxes, excess-profits taxes, franchise taxes, sales taxes, and numerous excise taxes imposed under Federal and state laws.

Where other types of accrued expenses are encountered the auditor should familiarize himself with the methods of calculation, dates of payment and other relevant facts, and check the accruals shown against such information available.

**Liability Certificate.** In all audits of liabilities, the auditor should obtain a certificate from the responsible officials stating that all known liabilities are included in the books, and that there are no legal claims, lawsuits involving additional liability, or damage claims existent. Where such claims are existent they should be investigated. If the auditor is unable to determine the probable liability, or if the attorneys of the company believe no liability exists as the result of such items, conservative practice demands that the possible contingent liability be mentioned either in a footnote to the balance sheet, or in the auditor's certificate.

## AUDITING PROCEDURE APPLICABLE TO ACCRUED LIABILITIES

### In an "Examination of Financial Statements"

"1. Interest, taxes, wages, etc., which have accrued to the end of the period under review but are not due and payable until a later date, are grouped on the balance sheet under 'accrued liabilities.' Special attention is directed to the following liabilities:

"2. *Interest Payable.* Make inquiries to ascertain whether provision has been made for interest due or accrued. See that interest on bonds and notes payable has been provided for and give consideration to the possibility that interest may be payable on past-due book accounts, on loan accounts of officers or directors and on judgments, overdue taxes and other liens.

"3. *Taxes*. Ascertain the amount of accrued Federal, state and local taxes including any liability for taxes withheld. In the case of some local taxes it may be necessary to inquire of the taxing authority as to the period for which taxes accrue. Determine the present situation relative to Federal income taxes for the current and prior years, i. e., what years have been examined, and what years have been finally closed. If there are in dispute any items of material importance on which a difference of opinion exists, adequate provision should be made or the situation should be disclosed in a footnote to the balance sheet, failing which reference should be made in the accountant's report.

"4. *Salaries and Wages*. If the date of the balance sheet does not coincide with the date to which the last pay roll of the period under review has been computed, ascertain the amount accrued to the date of the balance sheet. Inquiries should also be made as to any profit-sharing or bonus plans.

"5. *Traveling Expenses and Commissions*. See that provision has been made for unreported expenses of traveling salesmen and for accrued commissions.

"6. *Legal Expenses*. Provision should be made for any accrued liability for legal expenses.

"7. *Damages*. Inquire if there are any claims or suits for damages not covered by insurance; if any evidence is found indicating such liability, obtain information on which to base an opinion as to the amount that should be set up as an accrued liability or as a reserve against probable loss."

### Modifications of Audit Program for Larger or Smaller Concerns

"In endeavoring to see that all liabilities are reflected in the balance sheet, the accountant should not go to the extreme of providing meticulously for every minor item that he happens to discover. There will always be overlapping items between years, which have no important bearing on the accounts. His function is to see that liabilities ascertainable by a reasonable examination are included in the balance sheet."

## CONTINGENT LIABILITIES

In addition to the liabilities which are shown on the books of account, there may be contingent liabilities. Contingent liabilities arise from the endorsement of notes, guarantees of merchandise or services, damages, assessment of additional Federal income taxes, etc. It is the duty of an auditor to discover and report upon liabilities of every description whether recorded upon the books or not and whether they represent actual or contingent obligations. Contingent liabilities should appear as footnotes on the liability side of the balance sheet.

Contingent liabilities may at times bear considerable significance to the financial condition of a business, and the omission of such information from the balance sheet may so distort the financial condition of the company as to present an exceedingly erroneous statement.

There appears to be a tendency on the part of business men to overemphasize the importance of the properties owned, and to minimize the importance of liabilities which are not due for some time to come, or which may never come due, if business conditions continue favorable. This tendency is found to result frequently in failure to record important transactions, which, though they may never affect the financial condition of the company concerned, may on the other hand seriously impair the solvency of the enterprise in times of stress.

One of the more important duties of the auditor consists in determining whether such items really do exist, and in case they do, to what extent the enterprise concerned may be involved. As such items are usually not entered in the records, their existence must oftentimes be determined from outside sources, from records which may lend a clue to their existence, or from statements of the client or his employees.

### AUDITING PROCEDURE APPLICABLE TO CONTINGENT LIABILITIES

#### In an "Examination of Financial Statements"

"1. Make inquiries relative to the existence of contingent liabilities. Such liabilities will usually be of the following nature:

"2. *Notes Receivable Discounted.* (See procedure suggested under notes receivable.)

"3. *Endorsements and Guaranties*. Ascertain from responsible officers of the company whether any endorsement of unrelated paper or any guaranties have been made and if so what security has been received to protect the company. This inquiry is especially necessary if it is known that any of the officers are interested in other enterprises.

"4. *Judgments*. Any liability for judgments not appearing on the records of the company may be discovered by searching the public records; but this is within the province of lawyers, not of accountants. Many business men will not permit entry in their books of a judgment from which they intend to appeal, and it becomes difficult for the accountant to find any evidence of such a liability except by inquiry of responsible officials. Make such inquiries. If any liability exists, though not finally determined, appropriate mention of the facts should be made in a footnote to the balance sheet.

"5. *Unfulfilled Contracts*. Where the nature of the business requires large purchase orders for future delivery ask for copies of such purchase orders. If the contract prices are higher than market prices and the purchase contracts are not protected or only partly protected by firm sales orders, it may be necessary to set up a reserve for possible loss.

"6. *Damages*. There may be claims or suits for damages not covered by insurance or by reserves provided therefor. If evidence is found indicating a liability of this nature, request full information so as to be able to form an opinion as to the amount which should be stated as a contingent liability.

"7. *Liability for Real Estate Bonds and Mortgages*. Investigate the possibility that any liability may result from the sale by the company of property subject to mortgage. If property subject to a mortgage has been sold there may be a contingent liability under the bond unless the mortgage has been satisfied, the satisfaction recorded and the bond canceled.

"8. Notation should be made on the balance sheet relative to contingent liabilities where the amounts involved are or may become material. In case of claims, litigation, and other matters involving a legal determination it may be advisable for the accountant to obtain information, preferably in writing, from the company's legal advisors as to the probable extent of the liability."

### Modifications of Audit Program for Larger or Smaller Concerns

"Contingent liabilities are apt to be numerous in large companies. In the ordinary course of business there is frequently a large number of outstanding claims or suits for damages and commitments of various kinds. It is often very difficult, if not impossible, to determine the amount in money that may be involved, since the nominal amount of a suit is no measure of the maximum amount that may have to be paid. It is generally recognized that such conditions exist and it is only necessary to refer to major or unusual situations. In case of claims, litigation, and other matters involving a legal determination it may be advisable for the accountant to obtain information, preferably in writing, from the company's legal advisors as to the probable extent of the liability."

## APPLICATION OF PRINCIPLES
### AUDIT OF THE BLANK MANUFACTURING COMPANY (Continued)

**Notes Payable.** In continuing the audit of The Blank Manufacturing Company, J. I. King, one of the junior accountants in the employ of Stevenson and Bennett, was assigned to audit the current liabilities. He prepared a schedule of the notes payable (see Illustration No. 25), and computed the interest accrued to December 31, 1937.

As the notes were all for amounts in excess of one thousand dollars, it was decided to confirm them by correspondence with the creditors. No differences were noted.

**Accounts Payable.** The accounts payable, as shown by the balance of the general ledger controlling account, amounted to $39,462 at December 31, 1937. Mr. King checked the items on the bookkeeper's schedule of accounts payable with balances in the respective subsidiary ledger accounts. No differences were discovered. The total of the accounts payable in the subsidiary ledger agreed with the general ledger balance.

Included in the list of accounts payable were amounts totaling $7,681.50 representing unclaimed salaries owed to officers of the company. The officers were permitted to draw salary funds as needed and as a result there were times when their accounts were either overdrawn, or there were amounts still owed to them. (See Illustration No. 26.)

(*Continued on page 262*)

## THE BLANK MANUFACTURING COMPANY

### Notes Payable

### December 31, 1937

| Payee | Date of Note | Maturity Date | Amount | Interest Rate | Accrued Interest | Collateral Pledged | Remarks |
|---|---|---|---|---|---|---|---|
| Apex Manufacturing Co. | 12– 4–37 | 3– 4–38 | 1,500.00 | 6% | 6.75 | none | confirmed |
| Cyrus & Parks, Inc. | 12–20–37 | 2–20–37 | 2,535.00 | 6% | 4.65 | none | confirmed |
| Johnson Supply Co. | 11–15–37 | 2–15–38 | 15,100.00 | 6% | 115.78 | none | confirmed |
| Mason George & Co. | 10–25–37 | 1–25–38 | 1,865.00 | 6% | 20.84 | none | confirmed |
| Total | | | 21,000.00 | | 148.02 | | |

*The above list of notes comprises the notes payable of The Blank Manufacturing Company at December 31, 1937, as shown by the notes payable register. The total of $21,000 agrees with the balance shown by the notes payable account in the general ledger. All of the notes were confirmed by correspondence with the holders of the notes.*

*(Schedule No. 12)*

J. I. King
(Junior Accountant)

**Illustration No. 25. Analysis of Notes Payable**

## THE BLANK MANUFACTURING COMPANY

### Accounts Payable—December 31, 1937

Balance per general ledger account...................... $39,462.00

Less amounts due to officers of the company, to be shown
 separately.......................................... 7,681.50

Amount due to trade creditors........................... $31,780.50

    The adding machine tape prepared by the company's bookkeeper was checked with the individual ledger accounts. The tape was footed and the total agreed with the general ledger controlling account.

    The unpaid invoice file and the disbursement record for the first three weeks of January were checked for unrecorded liabilities as of December 31, 1937. None were found.

*(Schedule No. 13)*

*J. I. King*
*(Junior Accountant)*

**Illustration No. 26.  Analysis of Accounts Payable**

## THE BLANK MANUFACTURING COMPANY

### Accrued Pay Roll—December 31, 1937

The accrued pay roll at December 31, 1937, consisted of the following:

Factory wages, five days' wages as per pay roll......... $ 4,980.20
Salaries of salesmen, five days' wages as per pay roll... 585.00
Delivery salaries, five days' wages as per pay roll...... 120.00
Office salaries, five days' wages as per pay roll........ 626.00

    Total accrued pay roll........................... $ 6,311.20

    Employees are paid each Thursday for the work performed during the preceding week. Five days' wages were accrued at December 31, 1937. The above figures were taken from the pay roll for the last week of December. This pay roll, together with three other pay rolls taken at random, were footed, the pay roll summaries checked, and the amounts traced into the ledger accounts. The names of the employees appearing on the last pay roll for December were checked with the employees' personnel records. Time clock cards were also checked with this pay roll as to names and time recorded. No differences were noted.

*J. I. King*                              *(Schedule No. 14)*
*(Junior Accountant)*

**Illustration No. 27.  Analysis of Accrued Wages Payable**

**Taxes Payable.** An investigation of the company's tax liability revealed that all property taxes assessed for the year 1937 have been paid. The capital stock tax assessed as of June 30 was paid in full on July 31. Examination of the duplicate copy of the return revealed that a declared value of $650,000 was placed on the stock. The liability for the capital stock tax due July 31, 1938, must be set up before preparing a balance sheet as of December 31, 1937, for the liability is incurred when the company has operated for any part of the year ending June 30, 1938. The company's liability for pay roll taxes imposed under the Social Security Act and under the State Unemployment Compensation Acts has also been recorded correctly. See Illustration No. 28 for detailed verification of the liabilities incurred on account of pay roll taxes. The computation of pay roll taxes imposed for the purposes of old-age benefits is based on the assumption that the accrued wages payable on December 31, 1936, were the same as on December 31, 1937. Otherwise it would be necessary to distinguish between the amount of wages actually or constructively paid during the year and the amount of wages payable for services rendered during the year. Also see Illustration No. 30 for the adjusting entries required to record the pay roll taxes on wages accrued December 31, 1937. The taxes imposed under Title VIII of the Social Security Act are not applicable to accrued wages payable but are imposed only on wages actually or constructively paid during the taxable year. The company's liability for Federal income taxes cannot be determined until the audit is completed and the company's net profit for the period is determined.

**Unrecorded Liabilities.** Mr. King examined the bills and vouchers in the unpaid invoice file to ascertain that there were no amounts representing liabilities at December 31, 1937, which had not been entered in the accounts at that date. He also scrutinized the entries in the January, 1938, cash disbursements record for liabilities existing at December 31, 1937, which were entered in the books in January, 1938. No liabilities were found applicable to December 31, 1937, which had not already been entered as of that date.

**Pay Rolls.** An examination was made of four of the company's weekly pay rolls taken at random throughout the year.

(Continued on page 265)

## THE BLANK MANUFACTURING COMPANY
### Analysis of Pay Roll Taxes for Year Ending December 31, 1937

| UNEMPLOYMENT COMPENSATION CONTRIBUTIONS | TAX. WAGES | TAX RATE | AMOUNT | REMARKS |
|---|---|---|---|---|
| Factory Pay Roll | 305,180.20 | 2% | 6,103.60 | |
| Delivery Salaries | 8,720.00 | 2% | 174.40 | |
| Salaries of Salesmen | 30,835.00 | 2% | 616.70 | |
| Office Salaries | 38,186.00 | 2% | 763.72 | |
| Total | 382,921.20 | | 7,658.42 | |
| Distribution: | | | | |
| State Contributions Paid at 1.8% | 5,169.57 | | | |
| Amount Due States for Quarter Ended Dec. 31, @ 1.8% | 1,723.01 | | | |
| Total | 6,892.58 | | | |
| Amount Due Fed. Gov't for Year Ended Dec. 31, @ .2% | 765.84 | | | |
| Total Unemployment Compensation Contribution | 7,658.42 | | | |

| OLD-AGE BENEFITS | TAXABLE WAGES | EMPLOYER | | EMPLOYEES | |
|---|---|---|---|---|---|
| | | TAX RATE | AMOUNT | TAX RATE | AMOUNT |
| Factory Pay Roll | 305,180.20 | 1% | 3,051.80 | 1% | 3,051.80 |
| Delivery Salaries | 8,720.00 | 1% | 87.20 | 1% | 87.20 |
| Salaries of Salesmen | 30,835.00 | 1% | 308.35 | 1% | 308.35 |
| Office Salaries | 38,186.00 | 1% | 381.86 | 1% | 381.86 |
| Total | 382,921.20 | | 3,829.21 | | 3,829.21 |
| Distribution: | | | | | |
| Excise Tax on Employer @ 1% | | 3,829.21 | | | |
| Income Tax on Employees (1% deducted from wages) | | 3,829.21 | | | |
| Employer's Total Liability | | 7,658.42 | | | |
| Amount Paid During 1937 | 5,743.96 | | 2,871.98 | | 2,871.98 |
| Amount Due for Quarter Ended December 31, 1937 | 1,914.46 | | 957.23 | | 957.23 |
| Total | 7,658.42 | | 3,829.21 | | 3,829.21 |

J. I. King
(Junior Accountant)

Illustration No. 28.   Analysis of Pay Roll Taxes

(Schedule No. 15)

---

### THE BLANK MANUFACTURING COMPANY
#### Indianapolis, Indiana
#### Liability Certificate

January 20, 1938

Stevenson and Bennett
Certified Public Accountants
9 West Third Street
Cincinnati, Ohio
Gentlemen:

 Relative to your examination of the accounts and statements of The Blank Manufacturing Company, we hereby certify that to the best of our knowledge and belief all liabilities of every character, either direct or contingent, existing at December 31, 1937, were included in the accounts at that date, or were otherwise disclosed to your representatives.

Sincerely yours,
L. W. SHIELDS
General Manager
HAROLD POND
Chief Accountant

LS/DS

---

Illustration No. 29. Liability Certificate

### THE BLANK MANUFACTURING COMPANY
#### Adjusting Journal Entries

| | | |
|---|---:|---:|
| Interest and Discount | $ 148.02 | |
|  Accrued Interest Payable | | $ 148.02 |
|   To record the accrued interest on notes payable as of December 31, 1937. | | |
| Accounts Payable | 7,681.50 | |
|  Accounts Payable—Officers | | 7,681.50 |
|   To reclassify the accounts payable for balance sheet purposes. | | |
| Factory Labor | 4,980.20 | |
| Salaries of Salesmen | 585.00 | |
| Delivery Expense | 120.00 | |
| Office Salaries | 626.00 | |
|  Accrued Wages Payable | | 6,311.20 |
|   To record accrued wages as of December 31, 1937. | | |
| Deferred Capital Stock Tax | 650.00 | |
|  Accrued Capital Stock Tax Payable | | 650.00 |
|   To record the estimated amount of the capital stock tax for the year ending June 30, 1938. | | |
| Federal Social Security Excise Tax (U. C.) | 12.62 | |
| State U. C. Contributions | 113.60 | |
|  Employer's Fed. Excise Tax Pay. (U. C.) | | 12.62 |
|  State U. C. Contributions Payable | | 113.60 |
|   To record pay roll taxes imposed under Title IX of the Social Security Act and under the State Unemployment Compensation Act on wages accrued December 31, 1937. | | |

J. I. King
(Junior Accountant)

Illustration No. 30. Adjusting Entries

The pay rolls were footed, the summaries were checked, and the amounts traced into the ledger accounts. The names on one pay roll were checked with the personnel department's records of employees to ascertain that all names on the pay roll represented individuals actually in the employ of the company. The accrued wages at December 31, 1937, were computed and the proper adjusting entries prepared. An analysis of the accrued pay roll is shown in Illustration No. 27 and the proper adjusting entries to record the accrued wages payable are shown in Illustration No. 30.

**Contingent Liabilities.** The Blank Manufacturing Company had endorsed notes discounted at the Merchants National Bank on which they were contingently liable at December 31, 1937, as follows:

Note signed by Alberts & Blackmar, principal $4,275 interest 6%, dated October 30, 1937, due January 30, 1938.

Note signed by R. O. Elmeier Co., principal $1,485.28, interest 6%, dated November 18, 1937, due February 18, 1938.

Mr. King made a memorandum on his comment sheet as a reminder that a footnote should be made on the balance sheet stating that the company was contingently liable in the amount of $5,760.20 at December 31, 1937, for discounted notes bearing its endorsement.

**Liability Certificate.** Illustration No. 29 shows the liability certificate obtained from The Blank Manufacturing Company. Note that the general manager and chief accountant have certified that in their opinions all liabilities of the company are reflected in the accounts.

## SUMMARY

The current liabilities must be carefully verified to ascertain that all such items are included in the balance sheet and that they represent bona fide indebtedness which must be paid within a year. The methods of verification will of necessity vary depending upon the accounting procedure and extent of internal check. The auditor should be most careful to see that any liability for goods received the last few days of the period is included in the accounts and that any liability for goods in transit in which ownership rests with the client is properly shown. Where goods are handled on consignment, the proper liability for sold portions should be determined and presented. Proper classification is important in the current liability section of the balance sheet to avoid misunderstanding. Amounts due officers, banks, and trade creditors should be presented separately to provide an adequate basis of judgment as to current financial condition. Accruals should be computed and checked against the proper records. A certificate should be obtained from the proper officer or officers certifying that all liabilities are properly stated.

It is the auditor's duty to determine whether there are any contingent liabilities existing which may affect the financial condition of the business. Contingent liabilities arising from endorsements, guarantees, royalties, and patent infringements are quite common and when found to exist should be provided for by either stating the liability in the balance sheet, by providing a reserve for such contingencies, or by mentioning it in a footnote to the balance sheet.

### AUDITING THEORY

**10—107.** What liabilities should be classified as current liabilities?

**10—108.** How should debit balances in creditors' accounts be disposed of?

**10—109.** Should amounts due creditors be verified through correspondence?

**10—110.** Should unpaid expense bills be treated as accrued liabilities at the close of a fiscal period?

**10—111.** What is meant by contingent liabilities? Name two common liabilities of this type.

**10—112.** How would you ascertain whether a balance sheet contains all the liabilities for purchases of supplies and raw material?

(C. P. A. Ind.)

**10—113.** (a) What different methods should be employed in books of account for recording notes endorsed for accommodation and notes endorsed in the regular order of business?

(b) How would you indicate in books of account the contingent liability arising in each case?

(C. P. A. Mich.)

**10—114.** You find that a group of accounts receivable have been assigned to secure a loan. Does that affect the value of any other creditor's claim in case of failure before the loan is paid? Should any reference to the fact be made in your report? How would you set up that fact in the balance sheet?

(C. P. A. Mich.)

**10—115.** What steps should an auditor take to insure, as far as possible, that accounts presented to him for audit contain all the liabilities of the company?

(A. I. A.)

**10—116.** How would you indicate on the balance sheet as of December 31:
(a) Preferred dividend (cumulative) due the previous November 1 not declared.

(b) Ordinary dividend for the year, declared the following January 22.

(c) Ordinary dividend declared December 30, payable February 1?

(A. I. A.)

**10—117.** You ascertain that a client owes a substantial amount on account of subscriptions to local charitable and fraternal organizations. No liability therefor appears on the books. How would you proceed to determine the amount due? How would you reflect such an amount on the balance sheet?

(A. I. A.)

**10—118.** In auditing the books of a corporation you find that certain officials, apparently without any authorization, are indebted heavily to the corporation. How would you proceed in such circumstances?

(A. I. A.)

**10—119.** In auditing the books of the A. B. Company you find an item of $1,000 debited to notes payable account, but no canceled note is produced in support thereof, nor can you find a similar amount previously credited to this account. For good and sufficient reasons you do not desire to question the officers of the company until you have more information regarding the transaction.

(a) How would you proceed to obtain that information?

(b) What may you expect to learn?

(A. I. A.)

## AUDITING PROBLEMS

**10—26.** While auditing the books of the E. F. Corporation you find an item of $5,000 debited to the notes payable account; that it is a part payment on a note for $15,000 signed by the president individually; that the proceeds of the note were used to purchase certain stocks for the corporation; and that the certificates for those stocks are in the name of the president personally. Against the loan of $15,000 were pledged other securities (belonging to the corporation) of the book value of $20,000. The only entry of these transactions on the books of the corporation is the $5,000 mentioned above. You note further that the president alone has access to the safe deposit box containing the corporation's securities.

(a) What is your opinion of the liability of the corporation on this note?

(b) What recommendations would you make?

(A. I. A.)

**10—27.** You are employed by The Central Manufacturing Co. to prepare and certify its balance sheet as of December 31, 1938. You are furnished with a balance sheet prepared by the bookkeeper at the end of the preceding fiscal period and a trial balance for December 31, 1938.

### THE CENTRAL MANUFACTURING CO.

#### Balance Sheet, December 31, 1937

##### Assets

| | | |
|---|---:|---:|
| Cash....................................... | $ 300.00 | |
| Accounts Receivable......................... | 1,570.00 | $ 1,870.00 |
| | | |
| Inventories: | | |
| Finished Goods........................... | $15,450.00 | |
| Goods in Process......................... | 835.00 | |
| Raw Material............................ | 5,500.00 | 21,785.00 |
| | | |
| Deferred Insurance.......................... | | 110.00 |
| Land....................................... | $ 4,000.00 | |
| Buildings.................................. | 9,400.00 | |
| Machinery and Fixtures..................... | 8,100.00 | 21,500.00 |
| | | |
| Deficit..................................... | | 5,285.00 |
| | | |
| Total Assets................................ | | $50,550.00 |

##### Liabilities

| | | |
|---|---:|---:|
| Notes Payable.............................. | $27,500.00 | |
| Accounts Payable........................... | 1,550.00 | |
| Reserve for Depr. of Buildings............... | 1,400.00 | |
| Reserve for Depr. of Machinery and Fixtures... | 2,100.00 | $32,550.00 |
| | | |
| Capital Stock: | | |
| Preferred................................ | $10,000.00 | |
| Common................................. | 8,000.00 | 18,000.00 |
| | | |
| Total Liabilities and Capital................. | | $50,550.00 |

In the course of a balance sheet audit you ascertain the following additional information:

(a) The company was incorporated January 2, 1932.

(b) Notes payable were renewed as they became due, except that notes amounting to $10,000 were donated to the company July 1, 1938.

### THE CENTRAL MANUFACTURING CO.

### Trial Balance, December 31, 1938

| | | |
|---|---:|---:|
| Capital Stock, Preferred..................... | | $10,000.00 |
| Capital Stock, Common...................... | | 8,000.00 |
| Cash....................................... | $ 1,230.00 | |
| Accounts Receivable......................... | 4,500.00 | |
| Inventories, December 31, 1937 | | |
|     Finished Goods..................... | 15,450.00 | |
|     Goods in Process...................... | 835.00 | |
|     Raw Material........................ | 5,500.00 | |
| Land....................................... | 4,000.00 | |
| Buildings................................... | 9,400.00 | |
| Res. for Depr. of Buildings................... | | 1,400.00 |
| Machinery and Fixtures...................... | 8,100.00 | |
| Res. for Depr. of Machinery and Fixtures...... | | 2,100.00 |
| Liberty Bonds.............................. | 500.00 | |
| Notes Payable.............................. | | 17,500.00 |
| Accounts Payable........................... | | 1,500.00 |
| Sales ..................................... | | 55,000.00 |
| Factory Insurance .......................... | 220.00 | |
| Purchases, Raw Material..................... | 34,700.00 | |
| Labor...................................... | 6,000.00 | |
| Manufacturing Expense...................... | 3,590.00 | |
| Selling Expense............................. | 3,500.00 | |
| Administrative Expense...................... | 2,490.00 | |
| Donation to Red Cross...................... | 200.00 | |
| Deficit..................................... | 5,285.00 | |
| Donated Surplus............................ | | 10,000.00 |
| | $105,500.00 | $105,500.00 |

(c) You are furnished with a certificate of inventory as of December 31, 1938, showing the following:

| | |
|---|---:|
| Raw Material on Hand..................... | $11,900.00 |
| Goods in Process........................... | 2,835.00 |
| Finished Goods............................ | 11,850.00 |

(d) Accrued interest on notes payable amounted to $250 on December 31, 1938.

(e) Factory insurance to be deferred amounts to $110.

(f) It is agreed that depreciation should be set up as follows:

| | |
|---|---:|
| Buildings.................................... | $200.00 |
| Machinery and fixtures ...................... | 300.00 |

From this information, draft the necessary adjusting entries and prepare a balance sheet which you would be willing to certify.

## AUDITING PRACTICE

### An Audit Case (Eighth Installment)

Ken B. Swift has now completed his verification of the asset accounts and is ready to proceed with the verification of the liability accounts. The trial balance at December 31, 1937 contains a number of current liabilities which do not appear in this year's trial balance. It will be necessary to prepare adjusting journal entries to record these items if they are found to exist as liabilities at December 31, 1938.

### Notes Payable

Analysis of the general ledger account with notes payable shows the following notes outstanding at 12–31–38:

| Payee | Date of Note | Maturity Date | Rate | Amount |
|---|---|---|---|---|
| Farmers' National Bank................... | 11–16–38 | 2–14–39 | 6% | $15,000.00 |
| Farmers' National Bank................... | 12– 1–38 | 1–30–39 | 6% | 10,000.00 |
| O. M. Grant and Co........................ | 10–20–38 | 1–18–39 | 6% | 5,000.00 |

Interest on the notes payable to the Farmers' National Bank, amounting to $325, was collected by the bank at the time the loans were made. The Beverly Supply Company's bookkeeper charged the interest to the account with interest on notes payable. Interest on the O. M. Grant and Company note is to be paid at the maturity of the note. The notes payable to the bank were confirmed as to dates and amounts by the letter received from the bank and illustrated in the second installment of the audit. It was not considered necessary to confirm the O. M. Grant and Company note.

The interest on notes payable account has a balance of $620, exclusive of accrued interest at 12–31–38.

### Accounts Payable

Mr. Swift checked the bookkeeper's schedule of the balances in the accounts payable ledger with the balances shown by the ledger accounts and found them to be in agreement. The trial balance total of $31,411.25 also agreed with the balance of the general ledger control account. One account in the accounts payable ledger had a debit balance of $500 representing an advanced payment on a contract for the purchase of merchandise.

A check of the unpaid invoice file disclosed the following invoices which had not been paid or recorded on the books at December 31, 1938:

| Creditor | Amount | Account to be Charged |
|---|---|---|
| J. A. McKarthy Co.............. | 400.00 | Cost of Sales (Merchandise Purchased) |
| The Chronicle.................. | 80.00 | Advertising |
| Clayton Garage................ | 120.00 | Delivery Expense (Repairs on Trucks) |
| Adamson Mfg. Co.............. | 1,100.00 | Cost of Sales (Mdse. in transit at 12–31–38 sent f.o.b. factory) |

The invoices were dated prior to December 31 and applied to purchases or expenses incurred prior to that date. Two of the invoices represented purchases of merchandise. The merchandise was included in the inventory at December 31, 1938.

### Property Taxes

Under the laws of California, in which the principal office of the Beverly Supply Company is located, city and county taxes are levied on property owned by taxpayers as of the first Monday of March in each year. The tax may be paid in two equal installments. The first installment is due November 1 and becomes delinquent December 5, the second installment is due January 20 and becomes delinquent April 20. The first half of the taxes assessed in March, 1938, amounting to $2,600, has been paid. The second half must be paid before April 20, 1939. The taxes assessed against the property but unpaid at the date the balance sheet is prepared, should be shown as an accrued liability. Therefore, it will be necessary to make an adjusting entry setting up an accrued liability for property taxes amounting to $2,600.

### Pay Roll Taxes

Employees of the Beverly Supply Company are paid on the fifth and twentieth of each month for the half month ending on the thirty-first and fifteenth, respectively. Following is a schedule of the wages paid and accrued for the year 1938:

| Pay Roll | Wages Accrued Dec. 31, 1937 | Wages Paid During 1938 | Wages Accrued Dec. 31, 1938 | Taxable Wages Title VIII S. S. Act | Taxable Wages Title IX S. S. Act |
|---|---|---|---|---|---|
| Office Salaries.......... | $ 200.00 | $ 4,420.00 | $ 200.00 | $ 4,420.00 | $ 4,420.00 |
| Administrative Salaries... | 408.00 | 10,492.00 | 408.00 | 9,400.00 | 10,492.00 |
| Sales Salaries........... | 518.00 | 14,200.00 | 618.00 | 12,700.00 | 14,300.00 |
| Delivery Salaries........ | 174.00 | 5,250.00 | 174.00 | 5,250.00 | 5,250.00 |
| | $1,300.00 | $34,362.00 | $1,400.00 | $31,770.00 | $34,462.00 |

The wages accrued at December 31, 1938 are not payable until January 5, 1939. The difference in the amount of wages taxable under Titles VIII and IX of the Social Security Act is due to the fact that under Title VIII wages paid to any individual in excess of $3,000 per year are not taxable, whereas under Title IX there is no such limitation. It should also be remembered that the taxes imposed under Title VIII of the Social Security Act apply only to wages actually or constructively paid during the taxable period, while the taxes imposed under Title IX apply to wages payable during the period.

The following additional information in regard to wages applicable to the quarter ended December 31, 1938 must be taken into consideration in computing the pay roll tax liability:

(a) Taxable wages under Title VIII of the Social Security Act actually paid during the quarter amounted to $8,200.

(b) Taxable wages under Title IX of the Social Security Act and under the State Unemployment Compensation Acts which were payable for services rendered during the quarter amounted to $8,400.

The company's trial balance shows that the bookkeeper has pursued a policy of recording the taxes imposed under the Federal Social Security Act and the State Unemployment Compensation Acts at the same time as wages were recorded. The pay roll tax accounts should be analyzed to ascertain if the taxes have been computed and recorded correctly. This analysis may be in form similar to Illustration No. 28. It will, of course, be necessary to draft the proper entries to record the accrued wages and the taxes imposed on the accrued wages as of December 31. Only the pay roll taxes imposed for unemployment compensation purposes need be accrued. The taxes imposed for old-age benefit purposes are imposed only on wages actually or constructively paid, hence need not be accrued. The procedure followed in the audit of The Blank Manufacturing Company will serve as a guide in completing this audit, but do not overlook the fact that the rate of the tax imposed for unemployment compensation purposes in 1937 was less than the tax imposed for 1938. For 1938 the rate of the tax imposed under Title IX of the Federal Social Security Act is 3% with a credit allowed for contributions to the state unemployment compensation funds for an amount not exceeding

90% of the tax imposed under the Federal Act. All of the states in which the Beverly Supply Company is liable for such contributions required contributions equal to 2.7% of the wages payable for services rendered in 1938. The contributions paid to the states were also payable on a quarterly basis. The following liabilities should appear on the balance sheet as of December 31:

(a) The Federal excise tax imposed on the employer under Title IX of the Social Security Act with respect to taxable wages payable for services rendered during the year ended December 31, 1938.

(b) The contributions imposed upon employers under the State Unemployment Compensation Acts with respect to taxable wages payable for services rendered during the quarter ended December 31, 1938.

(c) The Federal excise taxes imposed on the employer under Title VIII of the Social Security Act with respect to taxable wages paid for services rendered during the quarter ended December 31, 1938.

(d) The income taxes imposed on employees under Title VIII of the Social Security Act with respect to taxable wages received for services rendered during the quarter ended December 31, 1938. The employer is liable for the income taxes imposed on employees even though he is required to withhold the amount of these taxes from the wages paid to the employees.

These taxes are all payable on or before January 31, 1939.

### CAPITAL STOCK TAX

An examination of the duplicate copy of the capital stock tax return filed by the Beverly Supply Company on July 31, 1938 shows that an adjusted declared value of $150,000 was placed on the stock and the tax amounting to $150 was paid and properly charged to the capital stock tax account. A capital stock tax is imposed on every corporation which does business for any part of the year ending on June 30. Inasmuch as the Beverly Supply Company has already operated for six months of the year ending June 30, 1939, the company has incurred a liability for the entire amount of the capital stock tax due as of

June 30, 1939. Even if the company were to discontinue operations and be dissolved, it would be liable for the full amount of
the capital stock tax as there is no apportionment of the tax on
a basis of a fractional part of a year. It is, therefore, necessary
to set up the liability so that it may be reflected in the balance
sheet. Inasmuch as the capital stock tax paid for the year ended
June 30, 1938 will appear on the profit and loss statement as an
expense, the additional tax liability should not be treated as an
expense of the same period, but should be recorded as a deferred
item. In making the adjustment it may be assumed that the
tax liability is the same as the amount of the tax imposed for the
year ended June 30, 1938.

## INSTRUCTIONS

1. Read and study the auditing procedure suggested for the
verification of notes payable, accounts payable, accrued liabilities,
and contingent liabilities in an "Examination of Financial
Statements."

2. Prepare schedules for notes payable, accounts payable,
accrued pay roll, and pay roll taxes similar to the schedules shown
in the illustrative set of audit working papers. (See Illustrations
Nos. 25, 26, 27, and 28.)

3. Perform the audit work suggested for verifying current
liabilities, in so far as this procedure applies to the information
provided in this audit.

4. Prepare the required adjusting journal entries.

# CHAPTER ELEVEN

## FIXED LIABILITIES

1. Mortgages
   - (a) Classification
   - (b) Verification

2. Bonds
   - (a) Classification
   - (b) Recording the Bond Issue
   - (c) Verification of Bonds Payable

3. Amortization of Bond Premium and Discount
   - (a) Straight-Line Method
   - (b) Effective Rate Method
   - (c) Bonds Outstanding Method

4. Sinking Fund Provisions
   - (a) Sinking Funds
   - (b) Sinking Fund Reserves

5. Auditing Procedure

6. Application of Principles

7. An Audit Case—Ninth Installment

Fixed liabilities constitute the long term indebtedness or funded debt of a company. The Public Service Commission of New York defines funded debt as: "All debt which by the terms of its creation does not mature until more than one year after date of creation." If the fixed liabilities are secured, the securities usually take the form of real estate or chattel mortgages. If unsecured, the fixed liabilities represent a lien upon the general credit of the company. Funded indebtedness consists in most cases of mortgage and bonded indebtedness.

### MORTGAGES

A mortgage is a conditional title to property given by the owner to another to secure the payment of a debt or the discharge of some obligation. It is similar to a deed and conveys title to

275

the property on which the mortgage is placed in case the mortgagor fails to make payment of an obligation or debt at maturity. The tendency is to regard a mortgage as a lien on the property and not as an actual conveyance. The mortgagor retains physical possession of the property and is entitled to the income therefrom and may use the property just as though it were his own. Of course, he must not impair its value and he must comply with all the conditions in the mortgage contract.

**Classification of Mortgages.** Mortgages are known as either chattel or real estate mortgages, depending on the property which is the basis of the security. They sometimes are known as purchase money or building and loan mortgages, depending on the purpose of the mortgage. They also may be classified as to precedence, as first mortgages, second mortgages, etc. A first mortgage takes precedence over a second mortgage, and so on. In case of liquidation of capital assets, holders of mortgages stand in order according to the class of mortgage held.

Mortgages on chattel property usually are given for a short period of time and are classed as current liabilities, but mortgages on real property given as security for notes or bonds, due at some time in the future beyond that for which liabilities are classed as current, are considered fixed liabilities.

Mortgages used as security for notes usually are classed as mortgages payable on the books of account, while those used as security for bonds are classed as bonds payable. The usual procedure with mortgages payable is the same as with notes payable. The mortgages payable account is credited with each mortgage issued and is debited when the mortgage is paid.

Unlike bonds, mortgages are seldom originally sold at either a discount or a premium. The amount received usually is equal to the face of the mortgage, hence mortgages should be recorded, like notes, at their face or par value.

**Verification of Mortgages.** In auditing mortgages payable, the auditor should first secure from the bookkeeper a list of all mortgages payable and he should see that the totals thereof agree with the balance as shown on the books. It is the auditor's duty to examine copies of all mortgages, and he should note carefully all terms and special clauses in the instruments. For example, mortgages sometimes state that a certain ratio must be maintained between current assets and current liabilities so long as the mortgage is outstanding. The auditor must assure himself that any and all such stipulations are complied with.

The amount of mortgage indebtedness as shown by the books and other records of accounts, should be verified, the interest rates, due dates, and the property covered should be determined, and the purpose of the issue recorded. A certificate from the mortgagee will divulge all but the last, which may be ascertained from a copy of the mortgage, or from the minutes of the board at the time of authorizing the mortgage.

All mortgages to be legal liens must be registered in the public records. Theoretically the auditor should make or have made a search of the public records to secure a list of any liens recorded against the property of the client. Actually this is seldom done unless the auditor has reason to suspect that liabilities exist which have not been recorded in the accounts. Ordinarily an examination of the interest expense account, the tax receipts, the fire insurance policies, and the corporate minutes would be relied upon to disclose evidence of liens not recorded in the accounts. A liability certificate should also be obtained from the officers of the company in which they affirm or deny the existence of unrecorded liens.

## BONDS

A bond is a long-term note—an interest-bearing negotiable instrument, under seal, promising to pay a certain sum of money at a definite or determinable future date. It usually is secured by a pledge of certain properties, real or personal, as to either or both principal and interest.

A corporation may borrow money the same as an individual. If only a small amount is desired or if it is wanted for a short time only, notes usually are given. These notes may be secured or unsecured. If unsecured, they are recorded as notes payable and are classed as current liabilities. If secured by a mortgage, they usually are recorded as mortgages payable and may be classed as either current or fixed liabilities, depending on the length of time remaining until maturity.

When the amount to be borrowed is large and is desired for a long period of time, say from five to fifty years, bonds are issued instead of notes. A bond issue consists of a number of bonds, which may vary in denomination, but which are all of like general tenor, and if secured are all secured alike under one deed of trust.

A deed of trust is a mortgage on certain specified property placed in the hands of a trustee who represents the bondholders. The deed of trust states at length the terms and conditions under which the bonds are issued and under which the property for their security is held.   Reference is made in the bonds to the deed of trust by which they are secured.   It will be seen, therefore, that both the deed of trust and the bonds issued refer to each other in such a manner that all terms and conditions are clearly stated in both instruments.  The trustee has the right to act in behalf of the bondholders and may bring foreclosure proceedings if it becomes necessary to do so.   If the trustee fails to do so, any bondholder may bring foreclosure proceedings for the benefit of all the bondholders.  Of course, he must show the court that this action is necessary to safeguard the interest of the bondholders and that the trustee refuses to act.

**Classification of Bonds.**   Many classes of bonds may be encountered by auditors in their examinations of corporate records.   An auditor should be familiar with the more common types.  Bonds are commonly classified as to the purpose of the issue, the security back of the bond, the method of paying the bond interest, and the manner of providing for the repayment of the principal.  The following brief classification may be found helpful:

1. As to purpose of issue:

(a) *Improvement Bonds.* Where the purpose of issuing bonds is to derive funds for the construction of new buildings, such as an office building, or other types of permanent structures, the bonds may be classed as improvement bonds.

(b) *Purchase Money Bonds.* Bonds are sometimes issued in exchange for property, or as part payment on the purchase of property which has already been constructed.  Such bonds may be referred to as purchase money bonds.

(c) *Refunding Bonds.* Refunding bonds are issued to provide funds to be used in paying off bonds that are soon to become due, or they may be issued to derive funds with which to call in and retire outstanding bonds prior to their maturity date. If a company has an issue of bonds outstanding on which it is paying an interest rate which is 1% or 2% higher than the current market rate for a similar grade of bond, it would be advantageous to refinance by retiring the bonds outstanding and issuing bonds bearing a lower rate of interest.

(d) *Adjustment Bonds.* When companies that are in financial difficulties are being reorganized, it may become necessary to issue new types of securities to the holders of the securities already outstanding. The bondholders may be given new securities providing for a reduced rate of interest and an interest payment that is made only if the earnings permit. The new bonds are usually secured by a junior mortgage and foreclosure may be made for default of principal only.

2. As to security:

(a) *Debenture Bonds.* The term debenture is frequently used to denote a bond which has no security other than the general credit of the company.

(b) *Mortgage Bonds.* Mortgage bonds are secured by a mortgage on property. The security may be real estate, equipment, leaseholds, or other types of property.

(c) *Income Bonds.* Bonds may be indicated as income bonds when the interest payments are contingent upon the net income of the company and are payable at the discretion of the management. Bond interest must be paid before dividends may be paid to stockholders.

(d) *Guaranteed Bonds.* Bonds of subsidiary or affiliated companies are sometimes guaranteed as to payment of principal or interest by another affiliated company.

(e) *Collateral Trust Bonds.* Bonds that are secured by a deposit, with a trustee, of stocks, bonds, mortgages, or other securities are referred to as collateral trust bonds.

3. As to payment of interest:

(a) *Registered Bonds.* Bond interest may be paid either by check or by means of coupons attached to the bonds, which may be cashed through banks. If interest is paid by check, the names and addresses of the owners must be registered on the books of the company. Such bonds are known as registered bonds.

(b) *Coupon Bonds.* If coupons are attached to the bonds, the interest may be collected by cashing the coupons. The names of owners of coupon bonds are usually not recorded on the books of the company, although coupon bonds are sometimes registered as to principal and not as to payment of interest.

4. As to payment of principal:

(a) *Sinking Fund Bonds.* The bond indenture may require the issuing company to set aside funds annually in the hands of a trustee to accumulate principal and interest during the life of the bonds so that funds will be available to pay the bonds at maturity.

(b) *Serial Bonds.* Bonds may be issued in series so that a specified amount of the principal of the bonds matures each year. The bonds are thus paid off on an installment basis.

(c) *Convertible Bonds.* Bonds may be issued which contain a stipulation giving the owner of the bond the option of exchanging his bonds for stock of the company. This privilege may become a valuable one should the corporation's stock increase in value considerably above the market value of the bonds. In this event the bonds might be retired through the issuance of additional stock.

(d) *Local Improvement Bonds.* Bonds issued by local improvement districts frequently provide for the repayment annually of a portion of each bond. If the bonds were issued for ten years, each bond would contain ten coupons for the repayment of one-tenth of the principal each year. This type of bond has two kinds of coupons attached, (1) the coupons repaying the principal and (2) the coupons covering the interest payments. Such a bond issued for ten years would usually contain ten principal coupons, maturing serially at the end of each year, and twenty interest coupons, maturing at semi-annual intervals over the life of the bond.

**Recording the Bond Issue.** Most corporations sell issues of bonds to bankers or underwriters who, in turn, sell them to the investing public. When the bonds are disposed of in this manner, it is not necessary to provide subscription records and accounts.

Procedure in accounting for bond issues may vary with

different corporations, but usually when the bonds are authorized by the board of directors the issue is recorded in the minutes, no entry being made on the books of account until the bonds are sold. If an entire bond issue of $100,000 is sold in this manner at the par value, the transaction would be recorded as follows:

| | | |
|---|---|---|
| Cash..................................... | $100,000.00 | |
| Bonds Payable...................... | | $100,000.00 |

If, however, the bonds are sold directly to the investing public, a subscription record will become necessary. This will be similar to a stock subscription record. Accounts may be set up and the transactions recorded as shown in the following entries:

(1)

| | | |
|---|---|---|
| Unissued Bonds......................... | $100,000.00 | |
| Bonds Payable...................... | | $100,000.00 |
| To record the authorized issue of bonds. | | |

(2)

| | | |
|---|---|---|
| Bond Subscriptions Receivable........... | $100,000.00 | |
| Bonds Subscribed................... | | $100,000.00 |
| To record subscriptions to bonds. | | |

(3)

| | | |
|---|---|---|
| Cash................................... | $100,000.00 | |
| Bond Subscriptions Receivable....... | | $100,000.00 |
| To record the collection of cash from subscribers. | | |

(4)

| | | |
|---|---|---|
| Bonds Subscribed........................ | $100,000.00 | |
| Unissued Bonds.................... | | $100,000.00 |
| To record the issue of bonds. | | |

**Verification of Bonds Payable.** In verifying the bonds outstanding, the certification of the trustee should be obtained. If the bonds are registered, the amounts so recorded should be determined from the proper source. Occasionally bonds will be found authenticated by the trustee but held in the treasury, or they may be pledged as collateral for money borrowed. If in the treasury, they should be examined, the numbers and amounts recorded, and the unmatured coupons noted. If in the hands of banks or others securing loans, verification should be made through correspondence. If serial bonds are involved the periodic maturity date should be noted and stated on the balance sheet. Bond interest should be computed from the bond accounts, and compared with the charge to profit and loss for the period involved. If a discrepancy exists, it should be reconciled.

An auditor may find that bonds previously issued have been purchased for cancellation during the current period. The bonds may have been purchased at a price lower or higher than par value. The bonds may have been issued originally at a discount or premium and such discount or premium may not have been entirely written off when some of the bonds were purchased for cancellation. In verifying the record of such transactions it is necessary for the auditor to ascertain the book value of the bonds purchased for cancellation. The book value will be the difference between the par value and any unamortized discount or the sum of the par value and any undistributed premium. If the bonds are purchased for less than their book value the difference will represent a gain which should be recorded separately as it constitutes taxable income. If the bonds are purchased for more than their book value the excess represents a loss which may be claimed as a deduction in the computation of the taxable net income, hence it should be recorded separately.

Some accountants recommend that any gain derived from the purchase of bonds at less than book value should be credited to the unamortized discount account so as to reduce the charges in future periods as the remaining discount is written off. If this method is followed it is also reasonable to expect that should the bonds be purchased at a loss, the loss would be charged to the unamortized discount account, thereby increasing the charge against future periods as the discount is written off. This procedure conflicts with the treasury regulations, even though it may represent sound accounting procedure.

In no event should the loss or gain resulting from the purchase of bonds at more or less than their book value be treated as an operating loss or gain. The loss or gain is of a nonoperating or nonrecurring type and should be so listed in the statement of profit and loss.

Where bonds have been redeemed, the auditor should assure himself that they are properly canceled. If the trustees have destroyed the canceled bonds a certificate should be obtained so stating.

## AMORTIZATION OF BOND PREMIUM AND DISCOUNT

When the amount realized from the sale of bonds is less than par value, the difference should be charged to a bond discount and expense account, and written off over the life of the bonds. When the amount realized from the sale of bonds is greater than par value, the difference represents a premium. This should be credited to a bond premium account and should be written off over the life of the bonds. There are several methods by which the bond premium or discount may be written off or amortized over the life of the bonds. The decision as to which method to use is dependent somewhat on the type of bonds involved. Premium or discount on serial bonds should not be amortized in the same manner as premium or discount on bonds where the entire amount matures at one time. Three methods are discussed below:

(1) Straight-Line Method. Under this plan an equal amount of premium or discount is written off each year. The amount to be written off is determined by dividing the premium or discount by the number of years the bonds have to run. The simplicity of the plan commends it to the average business man.

(2) Effective Rate Method. The rate of interest at which a corporation can dispose of its bonds at par value is known as the true or effective rate of interest. When a corporation elects to issue bonds at any other rate of interest, they will sell at a premium or discount depending upon whether or not the rate is higher or lower than the effective rate. When the rate of interest is higher or lower than the effective rate, it is known as the nominal rate. In other words, the nominal rate of interest is the actual rate of interest paid on the bonds, while the effective rate of interest is the rate of interest which, if paid, would have resulted in the sale of the bonds at par value. Since the rate of interest paid on bonds is a determining factor in the selling price, it is logical that any premium or discount resulting from a sale of bonds at more or less than par value should be written off by adjusting the interest account.

Effective rates of interest are based upon compound interest calculations. When bonds are sold at a premium, the premium constitutes an excess payment which will be returned to the purchaser in the form of an annuity. The amount of the annuity will be the difference between the effective rate of interest and the actual or nominal rate of interest paid on the bonds. The purchaser may receive 6% interest on the bonds when, in reality, the effective rate is only 5%. The amount received in excess of the effective rate is the amount of the annuity and represents a return of the premium paid. This is the amount which should be credited to the interest account and debited to the bond premium account as a means of amortizing that account. Of course, when the bonds are sold at a discount, the procedure will be reversed and the difference between the nominal and effective rates of interest should be credited to the bond discount account and debited to the bond interest account.

(3) Bonds-Outstanding Method. When serial bonds are issued, the premium or discount should be written off in amounts proportional to the yearly balances outstanding. An example will illustrate the method followed. Assume that 4% serial bonds were issued in the amount of $50,000 to finance the construction of a building, and that the bonds mature in amounts of $10,000 annually for five years. If the bonds were issued at a discount of $2,000 and expenses of issuing the bonds amounted to $400, an amortization table should be set up as follows:

| Year | Bonds Outstanding During Year | Portion to be Amortized Annually | Amount to be Amortized Annually | Amount to be Amortized Semi Annually |
|------|-------------------------------|----------------------------------|---------------------------------|--------------------------------------|
| 1 | $50,000.00 | 5/15 | $800.00 | $400.00 |
| 2 | 40,000.00 | 4/15 | 640.00 | 320.00 |
| 3 | 30,000.00 | 3/15 | 480.00 | 240.00 |
| 4 | 20,000.00 | 2/15 | 320.00 | 160.00 |
| 5 | 10,000.00 | 1/15 | 160.00 | 80.00 |

In the illustration above, five times as much discount is amortized in the first year when the bonds outstanding are $50,000 as is amortized in the last year when the bonds outstanding have been reduced to $10,000. The amount written off each year declines as the amount of bonds outstanding is reduced.

## SINKING FUND PROVISIONS

**Sinking Fund.** When bonds are issued, the deed of trust may provide that a stipulated amount shall be set aside annually for the purpose of redeeming the bonds at maturity. The amount set aside for this purpose is known as a sinking fund. A trustee is usually appointed to take charge of the fund and is usually given authority to invest the fund in approved securities. The agreement may specify that any income earned on the securities purchased by the trustee may be added to the fund. If this is not specified, the income will revert to the company.

The trustee makes periodic reports setting forth the transactions completed during the period which relate to the fund. This report should show the amount of cash received for sinking fund purposes, the amount expended for securities and expenses, and the amount of interest received on securities purchased. When the trustee's report is received, it will be necessary to record his transactions on the books of the company.

Sometimes the trustee will purchase the company's own bonds. When this is done, the bonds may be held by the trustee as live bonds or they may be returned to the company for cancellation. When the bonds are carried as live bonds, it is a good plan to treat them the same as if they were outstanding. The interest on the bonds will then be paid to the trustee and will represent an addition to sinking fund income. The method of recording the bonds purchased by the trustee will be the same regardless of whether they represent the company's own bonds or the bonds of other companies. When the company's own bonds are purchased by the trustee and then canceled before maturity, it may be necessary to make an adjustment of any unamortized discount or premium. The method of amortizing the discount or premium on sinking fund bonds need not vary from the method of amortizing premium and discount on bonds issued. In other words, such premium and discount may be amortized on either a straight-line or effective rate basis.

Expenses incurred by the trustee should be charged to sinking fund expenses and credited to sinking fund cash. Interest collected on bonds held by the trustee should be charged to sinking fund cash and credited to sinking fund income.

The amount of the sinking fund generally is listed on the balance sheet as a fixed asset. The amount of cash and bonds held by the trustee should be listed separately in the following manner:

Sinking Fund:
    Cash in Hands of Trustee............ $x,xxx.xx
    Bonds Owned by Trustee............ x,xxx.xx    $xx,xxx.xx

**Sinking Fund Reserves.** Sinking fund provisions will require the earmarking periodically of a part of profits or surplus, the setting aside of cash or equivalent funds, or a combination of the two. The auditor should carefully read the agreement as to sinking funds or sinking fund reserves as stated in the bond indenture, and should verify the procedures of the corporation in respect thereto, assuring himself that the corporation has fully carried out the provisions of the indenture. Failure to do so should be mentioned in the audit report.

The indenture may simply provide that the mortgagor will set aside from profits or surplus periodically, amounts which will at maturity of the bond issues be sufficient to replace the issue. Such a provision probably means that a proprietary reserve must be set up only, and the auditor should assure himself that such has been done. In other cases, the company may be forced to set aside a certain amount of cash each period in the hands of a trustee for the purpose of retiring the issue at maturity. In the latter case it is usually assumed that the cash turned over to the trustee will earn a certain minimum return and the payments to the trustee and the earnings will retire the issue. In this case the auditor should obtain a certificate from the sinking fund trustee stating the condition of the fund, investments made, and all other relevant facts. If the condition of the sinking fund is such that the terms of the contract between the two parties is not being complied with, the auditor should state this fact in his report.

The reserve for sinking fund account is, in reality, an appropriation of surplus and should be listed in the net worth section of the balance sheet as follows:

### Net Worth

Capital Stock.....................                    $xxx,xxx.xx
Surplus:
    Reserve for Sinking Fund..... $xx,xxx.xx
    Unappropriated Surplus....... x,xxx.xx    xx,xxx.xx  $xxx,xxx.xx

When the bonds have been redeemed and the sinking fund accounts closed, the reserve for sinking fund should be closed into surplus. This addition to surplus is then available for dividends.

## AUDITING PROCEDURE APPLICABLE TO FUNDED DEBT
### In an "Examination of Financial Statements"

"1. Obtain from the trustee a statement of the amount of bonds outstanding, in confirmation of the liability shown on the balance sheet. Check the accrued liability for interest on outstanding bonds, and reconcile the relative interest expense taken up in the profit and loss account.

"2. Examine bonds redeemed during or prior to the period under review to see that they have been properly canceled, or, if they have been destroyed, the statement obtained from the trustee should show the net amount outstanding.

"3. Ascertain the sinking fund requirements of the bond indenture and see that due consideration has been given to them. Any default in the interest or sinking fund requirements that may exist should be mentioned on the balance sheet.

"4. Give consideration to any other important stipulation of the trust indenture concerning the accounts. Trust indentures, for example, sometimes stipulate that current assets shall be maintained at a stated amount in excess of current liabilities.

"5. Check the liability on account of mortgages or other liens so far as the company's records afford data. Confirm the amounts shown by the books of account and the interest rates, due dates, etc. This may be accomplished by obtaining certificates from the mortgagees.

"6. The balance sheet should show the amount of bonds issued and in treasury or sinking funds, and also the rates of interest and the dates of maturity or, in the case of serial bonds, the annual or periodical maturities. Serial bonds, notes, and mortgage installments due within one year should be separately disclosed and if material should be included with the current liabilities."

## APPLICATION OF PRINCIPLES
### AUDIT OF THE BLANK MANUFACTURING COMPANY (Continued)

W. H. Merz, the senior accountant in charge of the audit, verified the fixed liabilities which consist of an issue of first mortgage bonds amounting to $100,000. The bonds were issued January 15, 1936 at 92½. The discount amounted to $7,500, which is being amortized on a straight-line basis, 5% or $375 of

## THE BLANK MANUFACTURING COMPANY
### Verification of Fixed Liabilities

First Mortgage, 5%, Sinking Fund Bonds Outstanding
December 31, 1937.................................... $100,000.00

These bonds were issued January 15, 1936 at 92½ and will mature
in twenty years. The discount amounting to $7,500 is being writ-
ten off on a straight-line basis of 5% a year over the life of the bonds.
Interest payable semi-annually on January 15 and July 15. The
bonds are coupon bonds secured by a first mortgage on the company's
land, buildings, and equipment. The Merchants National Bank is
the trustee. Interest accrued December 31, 1937 amounted to $2,291.67.

Sinking Fund Reserve:

| | |
|---|---:|
| Amount previously reserved.......................... | $2,750.00 |
| Amount reserved December 31, 1937.................. | 2,750.00 |
| Accrued interest on investments..................... | 160.42 |
| Adjusted balance, December 31, 1937................. | $5,660.42 |

The amount credited to the reserve account was for the appropriation made on December 31, 1936. While an appropriation for
December 31, 1937 has been approved and the funds transferred to a
special bank account, no entry has been made on the books to increase the reserve to an amount equal to the sinking fund. The indenture provides that the sinking fund reserve must be maintained
at an amount equal to the sinking fund.

The following journal entries should be made to adjust the accounts:

| | | |
|---|---:|---:|
| Bond Interest....................................... | $2,291.67 | |
| Accrued Interest Payable.................... | | $2,291.67 |

To record interest accrued on first mortgage bonds outstanding at December 31, 1937.

| | | |
|---|---:|---:|
| Surplus............................................ | 2,910.42 | |
| Sinking Fund Reserve....................... | | 2,910.42 |

To increase the sinking fund reserve to an
amount equal to the sinking fund. Of the
amount reserved, $2,750.00 represents the re-
quired annual contribution and $160.42 rep-
resents the accrued interest on mortgages
included in the sinking fund.

W H. Merz
(Senior Accountant)                                    (Schedule No. 16)

### Illustration No. 31. Verification of Fixed Liabilities

the discount being written off annually. An examination of the
bond indenture revealed the following provisions:

(1) A sinking fund is to be established and maintained by
annual contributions of $2,750 on December 31 of each year.

(2) The Merchants National Bank is named as trustee of
the sinking fund.

(3) The sinking fund may be invested in first real estate mortgages only and such mortgages must bear interest at the rate of not less than 6%. In no event may the mortgages exceed two-thirds of the appraised value of the property.

(4) The bonds are 5% coupon bonds and are secured by a first mortgage on the company's land, buildings, and equipment.

(5) Interest on the bonds is payable semi-annually on January 15 and July 15.

(6) A sinking fund reserve must be maintained equal to the amount of the sinking fund.

An analysis of the sinking fund revealed that at December 31, 1937 it consisted of the following:

| | |
|---|---|
| (a) Cash......................................... | $2,750.00 |
| (b) Real estate mortgages........................... | 2,750.00 |
| (c) Accrued interest on mortgages................... | 160.42 |
| Total......................................... | $5,660.42 |

Provision for paying the bond interest due January 15, 1938 amounting to $2,500 was made by transferring $2,500 from the checking account to a special bond interest account. This transfer was confirmed by correspondence with the bank and by examination of the company's records. The working papers of the auditor are shown in Illustration No. 31.

### SUMMARY

The verification of the mortgage and bonds payable accounts in most cases is a question of determining from the public records the existence of such liens, the verification of the values, and the recognition of the terms of the indentures. The auditor should obtain a copy of the indenture stating the terms and important considerations accompanying each issue. The minutes of the board of directors should be examined as to the authority for an issue and the purpose of the loan. Certifications should be obtained from mortgagees, trustees, and registrars wherever possible. The auditor must at all times see that the legal requirements are being complied with, and that the interests of both parties are being recognized according to the contract. Sinking fund accounts should be carefully checked with the provisions under which the bonds were issued.

## AUDITING THEORY

**11—120.** What distinguishes fixed liabilities from current liabilities?

**11—121.** When a mortgage constitutes security for a note payable, how would you expect to find it recorded on the books?

**11—122.** (a) Is it necessary to have all mortgages registered in the public records?

(b) Should such records be checked as a means of verifying mortgages payable?

**11—123.** What is a sinking fund? Explain the accounting procedure in providing a sinking fund.

**11—124.** (a) How is a reserve for sinking fund created?

(b) What is the relation of a reserve for sinking fund to a sinking fund account?

**11—125.** If a 4% bond with a par value of $100 is purchased for $105, what is the actual percentage of income on the cost of the bond?

**11—126.** If a company sells its bonds at a premium, is the premium an operating profit of the company? Should the entire premium be considered a profit for the year in which the bonds are sold or should it be distributed over the life of the bonds?

**11—127.** Name five classes of bonds, describing briefly each class with regard to issue, purpose, redemption, etc.

(C. P. A. Mich.)

**11—128.** Do unsold bonds of a railroad company constitute a liability? If they do, under what account would they appear in the ledger?

(C. P. A. Mich.)

**11—129.** An issue of mortgage bonds of the par value of $100,000 and running for five years, has been sold at 90, the money to be used in the erection of new buildings. How should the transaction be recorded and why?

(C. P. A. Mich.)

**11—130.** Describe two different methods for writing off the premiums on bonds and state which, in your opinion, is the best method.

(A. I. A.)

## AUDITING PROBLEMS

**11—28.** A corporation has issued $1,000,000 of 6% twenty-year bonds at 90 and for eight years has written off 5% of the discount each year. Last year an opportunity occurred to buy in $200,000 of the bonds at 85, which was done and the bonds were canceled. The directors propose to take up into their year's revenue $30,000, the discount saved upon extinction of this liability.

As an auditor how would you record:

(a) The sale of the original issue of bonds?
(b) The amount of the discount written off each year?
(c) The bonds purchased and canceled?
Explain why you do or do not approve of the directors' proposal.

**11—29.** The Johnson Paint Co. issues bonds amounting to $1,000,000 (Denomination $1,000 each, dated January 2, 1936, bearing interest at 5% and maturing January 2, 1946). The bonds were sold at 80% of their par value.

The deed of trust provided for a sinking fund to be created by annual payments of $50,000 to a trustee. On December 31, 1937, the trial balance contained the following accounts:

Bond Discount............................. $160,000.00
Sinking Fund............................... 102,000.00
First Mortgage Bonds.......................                                $1,000,000.00

On January 2, 1938, the sinking fund trustee purchased 113 bonds at $900 each, paying for them out of the funds in his possession. These bonds were then canceled.

As auditor of the company you are consulted in regard to the recording of this transaction. Show by means of a journal entry how you would record it and explain how you would list the above accounts on a balance sheet prepared immediately after recording the transaction.

**11—30.** During the course of an audit of the books of The Race and Burnet Manufacturing Co. you find that during the period under audit, the company has purchased $50,000 of its own bonds in the open market which were subsequently canceled. In completing your investigation, you find that the bonds were issued five years previously. The original issue of bonds and the bonds purchased for cancellation were recorded as follows:

Cash....................................... $195,000.00
Unamortized Discount and Commission........    5,000.00
    First Mortgage Bonds....................                              $200,000.00
        To record the sale of an issue of 50-year 5% bonds at 98½ plus 1% commission.

Profit and Loss............................     100.00
    Unamortized Discount and Commission....                                 100.00
        To amortize discount and commission applicable to first mortgage bonds outstanding.

Note: A similar amount of discount and commission had been written off at the end of each year during the five years elapsing since the bonds were originally issued.

First Mortgage Bonds........................ $48,000.00
　　Cash...................................　　　　　　　　　　$48,000.00
　　　　　To record first mortgage bonds amount-
　　　ing to $50,000 par value, purchased for
　　　cancellation in the open market at 95 plus
　　　1% commission.

(a) Do you approve of the method used in amortizing the discount and commission on the bonds? Can you suggest a better method?

(b) Do you approve of the method used in recording the bonds purchased for cancellation? If not, how would you record the transaction?

## AUDITING PRACTICE
### An Audit Case (Ninth Installment)

On January 11, Ken B. Swift proceeds with the verification of the bonded indebtedness of the Beverly Supply Company.

The account with bonds payable appears as follows in the general ledger:

### First Mortgage, 5%, Serial Bonds

| Date | Items | Debit | Credit | Balance |
|---|---|---|---|---|
| 2–1–36 | Issued @ 98...................... | .......... | 100,000.00 | 100,000.00 |
| 2–1–37 | Series One retired.................... | 5,000.00 | .......... | 95,000.00 |
| 2–1–38 | Series Two retired.................... | 5,000.00 | .......... | 90,000.00 |

The bonds were issued February 1, 1936, and are repayable in installments (series) of $5,000 annually, commencing February 1, 1937. The third installment is due February 1, 1939. The bonds are secured by a first mortgage on the company's land and buildings.

The funds derived from the sale of the bonds were used in remodeling and enlarging the store building and in the construction of a warehouse for the storage of merchandise.

In response to his request, Mr. Swift received a letter from the Farmers' National Bank, the trustee named in the bond indenture, confirming the amount of bonds outstanding as being $90,000 at December 31, 1938. The letter also certified that bond series one and two, each for $5,000, had been redeemed and the certificates canceled.

Bond interest is payable semi-annually on February 1 and August 1. The bond interest account appears in the general ledger as follows at December 31, 1938:

### Interest on Bonds Payable

| Date | Items | Debit | Credit | Balance |
|------|-------|-------|--------|---------|
| 1-1-38 | Accrued 12-31-37.................... | .......... | 1,979.17 | 1,979.17 |
| 2-1-38 | Semi-annual interest payment.......... | 2,375.00 | .......... | 395.83 |
| 8-1-38 | Semi-annual interest payment.......... | 2,250.00 | .......... | 2,645.83 |

### Bond Discount and Expense

The bonds were originally sold at 98 and accrued interest. The bond discount is to be amortized each interest payment date.

The bond discount and expense account appears in the general ledger as follows:

### Bond Discount and Expense

| Date | Items | Debit | Credit | Balance |
|------|-------|-------|--------|---------|
| 1-31-36 | Discount on bonds sold @ 98.......... | 2,000.00 | .......... | 2,000.00 |
| 1-31-36 | Expense of issuing bonds.............. | 400.00 | .......... | 2,400.00 |
| 8- 1-36 | Amortization on straight-line basis....... | .......... | 60.00 | 2,340.00 |
| 2- 1-37 | Amortization on straight-line basis...... | .......... | 60.00 | 2,280.00 |
| 8- 1-37 | Amortization on straight-line basis....... | .......... | 60.00 | 2,220.00 |
| 2- 1-38 | Amortization on straight-line basis....... | .......... | 60.00 | 2,160.00 |
| 8- 1-38 | Amortization on straight-line basis...... | .......... | 60.00 | 2,100.00 |

Mr. Swift observed that bond discount and expense has been amortized on a straight-line basis during the past three years, whereas, he contends that it should have been written off by the bonds-outstanding method.

Mr. Knight, when consulted on the question, agreed with Mr. Swift that the bonds-outstanding method would be the proper one to follow in this case. After consultation with the client, Mr. Swift was instructed to compute the amortization of discount and expense by the bonds-outstanding method and to make an adjusting journal entry to reduce the account balance to an amount computed on this basis. In computing the amount to be written off by this method, it is necessary to set up a table showing the bonds outstanding during the period preceding each interest date over the 20-year period. Following is an illustration of the procedure which may be followed in computing the amount to be amortized each half year:

| Date | Bonds Outstanding | Portion to be Amortized |
|------|-------------------|-------------------------|
| 8–1–36 | $ 100,000.00 | 100/2100 |
| 2–1–37 | 100,000.00 | 100/2100 |
| 8–1–37 | 95,000.00 | 95/2100 |
| 2–1–38 | 95,000.00 | 95/2100 |
| 8–1–38 | 90,000.00 | 90/2100 |
| 2–1–39 | 90,000.00 | 90/2100 |
| etc. | etc. | etc. |
| Total | $2,100,000.00 | 2100/2100 |

The amount to be amortized August 1, 1936, is determined by taking a fractional part (100/2100) of $2,400. The amount to be amortized each interest period thereafter is denoted by the fraction determined by comparing the bonds outstanding each period with the total of the bonds outstanding as shown above.

The amortization table shown above differs from the one illustrated on page 284 in that the interval used in determining the portion to be amortized in the illustration on page 284 is a year, whereas the interval used above is a half year. The number of intervals resulting from using a half year is twice the number resulting from using a year. The method of computation and the results should otherwise be the same under the two methods.

## INSTRUCTIONS

1. Read and study the auditing procedure suggested for the verification of fixed liabilities (funded debt) and for deferred charges (bond discount) in an "Examination of Financial Statements."

2. Prepare a schedule showing an analysis of the entries in the bonds payable account.

3. Prepare a schedule showing the entries in the account with bond discount and expense as the entries would appear when the bonds-outstanding method is used instead of the straight-line method in writing off bond discount and expense.

4. Prepare adjusting journal entries, where necessary, to adjust the account balances.

# CHAPTER TWELVE

## NET WORTH

1. The Sole Proprietorship

2. The Partnership

3. The Corporation
   (a) Capital Stock
       (1) Examining the Charter, Minutes, Etc.
       (2) Verification of Capital Stock Records
       (3) No Par Value Stock
       (4) Auditing Procedure
   (b) Surplus
       (1) Auditing Procedure

4. Application of Principles

5. An Audit Case—Tenth Installment

The net worth of a business is the difference between the sum of the assets and the sum of the liabilities. In other words, it is the proprietor's equity in the assets. The proprietorship may be vested in a single individual, in two or more partners, or in the stockholders of a corporation.

### THE SOLE PROPRIETORSHIP

A business conducted by a single individual is known as a sole proprietorship. The individual contributes the capital, is entitled to the profits, and must stand the losses. The capital may represent accumulated earnings or contributions, or both. Usually it will be found that the proprietor has contributed at least a part of the present capital while the remainder represents profits which have been left in the business.

The capital invested or contributed by the proprietor is often referred to as paid-in capital, while the capital arising from accumulated profits is known as earned capital. However, it is not customary to distinguish between these two types of capital in setting up a balance sheet for a sole proprietorship.

In verifying the capital accounts of a sole proprietorship, the entries in the accounts should be examined to see that they are net worth items and that they are correctly recorded. There are seldom any documents to examine such as are found in a partnership or a corporate enterprise. A sole proprietorship does not have minutes of meetings, by-laws, charters, legal restrictions, and such matters which need to be investigated in examining the net worth accounts. All that is necessary is to check the entries in the capital account and the drawings or personal account, if one is maintained, to see that the entries have been correctly recorded.

The net worth of a sole proprietorship should be shown on the balance sheet in such manner as to indicate the present capital of the proprietor. The balance sheet may be supported by a schedule showing the proprietor's capital at the beginning of the period, the changes during the period, and the present capital at the end of the period.

### THE PARTNERSHIP

An association of two or more individuals in business may be brought about through the formation of a partnership. The investment of capital, the distribution of profits, the sharing of losses, and the distribution of assets in case of dissolution of the partnership are all subject either to agreement or to law. Hence, an auditor must examine the partnership agreement, which should be in writing, to determine these facts and to see that the accounting conforms to the agreement. In the absence of an agreement it will be necessary to account for the profits or losses in accord with the law.

The entries in the partners' capital accounts should be analyzed to see that they have been recorded correctly. The auditor should examine the entries for distribution of profit, interest on partners' capital, the amounts of withdrawals by partners, and similar entries to see that they conform to the provisions of the partnership agreement. If the partnership agreement is being violated, this fact should be mentioned in the auditor's report, together with suggestions for stating the accounts correctly.

The net worth of a partnership should be shown on the balance sheet or in a supporting schedule in such a way as to indicate the present capital of each of the partners. The following is a suggested classification of the proprietorship accounts of a partnership:

### Net Worth

| | | |
|---|---|---|
| John Jones, Capital at Beginning of Period.......... | | $x,xxx.xx |
| Plus: | | |
| Personal (Cr. Balance)................$xxx.xx | | |
| One-half Net Profit.................... xxx.xx | xxx.xx | |
| Present Capital..................................... | | $x,xxx.xx |
| Harry Smith, Capital at Beginning of Period......... | $x,xxx.xx | |
| Less—Personal (Dr. Balance)...................... | xxx.xx | |
| | $x,xxx.xx | |
| Add:   One-half Net Profit.......................... | xxx.xx | |
| Present Capital..................................... | | x,xxx.xx |
| Total Capital..  ................................... | | $x,xxx.xx |

## THE CORPORATION

**Capital Stock.** A business owned and operated by a group of persons whose ownership is represented by capital stock is conducted as a corporation. In a Supreme Court decision, a corporation has been defined as: "An association of individuals united for some common purpose, and permitted by the law to use a common name, and to change its members without dissolution of the association."

The organization of a corporation is different from that of a partnership. A partnership is formed by contract or agreement, either expressed or implied, between partners, but a corporation is created by the state in which it is organized and in accordance with the laws of that state. Persons desiring to incorporate must secure a charter from the state as provided by law. This charter bestows upon a corporation the powers specified in the application for a charter. It usually shows the name of the corporation, its object and purpose, amount and classes of capital stock authorized, place of business, and term of existence. In addition to these specified powers, certain general powers are conferred, whether specified or not.

**Examining the Charter, Minutes, Etc.** The charter or certificate of incorporation should be examined for information concerning the various classes of stock, including the number of shares authorized, the par values, stated values, and any preferences there may be as to dividends, voting privileges, rights in liquidation, and similar matters. The charter should also disclose the exact name of the corporation, the date of incorporation, the length of time the charter runs, and the state in which it is chartered.

The minutes of the meetings of the stockholders and board of directors should also be examined for information pertinent to the sale or retirement of stock, changes in the number of shares or in the par value, declaration of dividends, and such matters. Any changes in the capital structure should be authorized by the board of directors, and receive the sanction of the proper state authorities.

**Verification of Capital Stock Records.** If the company issues its own stock, the stock outstanding as shown by the balances of the accounts in the stockholders' ledger should be in agreement with the stock outstanding as shown by the capital stock accounts in the general ledger. A list of the stockholders should be prepared by company employees which may be used by the auditor in checking the balances in the stockholders' accounts. The amount of stock outstanding should not exceed the amount authorized in the charter and in the permits for issue received from the state authorities vested with the power of regulating corporate stock issues.

An examination should be made of the stock certificate books and tests should be made of the postings from the stubs to the stockholders' ledger accounts. Voided or canceled certificates should be attached to the certificate stubs or otherwise accounted for. Dividend lists should be examined to determine that the number of shares of each kind of stock receiving dividend payments agrees with the number of shares shown to be outstanding by the capital stock accounts.

The general ledger accounts should be analyzed and any changes during the current period should be checked to see that sales or retirements of stock were authorized by the board of directors and that permits, if required, were received from the

State Department of Corporations. The amounts received from the sale of stock should be checked to see that they were properly accounted for. If assets other than cash were received from the sale of stock, the auditor should examine the records to see that the sale conforms to the directors' authorization and that the assets were recorded at values approved by the board of directors. If stock is issued above or below par value, ascertain the manner of treating the premium or discount in the accounts.

If a company maintains the services of a registrar or transfer agent (usually a bank or trust company) in connection with the issuance of its stock and in the maintenance of its stockholders' records, a confirmation should be obtained from the registrar certifying to the amount of stock authorized and the amount outstanding at the close of the fiscal period. The figures in the registrar's certificate should agree with those shown by the records of the corporation.

Frequently stocks are sold to employees and customers on the installment plan. Such sales are evidenced by contracts between the company and purchaser which should be examined and the terms of sale noted. The total amount due on such subscriptions is usually stated as receivables and verified as such. The liability to deliver the stock on payment of subscription is also usually shown under a proper caption.

Treasury stock should be noted and stated depending on the policy of the company. If for purposes of retirement, it may well be deducted from stocks outstanding. If to be resold, the auditor may well present it under the asset accounts, though it should be clearly labeled.

**No Par Value Stock.** A share of no par stock is one in which the stock has no stated value but represents a certain share in the net assets of the business. Each share of stock of no par value represents an aliquot part of the net assets or net worth of the company. Since no value is specified in the stock certificate, there is less danger of the purchaser being deceived or misled as to the value of the stock. In some states no par value stock may be issued as a bonus, and stated at any arbitrary amount desired for financial purposes. It may be issued for $100 per share and the capital declared at $1 a share or any other value the directors may decide upon. For legal purposes, paid-in capital is apparently declared capital and dividends may be declared from surplus arising from stock contributions over and above the declared value. Such concepts of handling stock issues are legal rather than accounting, but the accountant must be prepared to cope with such situations. In verifying no par issues, a list of all stockholders and the total number of shares owned by each should be prepared by the client's staff, and verified along the same lines as stated for par issues. The auditor should determine the type and amount of property received in exchange for such stocks, and the method of accounting therefor. He must ascertain that such issues are properly accounted for according to the laws of the states concerned, the articles of incorporation, and the minutes of the board.

Prior to the year 1912 capital stock consisted of shares with stated par values on the face of the certificates. Since 1912 the use of no par stock has become popular. By 1928, the amount of no par value stock listed on the New York Stock Exchange alone had a market value of nearly 17 million dollars. According to an analysis prepared by the National Industrial Conference Board, no par stock issues are most popular among industrial service and finance corporations, but are found hardly at all in the field of railroad financing. Delaware leads all of the states in the amount of no par value stock issued. However, no par value stock may now be issued under the laws of most states.

### AUDITING PROCEDURE APPLICABLE TO CAPITAL STOCK
#### In an "Examination of Financial Statements"

"1. In the case of companies which issue their own stock, examine the stock records and stock certificate books to ascertain the amount of capital stock outstanding. See that the company is complying with the requirements of laws imposing transfer taxes.

"2. If a trust company is the registrar of the capital stock, obtain from the registrar and/or transfer agent a certificate as to the number of shares of capital stock issued and outstanding.

"3. If any stock has been sold during the period under review see that the cash or other consideration for which the stock was issued was in accord with authorization of the directors.

Make inquiries as to the existence of any stock options, warrants, rights or conversion privileges. If any exist, details should be given on the balance sheet.

"4. If stock has been subscribed on an installment plan ascertain whether or not any payments are in arrears. If special terms have been extended to any stockholder, examine the minutes of the board of directors to see that such terms have been approved.

"5. The capital stock or stated capital should be shown on the balance sheet in accordance with the statutes of the state under the laws of which the corporation is organized, the articles of incorporation and the corporation's minutes. It should be borne in mind that the laws of most states have special provisions relative to the acquisition of treasury stock by a corporation.

"6. Each class of stock should be stated separately on the balance sheet, with the amount authorized, issued and outstanding and the par value per share. If the stock is of no par value the stated or assigned value per share, if any, should be shown and the redemption price or the amount of preference upon liquidation. If any stock of the company is held in the treasury it should preferably be shown as a deduction from capital stock or from surplus or from the total of the two, at either par or cost, as the laws of the state of incorporation and other relevant circumstances require. If it is included on the asset side of the balance sheet the circumstances justifying such treatment should be indicated in the caption or in a footnote to the balance sheet.

"7. The total amount of dividends or the dividends per share on outstanding cumulative preferred stock which are in arrears should be stated on the balance sheet. All dividends declared but not paid at the date of the balance sheet should be included in the current liabilities."

**Surplus.** Any excess of net worth over the par or stated value of the capital stock outstanding represents surplus. In case the amount of the net worth is less than the par value or stated value of the capital stock outstanding, the difference represents a deficit. Surplus may arise from the following sources:

(a) It may represent capital in excess of the par value or

stated value of the capital stock. If subscribers pay more than the par value or stated value of the capital stock, the difference represents paid-in surplus. Many corporations, particularly banks, will sell their capital stock at a higher value than its par value. Such companies at time of organization may have a paid-in surplus.

(b) It may arise from an increase in value of capital assets or from a revaluation of capital assets. Such surplus is known as revaluation surplus and it is customary to state it separately on the balance sheet because it is not generally considered as being available for dividends.

(c) It may represent an increase in net worth arising from earnings. This type of surplus does not differ from the earned capital of the sole proprietorship or the partnership although it is stated differently in the balance sheet of a corporation.

In verifying the surplus accounts the auditor should prepare a work sheet showing surplus at the beginning of the period, changes during the period, and the surplus available at the end of the period. This should be done independently for earned surplus, appropriated surplus, capital surplus, or any surplus accounts existent in the particular case. The balances at the beginning and at the end of the period should agree with those shown on the books, and all changes in the accounts should be investigated to insure that they are proper surplus items.

A part of the profits may be carried to an account entitled Undivided Profits. Many corporations do not carry to surplus all of the profits of the period but will transfer to surplus only that part of the profits which the board of directors may contemplate distributing as dividends. In other cases that part of the profits will be carried to surplus which is to be retained in the business as working capital, the balance representing profits available for dividends. There is little uniformity in the distribution of profits in the accounts of corporations but for balance sheet purposes it is customary to show any excess of net worth over the par or stated values of capital stock as surplus. However, in stating the surplus it should be listed as follows:

(a) Capital or paid-in surplus
(b) Surplus arising from revaluation of capital assets
(c) Earned surplus (or deficit).

## AUDITING PROCEDURE APPLICABLE TO SURPLUS
### In an "Examination of Financial Statements"

"1. Analyze the surplus accounts for the period covered by the examination. Reconcile the opening balance with the surplus shown in the previous balance sheet and consider the propriety of the entries made in the surplus accounts.

"2. Check by reference to the minutes of directors' meetings the dividends declared or paid during the period under review. If stock dividends have been distributed, ascertain that the treatment on the books is in accordance with the minutes. Adequate disclosure should be made.

"3. Where practicable the nature of the surplus should be shown on the balance sheet divided under principal classifications such as:

(a) Earned surplus (or deficit).
(b) Capital or paid-in surplus.
(c) Surplus arising from revaluation.

If there are any restrictions on the surplus by reason of state laws, charter provisions, etc., such as in the case of reacquired shares, the nature of the restrictions should be indicated.

"4. The balance sheet should show as 'surplus arising from revaluation,' or by some similar title, any credit resulting from increasing the book value of capital or other assets by revaluation, whether on the basis of independent appraisal or otherwise.

"5. Unrealized profits should not be credited to income account either directly or indirectly, by charging against such unrealized profits amounts which would ordinarily be chargeable against income account. Profit is deemed to be realized when a sale in the ordinary course of business is effected, unless the circumstances are such that the collection of the sale price is not reasonably assured. An exception to the general rule may be made in the case of inventories in industries (such as the packing-house industry) in which it is a trade custom to take inventories at net selling prices which may exceed cost.

"6. Intercompany profits on sales of securities or other property should not be taken into the consolidated surplus account until realized by sale outside the group of affiliated companies.

"7. Capital surplus, however created, should not be used to relieve the income account of the current or future years of charges which would otherwise require to be made against income. This rule might be subject to the exception that where, upon reorganization, a reorganized company would be relieved of charges which would require to be made against income if the existing corporation were continued, it might be regarded as permissible to accomplish the same result without reorganization provided the facts were as fully revealed to and the action as formally approved by the stockholders as in reorganization.

"8. Earned surplus of a subsidiary company created prior to acquisition does not form a part of the consolidated earned surplus of the parent company and subsidiaries; nor can any dividend declared out of such surplus properly be credited to the income account of the parent company.

"9. If capital stock is issued nominally for the acquisition of property and it appears that at about the same time, and pursuant to a previous agreement or understanding, some portion of the stock so issued is donated to the corporation, it is not permissible to treat the par value of the stock nominally issued for the property as the cost of the property. If stock so donated is subsequently sold, it is not permissible to treat the proceeds as a credit to surplus of the corporation."

### Reserves

"1. Analyze all the reserves to determine the changes during the period, whether they be reserves deducted from the respective assets or shown on the liability side of the balance sheet. Give careful consideration to the accounting practices of the company in setting up reserves and in making charges against them.

"2. If the general or contingency reserves are of sufficient importance in comparison to the financial position or earnings of the company, it may be desirable for the company to include with its financial statements a summary of changes in reserves during the period."

### APPLICATION OF PRINCIPLES

### AUDIT OF THE BLANK MANUFACTURING COMPANY (Continued)

Mr. Merz, the senior accountant in charge of the audit, verified the capital stock and surplus accounts. Reference to his

## THE BLANK MANUFACTURING COMPANY
### Analysis of Proprietorship

*CAPITAL STOCK:*

| | |
|---|---:|
| *Capital stock authorized per articles of incorporation, 50,000 shares, par value $10* | *$500,000.00* |
| *Less unissued stock, 5,000 shares* | *50,000.00* |
| *Capital stock issued and outstanding, December 31, 1937* | *$450,000.00* |

> *The Merchants National Bank is the registrar and transfer agent. No stock options, warrants, rights, or conversion privileges have been issued by the company.*

*SURPLUS:*

| | | |
|---|---:|---:|
| *Balance, December 31, 1936* | | *$41,879.81* |
| *Less:* | | |
| *Dividend #1, 5% declared July 1, 1937* | *$22,500.00* | |
| *Organization Expenses charged off December 31, 1937* | *816.67* | |
| *Reserved for sinking fund purposes, December 31, 1937* | *2,910.42* | *26,227.09* |
| *Adjusted balance before adding net profit for 1937* | | *$15,652.72* |

> *Entire surplus earned. No paid-in or capital surplus. The dividend declared July 1 was paid and the amount charged to Dividend #1 as shown by the trial balance.*
>
> *The following journal entry should be made to adjust the accounts:*

| | | |
|---|---:|---:|
| *Surplus* | *$22,500.00* | |
| *Dividend #1* | | *$22,500.00* |

> *To transfer the dividend account to surplus.*

*W. H. Merz*
*(Senior Accountant)*                                        *(Schedule No. 17)*

**Illustration No. 32.  Analysis of Proprietorship**

working papers, which are shown in Illustration No. 32, will reveal the following information:

**Capital Stock.** At December 31, 1937 there were 45,000 shares of capital stock outstanding with a par value of $450,000. The charter shows that the corporation is authorized to issue 50,000 shares of $10 par value, but only 45,000 shares have been issued.

**Surplus.** At December 31, 1936 the surplus account had a credit balance of $41,879.81. On July 1, 1937 a dividend of 5%

was declared. This amounted to $22,500. When the dividend was paid it was recorded by debiting Dividend #1 and crediting Merchants Bank—Checking Account. On December 31, 1937 organization expenses were charged off amounting to $816.67 and there was reserved for sinking fund purposes, $2,910.42. After taking these items into consideration, the adjusted balance of the surplus account at December 31, 1937 amounted to $15,652.72 before adding the net profit for the year 1937. This is earned surplus, there being no paid-in or capital surplus.

## SUMMARY

In auditing net worth, the auditor should assure himself that the items stated are proper net worth items. With the rapid rise of no par stock and its use, there is still considerable variation in different state laws controlling its use, and wide variation in the methods of accounting for and presenting such values.

The laws of the state under which a corporation is organized, a corporation's charter and by-laws, and the minutes of the board of directors may all be of value in determining the proper handling of capital stock and surplus items. Surplus items should be so stated as to clearly distinguish between earned surplus and capital surplus.

### AUDITING THEORY

**12—131.** In the case of a business owned by an individual, how may his net worth be ascertained?

**12—132.** In a business organized as a partnership, how may the present capital of each of the partners be ascertained?

**12—133.** In a business organized as a corporation, how may the book value of each share of stock be computed?

**12—134.** Prepare an outline showing the procedure to be used in verifying the capital stock accounts of a corporation with both common and preferred stock outstanding.

**12—135.** (a) Distinguish between capital and earned surplus.

(b) Would you consider paid-in surplus as capital or earned surplus?

**12—136.** You are auditing the accounts of a concern preparatory to a change of policy. It is desired to change the stock from a par value of $100 a share to no par value. Explain how you would record the change in capital stock and state what effect the change would have on the surplus.

12—137. An audit of a corporation is under consideration.

(a) How would you show discount on capital stock in the balance sheet? Under what circumstances, if any, would you consider it proper to deduct it from the capital stock on the liability side?

(b) Would you consider the capital stock impaired as long as it carried discount on capital stock in excess of surplus?

(c) Can dividends be declared by a company which sold its capital stock at a discount, before the discount is extinguished?

(d) What is the fundamental difference between discount on bonds and discount on capital stock?

(e) Do you know of any circumstances that would justify or warrant premiums on capital stock being distributed as dividends?

12—138. Which of the following are liabilities, which are a part of net worth, and which are neither?

(a) Reserve for Bad Debts
(b) Reserve for Federal Income Tax
(c) Reserve for Undeclared Dividends on Cumulative Preferred Stock
(d) Reserve for Depreciation of Buildings
(e) Reserve for Contingencies
(f) Reserve for Appreciation of Assets
(g) Reserve for Sinking Fund.

(C. P. A. Ky.)

12—139. In making up a balance sheet for a corporation should the capital invested be included in the liabilities? State your reasons.

(C. P. A. Ohio)

12—140. How should the losses on shares of stock issued at a discount be dealt with in the accounts of a corporation?

(C. P. A. Ind.)

12—141. What is treasury stock, and state the difference, if any, between that and stock authorized but not issued. At what price may either be sold? How should they appear on the books of account?

(C. P. A. Ind.)

## AUDITING PROBLEMS

12—31. A corporation, being in debt and unable to finance its plans, decides to sell two-thirds of its property (real estate) for preferred stock of a new concern that will utilize the part sold. The capital stock will then be decreased to the value of the property retained. The present capital is $300,000 common. The new capital will be $150,000 common. The sale is made for $600,000 preferred stock. The debts of $150,000 will be paid with $300,000 of the preferred stock at 50, that being the best price obtainable. Each stockholder will receive for each two shares of the stock now held, one share of the new common and two shares of the preferred at 50. Make the proper entries to record:

(a) The sale of the real estate
(b) The payment of the debts
(c) The exchange of the stock.

**12—32.** The charter of a corporation, the books of which you are auditing, contains a provision for the payment of an amount equal to 3% of the preferred capital stock, originally issued, into a redemption fund. This fund, it is directed, is to be utilized in purchase of stock, at not exceeding 10% premium, and its cancellation and retirement. State in full detail how you would reflect transactions under this provision in your balance sheet. Draft proforma journal entries—(a) assuming stock acquired at a discount of 10%, and (b) assuming stock acquired at a premium of 10%.

(A. I. A.)

**12—33.** The Gibraltar Bronze Co. was incorporated February 1, 1938, with an authorized capital stock of $10,000,000, consisting of $4,500,000 (45,000 shares of $100 each) preferred 7% noncumulative stock, and $5,500,000 (55,000 shares of $100 each) of common stock. On the same date $2,000 of the common stock was subscribed for at par as follows:

| | | |
|---|---|---|
| A. Van Oss | 2 shares | $200.00 |
| T. L. W. Porte | 4 shares | 400.00 |
| Wiley T. Lyon | 4 shares | 400.00 |
| David Smith | 3 shares | 300.00 |
| William Leslie | 7 shares | 700.00 |

### Inventory of Property Purchased

| Factory | Raw Material | Finished Stock | Real Estate | Buildings | Machinery |
|---|---|---|---|---|---|
| A | $ 430,000 | $ 95,000 | $ 195,000 | $ 20,000 | $ 98,000 |
| B | 211,000 | 44,000 | 130,000 | 10,000 | 84,000 |
| C | 495,000 | 38,500 | 475,000 | 11,000 | 62,000 |
| D | 304,000 | 15,000 | 924,000 | 13,000 | 48,000 |
| E | 171,000 | 32,750 | 184,000 | 14,500 | 89,000 |
| F | 86,500 | 81,000 | 60,000 | 17,750 | 26,000 |
| G | 47,250 | 44,000 | 30,000 | 32,500 | 34,000 |
| H | 98,000 | 35,750 | 20,000 | 14,600 | 62,000 |
| I | 101,250 | 11,000 | 10,000 | 17,200 | 11,000 |
| J | 37,000 | 13,000 | 11,000 | 19,200 | 35,000 |
| K | 346,000 | 49,000 | 14,000 | 75,000 | 71,000 |
| L | 121,000 | 67,000 | 37,000 | 34,750 | 44,000 |
| Totals | $2,448,000 | $526,000 | $2,090,000 | $279,500 | $664,000 |

On February 4, these subscribers paid the amount of their subscriptions, and stock was issued to them. February 15, the balance of the authorized capital stock of the company, both preferred and common, was issued by resolution of the board of directors to A. A. Keiser, for and in consideration of $750,000 in cash and twelve (12) manufacturing plants. An inventory of the property purchased, made by authorized representatives of the company, is shown in the foregoing schedule.

Operations for the period ending December 31, 1938, resulted as follows:

(a) Gross Profit on Sales............................ $240,000.00
(b) Operating Expenses (not including depreciation).. 160,000.00
(c) Profit Derived from the Sales of Real Estate..... 45,000.00

You are employed to make an audit of the books of The Gibraltar Bronze Co. for the period intervening from date of organization to December 31, 1938, and you find the capital stock transactions recorded as follows:

### February 1, 1938

Unissued Capital Stock, Preferred..............$4,500,000.00
Unissued Capital Stock, Common............... 5,500,000.00
    Authorized Capital Stock, Preferred........                $4,500,000.00
    Authorized Capital Stock, Common.........                 5,500,000.00
    To record the authorized issue of capital stock.

Subscribers to Capital Stock, Common.........                2,000.00
    Capital Stock Subscriptions, Common.......                              2,000.00
    To record common stock subscribed for, at par, as follows:

A. Van Oss...........2 shares..........$200.00
T. L. W. Porte.......4 shares.......... 400.00
Wiley T. Lyon.......4 shares.......... 400.00
David Smith.........3 shares.......... 300.00
William Leslie........7 shares.......... 700.00

### February 4, 1938

Cash.......................................                2,000.00
    Subscribers to Capital Stock, Common......                              2,000.00
    To record cash receipts from subscribers to capital stock (as per list).

Capital Stock Subscriptions, Common...........                2,000.00
    Unissued Capital Stock, Common...........                              2,000.00
    To record stock certificates issued to subscribers.

## February 15, 1938

| | | |
|---|---:|---:|
| Cash............................................... | $750,000.00 | |
| Finished Stock: | | |
|    Factory A.................................. | 95,000.00 | |
|           B.............................. | 44,000.00 | |
|           C.............................. | 38,500.00 | |
|           D.............................. | 15,000.00 | |
|           E.............................. | 32,750.00 | |
|           F.............................. | 81,000.00 | |
|           G.............................. | 44,000.00 | |
|           H.............................. | 35,750.00 | |
|           I.............................. | 11,000.00 | |
|           J.............................. | 13,000.00 | |
|           K.............................. | 49,000.00 | |
|           L.............................. | 67,000.00 | |
| Raw Material: | | |
|    Factory A.................................. | 430,000.00 | |
|           B.............................. | 211,000.00 | |
|           C.............................. | 495,000.00 | |
|           D.............................. | 304,000.00 | |
|           E.............................. | 171,000.00 | |
|           F.............................. | 86,500.00 | |
|           G.............................. | 47,250.00 | |
|           H.............................. | 98,000.00 | |
|           I.............................. | 101,250.00 | |
|           J.............................. | 37,000.00 | |
|           K.............................. | 346,000.00 | |
|           L.............................. | 121,000.00 | |
| Plant Account................................ | 6,274,000.00 | |
|    Unissued Capital Stock, Preferred.......... | | $4,500,000.00 |
|    Unissued Capital Stock, Common.......... | | 5,498,000.00 |

By resolution of the board of directors, title to 12 manufacturing plants was acquired from A. A. Keiser in consideration of which there was paid $750,000 in cash and capital stock, common, par value, $5,498,000; capital stock, preferred, par value, $4,500,000.

In completing your audit you ascertain the following information:

(a) That the values placed upon the inventories of raw materials and finished stock acquired from A. A. Keiser, represented cost or market price whichever was the lower.

(b) That the value placed upon real estate is the result of an appraisal which Mr. Keiser had made by expert real estate appraisers just previous to the transfer of the property to the corporation.

(c) That the valuation placed upon the buildings and machinery represents cost less depreciation as shown by the books kept by A. A. Keiser.

(d) It is estimated that the buildings acquired from Mr. Keiser will depreciate at the rate of 2% and the machinery at the rate of 12% per year, based upon the value placed upon these assets at time they were acquired from Mr. Keiser.

From the preceding information, prepare a balance sheet giving effect to the transactions completed in connection with the organization of the company up to February 15, 1937, and explain any variations in the accounts shown on your balance sheet from the records of the corporation. Also state the net worth of the corporation as of December 31, 1937, and compute the book value of each share of common capital stock outstanding.

**12—34.** The Y Corporation was originally capitalized at $9,000,000 as follows:

50,000 shares preferred stock, cumulative, $100 par............ $5,000,000
400,000 shares common stock, no par, stated value $10.......... 4,000,000

At the beginning of 1938 it had a deficit of $500,000, and during the year it suffered an operating loss of $1,000,000.

To avoid showing a deficit of $1,500,000 at the end of the year, the corporation induced its preferred stockholders to exchange their shares of par stock for an equal number of no par shares with a stated value of $50 each, the new stock retaining all the guaranties of the original as to dividends, liquidating value and callable value. After sundry intangible and doubtful assets had been written off, the corporation's balance sheet as of December 31, 1938, showed (in totals):

| | | | |
|---|---|---|---|
| Total assets............ $9,000,000 | Total liabilities......... | $1,500,000 |
| | Preferred stock......... | 2,500,000 |
| | Common stock......... | 4,000,000 |
| | Surplus................ | 1,000,000 |
| $9,000,000 | | $9,000,000 |

As an auditor for the Y Corporation would you give an unqualified certificate to the balance sheet as stated? If not restate the balance sheet as you would have it appear in your report.                          (A. I. A.)

## AUDITING PRACTICE
### An Audit Case (Tenth Installment)

On January 12, Ken B. Swift audited the net worth accounts, capital stock, and surplus.

#### Capital Stock

The Beverly Supply Company does not have a registrar or transfer agent for its stock. The stock records are maintained by Mr. D. B. Beverly, the president of the company. Mr.

Beverly states there is no need of a registrar or transfer agent for the stock since the stock is not listed on any security exchange and there are very few transfers of stock.

The accounts with capital stock and unissued capital stock appear on the general ledger as follows:

### Capital Stock

| Date | Description | Debit | Credit | Balance |
|------|-------------|-------|--------|---------|
| 12–20–32 | 2,000 shares, $100 par value............ | ............ | 200,000.00 | 200,000.00 |

### Unissued Capital Stock

| Date | Description | Debit | Credit | Balance |
|------|-------------|-------|--------|---------|
| 12–20–32 | 2,000 shares, $100 par value............ | 200,000.00 | ............ | 200,000.00 |
| 12–31–32 | 1,000 shares, $100 par value............ | ............ | 100,000.00 | 100,000.00 |
| 9–30–33 | 500 shares, $100 par value............ | ............ | 50,000.00 | 50,000.00 |

No stock has been issued by the company since September 30, 1933.

Mr. Swift examined the stubs in the stock certificate book and the accounts in the stockholders' ledger and determined that the stock issued and outstanding agreed with the amounts shown in the general ledger accounts. An examination of the certificate of incorporation and the Commissioner of Corporation's permit to issue stock disclosed authority had been received to issue 2,000 shares of $100 par value. The records show that only 1,500 shares have been issued to date.

In checking the minutes of the board of directors, Mr. Swift learned that a 2% dividend had been declared out of current earnings by the directors, December 20, 1938, payable January 20, 1939 to stockholders of record December 31, 1938. No entry for this dividend has been made by the bookkeeper.

The following information is compiled from an analysis of the stockholders' ledger:

| Name | Cert. No. | Number of Shares |
|------|-----------|------------------|
| Donald B. Beverly.................... | 1–2 | 800 |
| H. E. Beverly........................ | 5 | 50 |
| I. C. Beverly........................ | 3 | 100 |
| Carl Knox........................... | 7 | 100 |

| | | |
|---|---|---|
| John D. Mizuno........................ | 14 | 25 |
| Gertrude Newcomb..................... | 10 | 50 |
| Joseph J. Parker....................... | 13 | 135 |
| Eugene C. Rollins...................... | 11 | 75 |
| Myrtle E. Scott........................ | 12 | 50 |
| Margaret Weitfle....................... | 4 | 100 |
| Treasury Stock........................ | 15 | 15 |
| | | |
| Total.............................. | | 1,500 |

Certificates 6, 8, and 9 have been canceled and are attached to the certificate stubs.

## Surplus

The surplus account appears on the general ledger at December 31, 1938, as follows:

### Surplus

| Date | Description | Debit | Credit | Balance |
|---|---|---|---|---|
| 1- 1-38 | Balance............................... | ........... | 3,133.71 | 3,133.71 |
| 3- 1-38 | Revaluation of land and buildings........ | ........... | 27,500.00 | 30,633.71 |
| 12-20-38 | Donated stock—15 shares............... | ........... | 1,500.00 | 32,133.71 |

The entry made March 1, 1938, crediting surplus with $27,500 was made to record a write-up in value of the land and buildings. This item was previously discussed in Installment Six under the heading of Fixed Assets.

## INSTRUCTIONS

1. Read and study the auditing procedure suggested for the verification of capital stock and surplus in an "Examination of Financial Statements."

2. Prepare schedules for capital stock and surplus using forms similar to those shown in the illustrative set of audit working papers. (Illustration No. 32.)

3. Perform the audit work suggested for verifying capital stock and surplus in so far as the procedure applies to the information provided in this audit.

4. Prepare adjusting journal entries, where necessary, to adjust the account balances.

# CHAPTER THIRTEEN

## THE PROFIT AND LOSS STATEMENT

1. **Extent of Verification**

2. **Sales, Cost of Sales, and Gross Profit**

3. **Selling, General, and Administrative Expenses**

4. **Other Income and Other Charges**

5. **Auditing Procedure**

6. **Application of Principles**

7. **An Audit Case—Eleventh Installment**

A balance sheet audit, or an examination of financial statements, comprehends the certification of a balance sheet and statements of profit and loss and surplus. In order to include the profit and loss and surplus statements within the scope of his certificate, the auditor must make a review of the profit and loss accounts. It may be claimed that if the balance sheets at both the beginning and the end of an accounting period have been verified that the net profit or loss for the period must axiomatically be correct, taking into consideration any changes in the capital accounts during the period. This statement is not exactly correct as the balance sheet and profit and loss statement are interrelated and the balance sheet cannot be completely verified independently of the items in the profit and loss statement.

When the auditor has completed his audit of the balance sheet accounts, he also will have completed or partly completed his examination of a number of the profit and loss accounts. Many of the profit and loss accounts must be considered in connection with the asset or liability accounts to which they relate. For example, depreciation expense should be checked at the time the fixed asset accounts are verified. Losses on bad debts should be verified in connection with the verification of accounts and notes receivable. Interest accounts should be reviewed in connection with the verification of investments, notes receivable, notes payable, mortgages, and bonds payable.

## EXTENT OF VERIFICATION

To what extent should the items in the profit and loss statement be verified independently of the examination made in connection with the verification of the balance sheet items? In audits classified as an "Examination of Financial Statements" conditions may vary so widely that it is not practicable to submit a program for the examination of the profit and loss statement. Certain suggestions only may be given relative to the individual classifications.

It is suggested that the accountant prepare a working profit and loss statement preferably in comparative form covering two or more years, and in as much detail as possible. If company budgets are maintained, comparisons should be made between budget figures and those in the profit and loss statement. Likewise, if monthly statements are available, these should be compared with the annual results. If there are substantial variations between the profit and loss figures of the current year and those for the preceding year, or substantial variations between the current profit and loss figures and those in the budget which are not readily accounted for by changes in the volume of sales or of production, these items should be investigated, or explanations obtained from officers of the company.

It is advisable in setting up the working profit and loss statements in comparative form to compute ratios of the individual expense items as percentages of sales so that comparisons may be made of percentages as well as of amounts.

### SALES, COST OF SALES, AND GROSS PROFIT

**Sales.** A schedule should be made of sales by months for the current and preceding periods. Any large variation in sales as between corresponding months should be investigated to account for differences. If statistics are available, it is desirable to reconcile the quantities of the principal products sold with the quantities of the inventory at the beginning of the period plus the purchases, less the inventory on hand at the end of the period. If a proper system of internal check is maintained, no detailed checking of the sales records will be necessary.

An investigation should be made to determine that the sales records were closed on the last day of the period and that only sales belonging in the current period were included. Reference should be made to the shipping records to see that no goods shipped after midnight of the closing date were included in the sales of the period. If the auditor is auditing the records for the first time, a similar investigation should be made of the records at the beginning of the period to determine that sales were properly accounted for on that date.

**Cost of Sales.** Cost of sales in a merchandising business consists of the value of the merchandise on hand at the beginning of the period, plus the net cost of purchases, less the value of the merchandise on hand at the end of the period. If any one of these three elements is stated incorrectly, cost of sales will, of course, be incorrect. The inventories at the beginning and end of the period should be verified in connection with the verification of the balance sheet items. The purchases account also should be investigated.

The purchases account should be examined or analyzed sufficiently to determine that the amounts seem reasonable. In checking the records for unrecorded liabilities, an examination should be made to determine that all invoices for merchandise purchases are recorded at the close of the period. Failure to record purchase invoices would have the effect of overstating the profit for the period. On the other hand, profits for the period may be understated by recording purchase invoices for goods that have not been received, or on which title has not yet passed, or by recording as purchases the cost of equipment which is chargeable to asset accounts. A schedule of purchases by months for the current and the preceding periods should be prepared as an aid in determining variations in purchases between corresponding months of the two periods. Large variations should be investigated to see that the purchases account contains entries for merchandise items only.

Cost of sales in a manufacturing business represents the cost of materials, labor, and manufacturing expenses connected with the manufacturing of the product. The auditor should investigate the accounting system to determine that it is adequate and reliable, and that the accounting records are being correctly maintained. Inquiry should be made as to the method of distributing the manufacturing expenses to the cost of the product. It should be ascertained that the manufacturing expenses do not contain items that should be charged to financial, administrative, or to selling expenses. Only expenses properly chargeable to factory operations should be included.

**Gross Profit.** If inventory losses, due to declines in market valuations, are of sufficient importance to affect the percentage of gross profits on sales it is desirable to show these losses as a separate item in the statement, otherwise, wide variations may occur in the rate of gross profit due to inventory write-downs from cost to market value. Comparisons should be made of the rate of gross profit between periods, but obviously this comparison would have little meaning if in one period the amount of gross profit was materially understated due to declines in inventory valuations. Likewise, if selling prices of company products have been changed, or new products have been introduced, these factors should be taken into consideration in comparing volume of sales or rates of gross profit.

### SELLING, GENERAL, AND ADMINISTRATIVE EXPENSES

Schedules should be made of expense accounts, unless a working profit and loss statement has been set up in considerable detail. This should be done so that comparisons may be made between the figures for the current period and those for the preceding period or periods. As previously stated, comparisons should also be made between the figures for the current period and budget figures if they are available. Figures that seem to vary considerably from the previous year or from the budget figures should be investigated to see that the expense items have been properly classified.

Care should be taken to see that a proper distinction has been made between capital and revenue expenditures. Expenditures chargeable to asset accounts if charged to expense would, of course, understate the profits for the period. On the other hand, if expenses of substantial amounts are recorded in fixed asset accounts, the operating figures would be distorted by overstating the profits for the period. If the auditor is in doubt about any of the expenses, the ledger accounts in questions should be analyzed and vouchers for the larger items examined to see that the entries are proper charges to the accounts.

It is advisable to examine the pay rolls for one or more pay roll periods. In so doing, the auditor should ascertain that the employees, whose names are on the pay rolls, are actually in the employ of the company. A comparison should be made of the names on the pay roll with records of employees maintained in the company's personnel department. Pay roll checks returned by the bank should be compared with the amounts on the pay roll. The pay roll should be footed and the amounts traced into the ledger accounts.

## OTHER INCOME AND OTHER CHARGES

In the *Other Income* and *Other Charges* sections of the profit and loss statements, three types of items may be shown as follows: (1) financial income and financial expense, (2) non-operating income and expense items commonly referred to as extraneous income and expense, and (3) adjustments applicable to profits of prior periods.

Under *Other Income* may be included the following items: interest on bonds, mortgages, and notes receivable, dividends on investments in capital stocks of other companies, cash discounts on purchases, profit on sale of securities, profit on sale of fixed assets, profit on retirement of bonded indebtedness, adjustments of prior years' profits, and items of like nature.

*Other Charges* may include interest on notes payable and bonded indebtedness, amortization of bond discount, loss on sale of securities, loss on sale of fixed assets, tax assessments for prior years, losses on foreign exchange, and adjustments of prior years' expenses.

Many of the items listed above as *Other Income* and *Other Charges* are sometimes shown as "special credits to profit and loss" and "special charges to profit and loss" in sections immediately following the sections for *Other Income* and *Other Charges*. In such a case the sections for *Other Income* and *Other Charges* usually contain only items of financial income and financial expense. Adjustments applicable to profits of prior periods and extraneous income and expense items, such as profit or loss on sale of fixed assets, would be shown in the special credits or charges to profit and loss sections.

Some accountants may maintain that nonoperating expense and income items and adjustments of prior years' profits should be shown in the surplus statement rather than in the profit and loss statement. The final results in so far as their effect on net worth is concerned will be the same under either method. Recent developments in accounting practice would seem to be in the direction of disclosing to the stockholders of a company rather complete information as to the net earnings of a company available for dividends. This would tend to justify showing all the income and expense items in the profit and loss statement before arriving at a figure showing the net profit or loss for the period, otherwise, the reader of corporate reports might be deceived as to the actual earnings of a company.

## AUDITING PROCEDURE APPLICABLE TO THE PROFIT AND LOSS STATEMENT

### In an "Examination of Financial Statements"

"1. Analyze the profit and loss account for the period and obtain or prepare a working profit and loss statement in as much detail as is readily available. The extent of the examination to be made is dependent upon the classification of the accounts and other factors previously outlined. The accountant should satisfy himself that the income received and the expenditures made are properly classified in so far as the facts are known to him or ascertainable by reasonable inquiry.

"2. The profit and loss statement should be prepared so that it will be reasonably informative. It is usually helpful to obtain corresponding figures for one or more preceding years for comparative purposes as an aid in ascertaining and inquiring into unusual items during the year under review. The budgets adopted by the company and monthly financial statements, where available, should also be obtained for comparison with the annual results. Determine so far as possible that the company has applied its accounting principles consistently throughout the period and see that adequate explanation is made in the profit and loss statement of any departure from such principles.

"3. A satisfactory form of profit and loss statement is given on page 323, but any other form giving similar information may suffice. Conditions vary so widely that it is not practicable to submit a program for the examination of the profit and loss statement. Certain suggestions only are given relative to the individual classifications."

### Sales and Cost of Sales

"1. Whenever the necessary statistics are available it is desirable to reconcile the quantities of the principal products sold with the production or purchases during the period, taking into consideration the inventories at the beginning and end of the period.

"2. Ascertain by reference to the shipping records that the sales books were closed as of the last day of the period, and that no goods shipped after that date are included in the sales of the period. When a first examination is made it is well to ascertain similarly that the sales at the beginning of the period were recorded in accordance with the dates of shipment.

"3. Allowances to customers for trade discounts, outward freight, reductions in price, etc., should be deducted from gross sales. It is sometimes difficult to distinguish between deductions from sales and selling expenses, and the classification adopted by the company should be accepted if reasonable and consistently applied. Price concessions, allowances, and discounts are sometimes treated differently in the same trade or business. The net sales figure, after making such deductions from the gross volume of business recorded on the books, should be shown in the profit and loss statement, unless undesirable for trade reasons. Inquire as to the methods adopted to safeguard credits to customers for returned merchandise, claims, rebates, etc. Make a test examination to find out if the procedure is being followed.

"4. Cost of sales includes all the costs in connection with buying and producing goods sold. Write-downs of inventory to market prices at the end of the period may have a material effect on the percentage of gross profit to sales, and where such write-downs result from general business conditions rather than from the buying or production policies of the company, it may be desirable to show them separately. See that interdepartmental profits and, in the case of consolidated statements, intercompany profits are eliminated; if this is impracticable, the reason should be stated. If the accountant is in doubt as to the adequacy of the current provision for depreciation he should make suitable comment in his report."

### Gross Profit on Sales

"Gross profit on sales is ascertained by deducting cost of sales from net sales. Compute the ratio of gross profits to net sales; compare it with that of previous years, and make inquiries to account for any marked variation."

### Selling, General, and Administrative Expenses

"Examine the ledger accounts for selling, general, and administrative expenses to see that they are properly classified and that credits which should be shown elsewhere are not improperly deducted. Extraordinary items of material significance should be shown separately."

### Net Profit on Sales

"Net profit after deducting expenses but before other income and other charges is usually a significant figure, and determination of percentage to sales and comparison with previous years is desirable."

### Other Income

"Income derived from sources other than sales, such as income from investments, interest, discounts, etc., should appear under the heading 'other income.' The accountant should assure himself of the propriety of including each item as income. If there is extraordinary income of a material amount, proper disclosure should be made. If stock dividends received have been included as income, that fact as well as the basis on which they have been taken up should be indicated. If the company holds any of its own capital stock in its treasury, dividends thereon should not be treated as a credit to the income account."

### Other Charges

"Interest charges on funded debt, notes payable and other obligations, losses on securities sold and other nonoperating or extraordinary charges are usually detailed under the heading 'other charges.' Investigate these generally and see that they are properly included under this heading rather than as cost of sales or expenses. Provision for income and capital stock and excess-profits taxes may be included here or deducted as a separate item in the profit and loss statement. Minor surplus adjustments affecting prior periods are preferably included under this caption since it is impossible to close the accounts of any one period without continual overlapping of miscellaneous income and expense items."

## Modifications of Audit Program for Larger or Smaller Concerns

"Reasonable substantiation of a condensed income account or profit and loss statement is usually not difficult whether in a large or a small company, and a great part of the work will already have been done in making the examination of the balance

### Form of Profit and Loss Statement

| | | |
|---|---:|---:|
| Gross sales. | $xxx.xx | |
| Less outward freight, allowances and returns | xx.xx | |
| | | |
| Net sales | | $xxx.xx |
| Cost of sales | | xxx.xx |
| | | |
| Gross profit on sales | | xxx.xx |
| Selling, general and administrative expenses | | xx.xx |
| | | |
| Net profit before other income and charges | | xx.xx |
| | | |
| Other income: | | |
| Income from investments | xx.xx | |
| Interest on notes receivable, etc. | xx.xx | |
| Other non-operating or extraordinary income (separately shown) | xx.xx | xx.xx |
| | | |
| | | xxx.xx |
| | | |
| Other charges: | | |
| Interest on funded debt (and amortization of bond discount) | xx.xx | |
| Interest on notes payable | xx.xx | |
| Other non-operating or extraordinary charges (separately shown) | xx.xx | |
| Provisions for income taxes | xx.xx | |
| | | |
| Total deductions | | xxx.xx |
| | | |
| Net profit (loss) for period carried to surplus | | xx.xx |

NOTE: It is desirable to indicate the amount of provision for depreciation, depletion, etc., for the period.

sheets at the beginning and end of the period. The separation of sales and deductions from sales, the determination of cost of sales and the classification of the various expenses and charges, however, are sometimes difficult in the case of a large company; and a good deal of reliance must necessarily be placed on the internal accounting classifications and control. Overhead is frequently distributed between operations or products or even between plants and this may make it difficult, if not impracticable, for the accountant to classify the summarized profit and loss statement in any greater detail than that followed by the company in its internal statements or to obtain the data necessary for that purpose from the underlying records. It is most important that the accountant obtain a thorough understanding of the accounting principles and classifications adopted by the company before making his examination of the profit and loss statement. It will then be necessary for him to use his judgment to determine the relative importance of the different items and the amount of detailed checking which he considers necessary."

## APPLICATION OF PRINCIPLES

### AUDIT OF THE BLANK MANUFACTURING COMPANY (Continued)

J. I. King and C. E. Shaw verified the profit and loss accounts of The Blank Manufacturing Company. The footings and balances of all accounts were checked and various tests were made to verify the accuracy of the postings. The following accounts were given special attention:

**Property Taxes.** After consultation of the general manager and checking over the tax receipts it was decided to distribute the property taxes on a basis of 90% to manufacturing and 10% to selling and administrative expenses. Since the company is engaged in manufacturing, it is important to make a proper allocation of all manufacturing costs.

**Insurance.** Expired premiums on insurance policies covering the plant and equipment amounting to $2,420 should be charged to manufacturing expense, while the expired premiums on insurance policies covering furniture and fixtures, merchandise, and delivery equipment amounting to $1,421 should be charged to selling and administrative expense. The proper entry to record the expired insurance has previously been made (see Illustration No. 22).

**Depreciation of Buildings.** In view of the fact that only a small part of the buildings is used for general office purposes, it was decided to charge the entire amount of depreciation of buildings to manufacturing expense. (See Illustration No. 20.)

**Interest and Discount.** The trial balance shows that separate accounts have been kept for interest and discount and for bond interest. The results of analyzing the interest and discount account are shown in Illustration No. 33.

### THE BLANK MANUFACTURING COMPANY

#### Analysis of Interest and Discount—December 31, 1937

| | | |
|---|---:|---:|
| *Interest and Discount Dr. Balance (per trial balance)* | $ 734.81 | |
| *Add Accrued Interest on Notes Payable* | 148.02 | |
| *Total Dr. Balance* | $ 882.83 | |
| *Deduct: Accrued Interest on Notes Rec.* 78.25 | | |
| *Accrued Interest on Marketable Securities* 77.08 | 155.33 | |
| *Adjusted Dr. Balance* | | $ 727.50 |
| *Distribution:* | | |
| *Interest Expense Dr.* | $1,512.00 | |
| *Interest Income Cr.* | 784.50 | |
| *Adjusted Balance* | | $ 727.50 |

#### Adjusting Journal Entry

| | | |
|---|---:|---:|
| *Interest Expense* | $1,512.00 | |
| *Interest Income* | | $ 784.50 |
| *Interest and Discount* | | 727.50 |
| *To reclassify interest and discount.* | | |

*C. E. Shaw*
*(Junior Accountant)*

*(Schedule No. 18)*

**Illustration No. 33. Analysis of Interest and Discount**

## SUMMARY

A profit and loss statement is usually included in an auditor's report covering a balance sheet audit. It should be submitted with the income and expenditures classified under appropriate captions, and, if possible, this statement should show the operations in comparative form. If a profit and loss statement is prepared for more than one year it should be set up in comparative form. If comparative figures for several years are submitted, the accountant must satisfy himself that the figures for all periods are prepared on the same basis. Instances are frequent where concerns make a liberal provision for depreciation, etc., in prosperous years, and reduce, or even eliminate, all depreciation in years during which business is poor and profits small. Occasionally, a basis of inventory valuation is adopted differing materially from the basis used the year before, and some concerns show a tendency to charge to capital during lean years, items of a nature which are absorbed in operating expenses during prosperous years.

Increases or decreases in sales should be carefully analyzed. Expenditures should be analyzed to ascertain that capital expenditures are not charged against current operations and that no current operating expenses are capitalized. The statement should be prepared in standard form and it should reflect the actual financial results of the operations of the business for the period under audit.

### AUDITING THEORY

**13—142.** Why is it necessary to include a profit and loss statement in the report covering a balance sheet audit?

**13—143.** Explain the following terms:

(a) Cost of sales (in a manufacturing business)
(b) Cost of production
(c) Gross trading profit
(d) Operating income
(e) Nonrecurring items
(f) Deductions from income

**13—144.** (a) Why do some companies have separate accounts for undivided profits and surplus?

(b) When both accounts are kept, to which account are dividends usually charged?

**13—145.** To what extent is it necessary to audit the items appearing on a profit and loss statement when making a balance sheet audit?

**13—146.** Explain why an auditor, in making a balance sheet audit, should examine income and expense accounts.

(C. P. A. Ohio)

**13—147.** You have been called to audit the books of a furniture company which sells on the installment plan. The books have been closed when you reach the office, and you are handed a completed profit and loss statement and balance sheet. The company has been in business one year only.

Upon investigation you find that all installment sales are credited to an account designated "Installment Sales." A controlling account and subsidiary ledger are kept for the installment customers.

You find that the total of the installment sales has been credited to the installment sales account, which has been closed into profit and loss.

All accounts, installment and otherwise, that were known to be uncollectible have been charged off. There are no reserves against balances due from customers on the books.

What criticisms or corrections have you to suggest as to the correctness of the balance sheet and profit and loss statement handed to you.

(A. I. A.)

## AUDITING PROBLEMS

**13—35.** The manager of The Arcola Heating Co. asks you to certify to its average annual operating profits for the past five years. After charging all costs, expenses, depreciation, and allowances for bad debts, it is found that profits for the first year were $30,000; second year, $37,500; third year, $35,400; fourth year, $43,200; fifth year, $38,700.

Included in the second year's profits is profit on sale of real estate, $3,750; in third year's profits, $7,500, profit on investments; in fifth year's profit, $8,600, profit on sales of real estate.

Prepare statement showing computation of the average annual operating profit.

**13—36.** A. Wells, a manufacturer of novelties, is joined by I. M. Anxious in partnership upon the following terms:

A. Wells is to receive a monthly salary of $100 for the first year, which shall be a first charge upon the profits after providing for the usual business expenses and before reckoning 3% upon the partner's capital. In the event of such profits during the first year, or any subsequent year, not exceeding 6% of the total capital (after payment of the salary), this salary shall be reduced to $75 per month the following year, and remain so until the yearly profit advances to more than 6% when such salary shall return to $100, commencing the year succeeding the one showing the required increase of profit. Should the profits in any one year amount to more than 10% upon capital, A. Wells shall be entitled (in addition to the salary he has received for that year) to a bonus of 33⅓% upon any sum in excess up to $1,500 and

25% upon any further excess profits and this bonus shall be a charge against profits, before allotting the interest at 3% upon capital. Any profit then remaining shall be divided equally.

When the partnership was organized five years ago, the partners made the following investments:

| | |
|---|---|
| A. Wells............................................. | $6,000.00 |
| I. M. Anxious...................................... | 5,000.00 |

Profit before deducting salary, interest or bonus:

| | |
|---|---|
| 1st year............................................. | $1,750.00 |
| 2d year.............................................. | 1,800.00 |
| 3d year.............................................. | 4,250.00 |
| 4th year............................................. | 5,000.00 |
| 5th year............................................. | 5,500.00 |

On account of a disagreement between the partners, you have been employed to make such an audit of the accounts as is necessary to establish the present capital of each of the partners at the end of the fifth year.

In making the audit you find that it has been the custom to pay in cash the salaries and bonuses when due. The interest on the partners' investments and the net profits for each year have been credited to the partners capital accounts.

From the information given, prepare a schedule showing your computation of the profits to be distributed between the partners at the end of each year, and prepare capital accounts for each of the partners covering the five-year period.

**13—37.** The Spring Grove Association was formed on January 2, 1923, for the purpose of acquiring and conducting a cemetery, and started business on that date with a capital stock of $100,000 paid for in cash. The association first purchased forty acres of land within easy access of a large city paying for same at the rate of $1,000 per acre. It proceeded to expend considerable sums of money in the purchase and planting of trees and shrubs, laying out drives, and pathways, sodding, building of glass houses, etc. The association withheld the selling of burial lots until after January 2, 1933, so as to allow the trees and shrubs to become more fully grown and in the expectation that with the growth of the city their property would become more valuable.

In the year 1933, the association commenced selling burial lots, and all lots were sold under a special provision whereby the association agreed to apply 50% of all cash received on sales in the purchase of 4% bonds until a total of $150,000 of such bonds had been purchased. The agreement further provided that after all the lots had been sold, the company would wind up its affairs and the above bonds, amounting to $150,000, would be given to the city, the income of such bonds to be used in keeping up the cemetery. It has been the custom of the association not to purchase bonds until after the close of each fiscal year and after the total sales for that year have been determined.

March 31, 1939, the directors of the association found that, while they believed the books to be in balance, no proper entries had been recorded showing the total amount of their investment, and that no entries had been made with respect to the fund of $150,000 from which said bonds were to be purchased. While cash dividends had been declared and paid, the directors were in ignorance of what their profits actually had been, and how much of the dividends so received represented a distribution of profits and how much represented liquidating dividends. They, therefore, employ you to audit the accounts, to make the necessary entries on the books to properly record the operations, to prepare a balance sheet as of December 31, 1938, and to prepare a profit and loss statement for the period from January 2, 1923, to December 31, 1938.

After determining the clerical accuracy of the books, you prepare the following comparative trial balances:

## THE SPRING GROVE ASSOCIATION

### Comparative Trial Balances

| Debits | Dec. 31, 1933 | Dec. 31, 1938 |
|---|---|---|
| Real Estate........................... | $ 40,000.00 | $ 40,000.00 |
| Improvements......................... | 45,000.00 | 45,000.00 |
| Bonds (4%)........................... | .......... | 125,000.00 |
| Administrative Expense............... | 20,000.00 | 46,000.00 |
| Upkeep of Cemetery................... | .......... | 45,000.00 |
| Dividends Paid....................... | .......... | 130,000.00 |
| Cash................................. | 7,000.00 | 40,800.00 |
| | $112,000.00 | $471,800.00 |

| Credits | | |
|---|---|---|
| Interest Income...................... | $ 12,000.00 | $ 12,000.00 |
| Bond Interest........................ | .......... | 9,800.00 |
| Sale of Lots......................... | .......... | 350,000.00 |
| Capital Stock........................ | 100,000.00 | 100,000.00 |
| | $112,000.00 | $471,800.00 |

During the course of the audit, you ascertained the following:

(a) The sales for the year 1935 amounted to $240,000 and, in accordance with the provision, 50% of this sum was invested in bonds. The following year, the sales amounted to $110,000 but, for some reason, only $5,000 was invested in bonds.

(b) The credit to the bond interest account is the result of interest at 4% on the bonds amounting to $120,000 for a period of two years and on $5,000 for a period of one year. The credit of $12,000 to interest income is the amount of interest at 4% on the unexpended cash balance.

(c) An inventory of unsold lots on December 31, 1938, showed ten acres of equally desirable character with that already sold.

(d) Improvements costing $45,000 were incurred during the period between January 2, 1923, and December 31, 1933, and represent an addition to the value of the real estate, and it was agreed that the amount spent for improvements should be charged to the real estate account.

(e) The cost of upkeep of the cemetery was incurred during the five-year period ending December 31, 1938, and represents a part of the operating expenses.

(f) An examination of the charter and by-laws of the association revealed that it had agreed to apply 50% of all cash received from the sale of lots, to the purchase of 4% bonds until a total of $150,000 of bonds had been purchased. These bonds were to be held in a sinking fund until all the lots had been sold, when the association would give the bonds to the city under an agreement that the income from the bonds was to be used in keeping up the cemetery. The trial balance on December 31, 1938, shows that bonds amounting to $125,000 were purchased during the period from December 31, 1933 to December 31, 1938. In view of the fact that the value of the lots sold amounted to $350,000 and there are no accounts receivable, it is evident that the lots were sold for cash. This indicates that the association must under its agreement set aside cash amounting to $25,000 to be used in the purchase of additional bonds. Upon your recommendation, the officials agree to do this and a check for $25,000 is drawn in favor of the sinking fund. After this adjustment is made, the sinking fund consists of bonds amounting to $125,000 and cash amounting to $25,000. It was also decided to set up a reserve for sinking fund amounting to $150,000 to be maintained until such time as the bonds are given to the city.

## AUDITING PRACTICE
### An Audit Case (Eleventh Installment)

Ken B. Swift has now completed the audit of the Beverly Supply Company's balance sheet accounts. The profit and loss accounts remain to be audited. A number of the profit and loss accounts have been partially or completely verified in connection with the verification of the asset or liability accounts to which they relate.

The following are the profit and loss accounts that have been partially or completely verified in connection with audit work performed in the preceding installments:

1. Insurance expense.................................Installment Seven
2. Store and office supplies used.......................    "        Seven
3. Property taxes.....................................    "        Eight
4. Bad debts.........................................    "        Four
5. Depreciation of furniture and fixtures...............    "        Six

6. Depreciation of delivery equipment..................Installment Six
7. Depreciation of buildings..........................    "    Six
8. Interest on notes receivable.......................    "    Four
9. Bond interest income..............................    "    Three
10. Dividends received...............................    "    Three
11. Interest on notes payable.........................    "    Eight
12. Capital stock tax................................    "    Eight
13. Pay roll taxes...................................    "    Eight

The only profit and loss accounts that have not been verified are the following:

1. Sales
2. Sales returns
3. Cost of sales
4. Sales salaries
5. Advertising
6. Delivery expense
7. Office salaries
8. Administrative salaries
9. Miscellaneous expense

The amount of verification of the profit and loss accounts will depend on circumstances encountered in each audit such as (1) the purpose of the audit; (2) the type of business; and (3) the extent of internal check and control within the organization.

The following suggestions are made, however, to assist in determining that the income and expenses have been properly classified in the accounts:

(1) Analyze the accounts for the period to see that the entries in the accounts are properly classified. It may be necessary to examine the vouchers supporting the entries and to test several pay rolls to see that they are distributed to the proper expense accounts.

(2) Reconcile, if possible, the quantities sold with the amount of purchases and the inventories at the beginning and end of the period. This reconciliation may be made by the "gross profit method."

(3) Ascertain by reference to the shipping records that the sales books were closed as of the last day of the period, and that no goods shipped after that date were included in the sales of the period.

## INSTRUCTIONS

1. Study carefully the suggestions made concerning the verification of the profit and loss statement and the items contained therein in an "Examination of Financial Statements."

2. Prepare a schedule of cost of sales from information contained in the merchandise stock and the cost of sales accounts (see Installment Five—Inventories) and from adjusting journal entries that have been prepared which affect the cost of sales.

3. No adjustment of the profit and loss accounts will need to be made other than those already provided for by the adjusting journal entries made in connection with previous installments of this audit.

# CHAPTER FOURTEEN

## CONCLUDING AN AUDIT

In any verification of accounts the auditor, of necessity, should be systematic in his work, should pursue a definite program, and should keep a permanent record of the information obtained. The audit working papers should be so prepared and assembled as to present an outline of what was done during the course of the audit, when it was done, who did it, and what changes or adjustments were made in arriving at or compiling the data or information which will be needed in preparing the final report.

The audit working papers are the auditor's source of information as to the condition of the company and as to all matters pertaining to the audit, once he has finished the engagement and returned to the office. Everything pertinent to the finished report, or to any future questions likely to arise as a result of the audit should be obtainable from the working papers. The working papers should be prepared for the purpose of providing the auditor with a permanent record of his engagement, to be filed for future reference, and to provide a complete history not only of the operations and condition of the enterprise concerned, but also of the routines and procedures of the auditor in verifying the results of those operations.

The type of working papers to be used will vary depending on the desires and aptitudes of the auditor, or the standard

practice adopted by the firm.  In the larger auditing firms standard papers are prescribed for auditing purposes, in order to
provide standardization in all the records of the company, and
to facilitate the preparation of reports, editing of the material,
and the proper handling of the routine of an engagement.  As a
rule, working papers which are simple and easily handled are
considered advisable.  Many firms use columnar analysis paper
of ten, twelve, or more columns for the actual record of the
engagement, supplemented by a different type of paper showing
the auditing schedule, preparation of the reports, etc., in order to
make the different sections of the work stand in relief one from
the other.  Where such paper is used, the columns may be used
for specific information, schedules easily drawn up, and the
headings, totals, and details easily set off so as to be readily
analyzed and interpreted.

In preparing working papers, the auditor should always keep
in mind that the papers are to be a permanent record, that paper
is cheaper than time, and that it pays to prepare them in such a
way as to leave plenty of space for analyses, schedules, and
adjustments, with explanations.  Orderliness should be paramount
in preparing all information.

The working papers represent the record of the auditor of
the engagement concerned.  Such being the case, they must
contain all the information pertinent to the engagement which he
may need for the preparation of the report to the client, or for
reference in relation to the work done in case a question may
arise in the future.

All working papers should be properly headed indicating
the identity of the client, the nature of the information recorded,
and the date of the audit.  The working papers should be numbered so that they may be indexed to the working trial balance.
Such a cross reference will facilitate locating any desired information relating to the audit.  Different systems are used in
indexing audit working papers.  Numbers or letters, or com-
binations of the two, may be used to identify the schedules.

The usual procedure in auditing is to start with the audited
account balances as of the close of the preceding period and end
with a list of the adjusted balances at close of the period under
audit.  When the working trial balance has been completed, it
should provide a ready reference to the accounts, working papers,

and adjustments deemed necessary to bring the books of account in accord with the auditor's final report.

In the verification of cash, notes payable to banks, and similar items, bank certificates should be filed with the working papers. The inventory certificate should be included with the working papers on inventories, and so on. Where income tax calculations are made, or any special reports are included, copies of each should be included in the file.

Some auditors also summarize the journal entries, making a summary of all entries made as a result of the audit. This is especially convenient when these entries are to be posted to the books by the staff of the client. In such a case the auditor, on the succeeding audit, if the books are not in agreement at the beginning of the period with the former audit report, may have a summarized list of entries to check with the books. This will be of particular value where several auditors are working on the same assignment and the adjustments affect two or more verifications under separate men.

The working papers prepared during the audit are directly made for the purpose of facilitating the preparation of the report to the client, and to furnish a permanent record of the audit for future reference. Their necessity for report purposes is easily to be seen. The auditor does his detail work in the office and place of business of the client. As soon as this is finished, the summary report of his findings is to be written, the greater part of which must be done in the auditor's office. Such being the case, the working papers must be prepared to facilitate the writing of the report. This, however, is not the only purpose of working papers. Frequently it becomes necessary for the auditor to refer to some audit previously made for purposes of advising clients or former clients as to previous financial situations, trends, or other information. The client may become involved in legal difficulties, and the former audit of the enterprise may be under question. The auditor must then be prepared to answer pertinent questions as to what he did, how he did it, and why, in court. Audit working papers are invaluable to the auditor, they are his property to be kept permanently, not only for the advantage to himself and his client in future work but as a protection against contingencies of the future, which may, through no negligence of his, involve the auditor in difficulties far reaching in character.

The profession has set up rather definite practices as regards working papers. As they are papers containing information of a confidential nature, they are not to be used outside of the office for the information of others, nor is their content to be divulged to others. In cases in which clients or former clients wish certain information from former audits, it is considered better practice to co-operate to the fullest extent, the auditor going so far as to prepare copies from his files of information wanted. Working papers themselves, however, are the property of the auditor, and as such should remain with the auditor, and should not be loaned, even to the client himself. Copies should suffice for the purpose of the client, originals are often of extreme value to the auditor.

## CORRECTING AND ADJUSTING ENTRIES

Journal entries should be made, together with full explanations, for all errors, whether clerical or in principle, that have been discovered during the course of an audit. These errors will be shown by the working papers prepared by the persons engaged on an audit. A separate entry should be made for each error found. Usually, after discussing the matter of errors with the client, the bookkeepers will be instructed to make similar correcting entries on the books of account. If this is done the books will show the same results as the statements prepared by the auditor. If, for any reason, the books of the client are not corrected, the auditor should proceed with his working papers in the same manner as outlined, for his statements must show the facts based upon sound accounting procedure.

There are certain facts which may not appear in the accounts at the close of the fiscal period, and in order that the books may show true conditions on that date, adjusting entries are required. Entries must be made for accrued assets, accrued liabilities, deferred charges to operations, deferred credits to income, depreciation, reserves, inventories, etc.

Frequently it is found necessary to draft adjusting entries to reclassify certain accounts. For instance, accounts receivable may be reclassified to distinguish between accounts with trade debtors and accounts with employees. Such reclassification of accounts is usually made to facilitate a proper listing of the accounts in the financial statements.

## BRINGING THE AUDIT TO A CLOSE

After the detailed work of verifying the accounts has been completed, the summarizing work in connection with the completion of the audit working papers remains to be done. The steps to be followed in completing the audit working papers and in bringing the audit work to a close may be listed as follows:

(1) The adjusting journal entries prepared during the course of the audit should be reviewed by the auditor before posting them to the working trial balance to see that they are correct both in amount and in the accounts affected.

(2) It is advisable to discuss with the client the proposed adjustments prior to the actual posting of the adjusting journal entries to the working trial balance. The client may be of assistance in justifying the procedure followed in recording the transactions in the accounts. He should at least be informed of the adjustments which the auditor proposes to make.

(3) After the entries have been reviewed and are found to be correct, they should be posted to the working trial balance.

(4) The working trial balance should be completed by extending the adjusted balances of the accounts to the balance sheet and the profit and loss columns.

(5) The schedules and analyses should be arranged in the order in which the accounts to which they relate appear in the working trial balance.

(6) Number the schedules and analyses and index them to the working trial balance.

(7) Compare the amount of the adjusted balance on each schedule with the amount of the adjusted balance in the balance sheet or profit and loss columns of the working trial balance to see that they agree.

(8) When the working trial balance has been completed, a final check should be made to see that no audit work has been overlooked that should have been performed and that no information has been omitted that will be needed in preparing the audit report. Writing the report is of course the last step.

## APPLICATION OF PRINCIPLES

### AUDIT OF THE BLANK MANUFACTURING COMPANY (Continued)

The audit of The Blank Manufacturing Company constituting an examination of financial statements has been completed so far as the verification of accounts is concerned. The auditors' working papers have been illustrated in the preceding chapters except for the information obtained by Mr. Merz in examining the certificate of incorporation and in reading the corporation minutes of The Blank Manufacturing Company. Mr. Merz's notes are shown in Illustration No. 34. The illustrations show what information was recorded by the auditors. The discussion of auditing procedure and the illustration of the auditors' working papers is continuous from Chapter Three through Chapter Fifteen, paralleling the subject matter of each chapter.

As was explained in Chapter Three, the auditors used a working trial balance prepared in two sections. The form of the working trial balance is shown in Illustration No. 5, pages 72 to 74. It will be noted that the first section contains the balance sheet accounts and the second section the profit and loss accounts. The illustration shows the working trial balance of the auditor after the auditor had recorded the bookkeeper's balances of all accounts kept in the general ledger as of the close of the period under audit. The auditor simply copied the account balances as appeared in the ledger. The only adjustment shown in that illustration is for an offsetting error of $30 affecting the accounts with salaries of salesmen and advances to employees.

As the auditors completed the audit, the required adjusting entries were drafted and are illustrated. These entries are now summarized in Illustration No. 35 which appears in this chapter. In Illustration No. 36, the working trial balance is shown in final form after the adjusting entries have been posted and the proper extensions made. The form of the working trial balance shown in this illustration is exactly the same as in Illustration No. 5. A careful examination of the final working trial balance will reveal that it provides the information which will be needed in preparing the financial statements which will appear in the final report to the client.

## THE BLANK MANUFACTURING COMPANY
### Excerpts from Corporation Minutes

### 1935

*Monthly Meeting—December 10, 1935:*

*Authorized an issue of 5%, twenty-year, sinking fund bonds amounting to $100,000. The bonds are to be dated and issued as of January 15, 1936. The bonds are to be coupon bonds, interest payable semi-annually, and they are to be registered with the Merchants National Bank as trustee.*

### 1936

*Monthly Meeting—January 10, 1936:*

*Accounting Department authorized to write off, against surplus, organization expenses amounting to $8,166.67. One tenth is to be written off annually over a period of ten years, commencing December 31, 1936.*

*Monthly Meeting—March 10, 1936:*

*Voted that the discount on bonds issued January 15, 1936, should be amortized over the life of the bonds (20 years) on a straight-line basis, 5% each year.*

### 1937

*Special Meeting—July 1, 1937:*

*Voted the declaration of a dividend of 5% payable August 1, 1937, to stockholders of record July 15, 1937.*

*Note: Directors' meetings were scheduled monthly, but only routine business was transacted except as noted above.*

*W. H. Merz*
*(Senior Accountant)*                                      *(Schedule No. 19)*

Illustration No. 34.  Analysis of Corporation Minutes

## THE BLANK MANUFACTURING COMPANY
### Adjusting Journal Entries—December 31, 1937

(1)

| | | |
|---|---:|---:|
| Salaries of Salesmen | $ 30.00 | |
| Salary Advances to Employees | | $ 30.00 |

To correct an offsetting error of $30 in the footing of each of the above accounts.  (Sch. 11)

(2)

| | | |
|---|---:|---:|
| Office Expense | 110.00 | |
| Miscellaneous General Expense | 70.00 | |
| Merchants Bank—Checking Account | | 180.00 |

To reimburse the petty cash fund as of December 31, 1937, and to record expense vouchers applicable to the year 1937, which were included in the petty cash fund at January 15, 1938. (Sch. 3)

(3)

| | | |
|---|---|---|
| Accounts Receivable—Trade Debtors.............. | $ 17.76 | |
| Merchants Bank—Checking Account.......... | | $ 17.76 |

To record bank debit memo for check returned on account of "Not Sufficient Funds". This check was included in the cash receipts of 12–31–37, and the bank deposit of 1–3–38. (Sch. 3)

(4)

| | | |
|---|---|---|
| Accrued Interest Receivable..................... | 77.08 | |
| Interest and Discount........................ | | 77.08 |

To record accrued interest on bonds at December 31, 1937. (Sch. 4)

(5)

| | | |
|---|---|---|
| Sinking Fund...................................... | 160.42 | |
| Sinking Fund Income........................ | | 160.42 |

To record interest accrued on sinking fund investments at December 31, 1937. (Sch. 5)

(6)

| | | |
|---|---|---|
| Accrued Interest Receivable..................... | 78.25 | |
| Interest and Discount........................ | | 78.25 |

To record accrued interest on notes receivable at December 31, 1937. (Sch. 6)

(7)

| | | |
|---|---|---|
| Notes Receivable—Officers..................... | 1,500.00 | |
| Notes Receivable—Trade Debtors............ | | 1,500.00 |

To show the notes of officers separately for balance sheet purposes. (Sch. 6)

(8)

| | | |
|---|---|---|
| Accounts Receivable—Trade Debtors.............. | 3,034.50 | |
| Customers' Overpayments................... | | 3,034.50 |

To properly classify accounts receivable in the working trial balance and to facilitate showing accounts with credit balances as a liability on the balance sheet. (Sch. 7)

(9)

| | | |
|---|---|---|
| Loss on Bad Debts............................. | 1,952.91 | |
| Reserve for Doubtful Notes and Accounts...... | | 1,952.91 |

To increase the reserve for doubtful notes and accounts to 2% of the amount of the notes and accounts receivable on hand at December 31, 1937. (Sch. 7)

(10)

| | | |
|---|---|---|
| Raw Materials Inventory......................... | 25,000.00 | |
| Good in Process Inventory........................ | 32,875.00 | |
| Finished Goods Inventory...................... | 80,000.00 | |
| Raw Material Purchases...................... | | 25,000.00 |
| Cost of Production........................... | | 32,875.00 |
| Cost of Sales................................ | | 80,000.00 |

To record inventories as of December 31, 1937. (Sch. 8)

(11)

| | | |
|---|---|---|
| Raw Material Purchases......................... | $ 37,310.50 | |
| Cost of Sales.................................... | 15,000.00 | |
|     Raw Materials Inventory..................... | | $ 37,310.50 |
|     Finished Goods Inventory................... | | 15,000.00 |

        To transfer inventories at beginning of period to the profit and loss section of the working trial balance. There was no inventory of goods in process on hand at beginning of period under audit. (Sch. 8)

(12)

| | | |
|---|---|---|
| Machinery....................................... | 215.00 | |
|     Tools and Implements....................... | | 215.00 |

        To transfer the cost of a machine amounting to $215 from the tools and implements account to the machinery account. (Sch. 9)

(13)

| | | |
|---|---|---|
| Depreciation—Office Furniture..................... | 260.05 | |
| Depreciation—Delivery Trucks..................... | 3,000.00 | |
| Depreciation—Machinery.......................... | 6,000.00 | |
| Depreciation—Buildings........................... | 3,750.00 | |
|     Office Furniture............................. | | 260.05 |
|     Reserve for Depreciation—Delivery Trucks..... | | 3,000.00 |
|     Reserve for Depreciation—Machinery.......... | | 6,000.00 |
|     Reserve for Depreciation—Buildings........... | | 3,750.00 |

        To record the depreciation of fixed assets for the period ended December 31, 1937. (Sch. 9)

(14)

| | | |
|---|---|---|
| Expired Insurance—Manufacturing................ | 2,420.00 | |
| Expired Insurance—Administrative................ | 1,421.00 | |
|     Prepaid Insurance........................... | | 3,841.00 |

        To record the insurance expired during the year ended December 31, 1937. (Sch. 10)

(15)

| | | |
|---|---|---|
| Office Supplies Used............................ | 230.00 | |
|     Office Supplies.............................. | | 230.00 |

        To record the cost of office supplies consumed during the year ended December 31, 1937. (Sch. 11)

(16)

| | | |
|---|---|---|
| Prepaid Advertising............................. | 12,575.00 | |
|     Advertising................................. | | 12,575.00 |

        To defer one-half of the advertising expense incurred during 1937. (Sch. 11)

(17)

| | | |
|---|---|---|
| Surplus........................................ | 816.67 | |
|     Organization Expense....................... | | 816.67 |

        To charge off 10% of organization expense. (Sch. 11)

(18)

| | | |
|---|---|---|
| Bond Discount Written Off....................... | 375.00 | |
|     Bond Discount.............................. | | 375.00 |

        To record the amount of bond discount written off for the year ended December 31, 1937. (Sch. 11)

(19)

| | | |
|---|---|---|
| Interest and Discount............................. | $   148.02 | |
|    Accrued Interest Payable..................... | | $   148.02 |

      To record the accrued interest on notes payable as of December 31, 1937.  (Sch. 12)

(20)

| | | |
|---|---|---|
| Accounts Payable............................... | 7,681.50 | |
|    Accounts Payable—Officers................... | | 7,681.50 |

      To reclassify the accounts payable for balance sheet purposes.  (Sch. 13)

(21)

| | | |
|---|---|---|
| Factory Labor.................................. | 4,980.20 | |
| Salaries of Salesmen............................ | 585.00 | |
| Delivery Salaries................................ | 120.00 | |
| Office Salaries.................................. | 626.00 | |
|    Accrued Wages Payable...................... | | 6,311.20 |

      To record accrued wages as of December 31, 1937.  (Sch. 14)

(22)

| | | |
|---|---|---|
| Deferred Capital Stock Tax....................... | 650.00 | |
|    Accrued Capital Stock Tax Payable............ | | 650.00 |

      To record the estimated amount of the capital stock tax for year ending June 30, 1938.

(23)

| | | |
|---|---|---|
| Federal Social Security Excise Tax (U. C.).......... | 12.62 | |
| State U. C. Contributions........................ | 113.60 | |
|    Employer's Fed. Excise Tax Pay. (U. C.)...... | | 12.62 |
|    State U. C. Contributions Payable............ | | 113.60 |

      To record pay roll taxes imposed under Title IX of the Social Security Act on wages accrued December 31, 1937.  (Sch. 15)

(24)

| | | |
|---|---|---|
| Bond Interest................................... | 2,291.67 | |
|    Accrued Interest Payable..................... | | 2,291.67 |

      To record interest accrued on first mortgage bonds outstanding at December 31, 1937.  (Sch. 16)

(25)

| | | |
|---|---|---|
| Surplus......................................... | 2,910.42 | |
|    Sinking Fund Reserve........................ | | 2,910.42 |

      To record the amount reserved for sinking fund purposes. Of the amount reserved, $2,750.00 represents the required annual contribution and $160.42 represents the accrued interest on sinking fund bonds.  (Sch. 16)

(26)

| | | |
|---|---|---|
| Surplus......................................... | 22,500.00 | |
|    Dividend #1................................. | | 22,500.00 |

      To transfer the dividend account to surplus. (Sch. 17)

(27)

| | | |
|---|---|---|
| Interest Expense................................ | 1,512.00 | |
|    Interest Income............................. | | 784.50 |
|    Interest and Discount....................... | | 727.50 |

      To reclassify interest and discount.  (Sch. 18)

(28)

Property Taxes—Manufacturing................... $ 1,809.00
Property Taxes—Administrative.................. 201.00
　　Property Taxes............................ $ 2,010.00
　　　　To reclassify property taxes.

**Illustration No. 35.  Adjusting Entries**

## SUMMARY

When an audit has been completed, the accountant in charge assembles the working papers before leaving the office of the client. He should check over the trial balance together with the various schedules, analyses, and summaries supporting it, and index the schedules to the trial balance, or to statements prepared from the trial balance. The reason for doing this work immediately and before leaving the place where the work has been carried on, is that if anything should develop which requires attention, access to the books is still possible. It is quite embarrassing to discover, perhaps several days after an audit has been completed, that certain information is needed and it is impractical to return to the office of the client. Satisfactory results in such cases often cannot be obtained by correspondence.

The proper handling of audit working papers is of vital importance, and the manner of so doing immediately stamps the auditor as good, poor, or average. Audit working papers of necessity vary with each engagement, with the desires and procedures of each firm of accountants and with individual accountants and auditors, hence no standardized set-ups, procedures, or practices have been presented.

## AUDITING THEORY

**14—148.** What are audit working papers, and what purpose do they serve?

**14—149.** What procedure should be followed in bringing an audit to a close? Discuss.

**14—150.** What form of working trial balance was used in the audit of The Blank Manufacturing Company? Name two other forms of working trial balances that could have been used.

**14—151.** Should an auditor's working trial balance be completed in the office of the client or in the auditor's office? Explain.

**14—152.** Name and discuss three types of journal entries that were classed as adjusting journal entries in the audit of The Blank Manufacturing Company.

(*Continued on page 348*)

## THE BLANK MANUFACTURING COMPANY

### Working Trial Balance, December 31, 1937

(Sec. 1)

| Sched. No. | Balance Sheet Accounts | Bookkeeper's Balances | Auditor's Adjustments | | Adjusted Balances |
|---|---|---|---|---|---|
| 1 | Petty Cash | 500.00 | | | 500.00 |
| 3 | Merchants Bank—Ck. Account | 20,179.76 | | (2) 180.00 (3) 17.76 | 19,982.00 |
| 3 | Merchants Bank—Div. Account | 2,050.00 | | | 2,050.00 |
| 3 | Merchants Bk.—Bond Int. Acct. | 2,500.00 | | | 2,500.00 |
| 4 | Marketable Securities | 20,225.00 | | | 20,225.00 |
| 6 | Notes Rec.—Trade Debtors | 7,145.72 | | (7) 1,500.00 | 5,645.72 |
| 6 | Notes Receivable—Officers | | (7) 1,500.00 | | 1,500.00 |
| 7 | Accounts Rec.—Trade Debtors | 81,687.00 | (3) 17.76 (8) 3,034.50 | | 84,739.26 |
| 7 | Reserve for Doubtful Notes and Accounts | 56.00 | | (9) 1,952.91 | 2,008.91 |
| 4, 6 | Accrued Interest Receivable | | (4) 77.08 (6) 78.25 | | 155.33 |
| 8 | Raw Materials Inventory | 37,310.50 | (10) 25,000.00 | (11) 37,310.50 | 25,000.00 |
| 8 | Goods in Process Inventory | | (10) 32,875.00 | | 32,875.00 |
| 8 | Finished Goods Inventory | 15,000.00 | (10) 80,000.00 | (11) 15,000.00 | 80,000.00 |
| 9 | Office Furniture | 2,600.50 | | (13) 260.05 | 2,340.45 |
| 9 | Delivery Trucks | 15,000.00 | | | 15,000.00 |
| 9 | Res. for Depr. of Del. Trucks, 20% | 3,000.00 | | (13) 3,000.00 | 6,000.00 |
| 9 | Tools and Implements (net) | 20,215.00 | | (12) 215.00 | 20,000.00 |
| 9 | Machinery | 100,000.00 | (12) 215.00 | | 100,215.00 |
| 9 | Res. for Depr. of Machinery, 6% | 6,000.00 | | (13) 6,000.00 | 12,000.00 |
| 9 | Buildings | 150,000.00 | | | 150,000.00 |
| 9 | Res. for Depr. of Buildings, 2½% | 3,750.00 | | (13) 3,750.00 | 7,500.00 |
| 9 | Land | 140,000.00 | | | 140,000.00 |
| 5 | Sinking Fund | 5,500.00 | (5) 160.42 | | 5,660.42 |
| 10 | Prepaid Insurance | 4,997.34 | | (14) 3,841.00 | 1,156.34 |
| 11 | Prepaid Advertising | | (16) 12,575.00 | | 12,575.00 |

| Acct. | Account | Balances from Sec. 2 Dr. | Balances from Sec. 2 Cr. | Adjustments Dr. | Adjustments Cr. | Dr. | Cr. |
|---|---|---|---|---|---|---|---|
| 11 | Deferred Capital Stock Tax | 980.00 | | | | | 650.00 |
| 11 | Salary Advances to Employees | 7,125.00 | | (1) 30.00 | | | 950.00 |
| 11 | Bond Discount | 7,350.00 | | (18) 375.00 | | | 6,750.00 |
| 11 | Organization Expense | | | (17) 816.67 | | | 6,533.33 |
| 11 | Office Supplies | 510.00 | | (15) 230.00 | | | 280.00 |
| 12 | Notes Payable | | 21,000.00 | | | | 21,000.00 |
| 13 | Accounts Payable | | 39,462.00 | | (20) 7,681.50 | | 31,780.50 |
| 13 | Accounts Payable—Officers | | | | | | 7,681.50 |
| 7 | Customers' Overpayments | | | (8) 3,034.50 | | | 3,034.50 |
| 15 | Employer's Fed. Excise Tax Pay. (O.A.B.) | | 957.23 | | | | 957.23 |
| 15 | Employees' Income Tax Payable | | | | | | 957.23 |
| 15 | Employer's Fed. Excise Tax Pay. (O.A.B.) | | 957.23 | | | | 957.23 |
| 15 | State U. C. Contributions Pay. (U.C.) | | 753.22 | (23) 12.62 | | | 765.84 |
| | | | | (23) 113.60 | | | 1,723.01 |
| 12,16 | Accrued Interest Payable | | 1,609.41 | (19) 148.02 | | | 2,439.69 |
| | | | | (24) 2,291.67 | | | |
| 14 | Accrued Wages Payable | | | (21) 6,311.20 | | | 6,311.20 |
| 3 | Accrued Capital Stock Tax Payable | | 2,050.00 | (22) 650.00 | | | 650.00 |
| 16 | Div. Pay.—Unclaimed Checks | | | | | | 2,050.00 |
| 16 | First Mortgage, 5%, 20-year bond | | 100,000.00 | | | | 100,000.00 |
| 17 | Unissued Capital Stock | 50,000.00 | | | 50,000.00 | 50,000.00 | |
| 17 | Capital Stock, 50,000 shares, $10 par value | | 500,000.00 | | | | 500,000.00 |
| 16 | Sinking Fund Reserve | | 2,750.00 | (25) 2,910.42 | | | 5,660.42 |
| 17 | Surplus | | 41,879.81 | (17) 816.67 | | | 15,652.72 |
| | | | | (25) 2,910.42 | | | |
| 17 | Dividend #1 | 22,500.00 | | (26) 22,500.00 | | | |
| | | 713,375.82 | | 120,132.42 | | 728,172.75 | |
| | | 10,849.08 | | 69,959.18 | | 59,110.10 | |
| 17 | Balances from Sec. 2 | 724,224.90 | 724,224.90 | 190,091.60 | 190,091.60 | 787,282.85 | 787,282.85 |

## THE BLANK MANUFACTURING COMPANY

### Working Trial Balance, December 31, 1937

(Sec. 2)

| Sched. No. | Profit and Loss Accounts | Bookkeeper's Balances | Auditor's Adjustments | | Adjusted Balances |
|---|---|---|---|---|---|
| .... | Sales—Less Returns and Allowances | 635,597.47 | | | 635,597.47 |
| 8 | Raw Material Purchases | 195,250.00 | (11) 37,310.50 | (10) 25,000.00 | 207,560.50 |
| .... | Freight In | 2,831.00 | | | 2,831.00 |
| 15 | Factory Labor | 300,200.00 | (21) 4,980.20 | | 305,180.20 |
| .... | Property Taxes | 2,010.00 | | (28) 2,010.00 | |
| .... | Property Taxes—Manufacturing | | (28) 1,809.00 | | 1,809.00 |
| .... | Property Taxes—Administrative | | (28) 201.00 | | 201.00 |
| .... | Capital Stock Tax | 650.00 | | | 650.00 |
| .... | Maintenance and Repairs | 13,471.00 | | | 13,471.00 |
| .... | Miscellaneous Factory Expenses | 615.00 | | | 615.00 |
| 8 | Cost of Production | | (10) 32,875.00 | (10) 32,875.00 | 32,875.00 |
| 8 | Cost of Sales | | (10) 80,000.00 | (10) 80,000.00 | 65,000.00 |
| 11, 15 | Salaries of Salesmen | 30,220.00 | (11) 15,000.00 (1) 30.00 (21) 585.00 | | 30,835.00 |
| 15 | Delivery Salaries | 8,600.00 | (21) 120.00 | | 8,720.00 |
| 11 | Advertising | 25,150.00 | | (16) 12,575.00 | 12,575.00 |
| 7 | Loss on Bad Debts | | (9) 1,952.91 | | 1,952.91 |
| 15 | Office Salaries | 37,560.00 | (21) 626.00 | | 38,186.00 |
| 1 | Office Expense | 12,875.00 | (2) 110.00 | | 12,985.00 |
| 1 | Miscellaneous General Expense | 910.00 | (2) 70.00 | | 980.00 |
| .... | Garage Expense | 2,000.00 | | | 2,000.00 |
| 10 | Expired Insurance—Manufacturing | | (14) 2,420.00 | | 2,420.00 |
| 10 | Expired Insurance—Administrative | | (14) 1,421.00 | | 1,421.00 |

| Acct | Account | Dr | Cr | Adj. Dr | Adj. Cr | Dr | Cr |
|------|---------|----|----|---------|---------|----|----|
| 11 | Office Supplies Used | 3,829.21 | | ⑮ 230.00 | | 3,829.21 | |
| 15 | Federal S. S. Excise Tax (O. A. B.) | 753.22 | | ㉓ 12.62 | | 765.84 | |
| 15 | Federal S. S. Excise Tax (U. C.) | 6,778.98 | | ㉓ 113.60 | | 6,892.58 | |
| 15 | State U. C. Contributions | | | ⑬ 260.05 | | 260.05 | |
| 9 | Depreciation—Office Furniture | | | ⑬ 3,000.00 | | 3,000.00 | |
| 9 | Depreciation—Delivery Trucks | | | ⑬ 6,000.00 | | 6,000.00 | |
| 9 | Depreciation—Machinery | | | ⑬ 3,750.00 | | 3,750.00 | |
| 9 | Depreciation—Buildings | | | | | | |
| | Dividends Received | 450.00 | | | | | 450.00 |
| | Rent Income | 250.00 | | | | | 250.00 |
| 16 | Bond Interest | 2,708.33 | | ㉔ 2,291.67 | | 5,000.00 | |
| 5 | Sinking Fund Income | | | | ⑤ 160.42 | | 160.42 |
| 18 | Interest and Discount (net) | 734.81 | | ⑲ 148.02 | ④ 77.08 ⑥ 78.25 ㉗ 727.50 | | |
| 18 | Interest Expense | | | ㉗ 1,512.00 | | 1,512.00 | |
| 18 | Interest Income | | | | ㉗ 784.50 | | 784.50 |
| 11 | Bond Discount Written Off | | | ⑱ 375.00 | | 375.00 | |
| | Balances to Sec. 1 | 636,297.47 | 10,849.08 | 84,328.57 | 69,959.18 | 676,007.29 | 59,110.10 |
| | | 647,146.55 | 647,146.55 | 154,287.75 | 154,287.75 | 735,117.39 | 735,117.39 |

Illustration No. 36.  Working Trial Balance

**14—153.** What is meant by indexing working papers? What system was used for indexing the working papers of The Blank Manufacturing Company?

## AUDITING PROBLEMS

**14—38.** You are given the following working papers and are requested to rearrange them in their proper order giving each one a designating symbol or number. List the papers in the order in which you would arrange them for filing.

(a) Cash reconciliation of First National Bank account

(b) Working trial balance as of end of period

(c) Analysis of building account

(d) Analysis of accounts receivable

(e) Detail statement of additions to Building No. 5, which account had been closed into the building account.

(f) Inventory test sheets of prices

(g) Statement of work done in checking the cash book

(h) Statement of notes payable

(i) Analysis of surplus

(j) Schedule of unexpired insurance

(k) Notes on examination of minutes not pertinent to other schedules

(l) Summary of properties including land, buildings, machinery, and vehicles

(m) List of stockholders of common stock and analysis of common stock account

(n) Adjusting journal entries

(o) Statement of accrued taxes

(p) Certificate from First Wisconsin National Bank

(q) Certificate of registrar of preferred stock

(r) Count of petty cash

(s) Analysis of reserve for depreciation of buildings

(t) Statement of count of securities

(u) Certificate from registrar of bonds payable

(v) Certificate from trustees of sinking fund

(w) Reconciliation of bank account of Second National Bank

(x) Notations with regard to subsequent audits

**14—39.** You are employed to make a balance sheet audit for The Passaic Falls Woolen Manufacturing Co. for the year ended June 30, 1938. Upon reporting for duty the bookkeeper gives you the balance sheet which he has prepared and you proceed with the audit. During the course of the audit you ascertain the following information:

(a) The book value of the land represents its cost when originally purchased. The company has had it appraised recently and desires to have its value adjusted to the appraised value of $15,000 to which you agree.

(b) The value of the fixed assets as shown by the balance sheet prepared by the bookkeeper represents the book value without any deduction

for depreciation for the current year. After consulting with the president
of the company, it is agreed that reserves for depreciation based upon the
book values of the fixed assets should be provided as follows:

| | |
|---|---|
| Brick Buildings | 2½% |
| Machinery | 7½% |
| Steam Power Plant | 10 % |

(c) An audit of the inventories taken by the bookkeeper, reveals an
undervaluation of $5,000 when valued at cost or market price, whichever is
the lower.

(d) The treasury stock which is listed on the balance sheet prepared
by the bookkeeper was found to consist of 250 shares of common stock,
par value of $100 per share, which had been acquired at a cost of $20,000.
You advise that this stock be adjusted to par value and that the difference
between the cost and the par value be credited to discount on treasury stock
which is to be treated as a deferred credit to profit and loss pending the subsequent sale of the stock when the actual profit or loss can be ascertained.

(e) You find that the preferred stock is cumulative as to dividends at
the rate of 7%, but that no dividends were declared or paid during the years
ended June 30, 1937, and June 30, 1938.


### THE PASSAIC FALLS WOOLEN MFG. CO.

#### Balance Sheet, June 30, 1938

| Assets | | Liabilities | |
|---|---|---|---|
| Land | $ 10,000.00 | Cap. Stock. Common, | |
| Buildings (brick) | 100,000.00 | par $100 | $125,000.00 |
| Machinery | 150,000.00 | Cap. Stock, Preferred, | |
| Steam Power Plant | 25,000.00 | 7% cumulative par $100 | 100,000.00 |
| Treasury Stock, Com. | 20,000.00 | Accounts Payable | 130,000.00 |
| Accounts Receivable | 50,000.00 | Undistributed Earnings | |
| Inventories (6-30-38) | 75,000.00 | (6-30-37) | 60,000.00 |
| Cash | 20,000.00 | Profits, year ended | |
| | | 6-30-38 | 35,000.00 |
| Total Assets | $450,000.00 | Total Liabilities | $450,000.00 |

From the information given, prepare the following:

(a) Required adjusting entries

(b) Balance sheet which you would be willing to certify.

## AUDITING PRACTICE
### An Audit Case (Twelfth Installment)

This installment concludes the audit of the Beverly Supply Company. The assets, liabilities, and profit and loss accounts have been verified to the extent recommended in an "Examination of Financial Statements" and after completing this assignment the auditor's working papers should provide all of the information needed in writing the final report which will go to the client.

### INSTRUCTIONS

1. Check carefully the adjusting journal entries, prepared in connection with the performance of the audit work of the first eleven installments, to see that the entries are correct both in amount and in the accounts affected.

2. After the adjusting journal entries have been checked and found to be correct, post them to the adjustments columns of the working trial balance. The adjusting journal entries should be numbered consecutively. These numbers should also appear to the left of the amounts posted in the adjustments column of the working trial balance.

3. Complete the working trial balance by extending the adjusted balances of the accounts into the proper columns. Total the columns.

4. Arrange the schedules in the order in which the accounts to which they relate appear on the working trial balance.

5. Number each schedule so that it may be indexed to the working trial balance.

6. The amount of the adjusted balance on each schedule should agree with the adjusted balance of the corresponding item on the working trial balance. Check the adjusted account balances on each schedule with the adjusted balances shown in the working trial balance to see that they agree.

# CHAPTER FIFTEEN

## THE AUDIT REPORT

1. Factors in Report Writing
   (a) Purpose of the Report
   (b) Form of the Report
   (c) Preparation of the Report
2. Scope of Audit Reports
   (a) Presentation and Letter of Transmittal
   (b) Exhibits
   (c) Schedules
   (d) The Accountant's Certificate
   (e) Comments on the Audit
3. Federal Regulation of Corporate Reports
   (a) Federal Laws of 1933 and 1934
   (b) Effect of Federal Regulation
4. Auditing Procedure
5. Application of Principles
   (a) An Audit Report Illustrated
6. An Audit Case—Thirteenth Installment

The final step in the completion of an audit and perhaps the most important part of an audit is the preparation of the report. An accountant may be skillful in auditing technique, but unless he puts into written form the results of his efforts and his observations while conducting an audit, much of the value derived from the audit may be lost. The report is frequently the only contact between the officials of a company and the auditor.

### FACTORS IN REPORT WRITING

**Purpose of the Report.** The audit report forms the connecting link between the auditor and those for whom the audit was performed, usually the board of directors or the officers of a corporation. The purpose of the audit report is to present the financial condition of the enterprise and its operating results for the period, and to comment upon the essential features of the work done and observations made by the auditor during the course of the audit. Corporate officials usually have little knowledge of auditing technique and are not interested so much in

351

how the results were obtained, as in what they signify. They wish to know whether the corporate records were correctly maintained, and they desire information which will help to interpret the financial condition of the concern and assist in bringing about increased efficiency in its operation. The report should therefore contain, in addition to a statement of the financial condition of the concern and its operating results for the period, comments by the auditor on such matters as: suggestions for improving the accounting records, a discussion of the financial condition of the company in respect to changes that have taken place since the close of the preceding period, and any other information, based on the audit, which might be of value to the client.

**Form of the Report.** The form of the report will depend somewhat on the type of audit performed. It should always be typed and should generally be bound in a folder or with front and back covers. The report may be bound so as to open from the side or from the top. It should be stapled together so that parts of the report may not become separated. Many of the large accounting firms type their reports on water-marked stationery bearing the firm name in the paper. This is a safeguard against the reports being recopied and changes made which might give misleading information. The paper should be thin enough so that from four to six copies may be made at one typing. The arrangement of the contents of the report may vary according to the type of audit performed and the ideas of the accountant preparing the report. Considerable standardization, however, is now taking place in regard to the form of the statements and in regard to other features of the report such as the accountant's certificate.

**Preparation of the Report.** In preparing the report, the auditor should have in mind the use that will be made of the information it will contain. He may be able to make his report cover items of special interest to those for whom the report is intended. For instance, the prospective purchaser of stock would be primarily interested in the earnings or dividends of the corporation and its value as a going concern. The prospective purchaser of bonds would be principally interested in the value of the property mortgaged, and the ability of the company to maintain its interest payments during the life of the bonds and to retire them at maturity.   The stockholder's chief interest is usually in the earning capacity of the corporation and in the successful operation of the business by the officers and directors chosen by the stockholders.

The procedure followed in preparing a report is not uniform. Some accountants advocate that the report should be prepared by the accountant in charge of the audit before he leaves the place in which the audit was conducted.   Others state that the report should be written in the accountant's own office.   Varying conditions will perhaps determine where and by whom the report should be written.   If the report is written in the accountant's office, it may be necessary on some occasions for him to make trips back to the place where the audit was conducted for information or explanations necessary in writing the report.   This would be impracticable if the audit was made at some distance from the accountant's office.   If the report is to be written in the accountant's office, it is advisable that the audit working papers be reviewed and the adjusted trial balance completed and checked to the working papers before the accountant leaves the office in which the audit was conducted, so that information needed in the report will not be overlooked.

The report is usually written by the accountant in charge of the audit based upon his observations during the audit.   He may or may not be skillful in writing reports.   Hence it is well to have one or more individuals in an accounting organization who excel in report writing and whose duty it is to review the reports before they are typed in their final form.   Some reports will need to be entirely rewritten in order to conform to the technical form and language necessary under the circumstances involved.   In large public accounting firms the report usually is reviewed by several individuals before it is released.

## SCOPE OF AUDIT REPORTS

The scope of an audit report will vary according to the type of audit performed.   The report for a special investigation may consist of a letter discussing the results of the work performed by the auditor.   The report for a cash audit may include a statement of cash receipts and disbursements with comments explaining features of the audit.   If an examination of financial statements or a complete or detailed audit was made, the report would probably comprise the following: (1) a presentation and letter of transmittal; (2) an accountant's certificate; (3) exhibits, consisting of a balance sheet and profit and loss statement; (4) schedules; (5) comments on features of the audit.

**Presentation and Letter of Transmittal.** Each report should contain a presentation or introductory section in which the auditor indicates to the client that an audit has been made and sets forth in detailed form what is included in the report. The presentation may be made in a letter accompanying the report or it may be embodied in the report itself and combined with the comments, both being set forth over one signature. Where this is done, the comments will precede the certificate and the financial statements in the report. The letter of transmittal may contain the introductory part of the report if the introduction is not combined with the comments. In this event, the comments will probably appear after the financial statements in the report.

**Exhibits.** The principal statements of an audit report are usually referred to as exhibits. The statements most frequently encountered are the balance sheet and the profit and loss statement. These exhibits should be prepared in standard form, keeping in mind the objectives or purposes of the audit, and the information which the client expects to obtain from the report. In writing the report every effort should be made to avoid technicalities. While the balance sheet and profit and loss statement are, of course, technical reports, it is possible to prepare them in such a way that they may be more easily interpreted by the average business man.

**Schedules.** Statements which provide analytical or statistical information in addition to that provided in the exhibits are usually referred to as schedules. Numerous schedules may be prepared which provide detailed information designed to support the information which is summarized in the balance sheet and profit and loss statement. For instance, the balance sheet may be supported by detailed schedules of securities, inventories, fixed assets, accrued and deferred items, where such information is not stated in detail in the balance sheet itself. The profit and loss statement may be supported by schedules which provide detailed information regarding manufacturing costs, cost of sales, operating expenses, etc.

Exhibits and schedules should be numbered so that there is a proper cross reference as an aid to tracing information which may be shown in summary form at one place and in detailed form in another place in the report.

**The Accountant's Certificate.** An accountant's certificate is a statement signed by the accountant in which he affirms that he has audited the accounts of a concern or has made an examination of its statements. He expresses his opinion regarding the financial condition of the company and the results of its operations for the period under review as set forth in the balance sheet and profit and loss statement to which the certificate relates. If for any reason he cannot vouch for the accuracy of items in the statements, he should call attention to these matters in the certificate. Certificates may therefore be qualified or unqualified.

An unqualified certificate is one in which the accountant makes no reservation as to the facts set forth in his report. A qualified certificate is one in which the accountant makes certain qualifications or reservations to call attention to the fact that certain items have not been provided for in the statements, or that the values shown are subject to question.

Certificates are sometimes referred to as short or long certificates. Short certificates are usually unqualified although they may be qualified briefly. Long certificates usually are statements certifying as to what has been done or to what has not been done in making the audit.

The relative advantages and disadvantages of different types of certificates vary. From the viewpoint of the banker, a short, unqualified certificate is undoubtedly advantageous. On the other hand, there are numerous occasions in which the certificate which accompanies an audit report must be qualified. An unqualified certificate should signify that the auditor has assured himself that the accounts are essentially correct. To do so there are certain procedures and safeguards which the auditor must apply in his engagement according to custom and accounting practice. Where foreign branch accounts, subsidiary accounts, or other types of transactions may not be audited, the auditor, for his protection, should so state. Where access to certain records are not provided, the auditor should prepare a certificate qualified in that respect. Examples of the different types of certificates are numerous and may be obtained from the published reports of practically all of the leading corporations of the country. The following examples are for illustrative purposes only:

We have audited the books and accounts of the Arnold, Constable Corporation and Subsidiary Companies for the year ended January 31, 1938, and hereby certify that the above balance sheet and the accompanying profit and loss and surplus accounts are in accordance therewith, and in our opinion, set forth the true financial condition of the corporation and its subsidiaries as of January 31, 1938, and the result of their operations for the year then ended.

S. D. LEIDESDORF & CO.

The above represents a certificate in which the books of all companies concerned have been audited by the auditors, and no qualifications are expressed. As against such a statement the following one limits the responsibility only to the parent company operations, though stating that the subsidiaries accounts are audited by chartered accountants.

We have audited the books and accounts of the American Chicle Co. as of December 31, 1938, and certify that in our opinion, this balance sheet is properly prepared to set forth correctly the consolidated financial condition of the company at that date; based on our audit of the parent company and on audit of foreign subsidiary by chartered accountants.

PHILIP N. MILLER & Co.<br/>Certified Public Accountants

Compared with the above certificates, the following certificate in the long form of presentation has much of interest:

Board of Directors and Stockholders,
Crown Central Petroleum Corporation,
Houston, Texas
Gentlemen:

We have examined the books of account and records pertaining to the assets and liabilities of the Crown Central Petroleum Corporation and Subsidiaries, as of the close of business December 31, 1938, and submit herewith condensed consolidated balance sheet as of that date and consolidated deficit account for the year 1938, the latter being without audit by us.

Capital assets are included at appraised sound value based on appraisal by Crandall & Osmond, March, 1935, plus additions subsequently. The Holmes-Manley-Light Oil Units are included at cost, their installation being completed in 1937. Warehouse stocks of miscellaneous equipment totaling $181,903.89 are without verification by us, as physical inventories had not been taken.

Only actual additions to the capital assets have been capitalized during the year. Detailed appraisal report of Crandall & Osmond was not submitted for our inspection, and the amount of appreciation included herein is shown in total only, as evidenced by correspondence on file. Depreciation and depletion in the amount of $408,647.64 has been charged to the current year's operations and $77,286.10 has been charged to surplus from appraisal of capital assets and surplus from appreciation of discovery value, based on the method used during the past four years.

Investments consist of stock in the Air Oil Company and other minor items. Good will is included as shown by the records and represents cost Cash on hand and on deposit, with the exception of a minor working fund. was verified by actual count or by correspondence with the depository banks, Accounts receivable representing approximately 77.5% of the total. were paid prior to March 1, 1939, and, in our opinion, the balances are collectible or reserved. Physical inventory of oil and gasoline on hand at December 31, 1938, aggregating $845,226.71, is stated at the lower of cost or market at that date. Items appearing under the caption "Other Assets" are, in our opinion, properly classified and have been satisfactorily accounted for by us. During the year an amount of $5,053.99 has been applied as a credit to the account receivable arising from sale of lease, representing the value of oil produced from the said lease.

Full provision has been made for all ascertained liabilities of the corporation at December 31, 1938, for bonded indebtedness and interest, notes payable and accounts payable, as well as accrued items. Bonded indebtedness and notes payable were satisfactorily confirmed. With the exception of minor items, the amount of current accounts payable has been paid prior to March 1, 1939. The corporation was liable at December 31, 1938, for crude oil in transit aggregating $50,685.80 not included in the inventory or accounts payable. Subsequent to December 31, 1938, judgment against the corporation for approximately $65,000 had been obtained by F. J. Bates for which appeal has been filed and will be heard by the Federal Circuit Court of Appeals at New Orleans, against which an appeal bond of $75,000 has been posted by the corporation. Reserve for contingencies has been provided for special prior year items applicable to expense of the White Oil Corporation. No provision has been made for bond sinking fund according to bond indenture which was in arrears $600,000 at December 31, 1938.

Subject to the foregoing WE HEREBY CERTIFY that, in our opinion, based upon the records examined and information obtained by us, the accompanying consolidated balance sheet conservatively sets forth the financial position of the CROWN CENTRAL PETROLEUM CORPORATION and subsidiary companies at December 31, 1938.

PHILIP N. MILLER & CO.

Certified Public Accountants

The reader is referred to the following qualifications:

1. As respects the valuation of the fixed assets
2. As respects warehouse stocks of miscellaneous equipment
3. Basis of charging depreciation
4. Condition of bond sinking fund.

The question immediately arises as to what the value of such a statement may be. Does the last paragraph of the certificate carry any meaning with the above qualifications? In the example, the fixed assets in themselves amount to approximately three-fourths of all the properties owned. Is such a statement of any great value to a banker or financial house expecting to sell securities of the company concerned?

It is probably better practice to issue short certificates wherever possible. The phraseology should be such as to eliminate any possibility of misunderstanding as to what the auditor is certifying to, and should be as free from qualifications as possible. Many auditors adopt the policy of issuing short certificates, placing any qualifications which may be necessary as to contingencies, bond sinking fund conditions, and similar items, in footnotes to the balance sheet. In many cases such a presentation is highly advantageous as it provides the necessary qualifications in connection with the balance sheet without affecting the certificate.

**Suggested Form of Certificate.** Through the cooperative efforts of the American Institute of Accountants and the New York Stock Exchange, an accountant's certificate was drafted which was suggested as a form to be used by accountants in connection with statements submitted in annual reports to stockholders and for credit purposes. A study for the year 1934 of corporate reports of 500 companies listed on the New York Stock Exchange showed that 95% of the certificates were in the recommended form shown in the following paragraphs or were an adaptation of the recommended form.

The following is the certificate suggested by the American Institute of Accountants and the New York Stock Exchange:

To the XYZ Company:

We have made an examination of the balance sheet of the XYZ Company as at December 31, 1938, and of the statement of income and surplus for the year 1938. In connection therewith, we examined or tested accounting records of the company and other supporting evidence and obtained information and explanations from officers and employees of the company; we also made a general review of the accounting methods and of the operating and income accounts for the year, but we did not make a detailed audit of the transactions.

In our opinion, based upon such examination, the accompanying balance sheet and related statement of income and surplus fairly present, in accordance with accepted principles of accounting consistently maintained by the XYZ Company during the year under review, its position at December 31, 1938, and the results of its operation for the year.

ABC
Certified Public Accountants

## NOTES

1. It is contemplated that, before signing a report of the type suggested, the accountant will be satisfied that his examination has been adequate and in conformity with the accepted principles of auditing.

2. The report should be addressed to the directors of the company or to the stockholders, if the appointment is made by them.

3. The statement of what has been examined would, of course, conform to the titles of the accounts or statements reported upon.

4. In the second sentence, any special forms of confirmation could be mentioned: e. g., "including confirmation of cash and securities by inspection or certificates from depositaries."

5. This certificate is appropriate only if the accounting for the year is consistent in basis with that for the preceding year. If there has been any material change either in accounting principles or in the manner of their application, the nature of the change should be indicated.

6. It is contemplated that the form of report would be modified when and as necessary to embody any qualifications, reservations or supplementary explanations.

**Comments on the Audit.** It is customary for the auditor to submit comments in connection with the statements prepared for the client. These comments are made to explain any unusual items appearing in the financial statement, to describe his investigation into certain matters, to make such criticisms as are considered desirable or necessary, to make suggestions that may be of value to the client, and, if so requested, to make whatever recommendations he considers advisable.

Properly prepared comments may be of great value to a client. They may be constructive and may lead to vast improvements in the accounting records and the means of keeping the records. If a proper method of internal check has not been maintained, he may make suggestions as to how to bring about a satisfactory system of internal checking. This is, undoubtedly, constructive. The auditor should use simple words, short sentences and nontechnical expressions as far as possible in preparing his report. He should express his ideas in a clear, concise way which the layman will understand. The professional auditor is not expected to be a literary expert. He is expected to understand accounting, and to be able to express clearly what he has to say on the subject.

### FEDERAL REGULATION OF CORPORATE REPORTS

**Federal Laws of 1933 and 1934.** The Securities Exchange Act of 1934 and its predecessor the Federal Securities Act of 1933 were enacted with the purpose in view of protecting the interests of security holders and the investing public. These acts stipulate that accurate and detailed information be made available concerning the financial affairs of corporations selling their securities to the public. The Federal Securities Act, as amended in 1934, provides for the registration of new security issues with the Securities and Exchange Commission. The registration is accomplished by the filing of a registration statement which includes the financial statements of the issuing company. The company's financial statements must be certified to by independent public or Certified Public Accountants. The Act further provides that accountants, together with officers of the company and investment bankers selling the securities, are liable to security holders for losses that may be incurred as the result of a misstatement by them of a material fact made in connection with the sale of securities.

The Securities Exchange Act of 1934 requires every corporation whose securities are listed on a security exchange to render an annual report to the Securities and Exchange Commission. This report must be prepared from the audit information obtained by an independent public accountant or Certified Public Accountant, not officially connected with the concern being audited. The annual report to the corporation's stockholders may be somewhat condensed in form but should not differ materially from the report rendered to the commission.

**Effect of Federal Regulation.** As a consequence of these regulatory acts it becomes essential that accountants give more consideration to the preparation of their audit reports. Balance sheets and profit and loss statements must be prepared in such a manner and with such notations as to set forth accurately the essential information and to present it in such a manner that it will not be misleading.

## PROCEDURE IN PREPARING THE AUDIT REPORT
### In an "Examination of Financial Statements"

"The accountant's report or certificate should be as concise as is consistent with a clear statement of his opinion on the financial statements submitted. Explanations and disclosures which he believes to be desirable regarding accounting principles adopted should be inserted in the financial statements or in his report. Attention is directed to the importance of stating any qualifications clearly and concisely. Distinction should be made between those comments intended to be merely informative or to state the limitations of the scope of the accountant's work (e. g., where part of the work has been performed by other accountants), and those which indicate dissent from particular practices of the company. Care should be exercised to avoid making any statement that is not literally true or which might give rise to unwarranted implications."

## APPLICATION OF PRINCIPLES

## AUDIT OF THE BLANK MANUFACTURING COMPANY (Continued)

In concluding the audit of The Blank Manufacturing Company, Mr. W. H. Merz, the senior accountant, prepared a report consisting of the following: (a) a presentation and comments, (b) an accountant's certificate, and (c) statements consisting of a balance sheet, profit and loss statement, and a statement of cost of sales.

After the report was completed, it was submitted to Mr. M. D. Stevenson for review. The report was then typed and was again reviewed by both Mr. Stevenson and Mr. Bennett before it was finally submitted for typing in its finished form.

Four copies were made of the report. Two copies were prepared for The Blank Manufacturing Company, one copy for the report file, and the fourth copy was placed in the folder with the working papers of The Blank Manufacturing Company audit. The copies for The Blank Manufacturing Company were sent by registered mail, with a return receipt demanded, to Mr. C. H. Bossard, Chairman of the Board of Directors. The duplicate copies were filed for future reference.

A copy of the report for The Blank Manufacturing Company is illustrated on the following pages.

**9 West Third Street,**
**Cincinnati, Ohio**

# STEVENSON AND BENNETT

## Certified Public Accountants

February 12, 1938

Board of Directors
The Blank Manufacturing Company
Indianapolis, Indiana

Gentlemen:

We have made an examination of the accounts and statements of The Blank Manufacturing Company for the year ended December 31, 1937, and submit our report which consists of the following:

Our certificate

Balance Sheet, December 31, 1937 (Exhibit A)

Statement of Earned Surplus for the year ended December 31, 1937 (Exhibit B)

Statement of Profit and Loss for the year ended December 31, 1937 (Exhibit C)

Statement of Cost of Sales for the year ended December 31, 1937 (Exhibit C, Schedule 1)

Our comments as follows:

### HISTORY

The Blank Manufacturing Company was organized July 15, 1935, under the laws of the State of Indiana. Authority was received from the state corporation department to issue 50,000 shares of capital stock of $10 par value, of which 45,000 shares with an aggregate par value of $450,000 was outstanding at December 31, 1937. In developing the corporate organization, expenses of $8,166.67 were incurred, which are now being written off on a ten-year basis by charges to the surplus account.

On January 15, 1936, first mortgage, 5%, twenty-year sinking fund bonds were issued in the amount of $100,000. In accordance with the provisions of the bond indenture, the president of the Merchants National Bank may invest the funds in first real estate mortgages, paying not less than 6% interest. The amount of a mortgage is in no event to exceed two-thirds of the appraised value of the real estate. The investment in the sinking fund at

**Illustration No. 37. Comments on Audit**

December 31, 1937, amounting to $5,660.42, was confirmed by com-
munication with the Merchants National Bank.

## FINANCIAL CONDITION

The Blank Manufacturing Company had current assets at December 31, 1937, aggregating $273,163.40 and current liabilities
of $79,350.70, resulting in a current ratio of approximately 3.44
to 1. The excess of the current assets over the current liabilities (the working capital) was $193,812.70.

The total assets amounted to $709,773.94 as compared with
total liabilities of $179,350.70. The total assets exceeded the
liabilities by $530,423.24, which represents the amount of the
stockholders' equity in the assets. This equity is represented by
capital stock of $450,000.00 par value and surplus amounting to
$80,423.24 of which $5,660.42 is reserved for sinking fund purposes. The book value of the 45,000 shares of capital stock outstanding at December 31, 1937, was $11.66 per share.

Net sales for the year ended December 31, 1937, totaled
$635,597.47. Gross profit on sales amounted to $180,680.37,
which is approximately 28½% of net sales. Net profit from
operations amounted to $64,352.18, which is approximately 10% of
net sales. There was net profit before provision for federal
income tax of $59,110.10. This is equivalent to approximately
9⅓% of net sales and resulted in earnings of approximately $1.31
per share of capital stock outstanding.

## NOTES RECEIVABLE--$7,145.72

Of the total notes receivable, notes amounting to $5,645.72
represented obligations of trade debtors, while notes amounting
to $1,500.00 represented the obligations of officers of the com-
pany. All of the notes were examined and accounted for as having
been collected or in the hands of the bank for collection at the
date of the audit. Consultation with the general manager, Mr.
Shields, revealed that he considered all of the notes collectible.

## ACCOUNTS RECEIVABLE--$84,739.26

The accounts receivable at December 31, 1937, are summarized by billing dates as follows:

| | |
|---|---:|
| December, 1937 | $72,897.80 |
| November, 1937 | 8,773.46 |
| October, 1937 | 2,158.00 |
| Prior to October, 1937 | 910.00 |
| Total | $84,739.26 |

The recorded customers' balances were confirmed by direct
correspondence with the debtors and only minor differences were
reported in the replies received. The accounts were reviewed in
detail with the credit manager. On the basis of the company's
past experience, the reserve of $2,008.91, which covers both
notes and accounts receivable, appears to be adequate to cover
probable losses in the collection of these items.

**Illustration No. 37. Comments on Audit (Continued)**

### INVENTORIES--$137,875.00

The inventories as stated in Exhibit A were determined by physical inventories taken by employees of the company as of December 31, 1937, and priced at the lower of cost or market.

While we did not supervise the taking of the physical inventories, we made selective tests of the quantities of various inventory items and made comprehensive tests of the pricing and computation of the detailed inventory records.

### PLANT, PROPERTY AND EQUIPMENT--$402,055.45

The gross book values of plant, property and equipment as stated in Exhibit A represent cost, with the exception of tools and implements which are stated on the basis of a physical inventory priced at cost or less, and office furniture which is stated at cost less depreciation.

Only minor additions were made in the property accounts during the year. Vouchers in support of the principal additions were examined by us.

Provision for depreciation of fixed assets was made in the amount of $13,010.05 during the year and was based upon the following annual rates:

```
Buildings...................... 2½% of cost
Machinery...................... 6%     "
Delivery trucks................20%     "
Office furniture...............10% of depreciated value.
```

These rates appear to be adequate except that no allowance has been made therein for obsolescence of machinery. We suggest that in future years the depreciation rate on machinery be increased to 10% per annum in order to make adequate provision for obsolescence.

### CURRENT LIABILITIES--$79,350.70

The accounts representing current liabilities were reviewed in detail and in our opinion all known or recorded obligations of this character are shown in the accompanying balance sheet.

A certificate was obtained from officers of the company stating that all liabilities, either direct or contingent, were recorded on the books at December 31, 1937.

### PROVISION FOR FEDERAL INCOME TAX

No provision has been made for Federal income tax for the year 1937, which we have estimated at approximately $11,913.17, based on the provisions of the Revenue Act of 1936 as amended by the Act of 1937. In view of the fact that the net profit amounts to less than 10% of the adjusted declared capital, there is no excess-profits tax liability.

**Illustration No. 37. Comments on Audit (Continued)**

### COST ACCOUNTING SYSTEM

It is our opinion that the installation of a cost accounting
system would be of inestimable value to the management as an aid
in determining accurate costs of production and of selling
prices.  It would be an aid in controlling and reducing expenses
and would also make it possible each month for the accounting
department to prepare statements of financial condition and of
income and expenses.  This would be of assistance in formulating
sales and production policies.

In conclusion, we wish to express our appreciation of the
co-operation rendered us during the audit.  We also wish to state
that the books of account have been well kept, which, of course,
was an aid to us in conducting the audit.


                                        Respectfully,

                                        STEVENSON AND BENNETT

                                        Certified Public Accountants


WHM/VL


**Illustration No. 37.  Comments on Audit (Concluded)**

**9 W. Third Street**
**Cincinnati, Ohio**

# STEVENSON AND BENNETT

## Certified Public Accountants

To the Board of Directors
The Blank Manufacturing Company:

We have made an examination of the balance sheet of The
Blank Manufacturing Company (an Indiana corporation) as at December 31, 1937, and of the statements of profit and loss and
surplus for the year 1937.  In connection therewith, we examined
or tested accounting records of the company and other supporting
evidence and obtained information and explanations from officers
and employees of the company; we also made a general review of
the accounting methods and of the operating and income accounts
for the year, but we did not make a detailed audit of the transactions.

In our opinion, based upon such examination and before
making any deduction for Federal income taxes, the accompanying
balance sheet and related statements of profit and loss and
surplus fairly present the position of The Blank Manufacturing
Company at December 31, 1937, and the results of its operations
for the year ended that date.  Further, it is our opinion that
the statements have been prepared in accordance with accepted
accounting principles consistently maintained during the year.

Stevenson and Bennett

Cincinnati, Ohio

February 12, 1938

**Illustration No. 38.  Accountants' Certificate**

### THE BLANK MANUFACTURING COMPANY
### (Incorporated in Indiana)

### BALANCE SHEET, DECEMBER 31, 1937

#### ASSETS

CURRENT ASSETS:

| | | | |
|---|---|---|---|
| Cash....................................... | | $ 25,032.00 | |
| Marketable Securities, at cost (market value, $28,980.63)..................... | | 20,225.00 | |
| Notes and Accounts Receivable: | | | |
|   Notes Rec.--Trade Debtors.. | $ 5,645.72 | | |
|   Accounts Rec.--Trade Debtors. | 84,739.26 | | |
| | $ 90,384.98 | | |
|   Less Res. for Doubtful Notes and Accounts....... | 2,008.91 | 88,376.07 | |
| Accrued Interest Receivable............. | | 155.33 | |
| Inventories (valued at the lower of cost or market): | | | |
|   Raw Materials.............. | $ 25,000.00 | | |
|   Goods in Process.......... | 32,875.00 | | |
|   Finished Goods............. | 80,000.00 | 137,875.00 | |
| Other Current Assets: | | | |
|   Notes Receivable--Officers............ | | 1,500.00 | |
|     Total Current Assets.................. | | | $273,163.40 |
| SINKING FUND............................. | | | 5,660.42 |
| PROPERTY, PLANT AND EQUIPMENT (Subject to mortgage, see contra.): | | | |
|   Land (at cost)......................... | | $140,000.00 | |
|   Buildings.................... | $150,000.00 | | |
|   Less Reserve for Depr...... | 7,500.00 | 142,500.00 | |
|   Machinery.................... | $100,215.00 | | |
|   Less Reserve for Depr...... | 12,000.00 | 88,215.00 | |
|   Tools and Implements (depr. value)...... | | 20,000.00 | |
|   Delivery Trucks.............. | $ 15,000.00 | | |
|   Less Reserve for Depr...... | 6,000.00 | 9,000.00 | |
|   Office Furniture (depr. value).......... | | 2,340.45 | |
|     Total Fixed Assets.................... | | | 402,055.45 |
| DEFERRED CHARGES: | | | |
|   Office Supplies........................ | | $   280.00 | |
|   Prepaid Insurance..................... | | 1,156.34 | |
|   Prepaid Advertising................... | | 12,575.00 | |
|   Salary Advances to Employees........... | | 950.00 | |
|   Bond Discount......................... | | 6,750.00 | |
|   Organization Expense.................. | | 6,533.33 | |
|   Deferred Capital Stock Tax............. | | 650.00 | |
|     Total Deferred Charges................ | | | 28,894.67 |
| TOTAL..................................... | | | $709,773.94 |

**Illustration No. 39.  Certified Balance Sheet**

THE BLANK MANUFACTURING COMPANY

BALANCE SHEET, DECEMBER 31, 1937

## LIABILITIES

CURRENT LIABILITIES:

| | | |
|---|---:|---|
| Notes Payable (unsecured)....$ | 21,000.00 | |
| Divid. Pay.--Unclaimed Checks | 2,050.00 | |
| Accounts Payable............. | 31,780.50 | |
| Accounts Payable--Officers... | 7,681.50 | |
| Customers' Overpayments...... | 3,034.50 | |
| Federal Social Security Taxes Payable.................... | 2,680.30 | |
| State U. C. Contributions Pay. | 1,723.01 | |
| Accrued Wages Payable........ | 6,311.20 | |
| Accrued Interest Payable..... | 2,439.69 | |
| Accrued Capital Stock Tax Payable.................... | 650.00 | |
| Total Current Liabilities............. | | $ 79,350.70 |

FUNDED DEBT:

| | | |
|---|---:|---|
| First Mortgage, 5% Bonds, due Jan. 15, 1956 (Secured by mortgage on property, plant and equipment. See contra.).... | 100,000.00 | |
| Total Liabilities..................... | | $179,350.70 |

## NET WORTH

CAPITAL STOCK:

| | | |
|---|---:|---|
| Authorized 50,000 shares of $10 each; outstanding 45,000 shares............. | | $450,000.00 |

SURPLUS:

| | | | |
|---|---:|---:|---:|
| Sinking Fund Reserve.........$ | 5,660.42 | | |
| Earned Surplus Avail. for Div. | 74,762.82 | 80,423.24 | |
| Total Net Worth....................... | | | 530,423.24 |
| TOTAL..................................... | | | $709,773.94 |

## NOTES

1. No provision has been made for Federal income tax for the year, which we have estimated at $11,913.17.

2. The company was contingently liable for discounted customers' notes at December 31, 1937, amounting to $5,760.28.

(EXHIBIT A)

**Illustration No. 39.  Certified Balance Sheet**

THE BLANK MANUFACTURING COMPANY

STATEMENT OF EARNED SURPLUS
FOR THE YEAR ENDED DECEMBER 31, 1937

| | | |
|---|---:|---:|
| Balance, December 31, 1936................ | | $ 41,879.81 |
| Add Net Profit for the Year 1937......... | | 59,110.10 |
| | | $100,989.91 |
| Deduct: | | |
|    Dividend #1 (5%)........................ | $ 22,500.00 | |
|    Organization Expense.................... | 816.67 | |
|    Amount Credited to Sinking Fund Reserve. | 2,910.42 | 26,227.09 |
| Balance, December 31, 1937................ | | $ 74,762.82 |

(EXHIBIT B)

**Illustration No. 40. Certified Surplus Statement**

THE BLANK MANUFACTURING COMPANY

STATEMENT OF PROFIT AND LOSS
FOR THE YEAR ENDED DECEMBER 31, 1937

| | | |
|---|---:|---:|
| NET SALES................................... | | $635,597.47 |
| COST OF SALES (Schedule 1)................ | | 454,917.10 |
| Gross Profit on Sales................... | | $180,680.37 |
| **SELLING, GENERAL AND ADMINISTRATIVE** | | |
| **EXPENSES:** | | |
| Salaries of Salesmen.. ................. | $ 30,835.00 | |
| Advertising............................. | 12,575.00 | |
| Loss on Bad Debts....................... | 1,952.91 | |
| Delivery Salaries....................... | 8,720.00 | |
| Garage Expense.......................... | 2,000.00 | |
| Expired Insurance--Administrative....... | 1,421.00 | |
| Property Taxes--Administrative.......... | 201.00 | |
| Capital Stock Tax....................... | 650.00 | |
| Pay Roll Taxes: | | |
| Fed. S. S. Excise Tax(O.A.B.)$ 777.41 | | |
| Fed. S. S. Excise Tax (U.C.)   155.48 | | |
| State U. C. Contributions..  1,399.34 | 2,332.23 | |
| Depreciation: | | |
| Office Furniture...........  $ 260.05 | | |
| Delivery Trucks............  3,000.00 | 3,260.05 | |
| Office Salaries......................... | 38,186.00 | |
| Office Supplies Used.................... | 230.00 | |
| Office Expense.......................... | 12,985.00 | |
| Miscellaneous General Expense........... | 980.00 | 116,328.19 |
| Net Profit from Operations............ | | $ 64,352.18 |
| **OTHER INCOME:** | | |
| Rent Income............................. | $   250.00 | |
| Dividends Received...................... | 450.00 | |
| Interest Income......................... | 784.50 | |
| Sinking Fund Income..................... | 160.42 | 1,644.92 |
| Gross Income.......................... | | $ 65,997.10 |
| **OTHER CHARGES:** | | |
| Bond Interest........................... | $ 5,000.00 | |
| Bond Discount Written Off............... | 375.00 | |
| Interest Expense........................ | 1,512.00 | 6,887.00 |
| NET INCOME.............................. | | $ 59,110.10 |

Note: No provision has been made for Federal income tax for the
      year, which we have estimated at $11,913.17.

(EXHIBIT C)

**Illustration No. 41.  Certified Statement of Profit and Loss**

THE BLANK MANUFACTURING COMPANY

STATEMENT OF COST OF SALES
FOR THE YEAR ENDED DECEMBER 31, 1937

RAW MATERIALS:
Inventory, December 31, 1936............ $ 37,310.50
Raw Material Purchases.................. 195,250.00
Freight In............................. 2,831.00
$235,391.50
Less Inventory, December 31, 1937....... 25,000.00 $210.391.50

FACTORY LABOR............................. 305,180.20

MANUFACTURING EXPENSES:
Property Taxes--Manufacturing........... $ 1,809.00
Maintenance and Repairs................. 13,471.00
Depreciation:
Machinery..................$ 6,000.00
Buildings.................. 3,750.00 9,750.00
Expired Insurance--Manufacturing........ 2,420.00
Pay Roll Taxes:
Federal Excise Tax(O.A.B.).$ 3,051.80
Federal Excise Tax (U. C.).. 610.36
State U. C. Contributions.. 5,493.24 9,155.40
Miscellaneous Factory Expenses.......... 615.00 37,220.40

TOTAL MANUFACTURING EXPENSE............... $552,792.10
Less Goods in Process Inv., Dec. 31, 1937 32,875.00

COST OF GOODS MANUFACTURED................. $519,917.10
Add Finished Goods Inv. Dec. 31, 1936... 15,000.00
$534,917.10
Less Finished Goods Inv., Dec. 31, 1937. 80,000.00

COST OF SALES............................. $454,917.10

(EXHIBIT C, SCHEDULE 1)

**Illustration No. 42. Certified Statement of Cost of Sales**

## AUDITING THEORY

**15—154.** What is the purpose of an audit report and of what does it consist?

**15—155.** (a) What is an audit certificate?

(b) Why is it necessary in some cases for an auditor to qualify his certificate?

**15—156.** If engaged to make a balance sheet audit for credit purposes would you deem it advisable to incorporate in the report suggestions which might enable your client to make improvements upon the accounting system in use which would promote economy and at the same time provide more information for current use?

**15—157.** What advantages may be derived from the preparation of accounting statements in comparative form?

**15—158.** (a) Distinguish between exhibits and schedules in accounting reports.

(b) Name one schedule which usually accompanies a profit and loss statement for a manufacturing business.

**15—159.** You are auditing the books of a corporation. The books reflect no notes payable. The bank verification discloses notes payable aggregating $50,000 evidenced by four notes signed by the corporation per the president. How would you handle this item in your audit report and what procedure would you follow to disclose whether or not this was a defalcation or an understatement of liability?

**15—160.** Give your opinion of the following form of certificate to a balance sheet:

"I have examined the above balance sheet and certify that it is in accordance with the books of the company."

(Signed) Charles E. Wilson

(C. P. A. Ill.)

**15—161.** What is meant by a qualified certificate? Give an illustration of a case in which a qualified certificate might properly be given and draft a qualification applicable to that case.

(A. I. A.)

**15—162.** Draft a form of audit certificate to accompany a balance sheet which is to be published in the annual report of a corporation.

(A. I. A.)

## AUDITING PROBLEMS

**15—40.** In the course of your audit of the accounts of The Illinois Corporation, Chicago, Ill., for the year ended December 31, 1938, you find the following conditions existing:

(a) At the beginning of the year the corporation had an accumulated operating deficit of $125,000.

(b) During the year the corporation made a net operating profit of $80,000.

(c) During the year the corporation caused its factory site to be appraised by a reputable appraisal company, with the result that the appraisal value was found to exceed its book value (cost) by $175,000, and this appreciation in value was by order of the directors set up on the books and credited to the surplus account.

(d) During the year four equal quarterly dividends were paid to stockholders: $50,000 in all to preferred stockholders, and $40,000 to common stockholders.

(e) The company's balance sheet, to which you are required to certify without alteration, shows surplus account at $40,000 without any detail or comment.

Give the exact language which, under these circumstances, you would incorporate in your certificate and state your reason therefor.

(C. P. A. Ill.)

**15—41.** You are employed to make a balance sheet audit of the accounts of The McGregor Co. of Denver, Colo. Upon reporting for duty you are supplied with a trial balance as of December 31, 1938.

The president also furnishes you with a certificate of inventory showing merchandise on hand, December 31, 1938, valued at cost amounting to $4,460. In completing the audit you also ascertained the following:

(a) Prepaid advertising material not yet consumed amounts to $400

(b) $600 advanced to salesmen as an expense fund has been charged to salesmen's salaries

(c) Salaries accrued amount to $475

(d) Accrued interest on mortgage payable amounts to $100.

From the preceding information you are required to prepare an audit report which should contain the following:

(a) Auditor's certificate

(b) Balance sheet

(c) Profit and loss statement

(d) Adjusting, closing, and post-closing entries required to bring the books in accord with the auditor's report.

## THE McGREGOR COMPANY

### Trial Balance, December 31, 1938

| | | |
|---|---:|---:|
| Capital Stock Authorized...................... | | $ 25,000.00 |
| Unissued Capital Stock........................ | $  2,000.00 | |
| Merchandise Inventory (December 31, 1937)... | 5,500.00 | |
| Purchases.................................... | 28,300.00 | |
| Sales........................................ | | 57,690.00 |
| Sales Returns................................ | 4,900.00 | |
| Purchases Returns............................ | | 1,500.00 |
| Shipping Expenses............................ | 2,600.00 | |
| Accounts Receivable.......................... | 14,200.00 | |
| Accounts Payable............................. | | 7,800.00 |
| Notes Receivable............................. | 8,000.00 | |
| Notes Payable................................ | | 5,000.00 |
| Real Estate.................................. | 20,000.00 | |
| Advertising.................................. | 1,000.00 | |
| Real Estate Repairs.......................... | 875.00 | |
| General Expenses............................. | 4,800.00 | |
| Salaries..................................... | 5,600.00 | |
| Cash......................................... | 4,300.00 | |
| Petty Cash................................... | 100.00 | |
| Discount on Sales............................ | 460.00 | |
| Bank Discount................................ | 180.00 | |
| Discount on Purchases........................ | | 275.00 |
| Salesmen's Salaries.......................... | 2,000.00 | |
| Selling Expenses............................. | 800.00 | |
| Mortgage Payable............................. | | 6,000.00 |
| Interest Cost................................ | 150.00 | |
| Notes Receivable Discounted.................. | | 2,500.00 |
| | $105,765.00 | $105,765.00 |

15—42. You are engaged to audit the accounts of The Western Telephone Co., Seattle, Wash., for the six-month period ending December 31, 1938. Upon reporting for duty, you are furnished with a trial balance and in completing the audit, you ascertain the following information:

(a) It has not been the custom of the company to set up a reserve for depreciation of fixed assets. However, it has been the custom of the company to credit the asset accounts with an estimated amount of depreciation each year. After a consultation with the president of the company, your recommendation was accepted and it was decided to provide reserves for depreciation based upon the book values of the fixed assets as shown in the trial balance at the rate of 10% on furniture and fixtures and 5% on buildings, switchboards and booths, poles, wire lines, and telephones. You decide that is only necessary to set up two reserves for depreciation, one applicable to furniture and fixtures and the other to buildings and equipment.

(b) In investigating the account with material and supplies, you find that the entire amount charged to the account was consumed during the period.

(c) It was found that the accounts with supply sales had been credited with material and supplies sold by the exchanges. It was decided that the amount of the supplies sold should be treated as a deduction from the cost of materials and supplies consumed since it is impractical to attempt to ascertain the cost of the particular supplies sold, with a view to giving each exchange credit for any profit that may have been realized from the supply sales.

(d) The account with dividends paid amounting to $14,000 represents dividends declared and paid during the year. No entry was made at the time the dividends were declared, hence the amount of the dividends paid have not as yet been charged to surplus.

From the information given, prepare a report for your client consisting of the following:

(a) Auditor's certificate

(b) Balance sheet as of December 31, 1938

(c) General profit and loss statement for the six-month period ended December 31, 1938

(d) Schedule of operations showing the gross operating income of each exchange

(e) Adjusting entries required to bring books into accord with the auditor's report.

## THE WESTERN TELEPHONE CO.

### Trial Balance, December 31, 1938

| | | |
|---|---:|---:|
| Cash | $    300.00 | |
| Exchange Bank, Acton | 3,877.40 | |
| Central Bank, Burton | 793.20 | |
| J and A Bank, Castleton | 727.40 | |
| Accounts Receivable, Acton | 8,695.60 | |
| Accounts Receivable, Burton | 7,589.80 | |
| Accounts Receivable, Castleton | 5,328.00 | |
| Notes Receivable | 258.50 | |
| Accounts Payable | | $   3,976.00 |
| Notes Payable | | 53,200.00 |
| Interest Payable | | 1,052.00 |
| Material and Supplies | 20,146.50 | |
| Furniture and Fixtures | 12,253.50 | |
| Real Estate | 10,000.00 | |
| Buildings | 45,000.00 | |
| Switchboards and Booths | 23,115.40 | |
| Poles | 209,770.50 | |
| Wire Lines | 131,269.70 | |
| Telephones | 127,515.90 | |
| Capital Stock | | 350,000.00 |
| Surplus | | 181,572.30 |
| Tolls paid to foreign companies | 4,791.20 | |
| Rental allowances, Acton Exchange | 5,942.00 | |
| Rentals, Acton Exchange | | 44,077.50 |
| Rental allowances, Burton Exchange | 3,984.00 | |
| Rentals, Burton Exchange | | 26,425.30 |
| Rentals, Castleton Exchange | | 20,244.90 |
| Tolls, Acton Exchange | | 8,202.50 |
| Tolls, Burton Exchange | | 4,452.50 |
| Tolls, Castleton Exchange | | 2,800.70 |
| Pay Station Tolls, Acton | | 637.00 |
| Pay Station Tolls, Burton | | 727.50 |
| Pay Station Tolls, Castleton | | 988.60 |
| Supply Sales, Acton | | 126.80 |
| Supply Sales, Burton | | 57.50 |
| Refunds, Acton | 52.50 | |
| Salaries, central office | 3,000.00 | |
| General Expense | 13,121.30 | |
| Insurance | 745.90 | |
| Operators' wages, Acton | 6,935.00 | |
| Operators' wages, Burton | 4,890.00 | |
| Operators' wages, Castleton | 5,700.00 | |
| Repairs of wire plant | 14,022.00 | |
| Repairs of equipment | 14,435.30 | |
| Traffic Expense | 485.00 | |
| Profit and Loss | | 204.50 |
| Dividends paid | 14,000.00 | |
| | $698,745.60 | $698,745.60 |

15—43. Wood & Conn, Certified Public Accountants, are engaged by the National Candy Company to devise and install a system of accounts. The business had been in operation one year previous to their engagement. At the end of the first year, following the installation of the system, the accountants are again employed to make an audit. The following trial balance and other data are taken from the working papers prepared by the senior accountant in charge of the audit.

## THE NATIONAL CANDY CO.

### Trial Balance, December 31, 1938

| | | |
|---|---:|---:|
| Capital Stock, Common...................... | | $20,000.00 |
| Capital Stock, Preferred...................... | | 20,000.00 |
| Treasury Stock.............................. | $ 1,000.00 | |
| Sinking Fund Investments.................... | 2,500.00 | |
| Surplus...................................... | | 8,695.84 |
| Organization Expense........................ | 347.68 | |
| Bank........................................ | 8,342.91 | |
| Petty Cash.................................. | 50.00 | |
| Finished Goods Inventory, December 31, 1937... | 8,324.62 | |
| Raw Material Inventory...................... | 1,428.83 | |
| Sugar Inventory............................. | 542.61 | |
| Boxes Inventory............................. | 1,298.42 | |
| Merchandise Inventory....................... | 3,824.92 | |
| Accounts Receivable......................... | 12,422.98 | |
| U. S. Treasury Bonds........................ | 4,000.00 | |
| Machinery.................................. | 25,820.10 | |
| Miscellaneous Factory Equipment............. | 4,864.91 | |
| Garford Truck.............................. | 2,200.00 | |
| Dodge Car.................................. | 1,325.00 | |
| Warehouse Equipment........................ | 625.00 | |
| Office Equipment............................ | 1,610.12 | |
| Building, 2916 Wetmore...................... | 7,850.00 | |
| Lot 14, Block 462........................... | 6,828.12 | |
| Mortgage Bonds............................. | | 25,000.00 |
| Accounts Payable............................ | | 1,382.45 |
| Notes Payable First Nat'l Bank............... | | 6,000.00 |
| Reserve for Bad Debts....................... | 25.94 | 84.72 |
| Reserve for Depr. of Mach................... | 94.62 | 2,352.50 |
| Reserve for Depr. Misc. Factory Equipment..... | | 452.60 |
| Reserve for Depr. Garford Truck.............. | | 440.00 |
| Reserve for Depr. Dodge Car................. | | 265.00 |
| Reserve for Depr. Warehouse Equipment........ | | 62.50 |
| Reserve for Depr. Office Equipment........... | | 151.82 |
| Reserve for Depr. Building................... | | 235.50 |
| Raw Material Purchases...................... | 52,682.91 | |
| Raw Material Returns and Rebates............ | | 243.62 |
| Sugar Purchases............................. | 6,284.22 | |
| Boxes, Purchases............................ | 5,421.92 | |
| Repairs (See Schedule)....................... | 222.14 | |
| Productive Labor............................ | 19,241.68 | |
| Miscellaneous Factory Expense................ | 244.68 | |
| Fuel and Light.............................. | 562.81 | |
| Power....................................... | 493.84 | |
| Interest on Real Estate Investment............ | 1,172.85 | |
| Bldg. Expense and Income.................... | 93.28 | 1,172.85 |
| Garford Truck Operation..................... | 1,628.92 | |

*(Continued on next page)*

| | | |
|---|---:|---:|
| Insurance (See Schedule)...................... $ | 702.30 | |
| Stationery for Factory......................... | 32.84 | |
| Taxes (See Schedule).......................... | 3,197.67 | |
| Merchandise Purchases......................... | 41,421.62 | |
| Merchandise Rebates and Allowances........... | $ | 316.84 |
| Sales of Manufactured Goods.................. | | 106,824.64 |
| Rebates on Sales of Manufactured Goods........ | 826.28 | |
| Sales of Merchandise........................... | | 56,841.83 |
| Rebates on Sales of Merchandise................ | 563.18 | |
| Advertising.................................... | 1,324.83 | |
| Dodge Car Operation.......................... | 412.00 | |
| Salesmen's Salaries............................ | 3,354.62 | |
| Wrapping Materials............................ | 256.89 | |
| General Expense............................... | 86.21 | |
| Donations..................................... | 138.50 | |
| Officers' Salaries.............................. | 7,500.00 | |
| Office Expense................................. | 547.62 | |
| Office Salaries................................. | 2,480.00 | |
| Interest Expense............................... | 2,360.00 | |
| Sinking Fund Interest Income.................. | | 150.00 |
| Dividends Interim 5%, (July 1) Com............ | 2,000.00 | |
| Interest Income Liberty Bonds................. | | 123.13 |
| Bad Accounts Recovered....................... | | 31.24 |
| Purchase Discount............................. | | 1,428.94 |
| Sales Discount................................ | 1,675.43 | |
| | $252,256.02 | $252,256.02 |

## Other Data

Dodge Car used only by salesman. (⅛ of Garford Truck time used hauling
incoming freight from the depot and ⅞ used for delivery purposes.)
Building is of brick construction.
Material is unpacked in the factory.

## Inventories

(December 31, at cost or market, whichever is lower.)

| | | | | |
|---|---:|---|---|---:|
| Finished Goods........ | $10,384.92 | | Boxes.................. | $ 874.32 |
| Raw Material......... | 2,143.95 | | Merchandise........... | 4,015.83 |
| Sugar................. | 754.28 | | | |

## Accruals

Interest on U. S. Treasury Bonds ............................... $59.37

## Unpaid Bills (not recorded)

| | | | |
|---|---:|---|---:|
| Garage Bill Garford......... | $15.40 | Advertising................ | $ 45.82 |
| Garage Bill Dodge.......... | 12.82 | Salesman—Salary.......... | 112.00 |
| Stationery for Factory....... | 5.68 | Wrapping Material......... | 16.28 |
| Productive Labor........... | 75.84 | Office Expense............. | 5.94 |
| Plumbing Bill on Bldg....... | 19.45 | Int. due First Nat'l Bank... | 120.00 |

## Prepaid Items

| | | |
|---|---:|---|
| Advertising................. | $55.00 | Organization Expense to be written |
| Office Salaries.............. | 25.00 | off on a five-year basis. |

## Bad Debts

Write off bad debts........ $131.24　　accounts considered good (after
Reserve for bad debts should be　　deducting bad debts written off.)
increased to equivalent of 1% of

## Depreciation

Machinery 10%                         Warehouse Equipment 10%
Misc. Factory Equipment 10%           Office Equipment 10%
Garford Truck 20%                     Buildings 3%
Dodge Car 20%
No adjusting entries required for insurance and taxes.

## Distribution

Repairs:

| | | | |
|---|---|---|---|
| F. Ex. | Machinery | $ | 124.83 |
| F. Ex. | Miscellaneous Equipment | | 16.84 |
| Gar. Op. | Garford | | 25.68 |
| Dod. Op. | Dodge | | 2.42 |
| B. Ex. | Building | | 19.28 |
| F. Ex. | General Factory | | 26.84 |
| O. Ex. | Office Equipment | | 6.25 |

Taxes:

| | | |
|---|---|---|
| F. Ex. | Machinery and Factory Equipment | 425.62 |
| Gar. Op. | Garford | 32.61 |
| Dod. Op. | Dodge | 18.42 |
| B. Ex. | Building and Lot | 241.84 |
| F. Ex. | Raw Material | 39.68 |
| P. & L. | Finished Goods | 121.96 |
| P. & L. | Office Equipment | 24.86 |
| Surplus | Income paid during this fiscal period (applicable to previous period) | 2,182.68 |
| P. & L. | Corporation License | 15.00 |
| P. & L. | Capital Stock | 95.00 |

Insurance:

| | | |
|---|---|---|
| F. Ex. | Factory Plant | 380.00 |
| P. & L. | Office Equipment | 19.20 |
| B. Ex. | Building | 88.80 |
| Gar. Op. | Garford | 47.30 |
| Dod. Op. | Dodge | 27.00 |
| P. & L. | Finished Goods | 100.00 |
| P. & L. | Merchandise Stock | 40.00 |

Depreciation:

| | | |
|---|---|---|
| F. Ex. | Machinery | 2,582.01 |
| F. Ex. | Factory Equipment | 486.49 |
| Gar. Op. | Garford | 440.00 |
| Dod. Op. | Dodge | 265.00 |
| F. Ex. | Warehouse | 62.50 |
| O. Ex. | Office | 161.01 |
| B. Ex. | Building | 235.50 |

From the information given prepare a certified report for the National Candy Company. Your report should include the following:

(a) Auditors' certificate.
(b) Balance sheet.
(c) Statement of profit and loss.
(d) Manufacturing statement.
(e) Schedule of operating expenses.
(f) Adjusting entries required to bring the books in agreement with auditors' report.

**15—44.** As bookkeeper for The Blank Manufacturing Company, draft the entries required in journal form to close the profit and loss or temporary proprietorship accounts, assuming that all adjustments included in the report of the auditors, Stevenson and Bennett, were recorded on the books so as to bring the accounts in accord with the auditors' report.

## AUDITING PRACTICE

### An Audit Case (Thirteenth Installment)

The next step is the writing of a report. This is done after the audit work has been completed and the working papers arranged in order and indexed to the working trial balance or working sheet. The report usually consists of a balance sheet, a statement of profit and loss, comments concerning important features of the work done by the auditor, or matters which the auditor believes should be called to the attention of the management or owners of a concern, an auditor's certificate, and a letter of transmittal addressed to the person or persons for whom the audit was performed.

Inasmuch as no provision has been made for the Federal income and excess-profits taxes, this should be given consideration in drafting the report. It will be noted that the engagement does not involve the preparation of an income tax return for the Beverly Supply Company, but obviously the balance sheet and profit and loss statement cannot be certified without reference to the income tax and excess-profits tax liability. The audit has revealed that capital stock taxes amounting to $150 were paid for the year ended June 30, 1938. This indicates an adjusted declared capital of $150,000. Since a corporation is permitted to earn 10% of its adjusted declared capital without having to pay any excess-profits taxes, it will be found that the Beverly Supply Company has incurred no excess-profits tax liability. There is, of course, an income tax liability to be considered. Since the audit was for the calendar year 1938, the provisions of the Revenue Act of 1938 will apply in computing the tax.

## INSTRUCTIONS

Prepare an audit report consisting of the following:

1. A balance sheet
2. A statement of profit and loss
3. An accountants' certificate
4. Comments on important features of the audit, suggestions for improvement of the accounting system, etc.

After preparing the audit report, draft in journal form the entries required to close the profit and loss or temporary proprietorship accounts and prepare a post-closing trial balance.

# CHAPTER SIXTEEN

## DETAILED AUDITS

1. Auditing the Books of Original Entry
   (a) Cash Records
   (b) Sales Records
   (c) Purchase Records
   (d) General Journal

2. Auditing Pay Roll and Expense Records
   (a) Pay Roll Records
   (b) Expense Records

3. Use of Accounting Machines

The preceding chapters have been devoted to the presentation of principles and procedures applicable to a balance sheet audit or an examination of financial statements. Most audits are of this type.

Where such an audit is made periodically by a firm of reliable auditors, and where the accounting procedure is worked out through close co-operation of the parties, the balance sheet audit is the most satisfactory. As a result, annual and semi-annual statements as issued by the modern corporation and certified by practicing independent auditors are, as a whole, verified by the balance sheet audit procedure as previously outlined.

On the other hand, in many business enterprises, especially those whose securities are not listed on the various stock exchanges, the annual reports are not certified by public auditors. The statements prepared are not for publication, so there is a tendency toward poorer accounting records, and poorer internal checks. The extent to which errors creep in depends upon the degree in which proper practices are set up. The managers may receive a report which their knowledge of conditions leads them to doubt. Perhaps they may find that cash resources are low for some unexplainable reason; or some other factor may arise, which will necessitate a careful detailed check of all the transactions (or of a sufficient number to determine the difficulty) for a period or number of periods. Such an audit is known as a detailed audit to differentiate it from the balance sheet audit.

In a small concern a detailed audit may involve checking each transaction, voucher, posting, addition, and balance. This routine is usually impossible in a large enterprise unless performed daily by an internal auditing group, and even then the verification becomes to a large extent only a routine check of certain of the transactions. Too much detailed checking may result in increasing the cost of an audit without correspondingly increasing the benefits derived. Testing has been substituted to a great extent with the result that an auditor may verify certain sections or periods only, provided his investigation shows the records are properly maintained. The amount of testing, the frequency of the transactions tested, and the particular transactions verified will all depend upon the conditions encountered. With well kept books, a good system of internal check, and adequate office methods, the work may be reduced to a minimum.

The detailed audit involves then just what its name implies; a detailed verification of the recording of the transactions for the period. Such an audit not only verifies the correctness of the balance sheet items, but goes further, and determines that all revenue, expense, and capital items have been properly recorded, and that the financial statements correctly set forth the financial condition of the company and its operations for the period. A detailed audit involves an inspection of the following records, in addition to the procedure discussed in the preceding chapters:

(a)  Cash records
(b)  Sales records
(c)  Purchase records
(d)  General journal entries
(e)  Pay roll records
(f)  Expense records.

## AUDITING THE BOOKS OF ORIGINAL ENTRY

**Cash Records.**  The method of verification of the cash records is usually much the same as in a balance sheet audit, except for detail and emphasis. In the case of the balance sheet audit the emphasis is on the correctness of the balances shown on the financial statements. In the case of the detailed audit the emphasis is on the correctness of the individual transactions as recorded in the books of original entry and in the correctness of the postings of the transactions to the ledger accounts. The detailed audit, therefore, involves a large amount of checking of transactions. Cash receipts registers should be scanned to see that all receipts are properly recorded. Footings of all journals should be verified and tests should be made of the postings to the ledger accounts. Cash disbursements may be checked by comparing the canceled checks with the entries in the cash disbursement register. In this comparison, there should be care in determining to whom the checks are drawn, by whom endorsed, and whether they are made out to persons or firms ordinarily doing business with the company. If made out to members of the firm or employees (other than pay roll items) they should be carefully investigated. Checks made out to "Cash" usually will bear checking. In order to verify doubtful items, vouchers and invoices may be examined. Where invoices are not available the auditor should consult the proper officials for explanations.

**Sales Records.** The procedure to be employed in verifying the sales records in a detailed audit necessarily depends on the sales records maintained by the concern being audited. There are at least four types of sales transactions ordinarily encountered, anyone or all of which may exist in a given enterprise. The first type to be considered is the cash sale.

A record of receipts from cash sales is usually made on adding machine tapes contained within cash registers in which all cash received is entered. Cash registers contain one or more adding machine units in which the cash entries are accumulated. Some cash registers contain a number of separate adding machine units so that separate daily totals may be obtained of the cash entered in the cash register by different salespeople, or so that totals may be obtained of the amounts of sales of various lines of merchandise. Most of the adding machine units may be cleared of their totals whenever desired, usually daily. The "control" adding unit cannot be cleared of its totals, consequently, the amounts accumulate from day to day. Cash register readings are usually made at the beginning and end of each business day. The difference between the readings of the "control" unit should ordinarily represent the cash receipts for the day, except for errors or adjustments.

In verifying the cash sales, comparisons may be made of the daily totals of cash sales in the sales record with the amounts shown to have been received by readings on the cash register tapes. If separate cash registers are maintained for each sales department, the total cash receipts indicated by all the cash registers should correspond with the cash sales shown by the sales tickets and the entries in the sales journal for the day or period concerned.

Tests may be used to advantage in doing this. The total of sales slips (where used) should be verified and checked with the cash register reading. In theatres and similar enterprises, the cash receipts will represent sales and the tickets issued by the cashiers will be numbered numerically. In such cases the number of tickets of each class sold may be determined from those remaining on the rolls, and the cash value calculated by multiplying the number of tickets sold by the prices of each class. Where the client has collecting agents, the reports of agents should be checked with the cash receipts. In all cases cash received should be checked with the bank records.

A second type of sale to be considered is the one made on credit terms of thirty, sixty, or ninety days. In verifying credit sales, the auditor should make a comparison of the entries in the sales register with the shipping order, the manufacturing order, the charge slip, or whatever the record may be.

If duplicate sales invoices are maintained they should be compared with the entries in the sales register as to names and amounts for certain months depending on the extent to which testing is being employed in the audit. Tests may also be made of the postings from the sales record to the customers' ledger accounts. The sales register should be footed and the totals traced to the general ledger accounts. If the sales invoices are numbered, it is desirable that the numbers should all be accounted for. If the concern being audited has an internal auditing group which makes a daily audit of sales and accounts for all sales tickets, comparatively little detail work will need to be done by the auditor except to investigate the system and see that it is working properly.

The sales invoices of the last few days of the period should be checked to see that the goods were actually shipped and were not still on hand and included in the inventory. Care should be taken to see that the sales record was closed at the end of the audit period and that it does not include sales made in the following period. If there is doubt concerning the propriety of the sales for the last few days of the period, comparisons may be made of the sales record with the shipping records to determine when the goods were delivered.

Sales returns and allowances should be carefully verified. Many large stores have special departments which issue credit slips for returned goods. In any case there will be some individual or department whose duty it will be to pass on all such items. The auditor should satisfy himself that all such items are properly vouched, properly recorded, and properly posted to the subsidiary ledger and controlling accounts.

A third type of sales transaction is that represented by the installment sale. The goods are sold under the terms of a chattel mortgage, and payments are made weekly, monthly, or on some other set basis. Such transactions will usually be recorded in an installment sale register, and the signed contract will be on file. The auditor should verify the sale with the contract, see that all payments and adjustments are properly recorded, see that the charges to the customers have been properly made in the journals and ledgers, and see that the contracts are being properly carried out.

In most concerns the three types of sales transactions mentioned above will be fairly well handled. Internal checks of some sort will be in operation, and the work of the auditor, although routine and detailed, will be comparatively simple.

The fourth type of sale, however, is usually an exception in an ordinary enterprise and adequate means for handling such sales rarely exist. This class of transactions consists of sales of such property, as real estate, scrap, or other items not constituting merchandise. In such cases the auditor must ascertain from the facts of each particular case whether the transaction is properly recorded. In the case of real estate sales, contracts of sale may be examined, the cash receipts traced to the book of entry and bank records, and any credit instruments which are received in exchange should be checked to the proper records.

**Purchase Records.** The method of accounting for purchases will control, to a large extent, the auditor's procedure in checking such transactions. Many small concerns enter purchases in the cash book only at the time of their payment. In such cases order files, unpaid voucher files, or similar records will usually be found, or the memory of the client may have to be resorted to. In the latter case, the records of payments for thirty or sixty days after the closing of the books will be of considerable value. On the other hand, many larger enterprises will have well organized methods for purchasing, checking of invoices, recording of invoices in the purchase or voucher records, and paying of such items. Between these extremes will be found all types of procedure.

The auditor's first duty is to acquaint himself with the methods in existence, the records available, and the provisions existent for insuring that all transactions are recorded in the right accounts at the proper values. Errors of omission in purchase records (provided the periodic method of inventorying is in use) will result in higher profits, which must be carefully watched. The auditor should verify purchase transactions from the invoices to the books and vice versa. Where a receiving record is maintained, it should be checked against the invoices and purchase records for a sufficient period to assure the auditor that the records are reliable. The records at the beginning and end of the period should be checked against the receiving records to determine whether all entries for purchases are entered during the proper period. Many concerns purchase on long term contracts. In such cases the auditor should review the contract, and from its terms, determine whether the prices recorded are bona fide.

Where prices are not governed by long term contracts they should follow closely market prices. A test of invoices against market values may often be of advantage, and where discrepancies of any appreciable amount exist, they should be investigated. Where perpetual inventory records are maintained, checks of the inventory cards with the voucher or purchase record are often of value in determining whether the two are being properly maintained. Vouchers should be checked for extensions, and footings in sufficient number to satisfy the auditor that the vouchers have been properly handled. In the larger organizations, invoices are stamped when received, and the history of the invoice shown thereon from the time of arrival in the office till paid and filed. Where such a routine is followed the work of the auditor may usually be limited to satisfying himself that the routine is being properly followed through.

Discounts, allowances, and returned purchases necessitate careful attention on the part of the auditor. In some cases invoices are entered in the accounts payable or voucher register at the net value, the discounts being deducted on the face of the invoice. Again such discounts are treated as miscellaneous income items. The policy of the client should be determined and sufficient invoices checked against the records to assure that these items are properly reflected in the records. The method of handling allowances and returned purchases should be carefully followed through.

In verifying purchases, the auditor should assure himself that capital expenditures are properly handled and not included as a part of purchases. In other words, voucher register distributions should be carefully watched. Where budgets are in existence, comparisons of budgetary and actual commitments are well worth while and may be made a part of the report, as they should aid materially in shaping management policy and commitments.

Lastly, there are several criteria which may be used to assure roughly that purchases are properly stated. The gross profit ratio may be used to determine whether cost of sales is in line with past experience (this, of course, includes the factory pay roll and expense sections in manufacturing concerns). Debit balances in the payable register may signify omission of invoices. Exceptionally small credit balances of creditors' accounts may show failure to properly handle returns or allowances. All means of checking should be utilized by the auditor, for they often furnish leads to errors which it is highly important to reveal.

**General Journal.** Special attention should be given to all transactions recorded in the general journal as to regularity, proper posting, and proper vouching. In many businesses, general journal entries are primarily for correction transactions, or transactions out of the ordinary for which the special journals make no provision.

Certain entries customarily recorded in the general journal, or on journal vouchers if no general journal is maintained, need special attention by the auditor to determine that they have been correctly recorded. Entries which reduce the value of asset accounts such as credits to accounts and notes receivable or to fixed asset accounts should be carefully examined to ascertain that the entries have been authorized and that the correct accounts and amounts are indicated. It would be possible in some instances with customers' accounts and notes to misappropriate cash collections and later to conceal the abstraction by writing off amounts or by posting unauthorized credits to the accounts. All journal entries, crediting customers' accounts should be approved by some authorized official, and the journal voucher or journal entry should bear this individual's signature. Journal entries affecting fixed asset accounts are usually verified in connection with the verification of the balance sheet accounts. All changes in fixed asset accounts are verified by examination of vouchers, contracts, and other evidences indicating the propriety of the entries concerned. In so doing the journal entries will automatically be verified.

All or part of the journal entries for the audit period should be scanned and unusual entries should receive special attention. Adjusting and closing entries and regular monthly entries should be tested as to amounts and postings to see that they are correctly prepared and recorded. There will ordinarily be comparatively few general journal entries other than those mentioned above and they may be verified individually as to their propriety, amount, and posting to the ledger accounts affected.

### AUDITING PAY ROLL AND EXPENSE RECORDS

**Pay Roll Records.** In a detailed audit, pay roll practices and transactions require careful attention. The auditor should ascertain pay roll procedure prior to any attempt to verify the authenticity of the records. The internal procedure is of importance in that it tends to prevent fraud, if the procedure is effective. Pay roll discrepancies are of various types. Where a foreman makes out the pay roll and disburses the payments, he may easily pad the totals, appropriating the difference between the amount paid and received. The same may be true in case the paymaster prepares the pay roll and makes the expenditure.

Wherever possible, the pay roll division should be composed of clerical and disbursement divisions. The clerical group should collect the pay roll data, tabulate it, and prepare the pay envelopes. The disbursing group should make the payment to the employees. Under some such arrangement, fraudulent practices are limited, for by this method fraud or embezzlement of funds would involve collusion between two or more individuals.

Pay roll practices have undergone considerable change in the past few years. Robberies, the increased use of checks, and other changes have led to considerable improvement in pay roll procedure. Many companies now meet pay roll expenditures by checks entirely, using a separate pay roll bank account for the purpose. This procedure aids materially in verifying the pay roll. There are no unclaimed wages in the hands of the pay roll department—they are in the bank. The signatures on the canceled checks provide one more proof for the auditor. The whole procedure centers in the one bank account.

In auditing pay rolls the method existing for handling such items will govern the auditor's procedure. He should determine whether the system issued is adequate to prevent ordinary discrepancies. The method of verifying time, rates, and other items should be checked. Where an adequate cost system is in existence labor costs may often be checked against pay roll figures for a proof on the total pay roll figure of the factory, and in some cases this can be done for the general and selling groups. Where a pay roll check is made out and the bank fills the envelopes with the exact change, the pay roll should be confirmed, and the check drawn against the pay roll should be verified with the footings of the pay roll sheets. Where payments are made by check from a special bank account the charges to this account should agree with the total pay roll. The disbursements may also be checked in detail and compared with the individual items on the pay roll sheet. Where pay rolls are paid with currency, it is sometimes the practice to withdraw a sufficient amount to cover all payments and insure the proper change as well. This is in cases where the pay envelopes are not made up by the bank. In this case the auditor should assure himself that the excess drawn for purposes of making change is properly handled. The usual procedure is to reverse the original entry and deposit the excess cash in the bank.

In auditing pay rolls the principle of testing may be used. Pay rolls may be taken at random throughout the year and audited in detail. They should be footed and the amounts traced into the general ledger accounts. The names on one or more pay rolls should be checked against the personnel department's employee records to determine that the individuals named are actually in the employ of the concern being audited. The auditor may be present and supervise the paying of employees. If employees do not call to claim their pay envelopes, investigation should be made to determine that the individuals indicated are actually in the employ of the company.

Where it appears advisable, random transactions from time cards, cost sheets, or other records should be checked with the pay roll. This may be a simple operation, but where a complicated wage system is in vogue, it is a very detailed and complicated one. In the latter case, however, pay roll and cost departments are more often adequately organized and their calculations are much more reliable. Payments made to officers may be verified by checking against the minutes of the board, or the articles of co-partnership, in case the firm is a partnership.

A detailed audit of pay roll may include a verification of commissions when salesmen are paid on a commission basis. The practice of the firm, the method of payment, and provisions of the individual contracts with the men should be determined in each case, and payments checked against the record of sales. Where payment of commissions is deferred, accruals should be carefully noted, assuring that the proper pay roll amounts are included in both the cost and the accrued liabilities. Where bonuses are paid, the agreement between the company and the officers or employees should be examined, and the transactions verified. Bonus payments are frequently calculated on a wrong basis, and the auditor should carefully examine such items.

**Expense Records.** Any complete audit will require the verification of all expense items. These will include such items as repairs and maintenance, depreciation, depletion, insurance, supplies, and other similar expenses. In auditing expense items a large amount of judgment must be exercised by the auditor. Certain principles must be applied, but they necessarily must be used with considerable leeway to meet different conditions.

Expenditures made for maintenance, repairs, alterations, and similar purposes should be carefully checked against the original records, appropriations, and authorizations. The auditor should assure himself that such items are properly classified, that expense items are not capitalized, and that capital expenditures are not charged to expense. Expenditures made for the purpose of increasing the earning capacity of a plant are usually considered to be capital items. On the other hand an outlay made simply to maintain earning capacity is an expense and should be so handled. The question of whether an expenditure merely maintains or increases earning capacity is, of course, a debatable one in many cases. The facts of the case in any specific instance will rule.

The handling of depreciation should be given careful consideration in the detailed audit, and its adequacy should be determined, the entries carefully verified, and the methods used reviewed. Prior to the war period, the proper handling of depreciation was a more or less debated matter. With the advent of the Federal income tax regulations, depreciation has now become widely recognized as a cost. The problem as to what constitutes proper depreciation charges is still a much discussed proposition. What the rate and the basis used in specific cases should be is open for debate in many instances. The Bureau of Internal Revenue has made some valuable studies on depreciation and has aided materially in setting standard rates and practices. The auditor should satisfy himself that such items are adequate, that the basis in use is fair, and that the accounts are properly handled. Each individual case must be separately considered where unusual conditions exist. Frequently physical property is constructed on leased real estate. In such cases or in cases of mining or other extractive industries, the life of the improvements is judged not by their condition in relation to operating efficiency, but by the remaining life of the mine, oil, or standing timber.

In the case of depleting properties, depletion should be charged as the minerals or other raw materials are consumed, at a rate sufficient to reduce the value of such properties to their surface values at the expiration of operations. In such cases, depletion charges are usually based on values stated in the books and accounts and the estimated amount of materials recoverable. Estimates of mining engineers, oil and geological experts, and expert scalers will usually be available for purposes of obtaining estimated recoverable quantities.

Insurance premiums, costs, and accruals should be verified and should be allocated to expense and deferred charges in the proper proportions. Frequently such premiums are charged to expense as paid, though they may involve expenditures made to cover several years' protection. The auditor should check the vouchers with the disbursement register, and the postings with the ledger.

Frequently in a detailed audit the verification will disclose various expenses included in the accounts for the audit period which should be charged to a prior period, and expenses omitted from the audit period operations and included in charges affecting the succeeding period. Such items usually include monthly bills, entered when received, but applicable to the month previous to the one in which it is received. The vouchers for payments should be carefully examined for at least the first and the last months of the period, and for the next succeeding one, and the auditor should assure himself that all expenses are included in the proper records. There are many current expenses which often amount to approximately the same total each period. Comparisons of the amounts of such items as insurance costs, utilities, etc., as well as unit costs of products for like periods, are often of considerable value in locating errors, both of omission and commission.

Many companies have considerable income resulting from investments, or outside activities which are usually classified under other income. These items should be examined and should be included in other income, not as a part of revenue from operations. The existence of investments will usually inform the auditor of the occasion for such items. Interest paid, taxes, and depreciation not otherwise accounted for are often to be found as "Deductions from Other Income." These should be verified from the proper records, and the auditor should assure himself that they are financial and not operating items.

In many cases a large number of adjustments, appropriations, and reserves are charged or credited to the surplus accounts. These entries should all be checked to assure their proper treatment, and to be sure that they are not expense items.

## USE OF ACCOUNTING MACHINES

No such discussion as this is complete without at least some mention of the use of machines in accounting and auditing procedure. The last few years have witnessed the introduction of several makes of machines for general and specialized purposes for use in accounting and auditing work. Bookkeeping machines, posting machines, banking machines, and so on, are becoming increasingly common. The auditor should acquaint himself in so far as possible with such equipment and its place in accounting work, for such machines, through their multiplicity of operations may supplant journals, make their tape entries and the ledger entries, and bring down balances in one operation. Analysis machines are also today being introduced which are revolutionizing accounting and auditing procedure, though principles remain the same. Where such machines are in use the accounting work is more quickly performed, is cheaper, and is better done in most cases, permitting the auditor a much better set of records and more possibilities of adequate checks.

## SUMMARY

The detailed audit is one in which are verified in detail, all the transactions for the period or enough of them to indicate the general accuracy of the books of original entry and the ledger accounts. Where all transactions are not verified, the number of transactions, as well as the particular ones chosen, will vary depending on the condition of the records, files, office organization, and methods of accounting.

A detailed audit is a balance sheet audit, coupled with a careful verification of the profit and loss records and the books of original entry. In such verifications there are generally certain types of transactions which need to be carefully checked. In other instances tests may be made with excellent results. Depreciation, depletion, taxes, and similar expenses should be carefully checked. The verification of pay rolls varies widely, and the procedure involved will usually depend on the system in use. The cash records and the voucher register are usually carefully verified. The comparison of vouchers with the voucher register entries also requires careful scrutiny. The detailed audit is for the purpose of verifying the accuracy of the accounting records. The auditor should cover in sufficient detail the balance sheet and profit and loss accounts in order to do so. Where this may be done by tests, they should be used. If the records are such that proper tests may not be applied, detailed checking of all transactions, additions, postings, and footings may be necessary.

## AUDITING THEORY

**16—163.** Name some of the conditions which would justify a detailed audit.

**16—164.** What results might be expected to be obtained from a detailed audit which would not be expected of a balance sheet audit?

**16—165.** Analyze the following and state whether you would recommend a balance sheet or detailed audit:

(a) In the case of a retail merchant, who keeps a modern set of records, employs a well trained competent accountant, and desires to have a balance sheet certified for submission to a banker for credit purposes.

(b) In the case of a state bank which has been closed by authority of the State Banking Department following a run caused by rumors to the effect that the bank is insolvent.

(c) In the case of a brokerage house which contemplates underwriting an issue of bonds for a corporation which has been in business for a number of years, but which has never employed certified public accountants to audit its books and certify its annual statements.

**16—166.** Wherein would your procedure be different in auditing cash when the engagement calls for a detailed audit rather than a balance sheet audit?

**16—167.** Explain why it is essential that great care be used in checking pay roll records when making a detailed audit.

## AUDITING PROBLEMS

**16—45.** The office of Olson and Owens, a firm of importers, was destroyed by fire on June 1, 1938. The entire stock of merchandise was destroyed and the books of account which had been fully posted were badly damaged.

You are employed to make a detailed audit of the accounts for the period from January 1 to June 1, 1938. In completing the audit you find the following ledger accounts to be legible:

| | |
|---|---:|
| Purchases......................................... | $69,000.00 |
| Discounts Allowed................................ | 640.00 |
| Discounts Received............................... | 3,450.00 |
| Sales............................................. | 54,000.00 |
| Notes Receivable................................. | 33,000.00 |

Inquiry at the Second National Bank disclosed that the company had a balance on deposit of $129,000. Notes receivable amounting to $45,000 had been discounted at the bank. An audit of the canceled checks obtained from the bank showed that $39,000 had been paid to creditors and $60,000 had been paid to apply on notes payable.

The following balance sheet, prepared at the close of the last fiscal period, was obtained from Mr. Olson:

## OLSON AND OWENS

### Balance Sheet, December 31, 1937

| Assets | | Liabilities | |
|---|---:|---|---:|
| Cash................ | $ 60,000.00 | Notes Payable......... | $ 60,000.00 |
| Notes Receivable..... | 102,000.00 | **Capital** | |
| Accounts Receivable.. | 126,000.00 | Wm. R. Olson, Capital | 218,000.00 |
| Real Estate.......... | 90,000.00 | David F. Owens, Capital................ | 100,000.00 |
| | | Total Liabilities and | |
| Total Assets......... | $378,000.00 | Capital............ | $378,000.00 |

From the preceding information, draft the necessary adjusting entries in journal form to record the operations of the business from the date of the last closing of the books to the date of the fire, and prepare a work sheet as a means of assembling the data required in preparing a trial balance and balance sheet as of June 1, 1938. After preparing the work sheet, set up a trial balance and balance sheet as of June 1, 1938 and a profit and loss statement for the period ending June 1, 1938, assuming that the firm carried no insurance.

(C. P. A. New York)

# CHAPTER SEVENTEEN

## CREDIT INVESTIGATIONS AND EXAMINATIONS IN CONNECTION WITH NEW ISSUES OF SECURITIES

1. **Purpose of Credit Investigations**
   (a) **Determination of Security**
   (b) **Determination of Earning Power**
   (c) **Valuation of Properties**

2. **Scope of Credit Investigations**
   (a) **History**
   (b) **Product**
   (c) **Management**

3. **Statement Analysis**
   (a) **Balance Sheet**
   (b) **Profit and Loss Statement**

4. **Audits in Connection with New Issues of Securities**

5. **The Prospectus**

Frequently public accountants are engaged for the purpose of making an audit, the results of which are to be used for the purpose of obtaining or granting of credit, or for the purpose of selling the properties of the enterprise, or parts thereof. Such an investigation or audit is commonly known as a credit investigation, and differs in several respects from other types of audits.

If securities are to be issued and sold in interstate commerce, the audit comes within the scope of the Federal Securities Act of 1933 and is therefore under the jurisdiction of the Securities and Exchange Commission. The Securities Act of 1933 provides for the filing, by corporations proposing to issue securities, of a registration statement with the Securities and Exchange Commission. The registration statement must include balance sheets, profit and loss statements, usually for a three-year period, and supporting schedules prepared and certified to by independent accountants or independent certified public accountants. Because of its importance, a separate section of this chapter is devoted to a discussion of this subject. See the discussion under "Audits in Connection with New Issues of Securities."

## PURPOSE OF CREDIT INVESTIGATION

The following are several circumstances under which an investigation or audit is often made:

**Determination of Security.** The individual, loaning funds on a mortgage for a long term security, wishes to be assured that the properties protecting the loan are valued at a fair price and that their earning capacity is sufficient to insure that fixed charges will be earned with a fair margin of safety.

**Determination of Earning Power.** In another case, the prospective purchaser of a new stock issue might wish to be assured that a company will continue to operate at a profit as it has done in the past. He wishes to know what earnings were made for several periods in the past, applicable to a return on the stocks which he is considering, whether dividend requirements have been safely met in the past, and what the possibilities of enhancement of values and earnings in the future may be.

**Valuation of Properties.** In a further case, a group of corporation officials are considering a merger or consolidation and are bargaining as to the proper method of exchange of securities, and the proper price to be paid for this corporation's property and for another company's good will.

In all three cases, there are certain fundamental considerations which require investigation. The earnings of the different enterprises for the past decade may have been such as to allow conservative valuation of physical properties, liberal appropriations for depreciation, maintenance, and property write-downs, and nominal valuations for the intangibles which may be the most valuable assets the companies possess. Dividends might have been paid regularly, and fairly large amounts might have been retained in the businesses annually. Possibly some corporations have had larger earnings than others, even though their charges to expense for property expirations have been on a higher basis than those of their competitors.

In such cases, the balance sheet audit usually made for annual report purposes would be of little use for credit purposes. The balance sheet audit is made to verify the financial statement on an operating basis. It is customary and advisable to make conservative statement of values, as well as nominal valuations of intangibles. For sale purposes, or for bond or stock purposes, the properties are not to be valued at book values but rather at capitalized values of earning capacity. Therefore an audit must be performed in such cases where it is necessary to furnish the information as to the earning capacity of the properties, and the values of the properties for sales exchange purposes.

In order to meet the need for information of such sort, a special type of audit has been developed, namely, the credit investigation.

A credit investigation places its emphasis upon a verification of earnings applicable to specific equity holders. If a corporation wishes to expand its operations and purchase more property, build more plants, and secure more equipment, it must usually resort to a source of funds beyond those at the immediate command of the company. This capital is often supplied by an issue of stocks or bonds. In order to sell such an issue to the best advantage, a credit investigation will often be made, which will state the earnings applicable to the new issue for a period of years, as well as the value of the properties concerned at the time of the issue. This information, provided the period of the investigation covers a sufficient length of time, will permit a fair judgment as to the minimum earnings to be expected in the future, and with the additional information on products, markets. and management, allows a decision as to possible future returns.

In the same way, such an investigation aids in mergers and consolidations. If two companies have the same properties valued at the same amounts, but one earns double that of the other, earnings being calculated on the same basis, the one company is obviously worth considerably more to the resultant organization than the other.

Credit investigations may be made to cover the earning capacity and values of all the properties of an enterprise, or of only a part thereof. In such cases, segregations of earnings are required with all the ramifications of expense divisions and

classifications.* In most cases certain expenses and revenues of a
nonrecurring nature will of necessity have to be omitted from the
adjusted earnings figures when finally obtained as they will
represent transactions which will not again occur, and hence will
have no effect on the earnings of the prospective business, or the
earnings available for bond interest or stock dividends.

### SCOPE OF CREDIT INVESTIGATION

The scope and content of a particular investigation may vary
considerably but the period covered by the audit is always the
first thing to be settled. The balance sheet and detailed audit
usually cover a verification of one period, while the credit investigation will cover the verification of earnings for a period of
from four to ten years, and will go even further in tracing the
activities of the enterprise as to policies, history, etc. The usual
procedure in a credit investigation is to start with a financial
statement some years back, and verify the changes for a period of
years, with a verification of the balance sheet items as of the
date of the refinancing, sale of assets, or other transaction.

**History And Organization Of The Company.** The
report on any credit investigation usually starts with a resumé of
the organization of the enterprise, and a summarized historical
sketch of the company's activities. The purpose of this sketch is
to inform the prospective purchaser of the properties or securities
as to the following facts: (a) the length of time the enterprise
has been in operation; (b) the leading features connected with
its existence; and (c) the way in which the activities affect its
profits and earning capacity. Such a statement in the report to
the clients necessitates a careful perusal of the charter of the
corporation (the credit investigation is almost always made for

---

*The simplest example of this condition is in the present practice of
many retail establishments. For several decades it has been the practice of
such establishments to own their property and pay their taxes, insurance,
and so on, and charge such items to operations. At the present time, however,
many such establishments are refinancing, divorcing all real estate operations
from the retailing operations, and leasing the real estate at certain contract
rates. As such reorganizations generally involve sales of new securities,
many credit investigations have been made based on the earning capacity of
the retail activities only.

corporate enterprises), and a review of the by-laws, minutes, and annual reports of the management since inception, or, where the company has been in existence for several decades, since the present management or policies have been in effect.

Not only is it desirable in many cases to trace the history of the present company, but it is often advisable to make a concise statement of the growth, operations, and policies of the previous organization, especially where the present organization has been in existence only a short time as a result of a consolidation or merger of several other organizations.

**The Product.**  In addition to a knowledge of past history, a summarized statement of the products of the company, competition, marketing procedures, and manufacturing problems, should be presented.  The audit should review a sufficient period of operations to allow the auditor to state whether or not the product is a seasonal one.  There should be a discussion of the products offered by the company and the effect that business depressions or slack business periods have on sales.  Some of the following questions must be answered:

1. Has the business had a gradual growth in the face of competition, is it based on patent protection, or how has it developed its position in the field?

2. Has the product been sold nationally, internationally, or locally?

3. How much and what kind of advertising does the company do, and what has been the result of such policies in the past?

4. Has the company enough outlets for satisfactory distribution of its products to the ultimate consumer, and what is it doing to further develop such an organization?

5. As the enterprise is increasing its volume of business, in what way is the increase being obtained?

6. Is the product being sold to a greater number of consumers in ever-widening markets, or more to the same consumers in a narrow sales area?

All of these factors may be of considerable importance in gauging the value of a security or business, and should be reviewed carefully by the auditor. In order to do so, sales statistics, the sales organization, and the history of the advertising policy for several years are necessary. The development of new products, or the improvement of the old, may be of importance in such fields as office and store equipment, electricity, and machinery.

As a careful study of the sales situation is necessary in order to adequately present the marketing and distribution policies and possibilities, it is often essential in a manufacturing concern to make a resumé of manufacturing conditions. If it is a nation-wide organization, the location of the facilities of the company and their strategic value should be mentioned. The condition of plants, whether old, out-of-date, or in modern condition with most up-to-date labor saving machinery and devices, is important. Are the plants manufacturing cheaply, or are costs relatively high as compared with competitors, or as compared with costs in similar lines, where patents are prohibiting effective competition in the specific field concerned? What are the tendencies in costs, are they on the up or down grade? Are the manufacturing facilities sufficient to care for possible increased business in the future? If not, what are the present plans to provide for such an increase in business?

In the case of companies operating in the extractive industries, the nature and sufficiency of the raw materials supply for the future may be of exceeding importance.

**The Management.** One of the most important factors in the welfare of any business, and one which cannot adequately be valued in dollars and cents for balance sheet purposes, is the management. The men at the top should be competent and aggressive, ever striving to become leaders in their field. Where a group of executives have built an enterprise into a coordinated, profitable organization, it is usually highly desirable, where financial interests are at stake, that the present management continue in control of the business. The auditor may ascertain the key men in the organization, the length of time they have been with the company, and the financial interest of each in the different types of securities outstanding. Where the officers and directors are heavily interested in the concern financially, have grown with the organization, and are responsible for its growth, it is more likely that the company will continue to grow and prosper with these officers at the head of it, than if a new set of executives were given control. If the leading executives are heavily interested financially the auditor should so state in his report.

## STATEMENT ANALYSIS

**Balance Sheet.** Most credit investigations include a careful balance sheet analysis, accompanied by detailed schedules supporting the financial statement. The auditor should verify the accuracy of the items in the balance sheet as of the date on which the statement was prepared. In addition, much valuable information is available as to financial trends through a careful analysis of the different items on the balance sheet from the date of the first period under investigation until the end of the period as presented on the last financial statement. Analyses of changes in working capital over the period, the sources of additional capital invested in the business, a statement of application of funds for the period, and other statements designed to present the transactions in a summarized form, may well be drawn up and presented. An analysis of the surplus account for the period under review showing the source of all surplus additions, and the distribution thereof, is always of considerable value.

Special attention is usually given to all reserves, especially the valuation items, to ascertain that they have been adequately stated, and to make sure that the asset which the reserve evaluates has not expired.

**Profit and Loss Statement.** As the credit analysis is primarily made to determine the value of the properties for purposes of obtaining credit or for sale of a part or of the whole business, and as the value of those properties depends in the last analysis on the earning capacity of the business itself, the analysis of income and profit and loss accounts receives much emphasis. The purpose of the income and profit and loss analysis is usually to determine the proper amount of earnings over a number of periods applicable to certain equity holders, usually bond or stockholders. The auditor then will analyze all revenue and expense items carefully, and determine the accuracy of the books, paying special attention to debatable items such as maintenance, repairs, and depreciation charges. The audit serves as a method of restating the earnings and expenses in relation to some predetermined purpose. In the case of a merger or consolidation, the auditor will audit the records to see that the proper charges have been made to capital, to expense, and that deferred items are properly recorded. He will verify the accuracy of the accounts and will adjust their valuations to the bases prearranged for merger purposes.

Where the investigation is made to sell bonds or stocks, the problem becomes more varied. In this case, the purpose of the investigation is to determine the profits available to the particular issue to be sold, assuming that the profits are available at the time of issuing the stock or bonds. In other words, the auditor will attempt to allocate earnings of the past to security issues not issued, but to be issued in the future. This situation requires considerable adjusting of accounts and rearranging of the financial data.

All nonrecurring items are usually eliminated for the purpose of showing adjusted profits. For example, a company has been charging patent costs to expense over a period of years until the patents are not now stated in the balance sheet. Such costs are nonrecurring items which will not be existent in the future as charges against earnings, and in order to show earnings available for the securities to be issued should be eliminated from the net earnings figures throughout the period analyzed. Depreciation charges usually require adjustment, as do such items as maintenance, bad debt expense, and other similar items.

## AUDITS IN CONNECTION WITH NEW ISSUES OF SECURITIES

Persons or corporations wishing to offer a new issue of securities for sale to the public in interstate commerce are required under the Federal Securities Act of 1933, as amended, to file a registration statement with the Securities and Exchange Commission giving information in detail concerning the financial condition of the company and the securities it proposes to issue. The registration statement must include a balance sheet, a profit and loss statement, and supporting schedules certified to by an independent public or independent certified public accountant. Copies of the prospectus (in pamphlet form) prepared for distribution to the public as a means of advertising the proposed security issue must also be filed with the Commission.

The purpose of the registration statement as explained in the instructions issued by the Commission is two fold: "(1) It provides investors with a source of information on the securities to be offered for sale, and (2) It stands as a record of the representations made at the time the securities were sold with civil liabilities and criminal penalties for material misstatements or omissions."

**Information Required by the S. E. C.**  A number of registration forms, to be used in connection with the registration of new issues of securities, have been prepared by the Commission.  New and unseasoned enterprises are required to file a registration statement on one form (Form A-1), whereas seasoned corporations, which file profit and loss statements for three years, may file subject to certain limitations, a registration statement on a second form (Form A-2).  In order for a seasoned corporation to qualify for use of Form A-2, it must meet one of two conditions; either (1) have made available to its security holders for at least ten years, annual reports containing balance sheets and profit and loss statements, or (2) have had a net income for any two fiscal years of the five fiscal years preceding the date of the latest balance sheet filed with the Commission.

Other special forms are provided for mining companies, unincorporated investment trusts, securities issued in reorganizations, voting trust certificates, oil and gas royalty interests, and certificates of deposit.

The registration statement provides for detailed information concerning the issuing corporation and the proposed security issue.  Included in the information are the following: the name and location of the business; its history and organization; a description of its plants, properties, and capital structure; information concerning the officers, directors, and principal stockholders and their remunerations; a description of the securities to be offered for sale; the names of underwriters and principal provisions of the underwriting agreement; balance sheets, profit and loss statements, and supporting schedules prepared by independent public or independent certified public accountants together with their consent to use their report in the registration statement.

**Type of Audit to be Performed.** A question, frequently asked, concerns the type of audit or examination which should be performed by accountants in order to present a balance sheet, a profit and loss statement or statements, and supporting schedules required as part of a registration statement.

The extent of the audit or examination will depend upon circumstances involved in each case. If a concern's accounting organization is maintained with a reasonable system of internal check and control, the principles and procedures outlined in the preceding chapters for an examination of financial statements should prove adequate. If the accounting system lacks sufficient internal check and control, a more detailed examination will be necessary. In any event, for audits of seasoned corporations, the examination of profit and loss accounts should cover a three-year period in order for the accountant to certify to the profit and loss statements as required in the registration statement.

The Securities and Exchange Commission has not issued regulations requiring that any particular type of audit be performed. The auditor is sole judge of the type of examination necessary in order to present the financial statements, accompanied by a reasonably unqualified certificate. Responsibility for certification of the financial statements rests upon the accountant.

**Form of Financial Statements.** No particular form of balance sheet or profit and loss statement has been prescribed by the Securities and Exchange Commission. The instructions accompanying registration statements provide as follows: "The registrant may file statements and schedules in such form, order, and using such generally accepted terminology, as will best indicate their significance and character in the light of the instructions." The attitude of the Commission has been to cooperate with accountants and accounting organizations where possible in simplifying the task of the accountant. Registration statements are filed by innumerable types of business concerns and it obviously seems impracticable to prescribe a single form and procedure which would be applicable to all types of business.

**Accountants' Certificates.** Accountants' certificates accompanying registration statements, according to the rule of the Securities and Exchange Commission, "shall be dated and shall be reasonably comprehensive as to the scope of the audit made and shall state clearly the opinion of the accountant or accountants in respect of the financial statements of, and the accounting principles and procedures followed by the registrant."

"In certifying to the financial statements of the registrant, independent public or independent certified public accountants may give due weight to an internal system of audit regularly maintained by means of auditors employed on the registrant's own staff." If an internal audit system is maintained, the independent accountants should review the accounting system and satisfy themselves that such accounting procedures are actually being followed. "Nothing in these instructions shall be construed to imply authority for the omission of any procedure which independent public or independent certified public accountants would ordinarily employ in the course of a regular audit."

It is important from the investor's point of view to know the nature and extent of the examination upon which the accountant is basing his opinion. If the extent and limitations of his examination are not stated, an investor may interpret an unqualified statement as meaning that a complete or detailed examination was made of the books and accounts of the registrant, whereas the auditor may have limited the scope of his audit to that of an examination of financial statements.

**Who is an Independent Public Accountant?**  To be considered an independent public accountant, according to the rules of the Commission, one must be neither an employee, officer, or director of the registrant, nor the owner of a material interest in the business of the registrant. The ownership of a comparatively few shares of stock of the company may be construed as a material interest.

The Securities and Exchange Commission has not as yet indicated specific qualifications for accountants who certify to balance sheets and profit and loss statements filed with the Commission. The certifications of some accountants have been rejected because the accountant could not qualify under the rules of the Commission. It would seem that, to be qualified as an accountant, one must have had basic training and experience as an accountant and must actually hold himself out to the public as a practicing accountant and actually be engaged in a variety of accounting work.

**Are Registered Securities Good Investments?**  The Securities and Exchange Commission does not warrant the validity of the information contained in prospectuses issued in connection with the sale of securities, nor does the registration of a security signify that it is a good investment. Instructions issued by the Commission read as follows: "The Securities and Exchange Commission does not pass on the merits of securities registered with it. It does not guarantee any securities, nor can it guarantee the correctness or accuracy of information filed with them in registration statements. The investor must make his own interpretation of the relative merits of the securities. The registration statement merely makes the information available to investors and provides penalties for the misstatement of material facts therein."

The Federal Securities Act of 1933 and the rules laid down by the Securities and Exchange Commission, require that prospectuses containing a summary of the information in the registration statement be made available to the prospective purchasers of the securities at the time of the sale. Copies of the prospectus must be filed with the Commission at the time the registration statement is filed. Some of the information contained in the registration statement may be omitted from the prospectus. Photostatic copies of the information contained in a registration statement may be obtained from the Commission by request and upon the payment of a small fee to cover the cost of duplicating the information.

## THE PROSPECTUS

When an audit is made in connection with a new issue of securities, the result is published in summary form in a circular issued by the financial house or houses floating the security issue, or by the corporation whose securities are being issued. In such a circular, or prospectus as it is called, information is presented citing the characteristics of the business, the history, location of the business, physical property, proposed capitalization, earnings as adjusted in the past, the dividend record, the make-up of the management, and other items of importance.

A balance sheet is presented accompanied by a profit and loss statement in comparative form for a period of three or more years. Numerous footnotes and schedules may also be presented. In addition to the financial statements, a pro forma balance sheet may be included.

**Pro Forma Balance Sheet.** Balance sheets which portray the results of financial transactions to be performed in the future and which have not at the time of preparing the statement been consummated, are referred to as pro forma balance sheets. Care should be taken in the preparation of pro forma balance sheets to insure that they are not used to mislead or deceive investors. A committee of the American Institute of Accountants recommended as early as the year 1923 that an accountant should certify to a pro forma balance sheet only: (1) if there is a contract or agreement between the company and responsible bankers assuring that the subsequent transactions will be consummated; (2) if the time elapsing between the date of the statement and the date of the subsequent transactions is comparatively short, usually not to exceed four months; (3) if the accountant is convinced after investigation that other transactions or developments during the interval will not affect adversely the position of the company; and (4) if the character of the transactions to which effect is being given is clearly disclosed on the face of the statement or in the certificate.

A rule of the Securities and Exchange Commission concerning the preparation of pro forma balance sheets, effective March 1, 1938, is very similar to the one outlined in the preceding paragraph. Pro forma balance sheets are not permitted except where the securities are underwritten and the underwriters are irrevocably bound.

**A Pro Forma Balance Sheet Illustrated.** The reader will note that the pro forma balance sheet on the following page is a statement of financial condition which would have existed had the subsequent transactions been consummated at the time of the statement. It is a simplified statement issued at the time of the prospective merging of three companies. The A Corporation amended its charter and changed its capitalization. The outstanding shares of the corporation at the time were to be exchanged for the new shares on a prearranged basis the terms of

(Continued on page 413)

## THE A CORPORATION
### Pro Forma Balance Sheet as of June 30, 1938*

ASSETS:

Property—at sound value as appraised by
the Z Appraisal Company, adjusted to
July 1, 1937, with respect to additions
and depreciation:

| | | |
|---|---:|---:|
| Land.............................$ | 250,000.00 | |
| Buildings......................... | 800,000.00 | |
| Machinery and Equipment......... | 1,200,000.00 | |
| Motor Vehicles................... | 20,000.00 | |
| Office Furniture and Fixtures....... | 15,000.00 | $2,285,000.00 |

Current Assets:

| | | |
|---|---:|---:|
| Cash.............................. | $524,500.00 | |
| Due from customers less reserve for doubtful accounts................. | 375,000.00 | |
| Sundry Receivables................. | 2,500.00 | |
| Notes Receivable.................. | 3,000.00 | |
| Inventories (at cost, and certified to by company officials)................. | 240,000.00 | 1,145,000.00 |

| | |
|---|---:|
| Investments...................................... | 10,000.00 |
| Cash Surrender value of Life Insurance Policies..... | 3,500.00 |
| Deferred Charges................................ | 35,000.00 |
| Total.......................................... | $3,478,500.00 |

LIABILITIES:

| | | |
|---|---:|---:|
| First Mortgage Ten-Year Gold Bonds—to be issued..... | | $1,500,000.00 |
| Current Liabilities: | | |
| Accounts Payable.................... | $360,000.00 | |
| Accruals.......................... | 70,000.00 | 430,000.00 |

Capital and Surplus:

| | |
|---|---:|
| Authorized, 350,000 shares, presently to be issued 200,000 shares............................... | 1,548,500.00 |
| Total.......................................... | $3,478,500.00 |

### Illustration No. 43.   Pro Forma Balance Sheet

---

*Giving effect to the subsequent acquisition of the B Company, the X
Company, and the issue of 200,000 shares of no par common stock, and to
the receipt of the proceeds of $1,500,000 principal amount of first mort-
gage 10-year sinking fund gold bonds, and to the application of the proceeds
to payment of mortgages, notes payable, and estimated organization expenses,
and to increase cash.

which were covered by contract as of June 30, 1938. The stockholders of the B and X Companies had contracted to sell their respective properties in exchange for the stocks to be issued by the A Company. The bond issue was sold to a firm of investment brokers, which wanted this statement, as did the stockholders and directors of the old companies, for purposes of showing the condition of the consolidation on the date when the agreement was to be effected. Such a statement presents the financial condition of the new organization as if it were existent, and is for purposes of illustration only.

## SUMMARY

A credit investigation may differ from a balance sheet audit from the standpoint of scope, procedure, and purpose. Those concerned may be more interested in ascertaining the earning power of a company than in a verification of the assets and liabilities. When a company wishes to obtain additional working capital through the purchase of materials and supplies on credit, by borrowing from the bank on notes payable, through the sale of preferred stock, or through the sale of bonds, those concerned may wish to know both the financial condition of the business and what its earning power has been over a period of years. In other words, they want to know something of the "margin of safety." Those who extend credit have a right to information regarding the ability of the company to pay the interest on its indebtedness and to pay its obligations at maturity.

In the event a company contemplates the sale of bonds secured by a mortgage on a part or all of its fixed assets, the prospective purchaser of such bonds is interested in an unbiased report, setting forth the value of the properties in addition to information regarding the earning power of the company and its financial condition. The scope of an audit in connection with a credit investigation will depend upon many variable factors. However, the auditor should thoroughly acquaint himself with the terms of the engagement and the purpose which his report is to serve, as these factors will have a large influence upon the auditor's procedure as well as the scope of the audit.

An audit report covering a credit investigation may involve an analysis of the financial statements. Ratio analysis is an aid to administrative interpretation of financial statements.

## AUDITING THEORY

**17—168.** What is the purpose of a credit investigation?

**17—169.** It is said that, "The balance sheet audit usually made for annual report purposes is of little use in a credit investigation." Explain what is meant by this statement.

**17—170.** What is meant by analysis of financial statements?

**17—171.** Distinguish between the following:
(a) A balance sheet and a financial statement
(b) A condensed balance sheet and a classified balance sheet
(c) A consolidated balance sheet and a comparative balance sheet.


## AUDITING PROBLEMS

**17—46.** You are employed to prepare a statement for credit purposes as of June 30, of the current year, from data submitted to you in the following letter from The Western Mfg. Co.:

The plant stands at cost price, $90,600. There is a reserve for depreciation of $15,300. There is a mortgage of $30,000 on the plant and interest on the mortgage is at 6% and is paid to within three months of date of your proposed statement. The company holds $15,000 of notes receivable and has discounted notes at bank amounting to $37,500. Accounts receivable considered good, amount to $27,000, including $4,500 due from an employee on personal account. Accounts with trade customers are subject to 5% discount if paid at due date, and $15,000 is now past due. Suspense accounts amount to $6,000, 50% of which are believed to be good. A new machine has been ordered from the Simplex Mfg. Co. but not yet delivered, which cost $9,000 and which was paid in advance. Recording of this payment has been deferred pending receipt of invoice.

The company has endorsed a note for $9,000 for Smith & Co., but it will, no doubt, be paid when due. Accounts payable amount to $63,000. Insurance costs $600 a year and the present policy has six months to run. The company owes a note at bank for $7,500, interest paid to date. There are 50 shares of stock owned which cost $4,200, but which is presumed to be worthless. Inventory was taken at a selling price of 10% more than cost. This amounts to $26,400. There are 500 shares of capital stock outstanding, par value $100 per share.

You are not asked to accept any responsibility for the figures in the statement but simply to prepare the statement in the best form you can from the information given.

(C. P. A. Ind.)

**17—47.** As auditor for The Scatterbolt Automobile Co. you are furnished with a consolidated balance sheet and are asked by the general manager to analyze the statement and submit a report which will provide the following information:

(a) Excess of current assets over current liabilities

(b) *Ratio of current assets to current liabilities

(c) Excess of total assets over total liabilities

(d) Ratio of total assets to total liabilities

(e) Ratio of capital to fixed assets

(f) Book value of each share of common stock outstanding

(g) Ratio of book value to current market value of one share of common stock. Assume that the stock is listed on the New York Exchange and that the current market quotation is $27 per share.

(h) Liquidation of accumulated but unpaid dividends on the preferred stock to December 31, 1938, aggregating $6,559,725 has been authorized by the board of directors to be made by the issuance on January 2, 1939, of common stock, par value $5 per share at a valuation of $25 per share. Show what effect this would have upon the balance sheet by resetting the Capital section.

(i) Assuming that the net profits for the ensuing year amount to $11,422,777.18, what will be the balance of the surplus account on December 31, 1939, after payment of the accumulated dividends to December 31, 1938, and the current dividend on the preferred stock for 1939?

(j) Assuming that the board of directors, following the close of business on December 31, 1939, declares a dividend of $10,000,000 on the common stock payable $2,000,000 in common stock and $8,000,000 in cash, draft journal entries to record the declaration and payment of the dividend. Again, compute the book value of each share of common stock outstanding.

---

*Ratios may be expressed on a basis of units, hundreds, or thousands. In solving this problem it is suggested that the ratios be based upon units, and be stated decimally, as for example 7.75 to 1.

## THE SCATTERBOLT AUTOMOBILE COMPANY
## AND SUBSIDIARY COMPANIES

### Consolidated Balance Sheet

### December 31, 1938

#### Assets

Current Assets:

| | | | |
|---|---|---|---|
| Cash | | $ 725,962.68 | |
| Time Certificates of Deposit | | 7,010,000.00 | |
| Notes Rec. | $3,289,821.87 | | |
| Accts. Rec. | 4,452,528.76 | $ 7,742,350.63 | |
| Less Allowance for Doubtful Accounts | | 764,458.60 | 6,977,892.03 |
| Merchandise Inventories. | $27,300,995.46 | | |
| Less Reserve for Inventory Shrinkage | | 1,208,560.47 | 26,092,434.99 |
| Due from Affiliated Companies | | | 1,970,476.23 |
| Miscellaneous Notes, Accounts, Advances, etc. | | | 700,204.25 |
| Insurance and Other Claims Receivable | | | 543,435.41 |
| Total Current Assets | | | $44,020,405.59 |

Fixed Assets:

| | | | |
|---|---|---|---|
| Investments in Affiliated and Other Companies | | $ 1,286,039.68 | |
| Land | | 1,858,047.81 | |
| Buildings | $21,310,592.79 | | |
| Machinery, Equipment, etc. | 21,624,078.01 | | |
| | $42,934,670.80 | | |
| Less Allowance for Depreciation and Losses | 17,282,184.14 | 25,652,486.66 | |
| Total Fixed Assets | | | 28,796,574.15 |

Intangible Assets:

| | | | |
|---|---|---|---|
| Good Will, Patents, etc. | | | 1.00 |

Deferred Charges:

| | | | |
|---|---|---|---|
| Unamortized Bond Discount | | $ 393,939.39 | |
| Prepaid Advertising, Taxes, Insurance, etc. | | 656,726.79 | |
| Total Deferred Charges | | | 1,050,666.18 |
| Total Assets and Deferred Charges | | | $73,867,646.92 |

## Liabilities

Current Liabilities:

Accounts Payable:

| | | |
|---|---:|---:|
| For Purchases, Expenses, etc.......... | $ 1,719,423.03 | |
| Unpaid Pay Roll..................... | 197,557.54 | |
| Stock Purchase Contract and Interest (Due in 1939)..................... | 175,942.00 | |
| Excise Tax.......................... | 150,229.54 | |
| Refund Certificates.................. | 141,740.00 | |
| Bonuses—Dealers' and Others'........ | 109,877.49 | |
| Allowances for Price Reductions....... | 90,000.00 | |
| Dealers' Initial Payments............. | 42,140.69 | |
| Estimated Federal Income Tax for 1938.. | 1,740,000.00 | |
| Accrued Taxes, Interest, etc............ | 568,039.88 | |
| Total Current Liabilities.................. | | $ 4,934,950.17 |

Fixed Liabilities:

| | | |
|---|---:|---:|
| First Mortgage 6½% Sinking Fund Gold Bonds: Dated September 1, 1933, Redeemable $1,000,000 annually, Authorized $10,000,000; Less Retired, $2,000,000; and Purchased for Retirement, $525,000........... | $ 7,475,000.00 | |
| Stock Purchase Contract: Balance Payable $153,140 Annually Beginning in 1937.................. | 609,960.00 | |
| Total Fixed Liabilities.................... | | 8,084,960.00 |

## Capital

Capital Stock:

| | | |
|---|---:|---:|
| Preferred 7% Cumulative Authorized............$22,199,100.00 Less: Unissued....... 149,600.00 | $22,049,500.00 | |
| Common—Par Value $5 Authorized............ $15,000,000.00 Less: Unissued....... 3,676,695.00 | 11,323,305.00 | |
| Common Script........................ | 871.25 | |
| Reserve for Contingencies ................ | 1,654,478.29 | |
| *Surplus............................... | 25,819,582.21 | |
| Total Capital........................... | | 60,847,736.75 |
| Total Liabilities and Capital.............. | | $73,867,646.92 |

*Dividends on cumulative preferred stock in arrears but not declared amount to $6,559,725.

## AUDIT PROJECT No. 1

John A. Pendery, an employee of Stevenson and Bennett, Certified Public Accountants, has been engaged in making an examination of financial statements for The Carew Manufacturing Co. The work at the office of the client has been completed except that a summary work sheet has not been prepared. Mr. Pendery's working papers are reproduced on the following pages. An audit report is to be prepared from the information provided in the audit working papers. Mr. M. D. Stevenson, president of the firm of accountants, asks you to prepare a work sheet and a report for the client. The report is to be submitted to Mr. H. M. Carew, president of the Carew Manufacturing Co. and is to include the following:

Exhibit A —Balance Sheet as of December 31, 1938

Exhibit B —Profit and Loss Statement for the year 1938

Schedule A1—Analysis of Surplus for the year 1938

Scuedule B1—Statement of Cost of Manufactured Goods Sold during the year 1938

Schedule B2—Statement of Cost of Purchased Goods Sold during the year 1938

Schedule B3—Statement of Selling Expenses for the year 1938

Schedule B4—Statement of Administrative and General Expenses for the year 1938

The report should be accompanied by a letter of transmittal, an accountant's certificate, and any comments on the audit which you think would be of interest or value to the client.

Index to Working Papers of

THE CAREW MANUFACTURING CO.

For Year Ending December 31, 1938

J.A.P.

## THE CAREW MANUFACTURING CO.
### Trial Balance, December 31, 1938

| | | |
|---|--:|--:|
| Cash on Hand..................... $ | 3,500.00 | |
| Cash in Bank...................... | 12,500.00 | |
| Notes Receivable on Hand........... | 78,250.00 | |
| Notes Receivable Discounted........ | 12,250.00 | |
| Accounts Receivable on Hand........ | 175,000.00 | |
| Accounts Receivable Assigned....... | 18,200.00 | |
| Inventories and Purchases: | | |
|   Pig Iron....................... | 67,500.00 | |
|   Scrap Iron..................... | 63,950.00 | |
|   Bar Steel...................... | 89,300.00 | |
|   Sheet Steel.................... | 25,000.00 | |
|   Lumber......................... | 172,750.00 | |
|   Factory Supplies............... | 21,500.00 | |
| Goods in Process, Dec. 31, 1937.... | 50,000.00 | |
| Inv. of Fin. Goods, Dec. 31, 1937.. | | |
|   Manufactured................... | 50,000.00 | |
|   Purchased: | | |
|     Chairs...................... | 10,000.00 | |
|     Castings.................... | 10,000.00 | |
| Uncompleted Contracts.............. | 25,000.00 | |
| Advances on Contracts.............. | | $ 15,000.00 |
| Securities Readily Salable......... | 5,000.00 | |
| Notes from Officers and Employees.. | 5,000.00 | |
| Accounts of Officers and Employees. | 7,500.00 | |
| Prepaid Insurance.................. | 15,450.00 | |
| Prepaid Interest................... | 2,450.00 | |
| Prepaid Office Supplies............ | 500.00 | |
| Prepaid Advertising................ | 8,500.00 | |
| Land............................... | 25,000.00 | |
| Buildings.......................... | 257,500.00 | |
| Machinery and Equipment............ | 45,000.00 | |
| Jigs, Dies, and Fixtures........... | 27,500.00 | |
| Small Tools....................... | 3,000.00 | |
| Patterns and Drawings.............. | 3,000.00 | |
| Furniture and Fixtures............. | 5,500.00 | |
| Securities Not Readily Salable..... | 5,000.00 | |
| Patents and Copyrights............. | 50,000.00 | |
| Good Will.......................... | 50,000.00 | |
| Notes Payable: | | |
|   Banks.......................... | | 42,500.00 |
|   Brokers........................ | | 14,000.00 |
|   Trade Creditors................ | | 45,000.00 |
|   Officers and Employees......... | | 2,500.00 |
| Accounts Payable (Trade)........... | | 112,500.00 |
| Accounts Payable (Officers)........ | | 1,000.00 |
| Notes Receivable Discounted........ | | 12,250.00 |
| Accounts Receivable Assigned....... | | 18,200.00 |
| Notes Payable Secured by Liens..... | | 10,000.00 |
| Notes Payable Secured by Collateral | | 20,000.00 |
| Accrued Interest Payable........... | | 3,600.00 |
| Carried Forward................... | $1,400,600.00 | $296,550.00 |

### THE CAREW MANUFACTURING CO.

#### Trial Balance--Continued, December 31, 1938

| | | |
|---|---:|---:|
| Brought Forward...................... | $1,400,600.00 | $  296,550.00 |
| Employer's Federal Excise Tax Payable (O.A.B.).................... | | 902.50 |
| Employees' Income Tax Pay. (O.A.B.) | | 902.50 |
| Employer's Fed. Exc. Tax Pay. (U.C.) | | 1,336.65 |
| State U. C. Contributions Payable.. | | 2,840.60 |
| Mortgages Payable: | | |
|   On Land........................... | | 15,000.00 |
|   On Plant.......................... | | 20,000.00 |
|   On Machinery and Equipment....... | | 10,000.00 |
| Bonded Debt........................ | | 150,000.00 |
| Reserves for Depreciation: | | |
|   Buildings........................ | | 15,000.00 |
|   Machinery and Equipment.......... | | 10,000.00 |
|   Jigs, Dies and Fixtures.......... | | 5,000.00 |
|   Small Tools...................... | | 1,000.00 |
|   Patterns and Drawings............ | | 1,000.00 |
|   Office Furniture and Fixtures.... | | 1,000.00 |
| Reserve for Doubtful Accounts...... | | 8,000.00 |
| Preferred Dividends................ | 10,500.00 | |
| Common Dividends................... | 3,750.00 | |
| Corporation Insurance.............. | 125.00 | 10,000.00 |
| Capital Stock Authorized: | | |
|   Preferred........................ | | 200,000.00 |
|   Common........................... | | 100,000.00 |
| Capital Stock Unissued: | | |
|   Preferred........................ | 25,000.00 | |
|   Common........................... | 25,000.00 | |
| Sales.............................. | | 975,700.00 |
| Discount Earned.................... | | 2,250.00 |
| Interest Income.................... | | 1,550.00 |
| Income from Securities............. | | 1,450.00 |
| Old Accounts Collected............. | | 500.00 |
| Freight Out........................ | 22,500.00 | |
| Returns and Allowances............. | 8,500.00 | |
| Sales Discounts.................... | 15,700.00 | |
| Chairs Purchased................... | 17,250.00 | |
| Castings Purchased................. | 18,750.00 | |
| Productive Labor................... | 355,000.00 | |
| Nonproductive Labor................ | 26,000.00 | |
| Light and Power.................... | 14,500.00 | |
| Fuel Expense....................... | 3,500.00 | |
| Property Taxes..................... | 3,225.00 | |
| Maintenance of Buildings........... | 2,800.00 | |
| Maintenance of Machinery........... | 1,500.00 | |
| Freight-In......................... | 8,000.00 | |
| Salary of Purchasing Agent......... | 3,500.00 | |
| Traveling Exp. of Purchasing Agent. | 950.00 | |
| Sundry Buying Expense.............. | 1,500.00 | |
| Carried Forward.................... | $1,968,150.00 | $1,829,982.25 |

## THE CAREW MANUFACTURING CO.

### Trial Balance--Continued, December 31, 1938

| | | |
|---|---:|---:|
| Brought Forward..................... | $1,968,150.00 | $1,829,982.25 |
| Sales Manager's Salary.............. | 10,000.00 | |
| Salesmen's Salaries................. | 10,000.00 | |
| Commission and Brokerage........... | 2,500.00 | |
| Traveling Expense--Manager......... | 250.00 | |
| Traveling Expense--Salesmen........ | 6,500.00 | |
| Catalogs........................... | 1,500.00 | |
| Circular Matter.................... | 950.00 | |
| Stationery......................... | 2,650.00 | |
| Postage............................ | 925.00 | |
| Sales Office Expense............... | 1,650.00 | |
| Administrative Salary.............. | 30,000.00 | |
| Administrative Expense............. | 1,450.00 | |
| Office Salaries.................... | 11,050.00 | |
| Telegraph.......................... | 275.00 | |
| Collection and Expense............. | 225.00 | |
| Legal Fees......................... | 800.00 | |
| Audit Fees......................... | 1,500.00 | |
| Dues and Donations................. | 1,500.00 | |
| Federal S. S. Excise Tax (O.A.B.).. | 3,810.00 | |
| Federal S. S. Excise Tax (U. C.)... | 1,336.65 | |
| State U. C. Contributions.......... | 12,029.85 | |
| Income Taxes (1937)................ | 2,400.00 | |
| Surplus............................ | | 241,469.25 |
| | $2,071,451.50 | $2,071,451.50 |

### Notes on Trial Balance

(a) Upon reporting for duty, I was furnished with the
preceding trial balance which had been prepared by the bookkeeper at the close of the period on December 31, 1938.  It
was verified by checking it with the general ledger accounts.
The account footings and balances also were verified, no errors
being found.

(b) In addition to making a general audit of all the
accounts included in the trial balance, a more detailed audit
was made of certain accounts as indicated in the accompanying
working papers, A2 to A16 and B1 to B4 inclusive.

J.A.P. #A1

THE CAREW MANUFACTURING CO.

Reconciliation of Cash Balance

As of December 31, 1938


Balance in Banks per bank statements.................$14,250.00
Deduct Checks Outstanding............................ 2,250.00
                                                    _____
                                                     $12,000.00
Add Items in Transit.................................    500.00

Balance per cash book................................$12,500.00
Add Cash on Hand verified by count................... 3,500.00
                                                    _____
Total Cash Balance...................................$16,000.00


                  List of Checks Outstanding

            #2223.........................$    50.00
             2224.........................    750.00
             2329.........................    650.00
             2400.........................    800.00
                                           _____
             Total Outstanding............$2,250.00


                    List of Transit Items

            December 31, 1938.............$   300.00
            December 31, 1938.............    200.00
                                           _____
                                          $   500.00


J.A.P. #A2

THE CAREW MANUFACTURING CO.

List of Customers' Notes Receivable on Hand

As of December 31, 1938

| Name of Maker | Date | Maturity | Int. Rate | Amount | Interest Accrued to 12-31-38 | Remarks |
|---|---|---|---|---|---|---|
| Stewart Engineering Co. | 1-15-36 | 5-15-39 | 6% | $50,000.00 | $3,000.00 | Chattel Mortgage as Security |
| T. F. Randall & Co. | 2-20-37 | 2-20-39 | 6% | 10,000.00 | 600.00 | Secured by Endorsement |
| Thomas Byer Co. | 3-30-37 | 3-30-39 | 6% | 10,000.00 | 600.00 | Not seen by auditors |
| The Supply Co. | 4-10-37 | 4-10-39 | 6% | 8,250.00 | 495.00 | Paid January 25, 1939 |
| Total | | | | $78,250.00 | $4,695.00 | |

Adjustment Required:
(1) Accrued Interest Receivable...... $4,695.00
    Interest Income...... $4,695.00

J.A.P. #A3

## THE CAREW MANUFACTURING CO.

### List of Customers' Notes Receivable Discounted

### As of December 31, 1938

| Name of Maker | Date | Maturity | Int. Rate | Amount | With Whom Discounted |
|---|---|---|---|---|---|
| John P. Child Co.............. | 4-1-38 | 10-1-39 | 6% | $ 6,000.00 | Security National Bank |
| Deering Bros................. | 5-1-38 | 10-1-39 | 6% | 5,000.00 | Bank of Sheboygan |
| D. A. Pierce & Co............ | 6-1-38 | 10-1-39 | 6% | 250.00 | Citizens State Bank |
| Whalen Construction Co....... | 7-1-38 | 11-1-39 | 6% | 1,000.00 | Farmers & Merchants Bank |
| Total........................ | | | | $12,250.00 | |

J.A.P. #A4

THE CAREW MANUFACTURING CO.

List of Officers Notes Receivable

As of December 31, 1938

|  | Date | Due Date | Amount |
|---|---|---|---|
| H. M. Carew, Pres............... | 1-1-38 | 1-1-39 | $2,000.00 |
| M. S. Hastings, Treas............ | 1-1-38 | 1-1-39 | 2,000.00 |
| J  W. Kendall, Sales Mgr......... | 1-1-38 | 1-1-39 | 1,000.00 |
| Total............................................... | | | $5,000.00 |

These notes represent accommodation loans and were found to be properly authorized.

J.A.P. #A5

THE CAREW MANUFACTURING CO.

Analysis of Accounts Receivable

For the Year Ended December 31, 1938

Balance of Accounts Receivable on Hand and

    Assigned January 1, 1938........................ $  120,000.00

Net Sales for Year...............................    944,700.00

Total to be Accounted for........................ $1,064,700.00

Total Collections for Year.......................    871,500.00

Balance, December 31, 1938....................... $  193,200.00

        On Hand................... $175,000.00

        Assigned..................   18,200.00

                       $193,200.00

    In addition to the above there were found to be accounts
receivable from officers and employees amounting to $7,500.

J.A.P. #A6

## THE CAREW MANUFACTURING CO.

### Aging Customers' Accounts Receivable

#### December 31, 1938

| Accounts | Debit Balances | When Charged | | | |
|---|---|---|---|---|---|
| | | December and November 1938 | October and September 1938 | August July and June 1938 | Prior to June 1938 |
| G. W. Spink Co. | $ 26,500.00 | $ 8,500.00 | $ 8,000.00 | $ 5,000.00 | $ 5,000.00 |
| A. R. Tarvin Co. | 20,000.00 | 5,000.00 | 5,000.00 | 5,000.00 | 5,000.00 |
| Gabriel Supply Co. | 15,650.00 | 5,000.00 | 5,000.00 | 5,000.00 | 650.00 |
| Hunter Mfg. Co. | 14,000.00 | 6,250.00 | 5,000.00 | 2,000.00 | 750.00 |
| M. S. Rogers Co. | 17,000.00 | 5,000.00 | 5,000.00 | 5,000.00 | 2,000.00 |
| Grey Supply Co. | 16,000.00 | 7,000.00 | 8,000.00 | 500.00 | 500.00 |
| Ritter & Thurner | 18,000.00 | 6,000.00 | 6,000.00 | 3,000.00 | 3,000.00 |
| Lampe Publishing Co. | 25,500.00 | 10,500.00 | 5,000.00 | 5,000.00 | 5,000.00 |
| J. D. Simpson Co. | 22,350.00 | 12,000.00 | 5,350.00 | 3,000.00 | 2,000.00 |
| Total | $175,000.00 | $65,250.00 | $52,350.00 | $33,500.00 | $23,900.00 |

J.A.P. #A6a

THE CAREW MANUFACTURING CO.

Analysis of Reserve for Doubtful Accounts

December 31, 1938

| | | |
|---|---|---|
| Balance of Reserve, January 1, 1938..... | | $ 9,500.00 |
| Bad Debts Charged Off During Year....... | | 1,500.00 |
| Balance................................. | | $ 8,000.00 |
| Additions to Reserve: | | |
| For 1937............................. | $2,750.00* | |
| For 1938............................. | 2,500.00 | |
| | | 5,250.00 |
| Total Reserve, December 31, 1938........ | | $13,250.00 |
| Adjustment Required: | | |
| (2) Loss on Doubtful Accounts........... | $2,500.00 | |
| Reserve for Doubtful Accounts..... | | $2,500.00 |

*The addition to the reserve for doubtful accounts of
$2,750 is to cover the earliest portion of the J. D. Simpson
Company account, amounting to $2,000, and the Hunter Manu-
facturing Company, amounting to $750. This addition to
the reserve is charged to surplus because the accounts date
back prior to the current year. The firms named now owe
$22,350 and $14,000 respectively, as shown by working paper
No. A6a. The adjusting entry for adding the $2,750 to the
reserve for doubtful accounts will be found on working paper
No. A17.

J.A.P. A6b.

THE CAREW MANUFACTURING CO.

Analysis of Inventories

December 31, 1937 and 1938

| Classification | 1938 | 1937 | Increase (+)<br>Decrease (-)<br>in 1938 |
|---|---|---|---|
| Raw Material............ | $ 78,500.00 | $100,000.00 | $21,500.00 - |
| Purchases in Transit.... | 7,500.00 | 20,000.00 | 12,500.00 - |
| Goods in Process........ | 69,500.00 | 50,000.00 | 19,500.00 + |
| Finished Goods.......... | 89,950.00* | 70,000.00 | 19,950.00 + |
| Uncompleted Contracts... | 10,000.00 | 30,000.00 | 20,000.00 - |
| Supplies, etc........... | 16,750.00 | 20,000.00 | 3,250.00 - |
| | $272,200.00 | $290,000.00 | $17,800.00 - |

*Finished Goods Inventory consists of the following:

| | |
|---|---|
| Manufactured Goods.................................. | $62,500.00 |
| Purchased Chairs.................................... | 18,000.00 |
| Purchased Castings.................................. | 9,450.00 |
| Total.............................................. | $89,950.00 |

J.A.P. #A7

---

THE CAREW MANUFACTURING CO.

Verification of Inventory Prices

December 31, 1938

| Commodity | Cost<br>Price<br>per Unit | Present Market<br>Price<br>per Unit | Inventory<br>Price<br>per Unit |
|---|---|---|---|
| Raw Materials: | | | |
| Pig Iron.......... $ | .18 lb. | $ .21 | $ .18 lb. |
| Scrap Iron........ | .06 lb. | .085 | .06 lb. |
| Bar Steel......... | .30 lb. | .33 | .30 lb. |
| Lumber............ | 38.00 per M | 56.00 per M | 38.00 per M |
| Purchased Finished Goods: | | | |
| Finished Chairs... | $17.90 each | $19.20 each | $17.90 each |
| Finished Castings. | 6.00 each | 6.50 each | 6.00 each |

J.A.P. #A7a

THE CAREW MANUFACTURING CO.

Inventory Certificate

December 31, 1938

I HEREBY CERTIFY:

(1) That the inventories at December 31, 1938, amounting to $272,200, were taken by the company's employees according to my instructions and under my supervision.

(2) That the quantities were determined by actual count, weight or measurement, or by conservative estimates where actual count was impracticable.

(3) That the stock manufactured by us or in process of manufacture has been valued according to the cost records, which are based on not exceeding cost in labor, material, and a fair proportion of overhead manufacturing expense. The prices of raw material and operating and other supplies are stated at cost to company, less all trade discounts. Where market price of the day is less than the cost price to the company, the former has been adopted.

(4) That the signatures on each inventory sheet are those of the employees who respectively made the physical check of the stock, set the prices, and made the calculations.

(5) That adequate provision has been made for imperfect goods and for possible depreciation of stock regarded as obsolete or inactive.

(6) That in my opinion the amount stated above is a fair and proper valuation of said stock.

(7) That all stock has been paid for or the liability therefor has been set up on the books.

(8) And that all merchandise which has been charged out to customers or included in cash sales, but not actually delivered, prior to the date the inventory was taken, has been excluded from the inventory.

THE CAREW MANUFACTURING CO.
Per M. S. Hastings,
Treasurer

J.A.P. #A7b

THE CAREW MANUFACTURING CO.

Adjustments Required to Give Effect to

Inventories as of December 31, 1938

(3) Inv. of Raw Materials, Dec. 31, 1938 $78,500.00
    Inventories and Purchases.........        $78,500.00
       Pig Iron............. $23,500.00
       Scrap Iron........... 18,450.00
       Bar Steel............ 19,550.00
       Sheet Steel..........  4,750.00
       Lumber............... 12,250.00

       Total............... $78,500.00

(4) Inv. of Goods in Proc., Dec. 31, 1938 69,500.00
    Inv.of Goods in Proc.,Dec. 31, 1937      69,500.00

(5) Inv. of Finished Goods, Dec. 31, 1938 89,950.00
    Inv. Fin. Goods, Dec. 31, 1937....      89,950.00
       Manufactured Goods... $62,500.00
       Purchased Chairs..... 18,000.00
       Purchased Castings...  9,450.00

       Total.................$89,950.00

(6) Inventory of Supplies, Dec. 31, 1938 16,750.00
    Inv. of Supplies, Dec. 31, 1937...      16,750.00

J.A.P. #A7c

THE CAREW MANUFACTURING CO.

List of Securities

December 31, 1938

| Bonds: | December 31, 1937 Par Value | Book Value | Pur-chased During Year | Sold During Year | December 31, 1938 Par Value | Book Value | In-come per Year | Interest Accrued to 12-31-38 | Remarks |
|---|---|---|---|---|---|---|---|---|---|
| School District | $10,000.00 | $10,000.00 | None | $ 9,500.00 | $ 500.00 | $ 500.00 | 4½% | $ 4.50 | Seen by us |
| Chain Belt Co.. | 12,000.00 | 10,000.00 | None | 10,000.00 | | | 6% | | |
| Municipal...... | 5,000.00 | 5,000.00 | None | 500.00 | 4,500.00 | 4,500.00 | 6% | 90.00 | Examined at Bank |
| Equity Mfg. Co. | 5,000.00 | 5,000.00 | None | | 5,000.00 | 5,000.00 | 6% | 125.00 | Pledged as Collateral |
| Total.......... | $32,000.00 | $30,000.00 | | $20,000.00 | $10,000.00 | $10,000.00 | | $219.50 | |

Adjustment Required:
(7) Accrued Interest Receivable.................. $219.50
    Income from Securities....................          $219.50

J.A.P. #A8

THE CAREW MANUFACTURING CO.

Analysis of Deferred Charges to Operations

December 31, 1937 and 1938

| Accounts | 1938 | 1937 | Increase (+) Decrease (-) in 1938 |
|---|---|---|---|
| Insurance Premiums........... | $7,448.61 | $5,000.00 | $2,448.61 + |
| Interest..................... | 1,250.00 | 1,500.00 | 250.00 - |
| Advertising.................. | 750.00 | 500.00 | 250.00 + |
| Office Supplies.............. | 250.00 | 500.00 | 250.00 - |
|  | $9,698.61 | $7,500.00 | $2,198.61 + |

Adjustments Required:

(8)  Insurance Expense.................... $ 8,001.39
      Prepaid Insurance.................                    $8,001.39

      Amount charged per trial balance.... $15,450.00
      Less Prepaid Ins. Premiums, 12-31-38   7,448.61

      Insurance Expense for 1938.......... $ 8,001.39

(9)  Interest Cost...................... $ 3,000.00
      Prepaid Interest...................                    $3,000.00

      Amount charged per trial balance.... $ 2,450.00
      Additional charge applicable to 1937   1,800.00*

                                           $ 4,250.00
      Less Prepaid Interest, 12-31-38.....   1,250.00

      Interest Cost for 1938.............. $ 3,000.00

(10) Advertising Expense................. $ 7,750.00
      Prepaid Advertising...............                    $7,750.00

      Amount charged per trial balance.. $ 8,500.00
      Less Prepaid Advertising, 12-31-38     750.00

      Advertising Expense for 1938...... $ 7,750.00

(11) Office Supplies..,................. $   250.00
      Prepaid Office Supplies...........                    $   250.00

      Amount charged per trial balance.... $   500.00
      Less Prepaid Office Supplies 12-31-38    250.00

      Office Supplies Consumed in 1938.... $   250.00

    *See working papers #A17.

J.A.P. #A9

## THE CAREW MANUFACTURING CO.
### Analysis of Insurance
### In Force December 31, 1938

| Company | Policy No. | Date | Term | Expires | Premium | Unexpired | Carried on Buildings and Equipment | Stock | Misc., such as Windstorm, Burglary, etc. |
|---|---|---|---|---|---|---|---|---|---|
| Phoenix......... | 1250 | 2-1-38 | 3 Yrs. | 2-1-41 | $ 5,000.00 | $3,472.22 | $250,000.00 | | |
| Globe.......... | 657 | 3-1-38 | 3 Yrs. | 3-1-41 | 4,000.00 | 2,888.89 | | $250,000.00 | |
| National Union.... | 1236 | 7-1-38 | 2 Yrs. | 7-1-40 | 1,450.00 | 1,087.50 | | | $30,000.00 |
| Total........ | | | | | $10,450.00 | $7,448.61 | $250,000.00 | $250,000.00 | $30,000.00 |

J.A.P. #A10

## THE CAREW MANUFACTURING CO.
### Analysis of Fixed Assets
### December 31, 1938

| | Cost At December 31, 1937 | Cost Added During Year | Disposed of During Year | Cost At December 31, 1938 | Depreciation Reserve At December 31, 1937 | Rate | Added During Year | At December 31, 1938 | Net Book Value At December 31, 1937 | At December 31, 1938 |
|---|---|---|---|---|---|---|---|---|---|---|
| Land............ | $ 25,000.00 | | | $ 25,000.00 | | | | | $ 25,000.00 | $ 25,000.00 |
| Buildings...... | 250,000.00 | $7,500.00 | | 257,500.00 | $15,000.00 | 3% | $7,500.00 | $22,500.00 | 235,000.00 | 235,000.00 |
| Mach. & Equip.. | 50,000.00 | | $5,000.00 | 45,000.00 | 10,000.00 | 10% | 5,000.00 | 15,000.00 | 40,000.00 | 30,000.00 |
| Jigs,Dies & Fix. | 25,000.00 | 2,500.00 | | 27,500.00 | 5,000.00 | 10% | 2,500.00 | 7,500.00 | 20,000.00 | 20,000.00 |
| Small Tools.... | 2,500.00 | 500.00 | | 3,000.00 | 1,000.00 | 20% | 500.00 | 1,500.00 | 1,500.00 | 1,500.00 |
| Pat. & Drawings | 2,500.00 | 500.00 | | 3,000.00 | 1,000.00 | 20% | 500.00 | 1,500.00 | 1,500.00 | 1,500.00 |
| Of. Fur. & Fix. | 5,000.00 | 500.00 | | 5,500.00 | 1,000.00 | 10% | 500.00 | 1,500.00 | 4,000.00 | 4,000.00 |
| Total.......... | $360,000.00 | $11,500.00 | $5,000.00 | $366,500.00 | $33,000.00 | | $16,500.00 | $49,500.00 | $327,000.00 | $317,000.00 |

Adjustments Required:

(12) Depr. on Bldgs., Mach. and Equip............ $16,000.00
    Res. for Depr. on Buildings............. $7,500.00
    Res. for Depr. on Mach. and Equip...... 5,000.00
    Res. for Depr. on Jigs, Dies and Fix... 2,500.00
    Res. for Depr. on Small Tools.......... 500.00
    Res. for Depr. on Patterns and Drawings... 500.00

(13) Depr. on Office Furn. and Fix........ 500.00
    Res. for Depr. on Office Furn. and Fix...... 500.00

J.A.P #A11

**THE CAREW MANUFACTURING CO.**
Analysis of Notes Payable
December 31, 1938

| | Outstanding at December 31, 1938 | Due January 1939 | Due February 1939 | Due March 1939 | Due Subsequent to March 31, 1939 | Interest Accrued | Interest Prepaid |
|---|---|---|---|---|---|---|---|
| Banks: | | | | | | | |
| Bank of Commerce...... | $ 15,000.00 | $ 500.00 | $ 500.00 | $ 500.00 | $13,500.00 | $1,500.00 | $ 500.00 |
| State Bank........... | 15,000.00 | 1,000.00 | 1,000.00 | 1,000.00 | 12,000.00 | | 250.00 |
| Lincoln Bank......... | 12,500.00 | | | 12,500.00 | | | |
| Brokers: | | | | | | | |
| Coleman & Co........ | 5,000.00 | 500.00 | 1,000.00 | 1,000.00 | 2,500.00 | 1,250.00 | |
| Westerman & Co...... | 9,000.00 | | 2,500.00 | | 6,500.00 | 1,250.00 | |
| Trade Creditors: | | | | | | | |
| Semple Steel Co...... | 10,000.00 | | | | 10,000.00 | 1,500.00 | |
| Central Gear Co...... | 10,000.00 | | | | 10,000.00 | 1,500.00 | 500.00 |
| American Tool Co..... | 15,000.00 | | 5,000.00 | 5,000.00 | 5,000.00 | 800.00 | |
| Potter Machinery Co.. | 10,000.00 | | 5,000.00 | 5,000.00 | | | |
| Officers and Employees: | | | | | | | |
| A. J. King.......... | 1,250.00 | | | | 1,250.00 | 50.00 | |
| J. W. Kendall....... | 1,250.00 | | | | 1,250.00 | 50.00 | |
| Total............... | $104,000.00 | $2,000.00 | $15,000.00 | $25,000.00 | $62,000.00 | $7,900.00 | $1,250.00 |

J.A.P. #A12

THE CAREW MANUFACTURING CO.

Analysis of Taxes

For Year Ended December 31, 1938

Property Taxes:
Accrued Taxes, December 31, 1937........$ 3,500.00
Paid during 1938........................ 6,725.00

                                        $ 3,225.00
Accrued, December 31, 1938.............. 4,975.00

Total Charges to Manufacturing...........        $ 8,200.00

Income Taxes:
Income Taxes Paid Applicable to Prior
Year...................................         $ 2,400.00

Income Taxes For Current Year Accrued--
Estimated.............................          $   600.00

Capital Stock Tax:
Accrued, December 31, 1937..............$   500.00
Paid, July 31, 1938.................... 500.00

Accrued, December 31, 1938..............         $   500.00

Pay Roll Taxes:
Federal S. S. Excise Tax (O.A.B.).......         $ 3,810.00
Federal S. S. Excise Tax (U.C.)........$ 1,336.65
Federal S. S. Excise Tax (U.C.) on
Accrued Wages........................ 70.50    1,407.15

State U. C. Contributions...............$12,029.85
State U. C. Contributions Accrued....... 734.50  12,764.35

Total Pay Roll Taxes Applicable to 1938...        $17,981.50

Adjustments Required:
(14) Property Taxes.......................$ 4,975.00
     Accrued Taxes Payable..............         $ 4,975.00
(15) Income Taxes........................ 600.00
     Accrued Income Taxes Payable.......            600.00
(16) Capital Stock Taxes.................. 500.00
     Accrued Capital Stock Taxes Payable            500.00
(17) Federal S. S. Excise Tax (U.C.)...... 70.50
     State U. C. Contributions............ 734.50
     Exployer's Fed. Exc. Tax Pay. (U.C.)            70.50
     State U. C. Contributions Payable..            734.50

J.A.P. #A13

THE CAREW MANUFACTURING CO.

Analysis of Accrued Wages and Interest

December 31, 1938

|  | 1938 | 1937 | Increase (+) Decrease (-) |
|---|---|---|---|
| Wages...................... | $23,500.00 | $15,000.00 | $ 8,500.00 + |
| Interest................. | 7,900.00 | 3,600.00 | 4,300.00 + |
| Total.................... | $31,400.00 | $18,600.00 | $12,800.00 + |

Adjustments Required:

| | | |
|---|---|---|
| (18) Productive Labor.................... | $23,500.00 | |
| Accrued Wages Payable............ | | $23,500.00 |
| (19) Interest Cost...................... | 4,300.00 | |
| Accrued Interest Payable........ | | 4,300.00 |
| Accrued Interest Payable, 12-31-38. | $ 7,900.00 | |
| Less Accrued Interest Payable per Trial Balance.................... | 3,600.00 | |
| Additional Accrued Interest to be recorded......................... | $ 4,300.00 | |

J.A.P. #A14

THE CAREW MANUFACTURING CO.

Liabilities Not Recorded

December 31, 1938

| Creditor | Invoice Date | Amount | Charge to | Remarks |
|----------|--------------|--------|-----------|---------|
| Wilson and Company | 12/25/38 | $7,000.00 | Purchases in Transit | Goods shipped but not received |
| Smith and Company | 12/30/38 | 500.00 | " | " |
| Total...................... | | $7,500.00 | | |

Adjustment Required:

(20)  Purchases in Transit................. $7,500.00
        Accounts Payable...................              $7,500.00

J.A.P. #A15

### THE CAREW MANUFACTURING CO.
### List of Stockholders
### December 31, 1938

| Preferred | Certificate Number | Number of Shares | Amount |
|---|---|---|---|
| H. M. Carew.............. | 1 | 750 | $ 75,000.00 |
| M. S. Hastings........... | 2 | 750 | 75,000.00 |
| J. W. Kendall............ | 3 | 250 | 25,000.00 |
| Total..................... | | 1,750 | $175,000.00 |

| Common | Certificate Number | Number of Shares | Amount |
|---|---|---|---|
| H. M. Carew.............. | 1 | 250 | $ 25,000.00 |
| M. S. Hastings........... | 2 | 250 | 25,000.00 |
| J. W. Kendall............ | 3 | 250 | 25,000.00 |
| Total..................... | | 750 | $ 75,000.00 |

J.A.P. #A16

THE CAREW MANUFACTURING CO.

Analysis of Surplus

December 31, 1938


Surplus per Trial Balance......................... $241,469.25


Additions:
  Prepaid Interest, 1937............... $ 1,800.00
  Interest Earned, 1937................    200.00
  Life Insurance Collected............ 10,000.00    12,000.00
                                               $253,469.25

Deductions:
  Reserve for Doubtful Accounts........ $ 2,750.00
  Dividends on Preferred Stock......... 10,500.00
  Dividends on Common Stock............  3,750.00
  Premium Paid on Life Insurance.......    125.00
  Income Taxes--1937..................  2,400.00   19,525.00

Adjusted Surplus, Dec. 31, 1938.................... $233,944.25


Adjustments Required:
(21) Prepaid Interest................... $ 1,800.00
    Income from Securities............    200.00
    Corporation Insurance............. 10,000.00
      Surplus.........................              $ 12,000.00


(22)  Surplus........................... 19,525.00
    Reserve for Doubtful Accounts...              2,750.00
    Preferred Dividends.............             10,500.00
    Common Dividends................              3,750.00
    Corporation Insurance...........                125.00
    Income Taxes....................              2,400.00


J.A.P. #A17

THE CAREW MANUFACTURING CO.

Sales Summary

For the Year Ended December 31, 1938

Classification of Sales

| | Castings | Chairs | Sundry | Total |
|---|---|---|---|---|
| January, 1938... | $ 22,500.00 | $ 25,000.00 | $ 2,500.00 | $ 50,000.00 |
| February....... | 36,500.00 | 30,000.00 | 3,500.00 | 70,000.00 |
| March.......... | 13,500.00 | 15,000.00 | 1,500.00 | 30,000.00 |
| April.......... | 44,000.00 | 40,000.00 | 6,000.00 | 90,000.00 |
| May............ | 20,500.00 | 65,000.00 | 4,500.00 | 90,000.00 |
| June........... | 71,500.00 | 25,000.00 | 3,500.00 | 100,000.00 |
| July........... | 57,500.00 | 45,000.00 | 7,500.00 | 110,000.00 |
| August......... | 58,500.00 | 25,000.00 | 6,500.00 | 90,000.00 |
| September...... | 58,250.00 | 27,500.00 | 4,250.00 | 90,000.00 |
| October........ | 63,750.00 | 32,500.00 | 3,750.00 | 100,000.00 |
| November....... | 54,850.00 | 42,500.00 | 2,650.00 | 100,000.00 |
| December....... | 27,050.00 | 26,500.00 | 2,150.00 | 55,700.00 |
| | $528,400.00 | $399,000.00 | $48,300.00 | |

Total............................................. $975,700.00

J.A.P. #B1

THE CAREW MANUFACTURING CO.

Schedule of Manufacturing Expenses

December 31, 1938

| | |
|---|---|
| Productive Labor.................................. | $378,500.00 |
| Nonproductive Labor.............................. | 26,000.00 |
| Federal S. S. Excise Taxes (O.A.B.)............... | 3,469.50 |
| Federal S. S. Excise Taxes (U.C.)................. | 1,213.50 |
| State U. C. Contributions......................... | 10,921.50 |
| Light and Power................................... | 14,500.00 |
| Fuel Expense...................................... | 3,500.00 |
| Factory Supplies.................................. | 4,750.00 |
| Property and Excise Taxes......................... | 8,200.00 |
| Maintenance of Buildings.......................... | 2,800.00 |
| Maintenance of Machinery.......................... | 1,500.00 |
| Freight In........................................ | 7,000.00* |
| Insurance Expense................................. | 8,001.39 |
| Depr. on Buildings, Machinery and Equipment....... | 16,000.00 |
| Total............................................. | $486,355.89 |

*Balance of freight in, amounting to $1,000, is applicable to purchased goods.

J.A.P. #B2

THE CAREW MANUFACTURING CO.

Schedule of Selling Expenses

December 31, 1938

| | |
|---|---:|
| Sales Manager's Salary | $10,000.00 |
| Salesmen's Salaries | 10,000.00 |
| Federal S. S. Excise Taxes (O.A.B.) | 130.00 |
| Federal S. S. Excise Taxes (U.C.) | 60.00 |
| State U. C. Contributions | 540.00 |
| Commission and Brokerage | 2,500.00 |
| Traveling Expenses - Manager | 250.00 |
| Traveling Expenses - Salesmen | 6,500.00 |
| Catalogs | 1,500.00 |
| Circular Matter | 950.00 |
| Stationery | 450.00 |
| Postage | 450.00 |
| Sales Office Expense | 1,650.00 |
| Advertising Expense | 7,750.00 |
| Total | $42,730.00 |

J.A.P. #B3

THE CAREW MANUFACTURING CO.

Schedule of Administrative Expenses

December 31, 1938

| | |
|---|---:|
| Administrative Salary | $30,000.00 |
| Administrative Expense | 1,450.00 |
| Office Salaries | 11,050.00 |
| Federal S. S. Excise Taxes (O.A.B.) | 210.50 |
| Federal S. S. Excise Taxes (U.C.) | 133.65 |
| State U. C. Contributions | 1,302.85 |
| Stationery | 2,200.00 |
| Postage | 475.00 |
| Telegraph | 275.00 |
| Collection and Expense | 225.00 |
| Legal Fees | 800.00 |
| Audit Fees | 1,500.00 |
| Dues and Donations | 1,500.00 |
| Office Supplies | 250.00 |
| Depr. of Office Furniture and Fixtures | 500.00 |
| Salary of Purchasing Agent | 3,500.00 |
| Traveling Expense of Purchasing Agent | 950.00 |
| Sundry Buying Expenses | 1,500.00 |
| Total | $57,822.00 |

J.A.P. #B4

## REVIEW QUESTIONS

### Based on the Audit Working Papers of
### The Carew Manufacturing Co.

**172.** Does this audit constitute a test audit or a complete audit?

**173.** What was the bank balance on December 31, 1938?

**174.** What was the total amount of notes receivable on December 31, 1938?

**175.** State the amount of The Carew Manufacturing Company's contingent liability on account of notes receivable discounted and outstanding on December 31, 1938.

**176.** Why is it customary to age accounts receivable in connection with an audit?

**177.** (a) Should purchases in transit be included in the inventory in preparing a balance sheet, if the goods were shipped f.o.b. point of origin? (b) Point of destination?

**178.** What is the purpose of an inventory certificate?

**179.** If the auditor is furnished with inventory figures by the client, should they be accepted without verification in making a balance sheet audit?

**180.** Are income taxes generally considered an operating expense?

**181.** What is the ratio of the current assets to the current liabilities on December 31, 1938?

**182.** What is the book value of each share of common stock outstanding on December 31, 1938?

**183.** Assuming a dividend of 5% on the preferred stock and 10% on the common stock was declared on December 31, 1938, payable March 1, 1939, to stockholders of record January 31, 1939, draft the necessary journal entries to record the declaration and payment of the dividends.

**184.** What was the percentage of net operating profit based upon net sales for the year 1938?

**185.** What was the percentage of productive labor based upon the net cost of goods manufactured during the year 1938?

**186.** What was the percentage of net cost of goods manufactured based upon total cost of sales for the year 1938?

# AUDIT PROJECT No. 2

As a junior accountant in the employ of Sanford and Marti, Certified Public Accountants, you are assigned to work on an audit of The Sawcut Lumber Co. You will receive your instructions from a senior accountant.

Before entering upon this engagement you familiarize yourself with the conditions and nature of the engagement as indicated by the following report:

### Memo of Engagement

Client. *The Sawcut Lumber Co.*

Address. *Missoula, Montana.*

Conference. *W. T. Hughes, President.*

Telephone. *2277.*

Report to be addressed to. *W. T. Hughes, President.*

Account to be charged to. *The Sawcut Lumber Co.*

Examination to be made of. *The Sawcut Lumber Co.*

Where located. *Office as above.*

Nature of business. *The manufacture and sale of lumber.*

Type of audit. *Examination of Financial Statements.*

When to commence. *January 15 this year.*

Probable time required. *Four weeks.*

Accountants required. *One senior and one junior.*

Rates. *Usual.*

Remarks. *Report desired March 1.*

NOTE. *Use the current year for the date of the audit, counting backward or forward as may be required to fit the conditions named in the problem.*

Upon reporting for duty you present your credentials to Mr. W. T. Hughes, president, and in your conference with him ascertain the following information:

The Sawcut Lumber Co. was incorporated January 1 (ten years ago) with an authorized capital of $350,000 divided into 3,500 shares of common stock, par value $100 per share. The company has issued 3,430 shares of which 165 shares have been purchased and are now being held in the treasury.

## Assets

| | |
|---|---:|
| Cash.................................................... | $ 12,136.65 |
| Notes Receivable........................................ | 48,359.59 |
| Accounts Receivable..................................... | 60,880.80 |
| Inventories: | |
|     Retail Merchandise................................. | 4,354.32 |
|     Retail Wood....................................... | 894.00 |
|     Lumber............................................ | 366,936.15 |
|     Mill Barn Supplies................................. | 2,266.35 |
|     Logs.............................................. | 5,568.50 |
| Mission Camp Equipment.................................. | 10,698.98 |
| Deposits Receivable..................................... | 5,727.22 |
| Investments............................................. | 55,372.88 |
| Furniture and Fixtures.................................. | 1,467.61 |
| Machinery and Equipment, Motors and Tractors ............ | 249,147.76 |
| Office Building......................................... | 2,832.13 |
| Lumber Sheds and Buildings.............................. | 13,498.02 |
| Saw Mill Building....................................... | 49,751.87 |
| Planing Mill Building................................... | 45,023.16 |
| Ravalli Railway......................................... | 38,869.29 |
| Spur Siding to Mill..................................... | 6,925.35 |
| Timber and Timber Lands................................. | 105,943.30 |
| Mill Site............................................... | 41,238.78 |
| | $1,127,892.71 |

## Liabilities

| | |
|---|---:|
| Notes Payable.......................................... | $ 5,000.00 |
| Accounts Payable....................................... | 9,214.70 |
| Advances on Lumber Deferred............................ | 52,125.98 |
| Accrued Liabilities: | |
|     Freight........................................... | 11,776.80 |
|     Wages—Camp...................................... | 3,160.85 |
|     Wages—Mill...................................... | 8,412.18 |
| Payables to Officers................................... | 2,094.03 |
| Reserve for Depreciation............................... | 158,540.93 |
| | $250,325.47 |

## Capital

| | | |
|---|---:|---:|
| Capital Stock............................... | $343,000.00 | |
|     Less Treasury Stock..................... | 16,500.00 | 326,500.00 |
| Surplus..................................... | | 551,067.24 |
| | | $1,127,892.71 |

The officers include Mr. W. T. Hughes, president, Mr. K. K. Good, vice-president and general manager, and Mr. Peter Lansing, secretary-treasurer. Mr. Lansing has charge of the accounts. The accounts are kept in three ledgers including a general ledger, an accounts receivable ledger, and an accounts payable ledger. Receipts and disbursements are recorded in a cash book. Small expense items are paid from a revolving fund kept for this purpose but no separate petty cash book is kept. The cashier is allowed $50 at the first of each month as a revolving fund out of which to pay small bills and make change. Any balance in the revolving fund is added as cash on hand in proving cash and in reconciling the bank statement.

The company purchases standing timber suitable for harvest, owns timber lands, and contracts for standing timber. The logs are delivered to the mill, sawed into lumber, cured in the yards, and dressed for sale by passing through the planing mill. The finished product is sold at wholesale prices in carload lots. The company also maintains a retail department and a retail wood department. Schultz & Co. of Buffalo and Pittsburgh serving as lumber brokers, handle any surplus lumber.

Mr. Lansing submits the accompanying statement of assets and liabilities as of the beginning of the year under audit.

Mr. Lansing also submits the following trial balance taken from the books at the end of the year under audit:

### THE SAWCUT LUMBER CO.
#### Trial Balance, December 31, 19—

| | | | |
|---|---:|---:|---:|
| Cash in Bank and Revolving Fund | | | $ 15,441.97 |
| Notes Receivable | | | 52,620.07 |
| Accounts Receivable (Trade) | | | 46,815.43 |
| Inventories: | | | |
| Retail Merchandise | $ | 4,354.32 | |
| Retail Wood | | 894.00 | |
| Lumber | | 366,936.15 | |
| Mill Barn Supplies | | 2,266.35 | |
| Logs | | 5,568.50 | 380,019.32 |
| Mission Camp Equipment | | | 10,698.98 |
| Investments | | | 59,372.88 |
| Timber and Timber Lands | | | 105,943.30 |
| Mill Site Lands | | | 41,238.78 |
| Side Track to Mill | | | 6,925.35 |
| Saw Mill Building | | | 49,751.87 |
| Planing Mill Building | | | 45,023.16 |
| Lumber Sheds and Shook Houses | | | 13,997.06 |
| Machinery and Equipment, Motors and Tractors. | | | 249,147.76 |
| Office Building | | | 2,832.13 |
| Furniture and Fixtures | | | 1,525.11 |
| Ravalli Creek Railway | | | 38,869.29 |
| Timber Deposits—Receivable | | | 18,726.05 |
| Notes Payable—Bank | | | $ 25,000.00 |
| Accounts Payable (Trade) | | | 10,476.64 |
| Advances on Lumber Contracts | | | 84,556.36 |
| Reserve for Depreciation of Fixed Assets | | | 158,540.93 |
| Capital Stock—Common | | | 343,000.00 |

(*Continued on next page*)

| | | |
|---|---|---|
| Treasury Stock............................... | $ 16,500.00 | |
| Surplus...................................... | | $549,997.82 |
| Retail Lumber Sales.......................... | | 18,776.23 |
| Retail Wood Sales............................ | | 20,163.08 |
| Wholesale Lumber Sales...................... | | 804,420.13 |
| Employer's Federal Excise Tax Pay. (O.A.B.).. | | 630.05 |
| Employees' Income Tax Payable (O.A.B.)..... | | 630.05 |
| Employer's Federal Excise Tax Payable (U.C.) | | 727.16 |
| State U. C. Contributions Payable............ | | 1,636.11 |
| Taxes on Timber and Timber Leases.......... | 12,162.31 | |
| Income Taxes............................... | 640.65 | |
| Capital Stock Tax........................... | 500.00 | |
| Interest Expense............................ | 7,454.55 | |
| Insurance................................... | 15,308.36 | |
| Selling Expenses—Lumber................... | 8,500.00 | |
| General Expense............................ | 10,357.06 | |
| Office Expense.............................. | 20,594.21 | |
| Traveling Expense........................... | 917.70 | |
| Saw Mill Expense............................ | 14,777.93 | |
| Saw Mill Labor.............................. | 89,264.21 | |
| Planing Mill Expense........................ | 7,979.20 | |
| Planing Mill Labor.......................... | 74,559.30 | |
| Wood Expense............................... | 13,667.84 | |
| Retail Lumber Expense....................... | 8,954.14 | |
| Yard Expense............................... | 10,885.23 | |
| Piling Expense.............................. | 15,828.94 | |
| Lath Expense............................... | 5,206.59 | |
| Workmen's Compensation Insurance.......... | 1,572.30 | |
| Sales Discounts............................. | 9,316.56 | |
| Commissions................................ | 12,610.44 | |
| Postage, Printing, and Stationery............ | 1,179.24 | |
| Lumber Journals and Association Dues........ | 6,250.29 | |
| Donations.................................. | 287.00 | |
| Logs Bought................................ | 167,153.02 | |
| Freight on Logs............................. | 41,697.28 | |
| Telephone and Telegrams.................... | 941.54 | |
| Planing Mill Oil............................. | 1,117.87 | |
| Saw Mill Oil................................ | 1,901.24 | |
| Mill Spur Repairs........................... | 279.45 | |
| Freight Paid on Lumber Shipments........... | 133,214.51 | |
| Cribbing Costs.............................. | 667.03 | |
| Mission Camp Expenses...................... | 79,101.39 | |
| Mission Camp Labor......................... | 78,563.20 | |
| Federal S. S. Excise Tax (O.A.B.)............. | 2,423.87 | |
| Federal S. S. Excise Tax (U.C.)............... | 727.16 | |
| State U. C. Contributions.................... | 6,544.44 | |
| | $2,018,554.56 | $2,018,554.56 |

On January 15 at 4 p. m., Mr. George Thompson, the cashier, in the presence of Mr. Lansing and yourself, makes a count of the cash as follows:

- 4 Five dollar bills
- 7 One dollar bills
- 4 Half dollars
- 8 Quarters
- 3 Dimes
- 5 Nickles
- 5 Pennies

The following cash items were found to be included in the cash balance:

**Checks:**

White Pine Moulding Co., dated 1/10............................ $227.10
J. R. Minty, dated 1/8........................................ 57.15
W. L. Boardman, dated 1/15.................................... 16.50
Stephenson Lumber Co., dated 1/14............................ 222.28
Eastman Coal Co., dated 1/12................................. 100.00
John Peleran, dated 1/25..................................... 12.50
M. T. Jones, dated 12/15..................................... 5.30

**Duplicate Receipts:**

Earl White, dated 1/15....................................... .40
Garden City Floral Co., dated 1/15........................... 3.50
Dan O'Connor, dated 1/15..................................... 7.47

**Receipted Bills:**

Postage on Incoming Mail since Jan. 1........................ .32
Express Charges since Jan. 1................................. 1.15
A. A. Rummel, dated 1/8 (Replacing a broken window).......... 4.75
Tony, dated 1/12 (For hauling sawdust)....................... 2.00

There also is found an I. O. U. signed by K. K. Good, an employee, dated 1/5, for $15.00, and an expense voucher signed by Mary Smith, a stenographer, for $1.25.

It was found that the check signed by M. T. Jones had been returned by the bank December 21 marked "Insufficient funds," the bank having been reimbursed in cash.

It is the custom of the cashier to make deposits daily in so far as possible. The bank book and cash receipts record show the following receipts and deposits since January 1:

| | Receipts | Deposits |
|---|---|---|
| Jan. 2 | $ 1,061.20 | $ 622.30 |
| 3 | 844.10 | 1,061.20 |
| 5 | 366.80 | 844.00 |
| 6 | 1,255.10 | 366.30 |
| 7 | 2,210.00 | 1,255.00 |
| 8 | 778.40 | 2,209.25 |
| 9 | 1,116.67 | 778.00 |
| 10 | 887.13 | 1,116.50 |
| 12 | 787.50 | 887.13 |
| 13 | 1,600.77 | 787.25 |
| 14 | 937.20 | 1,600.77 |
| 15 | 646.90 | 937.00 |
| | $12,491.77 | $12,464.70 |

The bank charges exchange on certain out-of-town checks which is deducted on the deposit ticket. During December the exchange amounted to $4.48, for which no adjustment had been made. A note signed by the Freeman Lumber Co. for $2,000 due January 10 was left at the bank for collection. The book-keeper stated that he had not had a report on the note but a telephone call at the bank revealed that the note was paid and credited to the company's account on January 12, interest at 6% for ninety days less a collection charge of 50 cents.

The cash book footings on January 15 show debits of $27,933.74, and credits $3,671.82. The bank was asked for a certified statement of the balance credited to the Sawcut Lumber Co. at close of business on January 15. This statement was received on the morning of January 16 and showed a balance of $28,241.77. All checks outstanding on December 31 aggregating $2,251.80 have been paid and were returned with the statement together with six checks issued and paid since January 1 amounting to $1,017.50. Exchange deducted from January deposits amounted to $2.71. The following checks issued since January 1 still are outstanding:

| | | |
|---|---|---:|
| No. 2782 | Missoula Mercantile Co. | $ 850.56 |
| No. 2786 | Armour & Co. | 1,229.54 |
| No. 2788 | Ryan Fruit Co. | 10.25 |
| No. 2776 | Stone, Ordean & Wells | 529.88 |
| No. 2787 | San Juan Fish Co. | 25.80 |
| No. 2789 | Perry Fuel Co. | 8.41 |
| | | $2,654.44 |

The bank statement for December 31 showed a balance of $17,016.87. The check book balance on January 15 was $23,562.55 and there was $20.23 in the revolving fund. Check No. 1822 in favor of P. D. Metz, a lumberjack, issued December 4 (two years ago) in payment of wages amounting to $13.50, has never been cashed, but during December (of the year under audit) payment was stopped and it was recorded in the cash book by debiting cash and crediting accounts payable.

Notes receivable, $52,620.07. Examination revealed a 90-day note signed by The American Sash & Door Co. for $10,650 due February 15 with 6%. A note signed by T. C. Ruffcorn Lumber Co., $17,882.50 dated November 1, six months, due May 1 with 6%. A note signed by Thomas Ludwig for $2,000 endorsed by Edward Hiner Co. for three months at 6%, due

December 12 was protested for nonpayment. Fees $2.50, charged to general expense. A note for $5,000 signed by William T. Hughes, dated July 1 for one year at 5%. A note for $12,500 signed by Knoxville Lumber Co. given for four months, dated November 6, at 7%. A note for $2,587.57 at three months, due January 15 with 8% interest, payable at the First National Bank; left for collection January 12; no report. A letter on file from Edward Hiner Co. promises settlement soon for Thomas Ludwig's note. A 90-day note for $2,000 signed by the Freeman Lumber Co., due January 12, with interest at 6%.

Accounts receivable, trade, $46,815.43. A reserve for loss on bad debts has not been created, but following a conference with Mr. Hughes and Mr. Lansing, it was decided that a reserve equal to 1% of the outstanding trade accounts receivable should be provided. Following is a list of the amounts due from customers on December 31 as shown by the accounts receivable ledger:

| | |
|---|---:|
| E. B. Owen | $ 104.25 |
| Earl White | .40 |
| Garden City Floral Co. | 3.50 |
| R. D. Stewart | 5.32 |
| M. H. Lind | 103.51 |
| Wm. Alderman | 221.23 |
| Steinman Lumber Co. | 1,705.85 |
| Producers Lumber Co. | 1,955.48 |
| Adams, Kennedy & Co. | 587.93 |
| American Sash & Door Co. | 1,412.70 |
| H. E. Ketcham | 1,140.00 |
| Stephenson Lumber Co. | 722.28 |
| Valley Lumber Co. | 400.00 |
| Loveland Lumber Co. | 101.63 |
| F. G. Haverty | 678.36 |
| Hasslem Lumber Co. | 4,880.07 |
| Gilting, Rewick Lumber Co. | 105.67 |
| Eastman Coal Co. | 100.00 |
| Charles H. Allen | 667.87 |
| K. K. Good, Vice-President | 3,113.66 |
| G. J. Deschamps | 250.32 |
| Ed Hayes | 80.00 |
| Don O'Connor | 7.47 |
| Leo J. Polleys | 371.25 |
| C. C. Willis | 1,358.27 |
| Bardford, Kennedy Lumber Co. | 763.52 |
| C. & N. W. Railway | 1,210.72 |
| Central Reserve Lumber Co. | 2,274.84 |
| Carlos Rugger Lumber Co. | 1,598.72 |
| Wm. Schultz & Co. | 676.18 |
| Edward Hiner Co. | 913.38 |
| Brown Lumber Co. | 5,725.64 |
| Patrick Lumber Co. | 678.11 |

(Continued on next page)

| | | |
|---|---|---:|
| Havelock Lumber Co. | $ | 965.91 |
| Maxwell Gold Co. | | 233.31 |
| J. D. Mercham Lumber Co. | | 1,896.42 |
| W. T. Hughes, President | | 1.76 |
| Gregory Lumber Co. | | 1,439.31 |
| Freeman Lumber Co. | | 1,650.37 |
| Bannock Lumber Co. | | 880.95 |
| Trenton Lumber Co. | | 1,828.78 |
| O. E. Renfrew Lumber Co. | | 1,755.80 |
| Gregg, Saddleberg Co. | | 454.32 |
| John Peleran | | 29.57 |
| Hutloff Lumber Co. | | 287.48 |
| R. G. Chesbro Lumber Co. | | 971.06 |
| M. H. Mason (Employee) | | 17.44 |
| Monarch Lumber Co. | | 484.82 |
| | | $46,815.43 |

Investments, $59,372.88. An examination of the securities by the senior revealed that all were intact. He also found that the securities had been recorded at cost including interest accrued at date of purchase. He prepared the following data and submits it to you for analysis:

10M M. K. & T. 1st gold 4's, 1990, J. & D.*, bought at 88⅝, $8,862.50, accrued interest $188.89, November 21 a year ago.

5M St. Joseph Gas Co. 1st Mortgage 5's, 1947, J. & J., bought at 92½, accrued interest $106.94, December 5 a year ago.

7M L. & N. gold 4's, 1950, J. & J., bought at 92⅜, $6,466.25, accrued interest $108.89, November 21 a year ago.

6M Erie conv. 4's series B, 1953, A. & O., bought at 69½, $4,170.00, accrued interest $1.33, October 3 a year ago.

10M B. & O. ref. 4's, 1951, M. & N., bought at 87, $8,700.00, accrued interest $92.22, January 23 of the year under audit.

10M Public Service of Indiana 1st and ref. 6's, 1952, F. & A., bought at 87, $8,700.00, accrued interest $288.33, January 25 of the year under audit.

10M C. B. & Q. 4's, 1949, J. & J., bought at 95½, accrued interest $194.45, June 26 of the year under audit.

5M Asso. Gas & Elec. Deb. 5's, 1950, F. & A., bought at 82½, accrued interest $103.47, July 1 of the year under audit.

2M Cent. Ohio Light 1st 5's, 1950, A. & O., bought at 82¼, accrued interest $19.44, December 10 of the year under audit.

---

*It is customary to indicate interest payment dates by abbreviations, hence "J. & D." indicates that the interest is payable semi-annually on June 1 and December 1.

50 shares Colgate-Palmolive-Peet Co. no-par common at $28.41 and brokerage $4.67, December 10 of the year under audit.

No coupons have been clipped and cashed.

Deposits receivable, $18,726.05. This represents a guarantee deposit placed with the Federal Forestry Department on timber tracts, returnable when the cut over lands are restored to the government with all terms of the contract fulfilled, such as clearing, burning of slashings, etc. No interest is allowed on the fund.

New inventory, $420,114.54, December 31. Peter Lansing certified to the inventory sheets as to quantity and quality. Costs were furnished by the bookkeeper. The extensions and footings should be verified.

Yard Stock:
```
    Pondosa Pine........ 15,221,237 ft.
    Fir and Larch........  1,921,769  "
                          ─────────────
                          17,143,006 ft. at $19.055........  $326,659.98
```
Shed Stock:
```
    Mouldings—Pine.....  1,320,966 ft.
    Fir and Larch........   397,740  "
                          ─────────────
                           1,718,706 ft. at $22.452........  $ 38,588.39
Lath....................    610,450 ft. at $3.91...........     2,386.86
Logs in the pond at mill...  1,425,000 ft. at $15.44..........    22,002.00
Logs in the woods.......................................      3,412.50
Retail Wood............  2,197.74 cords at $1.00........      2,197.74
Retail merchandise detailed on inventory sheet..............    23,921.31
Mill Barn Supplies......................................        945.76
```

Fixed Assets:
```
  Mission Camp Equipment (Inventoried)
        Camp Cots........................................  $  1,357.61
        Locomotives......................................       806.39
        Blacksmith Shop..................................       204.71
        Barns............................................       583.50
        General Supplies.................................     2,899.62
        Commissary.......................................     1,420.34
        Cook-house.......................................     1,993.10
                                                          ─────────────
                                                          $  9,265.27
Ravalli Creek Railway (Cost to build two years ago $54,000)
        Written down, book value.........................  $38,869.29
        Depreciation to be taken this year...............   10,970.72
```

This is a temporary railway connecting with the main line of the Northern Pacific.

Furniture and fixtures, $1,525.11. Additional charges during year amounted to $57.50. Depreciation is estimated as $32.14 for the year under audit.

Machinery and equipment, motors and tractors, $249,147.76. An analysis of this account revealed that the book value of the machinery and equipment amounted to $99,950.25, and the book value of the motors and tractors amounted to $23,974.18 at beginning of year under audit.

Reserve for depreciation of fixed assets, $158,540.93. Investigation reveals that it has not been customary to prepare a schedule of depreciation annually but instead a reasonable sum has been credited to the reserve each year, the amount depending upon the profits before deducting depreciation. As a result of a conference with the officials of the company it was agreed that the reserve for depreciation be analyzed as follows:

| For: | | |
|---|---|---|
| Saw Mill Building | $ | 15,400.70 |
| Planing Mill Building | | 14,620.20 |
| Machinery and Equipment | | 77,705.20 |
| Motors and Tractors | | 47,518.13 |
| Furniture and Fixtures | | 482.10 |
| Side Track to Mill | | 2,144.40 |
| Office Building | | 670.20 |
| | | $158,540.93 |

It also was agreed that depreciation for the current year be provided as follows:

| | | |
|---|---|---|
| Saw Mill Building | $ | 1,643.80 |
| Planing Mill Building | | 1,128.58 |
| Machinery and Equipment | | 7,496.27 |
| Motors and Tractors | | 4,794.84 |
| Lumber Sheds and Shook Houses | | 3,184.48 |
| Side Track to Mill | | 346.27 |
| Office Building | | 84.96 |

The saw mill building was built about ten years ago and is situated on the edge of the mill pond where the logs may be transferred from the pond to the mill by endless chain belts. It is modernly equipped.

The planing mill building houses the planing and shaping machinery, and has been in use for ten years. The mill site and lands valued at $41,238.78 represent a tract of about thirty acres situated on the Black River and include the cost of the land and development costs for log pond and yards. The side track to mill is a spur owned by the company connecting the yards and mill pond with the Northern Pacific and the Chicago, Milwaukee and Puget Sound Railways.

Timber and timber lands valued at $105,943.30 consist of 1,000 acres of good merchantable timber lands owned, and other lands which are leased and contracted for with the Federal government. Lumber camps have been established and the timber is being harvested.

Lumber sheds and shook houses, $13,997.06. Additional charges during year amounted to $499.04. It has been the policy of the company to write down this asset, crediting the depreciation direct to the asset account. The depreciation for the year under audit is estimated to be $3,184.48.

Notes payable, $25,000. All held by the First National Bank.

July 1, due in one year $ 5,000.00 First National Bank, Interest 6%
Sept. 1, due in one year $10,000.00 First National Bank, Interest 6%
Dec. 1, due in one year $10,000.00 First National Bank, Interest 6%

Accounts payable (trade), $10,476.64. Transcript of accounts payable ledger follows:

| | |
|---|---:|
| C. M. & P. S. Railway | $ 76.66 |
| Acme Lumber Co. | 12.72 |
| M. Wells & Co. | 35.71 |
| Hahn & Daly | 2,614.11 |
| Goshen Drug Co. | 11.13 |
| Wallace Powder Co. | 96.90 |
| Westinghouse Brake Co. | 14.29 |
| Peter Lansing, Manager | 910.45 |
| C. J. Black (employee) | 296.80 |
| Perry Fuel Co. | 34.57 |
| Atwater Paint Co. | 59.25 |
| Roslyn Coal Co. | 770.81 |
| Simmons Hardware Co. | 686.82 |
| Colossom Co. | 75.40 |
| Buffalo Chemical Co. | 91.00 |
| Ryan Fruit Co. | 10.25 |
| San Juan Fish Co. | 25.80 |
| E. F. Houghton & Co. | 117.56 |
| Elmer Johnson | 28.73 |
| Charles Stahl | 35.50 |
| Grant & Anderson | 162.43 |
| Stone, Ordean & Wells | 529.88 |
| Texas Oil Co. | 71.64 |
| Durant Steel Foundry | 63.00 |
| American Machine Co. | 12.50 |
| Chicago Lumberman | 11.00 |

(Continued on next page)

| | | |
|---|---|---:|
| Spokane Paper Co. | $ | 21.60 |
| Washington Machine Co. | | 219.33 |
| Fairbanks, Morse & Co. | | 115.05 |
| George Thompson, Cashier. | | 2.53 |
| Hallacter Co. | | 18.98 |
| Spokane Saw Works. | | 97.19 |
| Arquhorst Service Co. | | 82.09 |
| Nott, Aiken Co. | | 116.99 |
| Connelly, Mason Co. | | 230.40 |
| Henry Diston & Sons. | | 598.76 |
| Armour & Co. | | 1,229.54 |
| P. D. Metz. | | 13.50 |
| West Pine Mfg. Co. | | 25.21 |
| Missoula Mercantile Co. | | 850.56 |

$10,476.64

Accounts payable (special), $84,556.36. Schultz & Co. of Pittsburgh and Buffalo contract for ten million board feet of lumber to be delivered throughout the year, and the above represents cash advances made on dimension stuff and dressed lumber ordered, now in process of preparation.

Capital stock, common, $343,000. The authorized stock of the company is $350,000, or 3,500 shares of $100 par. An analysis of the stock certificate book reveals the following owners, as per stubs:

No. 1 W. T. Hughes...............................100 shares
2 K. K. Good....................................100  "
3 Peter Lansing................................100  "
4 C. R. Clinton................................100  "
5 M. M. Carson.................................100  "
6 Cancelled....................................
7 Cancelled....................................
8 W. T. Hughes................................200  "
9 Cancelled....................................
10 Cancelled....................................
11 K. K. Good.................................. 50  "
12 Peter Lansing............................... 50  "
13 P. T. Jones................................100  "
14 R. M. Ledyard..............................265  "
15 Cancelled....................................
16 Cancelled....................................
17 Held in treasury............................
18 W. T. Hughes...............................500  "
19 K. K. Good.................................200  "
20 Peter Lansing..............................200  "
21 C. J. Black................................100  "
22 J. W. Logan................................250  "
23 R. S. Allen................................250  "
24 W. T. Hughes...............................200  "
25 L. E. Freeling.............................100  "
26 M. J. Phillips.............................100  "
27 B. M. Wilding..............................100  "
28 K. T. McKesson.............................100  "

Certificate No. 17 originally was issued to D. R. Mondell for 165 shares. Mr. Mondell died two years ago and the secretary was authorized to buy his stock from the heirs with company funds and hold same in the treasury.

The following accruals and deferred items should be recorded.

| | |
|---|---:|
| Freight on Logs Accrued............................. | $9,109.60 |
| Mission Camp Wages Accrued........................ | 2,988.85 |
| Saw Mill Wages Accrued............................ | 4,026.14 |
| Planing Mill Wages Accrued......................... | 2,617.93 |
| Wood Expense Accrued............................. | 163.60 |
| Lumber Expense Accrued............................ | 165.25 |
| Yard Expense Accrued.............................. | 272.50 |
| Lath Expense Accrued.............................. | 298.95 |
| Piling Expense Accrued............................. | 692.10 |
| Capital Stock Tax Accrued.......................... | 500.00 |
| Employer's Federal Excise Tax Accrued (U. C.)........ | 28.90 |
| State U. C. Contributions Accrued................... | 260.09 |
| Saw Mill Expense Deferred.......................... | 945.76 |

The account entitled Logs Bought has been charged for the cost of 7,046,795 feet of logs bought during the year. The inventory shows that 1,425,000 feet of logs are in the pond at the mill at the end of the period, valued at $22,002.

It was found that the element of stumpage had never been taken into consideration in computing costs. In addition to the logs bought, the company has been cutting some of its own timber. An analysis of the records revealed that 16,878,040 feet of logs have been cut since the company was organized, including 2,109,650 feet during the period under audit.

In the lumber industry it is customary to obtain the operating charge for stumpage by dividing the cost of the tract, less the value of the land, by the estimated number of feet of logs obtainable. The estimate is based upon the results of a "cruise." In this case the stumpage rate was found to be $4.95 per 1,000 feet.

The amount of stumpage applicable to previous periods should be charged to surplus, while that applicable to the current period should be charged to an account with stumpage.

It is suggested that a reserve for depletion account be set up crediting it for the amount of the stumpage. When the timber owned has been completely cut, the reserve for depletion should theoretically exactly offset the balance of the timber account. However, there is certain to be some variation because of such factors as the natural growth of the timber, the extent to which dead or fallen trees can be utilized, the minimum size of the trees cut, and variations from the estimates based upon the original cruise. Under government scaling it is estimated that the over-run when logs are sawed will exceed the estimated log scale by from 15 to 20%.

The stumpage rate may be tested from time to time by comparing the log measure of a given section with the estimate based upon the cruise for that section. If the test shows that the actual production exceeds the estimate, an adjustment may be made for the excess by charging the reserve for depletion account and crediting surplus. On the other hand if the test shows that the production is less than the estimate, an adjustment may be made by debiting surplus and crediting the reserve account for the deficit. At the same time the depletion rate should be adjusted to conform with the test.

Property taxes amounting to $12,162.31 have been paid on timber and timber leases. Income taxes amounting to $640.65 were paid during the year. Since these taxes applied to the previous year's income and no provision was made therefor in the annual statements, the amount should be charged to surplus instead of current earnings. Insurance is an annual cost, and no portion of the unexpired insurance is considered. Selling expenses need no further analysis. General expenses are considered administrative costs. Office expenses are for office salaries and office supplies. Traveling expenses are for outside selling of lumber by salesmen. Saw mill, planing mill, wood, lumber, yard, piling, and lath expense are considered manufacturing expenses. Workmen's Compensation Insurance is for protection of workmen against accidents, and is therefore to be considered as a manufacturing cost.

Commissions are selling costs. Postage, journals, association dues, donations, telephone, and telegrams are office or administrative costs. Mill oil and spur repairs are manufacturing costs, as are cribbing costs. The surplus represents the accumulation of profits from former years. No bonded indebtedness exists.

## Audit Program

Prepare the following schedules and draft adjusting entries required to make the books conform to the audit report:

(1) Cash count.

(2) Reconciliation of bank balance.

(3) Analysis of securities showing date of purchase, par value, cost, book value, interest accrued at date of purchase, interest accrued on December 31 of previous year, and interest accrued December 31 year of audit.

(4) Analysis of notes receivable showing maker, date of note, date of maturity, principal, rate of interest, and interest accrued to December 31 of the year under audit.

(5) Analysis of accounts receivable classified on a basis of trade customers and others.

(6) Analysis of fixed assets showing cost, reserve for depreciation at beginning of year under audit, book value at beginning of year under audit, current depreciation, and book value at end of year under audit.

(7) Analysis of notes payable showing date of note, name of holder, principal, rate of interest, date due, and interest accrued to December 31 of the year under audit.

(8) Analysis of accounts payable classified on a basis of trade creditors and others.

Acting in the capacity of a senior accountant, and assuming that the working papers prepared by the junior accountant have been referred to you, prepare an audit report for The Sawcut Lumber Co. consisting of the following:

(a) Balance Sheet (Exhibit A).

(b) Profit and Loss Statement (Exhibit B).

(c) Letter of recommendation setting forth your views as to what changes in the accounting system should be made in order that the president might be furnished with more useful information.

# INDEX

465